RECREATION PLANNING AND DESIGN

McGraw-Hill Series in
LANDSCAPE AND LANDSCAPE ARCHITECTURE

Albert Fein, Ph.D., A.S.L.A.(hon.)   *Consulting Editor*

Bring and Wayembergh ■ Japanese Gardens: Design and Meaning
Gold ■ Recreation Planning and Design
Hudak ■ Trees for Every Purpose
Landscape Architecture Magazine ■ Landscapes for Living
Landscape Architecture Magazine ■ Water and the Landscape
Simonds ■ Earthscape

RECREATION PLANNING AND DESIGN

Seymour M. Gold, Ph. D., AICP

Associate Professor of Environmental Planning
Division of Environmental Planning and Management
University of California, Davis

McGraw-Hill Book Company

New York   St. Louis   San Francisco   Auckland   Bogotá
Hamburg   Johannesburg   London   Madrid   Mexico   Montreal   New Delhi
Panama   Paris   São Paulo   Singapore   Sydney   Tokyo   Toronto

Library of Congress Cataloging in Publication Data

Gold, Seymour M
Recreation planning and design.

(McGraw-Hill series in landscape and landscape architecture)
Bibliography: p.
Includes index.
1. Recreation—Planning—United States.
2. Outdoor recreation—Planning—United States.
3. Recreational surveys—United States. I. Title.
II. Series.
GV53.G635   790'.0973   79-13792
ISBN 0-07-023644-5

4 5 6 7 8 9 0   HDHD   8 9 8 7 6 5

The editors for this book were Jeremy Robinson and Joan Matthews, the designer was Elliot Epstein, and the production supervisor was Sally Fliess. It was set in Optima Medium by The Clarinda Company.

It was printed and bound by Halliday Lithograph Corporation.

The research for this book was supported by a grant from the Beatrix Farrand Fund, Department of Landscape Architecture, University of California, Berkeley.

CONTENTS

APPENDIXES

PREFACE

This book describes the process and products of urban recreation planning. The focus is on basic concepts, measures, methodology and the park and recreation plan. The objective is to improve the state of the art to meet the needs of Urban America in the 1980s.

The prospect of increasing levels of leisure and urbanization suggest an increased demand for recreation space, service, and facilities in cities. An energy crisis, decreasing personal income, and reduced public budgets will have a significant impact on the use of federal, state, local, and private recreation opportunities. This impact will be most conspicuous at the local level, where most people spend much of their leisure time.

The impact of increased use levels of reduced public budgets raises serious questions of funding, user fees, access, design, and management. It suggests changes in the proposed acquisition and development programs for the provision of public facilities and significant opportunities for the private sector. These changes will require a more sophisticated level of recreation planning to serve as a guide for public and private decisions.

The goal of this book is to improve the quality of life and environment in cities by the provision of more effective park and recreation opportunities. Professionals and students need better techniques to prepare local recreation plans. There is also a need to critically review the planning concepts used to provide public and private recreation opportunities in cities and develop alternatives.

The state of the art is characterized by tradition. Recreation planning has been dominated by the use of outmoded concepts. Demonstration and innovation are the exception in most communities. Studies of leisure behavior are not evident in most plans. The objectives of many public park and recreation systems often better accommodate the needs of the supplier than the user.

There are notable exceptions to this situation, but they are not commonly available to most professionals and students. The lack of new ideas or successful examples results in perpetuating traditional techniques which may be more part of the problem than part of the solution.

My previous book, *Urban Recreation Planning*, was written in the context of Urban America 1968. In the past 10 years much has changed. Many events, people, and places have influenced my thinking about cities and recreation planning. Extensive travel in this country, Canada, and Australia; library research; field study; and contact with thousands of professionals, students, and public officials have given me valuable insight and perspective. They have balanced idealism with practicality, fantasy with reality, and academia with professional practice.

I am indebted to the many planning and recreation agencies, professional organizations, and individuals who helped to make this book possible. Their experience and hopes are the basis of this effort. I am also grateful to the Beatrix Farrand Fund and the Department of Landscape Architecture at the University of California, Berkeley, for supporting this research during my sabbatical year. Most of all, I appreciate the patience of my wife Susan and sons Daniel, David, and Robert during the past two years. Susan's typing and editing of the final manuscript were heroic. The encouragement of my family was essential and will long be remembered.

These are challenging times for recreation planning. I hope my ideas will improve the state of the art and have every reason to be optimistic about the future.

Seymour M. Gold

RECREATION PLANNING AND DESIGN

INTRODUCTION

Recreation planning is a process that relates the leisure time of people to space. It uses the concepts and methods of many disciplines to provide public and private leisure opportunities in cities. In practice, recreation planning is a professional specialty that blends the knowledge and techniques of environmental design and the social sciences to develop alternatives for using leisure time, space, energy, and money to accommodate human needs.

Objectives

The objective of this book is to develop a conceptual understanding of selected aspects of recreation planning as they apply to urban environments. Because the state of the art is evolving, both traditional and innovative ideas will be described. Case study examples are used to describe successful ideas or techniques that can be adapted to many situations.

Detailed objectives of this book are to (1) familiarize the reader with the process, products, and methodology of recreation planning, (2) develop a critical and sophisticated perspective on the state of the art, (3) relate recreation planning to other types of planning and environmental design, (4) describe alternative approaches to recreation planning based on the current literature and practice, and (5) describe how, when, and where these approaches can be used in the review, preparation, or revision of park and recreation plans.

Scope

This book emphasizes the state of the art in Urban America. The problems and potentials of the central city and suburb are described in the context of the planning process. The author sees recreation planning and design as essentially the same process and will use these words interchangeably. Distinctions will be made between planning and design in terms of the scale, methods, client, or approach to problem solving. However, both words are intended to have the same professional meaning and social objectives.

The methods and concepts used to prepare the park, recreation, and open space elements of a comprehensive plan at the city or county level are the primary focus of this book. The emphasis is on systems planning instead of detailed site or project design. One objective of this book is to bridge the gap between systems and site planning to show how they relate in terms of providing leisure opportunities in cities that meet the needs of people.

Approach

The basic approach of this book is to relate time (leisure), activity (behavior), and space (environment) to a geographic area (the city) with a process (planning/design) by describing the techniques (concepts/methods) that are part of the process. Because rapid change is a characteristic of leisure behavior, cities, and the planning process, techniques will be labeled as either "traditional" or "innovative."

Traditional techniques will be described in terms of their problem-solving effectiveness. Innovative techniques will be shown as alternatives to be refined over time. The conceptual merits and shortcomings of each technique will be compared where appropriate and illustrated by case studies or references listed in the bibliography.

Where possible, the typical situation and general practice will be described. Where the traditional approach is criticized and no alternative is available, new techniques that offer hopeful solutions are described or developed by the author. In all cases, the emphasis will be on professional practice that works or has the potential for application to real situations with a reasonable expectation of success.

Assumptions

Any book of this type must make assumptions about the nature of leisure, cities, and planning process or become mired in academic debate and ambiguity. These assumptions describe the author's viewpoint. They are intended to give the reader a philosophical and pragmatic orientation. They are based on current facts and trends, the author's experience, and an interpretation of the literature. In a research context, these assumptions represent hypotheses to be tested. In an applied context, these assumptions are targets for professional practice. Both research and practice will be necessary to refine these ideas over time. The essence of recreation planning is based on these assumptions:

1 Public parks, leisure services, and open space are vital aspects of urban form and function.

2 Leisure services and spaces that are well designed, properly located, adequately maintained, and serve the needs of intended users can improve the quality of urban life and environment.

3 The planning and design process can provide a rational basis for community action to improve the quantity and quality of leisure opportunities in cities.

4 Social research techniques can be used to measure leisure behavior in terms of preference or satisfaction for different types of activities or environments.

5 These values can be translated into dimensions of time, space, and activity for different populations.

6 These factors can be related to the demand for and supply of existing or potential leisure opportunities to indicate need in terms of area or services for a specific activity or set of activities.

7 This need can be translated into measures of effectiveness or performance standards which reflect the values of people.

8 These measures can play an important role in the planning and decision process for the provision of leisure opportunities in cities.

9 The provision of leisure opportunities in cities can be a joint effort of the public and private sectors.

10 This effort is worthwhile in human terms and can be justified by its social, economic, political, and environmental benefits.

Reality Checks

Recreation planning is done in the real world. If it is to serve the needs of society, it cannot be an academic exercise. Urban America is not an easy place to do any type of planning or to implement public programs concerned with social services or the environment. The current and projected fiscal crisis of cities, the social problems associated with urban living, and the complexity of local government complicate an already difficult situation.

This book presents ideas in a pragmatic way that can be considered and applied in professional practice. Some ideas may not apply in all situations or need revision over time. Others may be too radical or inappropriate for some communities. The only way to discover what is workable is to try different approaches. Recreation planning will not be easy in Urban America, but it is worth trying.

Because the problems demand pragmatic solutions, theory will be minimized. Research is essential to advance the state of the art, but this takes time and resources that few clients, professionals, or consultants can commit to this effort. What seems most appropriate now is to begin asking the right questions in practice while universities and federal or state government agencies develop the theoretical foundations needed in this field.

Focus

Most books on recreation planning begin with answers. They become a "cookbook" of absolutes difficult to apply to different situations and changing circumstances. This book begins with questions and outlines a new approach to recreation planning that can apply to different situations and changing circumstances.

Detailed or theoretical discussions of a topic are omitted or referenced in the bibliography. Wherever possible, the focus will be on the practical results or implications of using a particular method instead of the theoretical results or abstract implications.

The rule rather than the exception is used to describe a complex process that can be generalized to many situations. To dwell on exceptions would add unnecessary length or detail that dilutes the conceptual focus of each topic. Where case studies apply, they are listed in the bibliography or illustrated in the text.

Some important aspects of recreation planning are not included in this volume. They are detailed in other books listed in the bibliography. These include topics such as tourism, management practices, administrative responsibility, fees and charges, site planning, and program leadership. There is also a substantial body of literature on the philosophy of leisure, recreation economics, project planning, maintenance and operations, creative play areas, and regional park systems that is omitted in order to focus on the process and methods used to prepare local recreation plans.

Format

This book is divided into three major parts. Part I (Chapters 1–6) outlines some basic definitions, relationships, and concepts of recreation planning. Part II (Chapters 7–12) describes selected methods and techniques used for preparing recreation plans. Part III (Chapters 13–15) concentrates on how to select alternatives and implement recreation plans with an emphasis on special problems and design opportunities.

The progression of ideas moves from awareness to problem solving. This book is intended both for beginners and experienced recreation planners. Beginners should try to understand the basic meaning of each chapter before proceeding to the next. The experienced recreation planner can use this book as a technical reference on each topic.

In either case, the reader is urged to read critically and apply or refine these ideas in practice. If successful, this book should raise more questions than it answers. It should leave the reader with a better understanding of recreation planning and motivation to help improve the state of the art.

RECREATION
AND PLANNING

1 | NATURE OF RECREATION PLANNING

Local government agencies and private developers share the responsibility for providing recreation spaces and leisure services in cities. Urban planners and landscape architects should play a primary role in the location, preservation, and design of open space, development of recreation facilities, and analysis of social programs to serve the leisure needs of people. They should also cooperate with other professionals in park and recreation agencies and the private sector who manage leisure opportunitites.

The preparation of the park, recreation, and open space element of a comprehensive plan is the joint responsiblity of most local planning and recreation agencies. These agencies are also responsible for processing, approving, or preparing public and private recreation development proposals, land use changes, environmental impact statements, and the capital improvement budget that can have a significant effect on the quantity and quality of leisure opportunities.

PROCESS AND PRODUCTS

Recreation planning is a process that relates the leisure time of people to space (Figure 1.1). It is an art and a science that uses the concepts and methods of many disciplines to provide public and private leisure opportunities in cities. In practice, recreation planning blends the knowledge and techniques of environmental design and the social sciences to develop alternatives for using leisure time, space, energy, and money to accommodate human needs.

The process results in products (plans, studies, information) that condition the public policy and private initiative used to provide leisure opportunities in cities. In the broadest sense, recreation planning is concerned with human development and the stewardship of land by helping relate people to their environment and to each other. In a narrow sense, recreation planning is most concerned with the variables of leisure behavior and open space.

Recreation planning is a hybrid of physical and social planning that has evolved from the professional fields of city planning, landscape architecture, recreation, and park administration. It now also includes aspects of public administration, sociology, civil engineering, forestry, geography, and environmental health. The evolution of urban recreation planning parallels the chronology shown in Figure 1.2.

Both the process and the products are evolving. The state of the art is crude compared to other types of functional planning. It lacks the necessary definitions, measures, theory, and precedent to produce credible or sophisticated plans. The process and the products still remain a mystery or abstraction to many people and professionals. However, this situation is changing. The current fiscal crisis of local government is forcing cities to do out of necessity what they might have done by choice.

Scope and Emphasis

The scope and emphasis of recreation planning have paralled the development of cities and the Park and Recreation Movement. The nature of recreation planning is rapidly changing in these ways:

TRADITIONAL EMPHASIS Recreation planning has been traditionally identified with resource planning or facility planning. The major emphasis has been on open space preservation and the development of these spaces for outdoor recreation. Before 1970, site design, organized competitive sports, and outdoor public spaces

FIGURE 1.1 Planning process/Edmonton, Alberta.

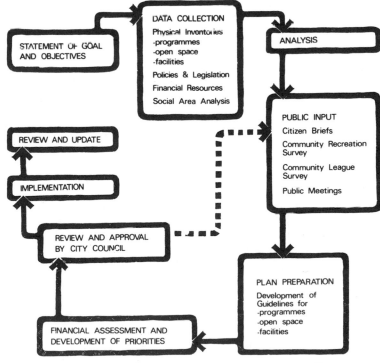

were the focus of most recreation plans. The philosophical basis of these plans was the Social Reform or City Beautiful Movement of the early 1900s. Public parks were viewed as natural refuges from the evils of the surrounding city. They were designed as pastoral retreats or escapes from the congestion and pollution of cities (Figure 1.3).

CURRENT EMPHASIS The current emphasis of recreation planning is on the relationship of public recreation opportunities to other types of land use, design, and access at the urban and regional scale. While the primary focus is still on the physical resource, this has been broadened to include social and environmental factors.

An expanded focus on urban beautification, commun-

FIGURE 1.2 Chronology of recreation planning/Bureau of Outdoor Recreation.

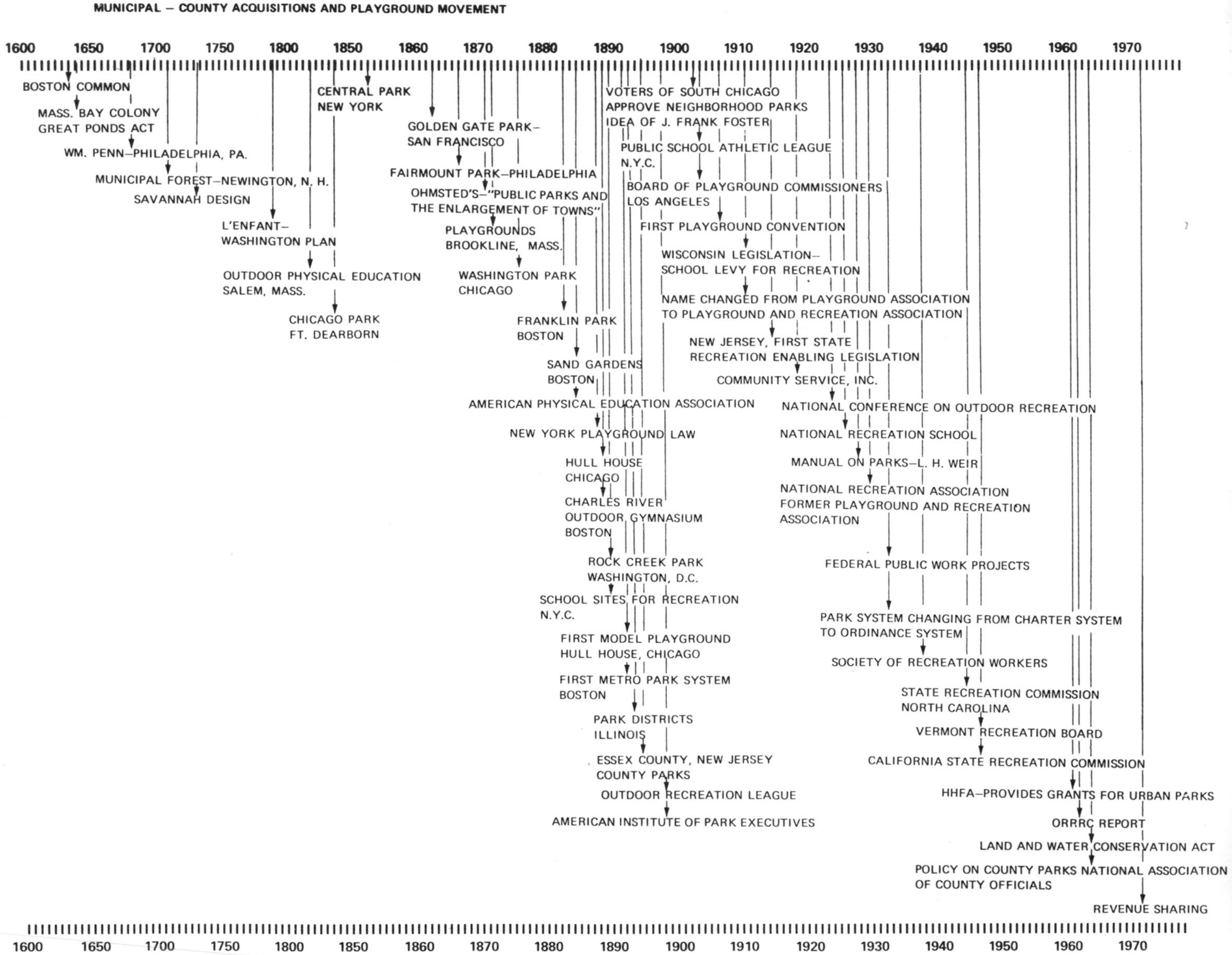

FIGURE 1.3 **Pastoral retreat concept of park design.** *(Top)* **The Terrace/Central Park, New York;** *(bottom)* **Reservoir Walk/Cleveland.**

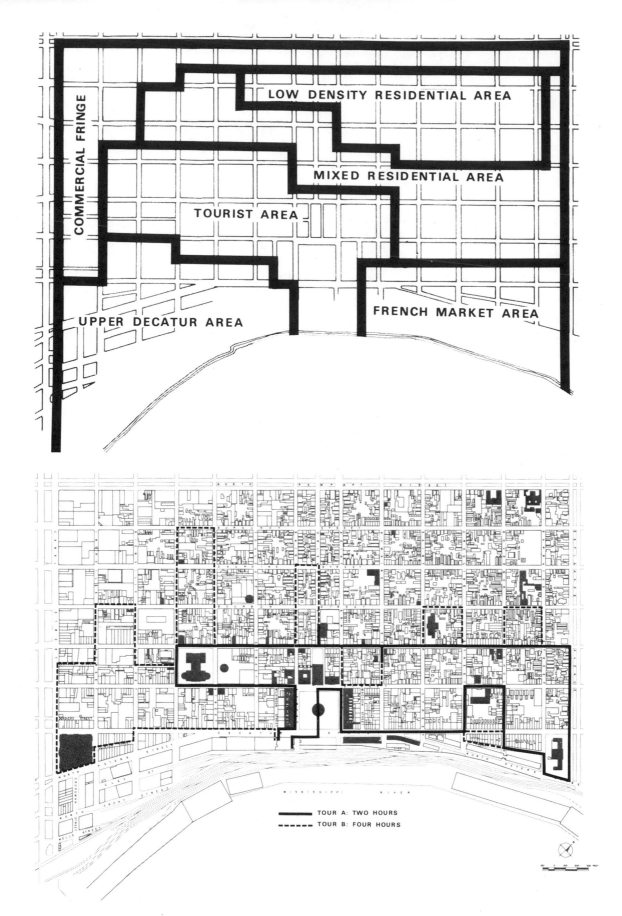

FIGURE 1.4 Historic preservation/Vieux Carre, New Orleans. *(Top)* Character areas; *(bottom)* proposed tourist trails.

ity development, historic preservation, environmental interpretation, multiple use of public and private spaces for recreation, and a broad range of organized recreation programs are now common in most communities. The philosophical justification of most efforts is to beautify or renew the city to make it a desirable place to live, work, or visit (Figure 1.4).

EMERGING EMPHASIS The emerging emphasis of recreation planning is a blend of environmental design, social science, and public administration to provide leisure opportunities as part of a human service and environmental management system. Both public and private spaces and services are included in a system of opportunities integrated at the neighborhood and metropolitan scale.

An emphasis on human development, environmental management, systems planning, self-generated design and management, recycling developed land into open space, noncompetitive self-programmed activities, creative play areas, and integration of the arts, culture, senior citizens, day care, and adult education programs with parks and recreation is emerging in many communities.

Special programs for the mentally retarded and physically handicapped are considered the responsibility of park and recreation departments. Community gardens, car care clinics, skateboard parks, and parcourse fitness are activities sponsored by park and recreation agencies. A new generation of spaces is being used to supplement existing resources in cities to include rooftops, cemeteries, pneumatic structures, air rights over parking lots, and the conversion of obsolete buildings to public or private recreational uses (Figure 1.5).

Previous distinctions between indoor and outdoor spaces and public vs. private opportunities are fading in a broader view of recreation planning that integrates space and services. The traditional parks or recreation department is becoming part of new agencies with a broader responsibility, e.g., human services, life enrichment, or environmental planning and management.

Recreation planning today requires more sensitive and sophisticated methods than the application of arbitrary standards and conventional thinking. New demands for citizen participation in the planning and design process, environmental and social impact assessment, and cost-effectiveness of public investments will make the traditional emphasis of recreation planning seem romantic.

These demands call for rethinking the objectives, purpose, approach, and methods of recreation planning to meet the needs of the present and future. They represent a hopeful mandate for recreation planners to help solve some of the physical and social problems of cities.

PURPOSE AND MISSION

Recreation planning deals with the future and develops alternatives for rational decisions by the public and private sector. It should be representative of what people want, imaginative in projecting what might be, and realistic in recognizing what is possible. It is based on the premise that (1) cities are for people, (2) change, complexity, and compromise are the essense of cities, and (3) planning is a means of anticipating, or reacting to, change.

FIGURE 1.5 Parcouse fitness course/San Francisco.

Purpose

The purpose of recreation planning is to meet events we expect to happen, accomplish things we want to happen, and prevent things we do not want to happen. If a city is to provide effective leisure opportunities, it can develop a course of action to solve current problems and anticipate future needs.

Recreation planning is one means of (1) obtaining a perspective on these problems, (2) developing realistic alternatives, (3) formulating goals, policies, and recommendations for public and private decisions, (4) developing criteria to measure change, and (5) involving people in the planning, design, and decision process.

Recreation planning is justified if it can describe issues to stimulate informed public discussion, consensus, and community action to solve common problems. Recreation planning can also become a guide for public or private decisions, coordination of effort, innovation or demonstration, and a vehicle to obtain federal, state, or private funds for public facilities.

Goals and Objectives

The overall goal of recreation planning is to improve the quality of life and environment in cities. The broad objective is to maximize human welfare by creating a better, more healthful, pleasurable, and attractive urban environment. The objectives of recreation planning are to:

1 Improve the physical environment of the community to make it more functional, beautiful, safe, exciting, and efficient.
2 Serve the public interest as defined by the courts and legislative or executive branches of government.
3 Inject long-range considerations into short-range decisions for the allocation of public and private resources.
4 Provide technical knowledge for political decisions concerning the social, economic, and physical development of a community.
5 Promote communication, cooperation, and coordination between all concerned with community development.

Professional Missions and Tasks

In a professional context, recreation planning has a mission that distinguishes it from other types of functional planning. This mission can be used to rationalize recreation planning as a function of local government. It can also be used to describe the operational tasks or responsibilities of a recreation planning unit or consultant to a public agency. This mission includes:

1 Providing objective, current, and relevant information to community decision makers about the quantity and quality of existing or potential leisure opportunities.
2 Improving the quantity and quality of the leisure experience for residents and visitors to the city.
3 Providing an optimum range, mix, and location of leisure opportunities for all people.
4 Preserving or developing appropriate recreation resources to serve their highest and best use.
5 Relating recreation plans to other types of planning and the comprehensive plan.
6 Promoting public understanding and support for more effective recreation planning at all levels of government.
7 Evaluating the effectiveness of existing and proposed public and private recreation development.
8 Encouraging public and private cooperation to provide leisure opportunities in or near cities.
9 Rationalizing existing and proposed park and recreation facilities and services.
10 Encouraging innovation, demonstration, and research to improve the state of the art.

PLANNING CONTEXT

The historical development and current orientation of recreation planning have paralleled the development of planning in this country. As a professional specialty, recreation planning and design have been associated with these types of planning:

RESOURCE PLANNING The allocation and development of natural or human resources in a rural context.

URBAN AND REGIONAL PLANNING The arrangement, form, and function of land use, housing, transportation, and community facilities in an urban context.

FACILITY PLANNING The provision and design of facilities such as highways, schools, parks, airports, and utilities.

ENVIRONMENTAL HEALTH PLANNING The protection of public health and safety, with emphasis on air and water pollution abatement, pest control, stress reduction, and the provision of health services.

SOCIAL PLANNING The development of institutions to carry out social goals with an emphasis on welfare programs, public housing, community organization, and social services.

ADVOCACY PLANNING   Planning for the objectives of a planning unit or special interest group with an emphasis on projects or services that meet the immediate needs of a special population or neighborhood unit.

ENVIRONMENTAL PLANNING   The integration of physical and social factors with an emphasis on natural ecosystems, environmental impact analysis, and the design and management of open space to provide for the public health, safety, and welfare.

Types of Planning

In an urban context, recreation planning has shifted from an identity with resource or facility planning to an identity with urban and environmental planning in the context of environmental design. In the future, recreation planning may develop closer associations with social and advocacy planning. However, its primary professional identity will remain with landscape architecture and urban planning.

There are two major types of plans: (1) single-purpose or project plans, which have a specific objective such as the development of a neighborhood park, and (2) policy or system plans, which have many objectives in a given planning area, such as the acquisition, development, and program in all city parks. The policy plan provides a framework for decision making, while the project plan provides a vehicle for implementing the policy plan.

Both types of plans should be based on people living with nature in a context of planned change and orderly development. If either type of plan cannot meet the conditions of rational land use, public interest, objectivity, and citizen participation, it should not be accepted as the type of recreation planning that is needed and possible.

PROJECT VS. SYSTEM PLANS   Figures 1.6 and 1.7 show the relationship between systems and project scale planning units in a small community. At the metropolitan or regional scale, the same differences of scale, time, service area, and political constituency are evident except the complexity or extremes are greater. Recreation planning must be done at both scales to be effective. The system should be viewed as a series of componenets in time and space. Likewise, each component should be viewed as part of an interrelated system in time and space that is constantly changing or responding to new influences of public values, technology, legislation, and funding (Figures 1.8–1.12).

Traditionally, too much effort has been placed on standardizing all parts of the system in time and space when greater diversity is necessary to serve most urban populations. For example, there is no reason why all neighborhood parks must be public, flat, square and contain a conventional mix of facilities. Likewise, there is no reason why parks should not be constantly renewed to reflect changing population, technology, or environmental conditions. The concept of standardizing public parks to simplify management or be consistent within the system is arbitrary because it will not accommodate the diverse and rapidly changing populations of cities.

A more constructive strategy is to tailor each component of the system to the levels of anticipated change and provide a maximum range of diversity in the system. In practice, the components determine the system instead of the system determining the components. It is also less difficult to change any individual component than the entire system to respond to rapid or unexpected changes in financing or life-style. The impact of a tax-payer revolt, energy crisis, racial or ethnic change, or aging population suggest this strategy as the best way to cope with change.

Types of Recreation Plans

Recreation plans can be classified by their scope, orientation, geographic area, or client. Most plans conform to the political jurisdiction of the planning unit, are comprehensive, and are oriented to serve the needs of the entire community. However, the community should be considered as a series of social groups or geographic areas with different values and needs. Planning for the mythical "average" person can be a serious mistake.

A component of recreation plans should be devoted to special populations, e.g., the handicapped or disadvantaged. There are also unique places or districts in cities, e.g., university campuses or historic districts, that require special plans. The private sector also needs special studies oriented to the location of, or demand for, recreation products and services, e.g., marinas, shopping centers, or entertainment districts (Figure 1.14).

Recreation plans can also be classified by the client, planning area, or level of government it serves. These differences determine the orientation, scale of analysis, and product of any recreation planning effort. They can also help determine the types of users, service area, and supplier of different kinds of recreation opportunities.

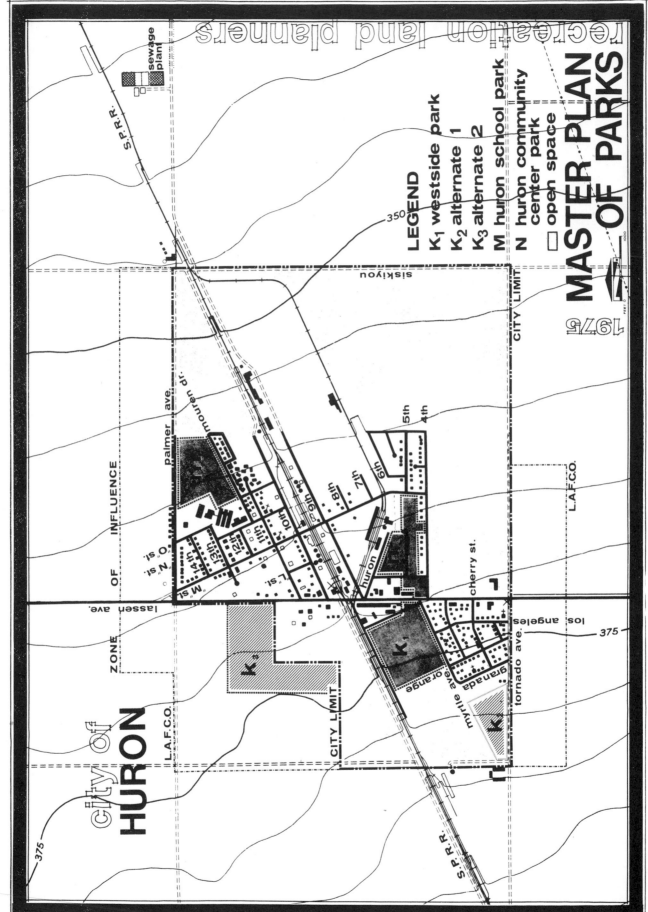

FIGURE 1.6 Systems scale planning unit/Huron California.

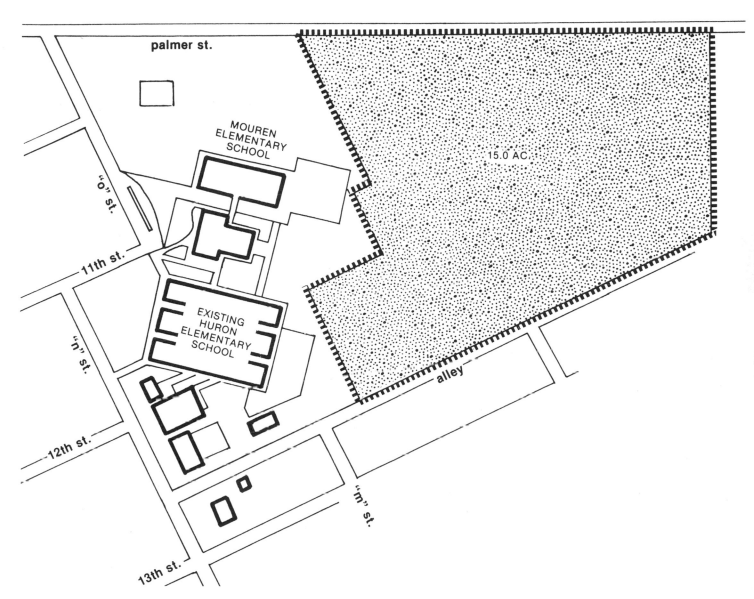

FIGURE 1.7 Project scale planning unit/Huron, California.

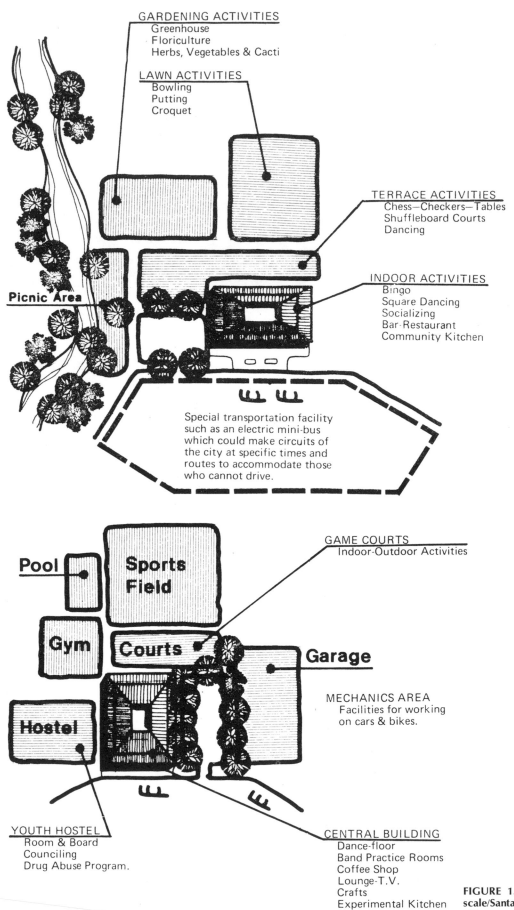

GARDENING ACTIVITIES
    Greenhouse
    Floriculture
    Herbs, Vegetables & Cacti

LAWN ACTIVITIES
    Bowling
    Putting
    Croquet

TERRACE ACTIVITIES
    Chess—Checkers—Tables
    Shuffleboard Courts
    Dancing

INDOOR ACTIVITIES
    Bingo
    Square Dancing
    Socializing
    Bar-Restaurant
    Community Kitchen

Picnic Area

Special transportation facility
such as an electric mini-bus
which could make circuits of
the city at specific times and
routes to accommodate those
who cannot drive.

Pool

Sports Field

Gym

Courts

Garage

Hostel

GAME COURTS
    Indoor-Outdoor Activities

MECHANICS AREA
    Facilities for working
    on cars & bikes.

YOUTH HOSTEL
    Room & Board
    Counciling
    Drug Abuse Program.

CENTRAL BUILDING
    Dance-floor
    Band Practice Rooms
    Coffee Shop
    Lounge-T.V.
    Crafts
    Experimental Kitchen
    Music Instruction

FIGURE 1.8 Neighborhood or district scale/Santa Cruz, California. *(Top)* Senior citizen center; *(bottom)* teen center.

West Orange Community Park

FIGURE 1.9   Community scale/West Orange Community Park, Orange, California.

15

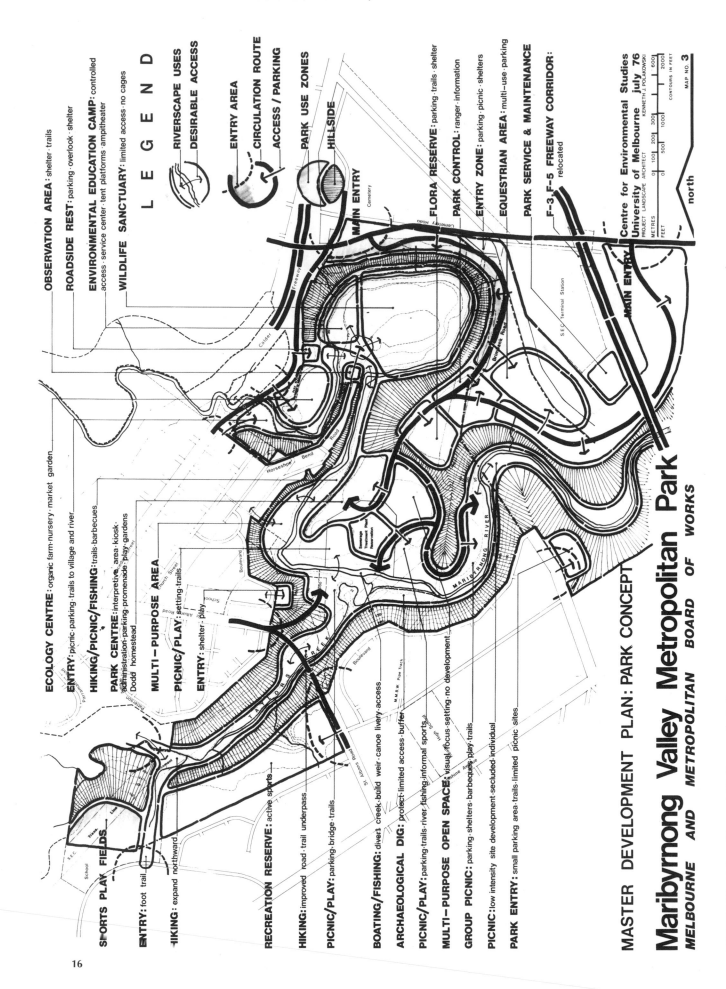

FIGURE 1.10 Metropolitan scale/Melbourne, Australia.

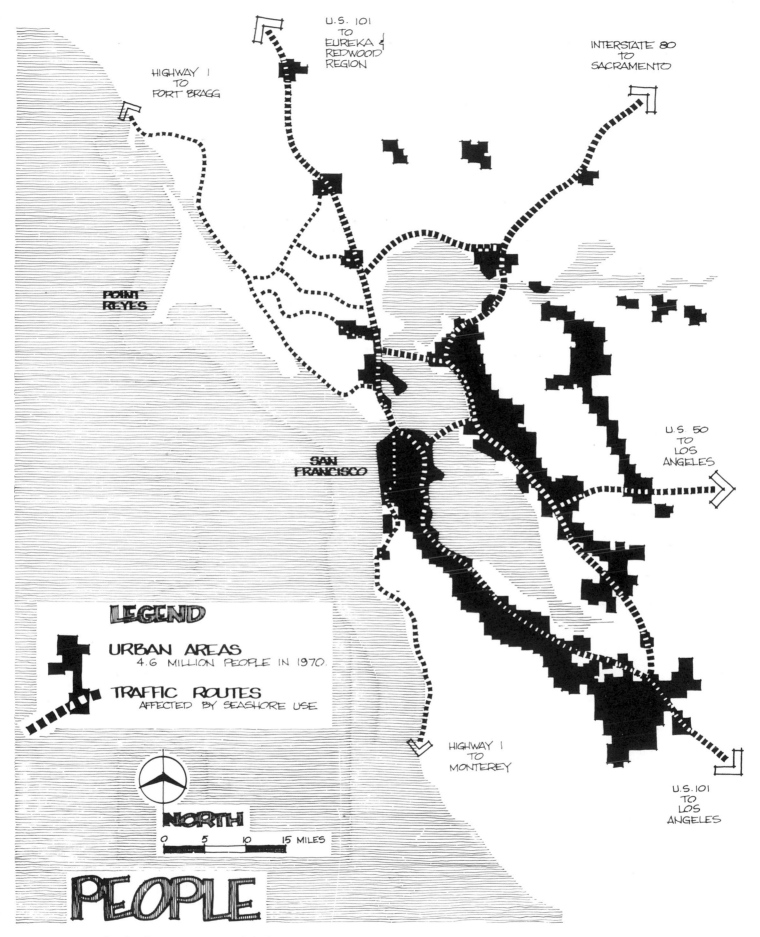

HIGHWAY 1
TO
FORT BRAGG

U.S. 101
TO
EUREKA &
REDWOOD
REGION

INTERSTATE 80
TO
SACRAMENTO

POINT
REYES

SAN
FRANCISCO

U.S. 50
TO
LOS
ANGELES

HIGHWAY 1
TO
MONTEREY

U.S. 101
TO
LOS
ANGELES

LEGEND

URBAN AREAS
4.6 MILLION PEOPLE IN 1970.

TRAFFIC ROUTES
AFFECTED BY SEASHORE USE

NORTH

0   5   10   15 MILES

PEOPLE

FIGURE 1.11   Regional scale/Pt. Reyes National Seashore, California.

17

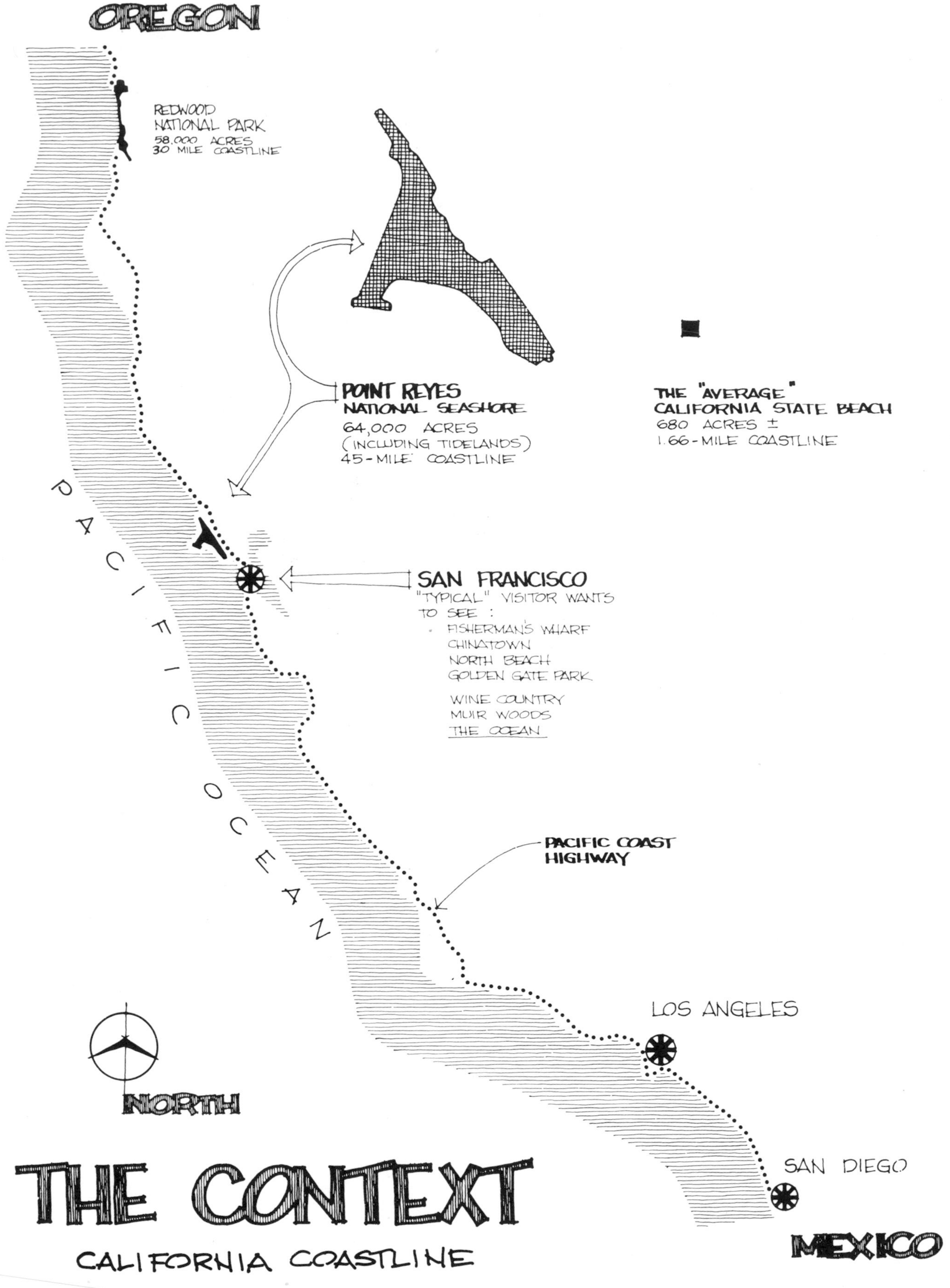

OREGON

REDWOOD
NATIONAL PARK
58,000 ACRES
30 MILE COASTLINE

POINT REYES
NATIONAL SEASHORE

64,000 ACRES
(INCLUDING TIDELANDS)
45-MILE COASTLINE

THE "AVERAGE"
CALIFORNIA STATE BEACH
680 ACRES ±
1.66-MILE COASTLINE

PACIFIC OCEAN

SAN FRANCISCO
"TYPICAL" VISITOR WANTS
TO SEE :
 · FISHERMAN'S WHARF
   CHINATOWN
   NORTH BEACH
   GOLDEN GATE PARK

   WINE COUNTRY
   MUIR WOODS
   THE OCEAN

PACIFIC COAST
HIGHWAY

LOS ANGELES

NORTH

SAN DIEGO

THE CONTEXT

CALIFORNIA COASTLINE

MEXICO

FIGURE 1.12   Regional context/Pt. Reyes National Seashore, California.

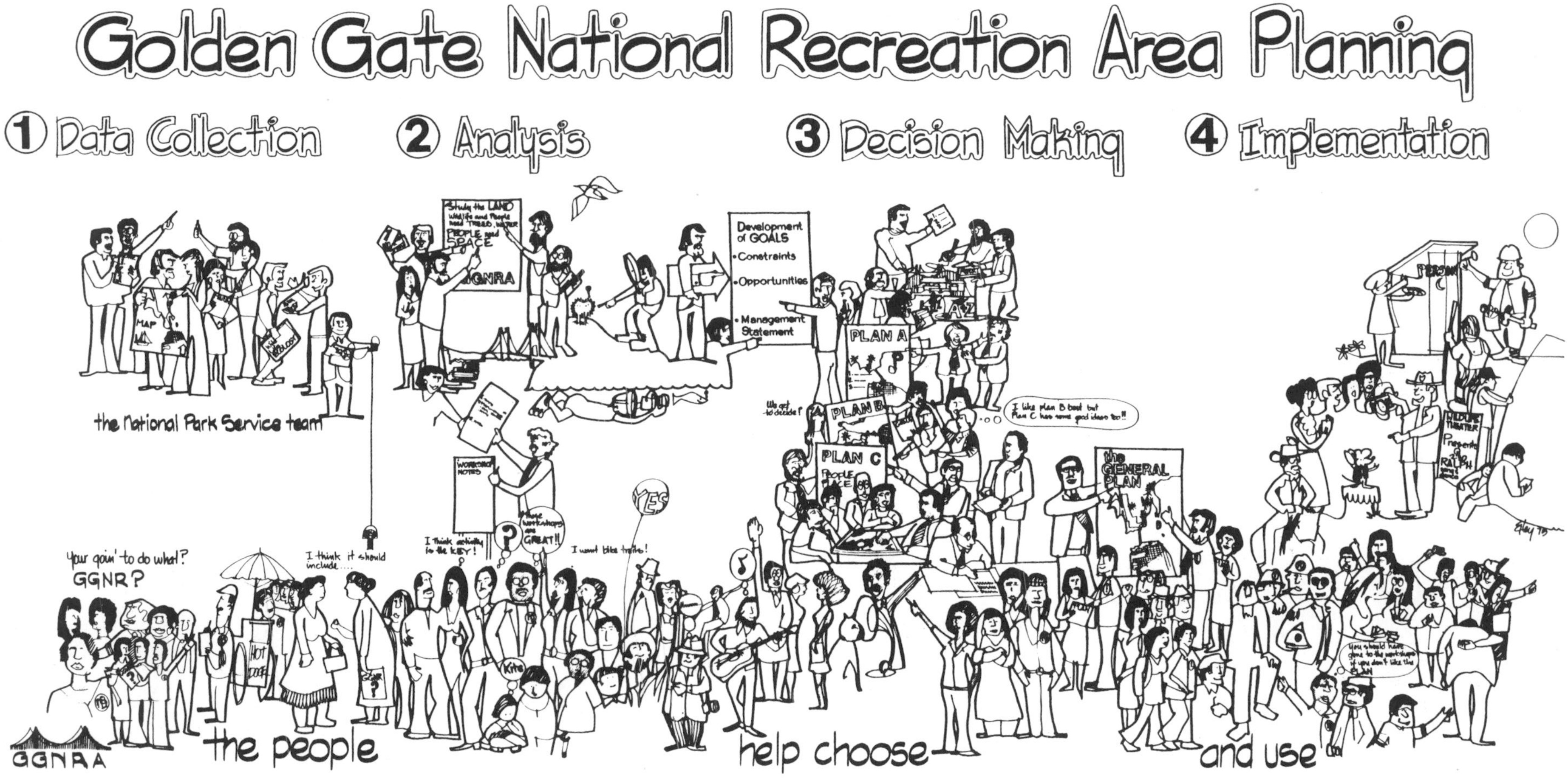

FIGURE 1.13 User-oriented approach to recreation planning/Golden Gate National Recreation Area, San Francisco.

19

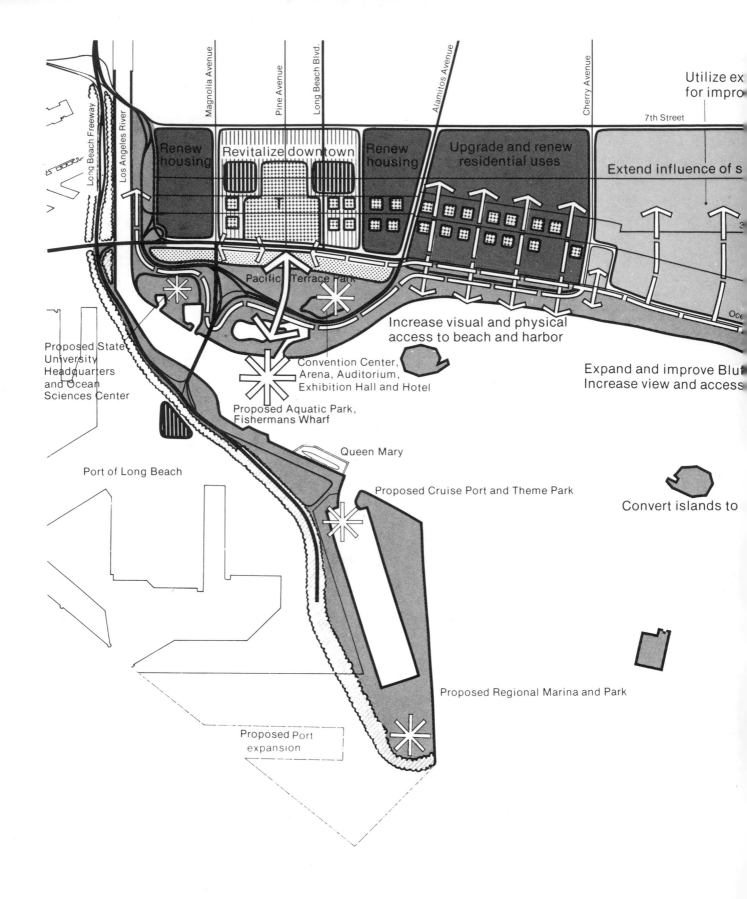

FIGURE 1.14 Waterfront recreation development/Long Beach, California.

20

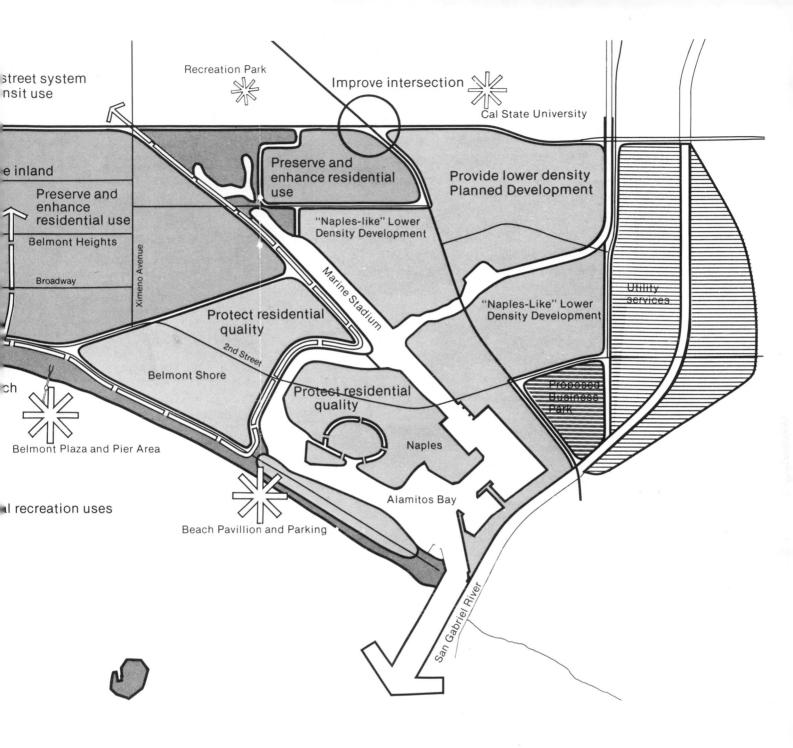

Recreation Park

Improve intersection

Cal State University

street system
nsit use

e inland

Preserve and
enhance
residential use

Preserve and
enhance residential
use

Provide lower density
Planned Development

Belmont Heights

"Naples-like" Lower
Density Development

Broadway

Utility
services

Ximeno Avenue

Marine Stadium

Protect residential
quality

"Naples-Like" Lower
Density Development

2nd Street

Belmont Shore

Protect residential
quality

Proposed
Business
Park

ch

Belmont Plaza and Pier Area

Naples

l recreation uses

Beach Pavillion and Parking

Alamitos Bay

San Gabriel River

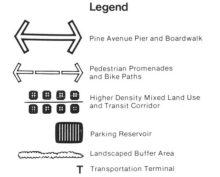

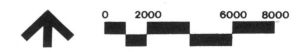

Legend

Pine Avenue Pier and Boardwalk

Pedestrian Promenades
and Bike Paths

Higher Density Mixed Land Use
and Transit Corridor

Parking Reservoir

Landscaped Buffer Area

T Transportation Terminal

Long Beach Shoreline Study

City Planning Department
City of Long Beach

The SWA Group
Formerly Sasaki, Walker Associates
Planning Consultants

0   2000   6000   8000

USER- VS. RESOURCE-ORIENTED PLANS   One basic distinction in most recreation plans is a difference in orientation. Traditionally, recreation plans at both the urban and nonurban levels have been resource-oriented. The dominant emphasis was on the preservation of open space. User behavior, programmed services, the private sector, and public involvement are token aspects of these plans. The predictable result is many current plans have little public understanding or support.

Although there is a strong logic for resource-oriented planning at the regional, state, and national levels for nonurban parks administered by public agencies such as the National Park Service, this orientation does not apply in urban areas, regardless of who supplies the recreational opportunities.

In many cases, the simple distinctions between user- and resource-oriented planning have not been observed. This is one cause of the planning problems commonly associated with federal or state efforts to provide urban recreation opportunities. Recent attempts to correct this problem are conspicuous in the user-oriented approach to recreation planning for the Golden Gateway Recreation Areas in New York and San Francisco (Figure 1.13). The success of these and similar projects can be measured against how well each accepts these conditions of user-oriented recreation planning:

1   More complexity, compromise, controversy, and unknowns.

2   Less sophisticated methodology, research base, and more experimental techniques.

3   Less lead time for planning and demonstration because of the urgent needs and political climate of most cities.

4   A range of user groups/activities that is probably 10 times that for most resource-oriented areas. This factor implies more actors in the planning process, a better understanding of user-resource relationships and more citizen participation in reviewing plans.

5   More intensive design, development, and maintenance.

6   Better access by mass transit, bicycles, and pedestrians.

7   More sensitive considerations of multiple-use, human-carrying-capacity, and design-load criteria for their impacts on both the user and the resource.

8   More detailed consideration of the environmental impact of park and recreation facilities on surrounding land use.

The preparation of a resource-oriented plan for nonurban areas is a relatively simple exercise compared to the preparation of user-oriented plans for urban areas. This is why most plans still reflect a resource orientation. The future trend, however, is toward recreation plans that reflect a balanced orientation between user needs and resource constraints. The result will be a greater sensitivity to social and natural factors that combines the methods of each orientation.

THE PLANNING PROCESS

Planning is a continuous and incremental process which develops guidelines for urban development. The concept of development includes preservation or renewal of spaces and services. The recreation planning process results in plans, studies, or information that can be used to make decisions regarding a city's changing leisure needs, problems, and opportunities.

Recreation planning is a systematic way of anticipating, causing, preventing, or monitoring change related to the provision of public and private leisure opportunities. It is a continuous process of change in response to new social values, life-style patterns, technology, legislation, and the availability of resources. Despite differences in the scope, scale, or orientation of recreation plans, the planning process should be:

1   *Evolutionary* instead of revolutionary. Radical changes may be necessary, but they will have a much greater chance of public acceptance if proposed in an incremental or demonstration program.

2   *Pluralistic* instead of authoritarian. The right choice is a matter of value, not fact, based on a consideration of alternatives from individuals or groups with different objectives.

3   *Objective* instead of subjective. The criteria or methodology used to describe alternatives should minimize distortion of the facts even though the final decision may be based on subjective values.

4   *Realistic* instead of politically naive. Parks and recreation should develop a constituency to compete effectively in the decision or budget process.

5   *Humanistic* instead of bureaucratic. Proposed plans, designs, or programs should be people-serving instead of agency-serving. The agencies responsible for providing leisure opportunities or preparing the plan should be accountable for their actions.

Steps, Stages, and Products

At the systems level, the planning process is organized into the sequence shown in Figure 1.15. At the site planning level, the design process is organized into the process shown in Figure 1.16. Although this process is common to most planning or design efforts, there is considerable difference in the approach, concepts, and methods used to apply this process at both the systems

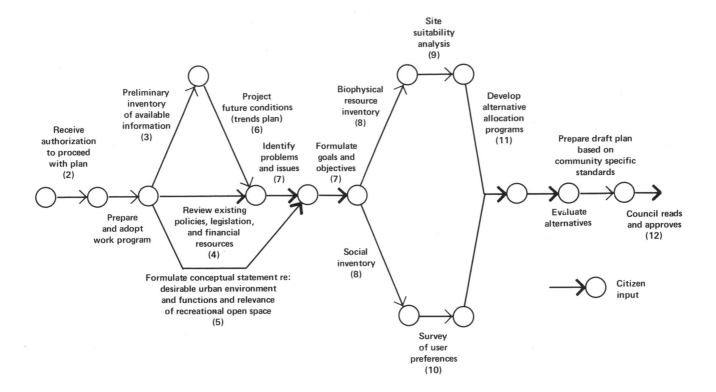

FIGURE 1.15 Planning process at the system level.

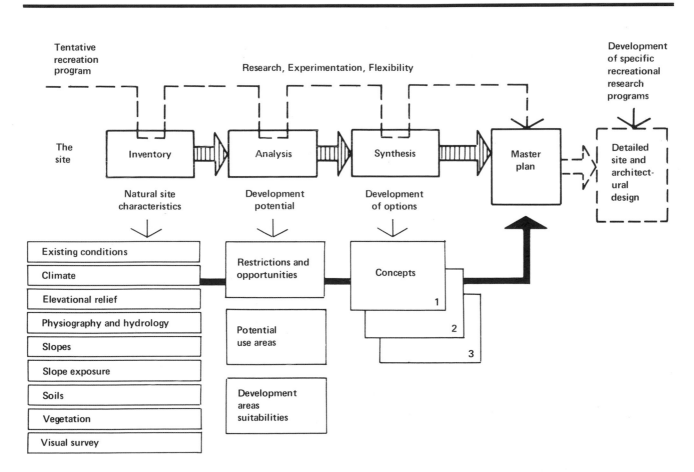

FIGURE 1.16 Design process at the site level.

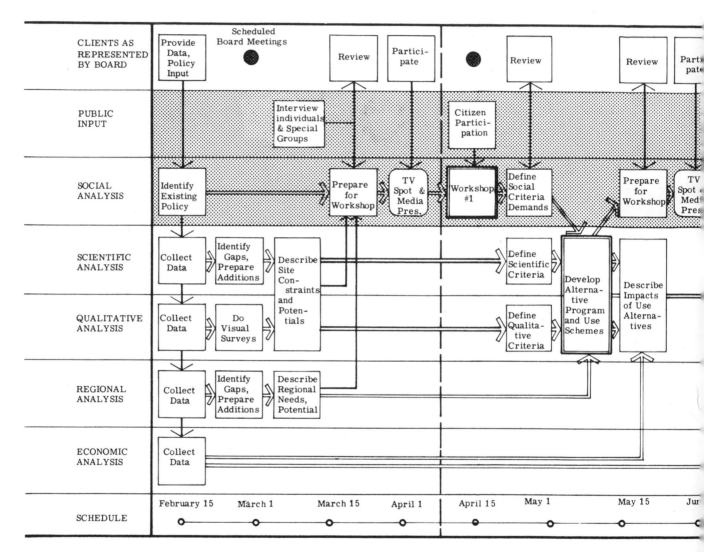

FIGURE 1.17 Work program for recreation planning/Shelby County, Tennessee.

and site planning level. These differences are conditioned by different views of the planning process.

TRADITIONAL VIEW   The traditional view of planning is a static and linear process that follows a series of logical and consecutive steps. Planners begin with defining the problem and end with recommendations to solve the problem. The emphasis is on the *output* or product instead of the *input* and process. A primary concern is on the *what* and *how* of planning, rather than *who* participates and *why*. The means often become ends. Imple-

menting the plan becomes the objective instead of the way to achieve an objective.

The traditional planning process attempts to reduce the complexity with arbitrary guidelines or standards to produce uniform spaces or services. Professionals superimpose their values on the process. Citizens are asked to participate in a token way by reviewing plans or proposals prepared by experts. Everything is organized and predictable in terms of timing, responsibility, and outcome. The product of this process is a two-dimensional physical plan that is inflexible, uniform, and

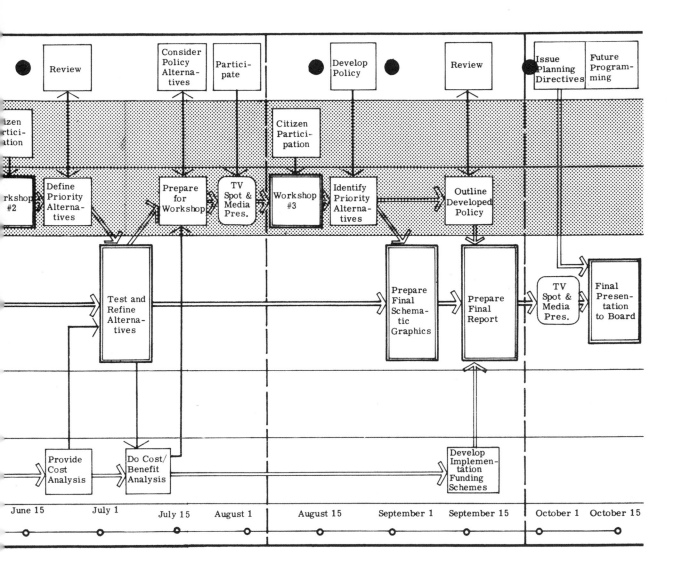

unrepresentative of many of the values or needs in a community.

NEW VIEW   The new view of planning sees the process as dynamic and incremental. It begins with the values, behavior, or priorities of many people and accommodates these through political compromise. The emphasis is on *input* and process. Change, controversy, compromise, and involvement at all stages of the planning process are expected. Ends are used to justify the means. Achieving these ends is more important than the plan

and the methods used to prepare it.

The new view attempts to encourage diversity with criteria sensitive to the particular needs of a social group or planning area. The objective is to provide *effective* spaces or services. Professionals act as resource persons to translate human values into *alternatives* that people, or their representatives, can consider and revise. Citizen participation is essential and taken seriously at every step in this process.

The outcome of the process is not predictable and the sequence of events may not flow smoothly or in any preconceived pattern. The product is normally a set of policies, priorities, or criteria that are relatively flexible, diverse, and representative of community values.

Approaches to Planning

Both the traditional and the new view of the planning process are the intellectual basis of different approaches to recreation planning and design. The gap between these approaches is the cause of much conflict associated with the planning process. An understanding of the differences between these approaches is fundamental to the application of methods and techniques described in this book.

TRADITIONAL APPROACH The traditional approach emphasizes these concepts: (1) quantity over quality, (2) physical over social objectives, (3) form over function, (4) growth or development over no-growth and preservation of natural resources, and (5) the community rather than the individual. These concepts are usually reflected in (1) the preparation of single-purpose, physical plans, (2) a terminal planning process, (3) a centralized planning function located outside the planning area, (4) long-range time horizons, and (5) rigid planning units related to political or physical boundaries.

NEW APPROACH The new approach to planning emphasizes a different set of values which rank (1) quality over quantity, (2) social over physical objectives, (3) function over form, (4) conservation over the development of natural resources, and (5) the individual over the community. These concepts are usually reflected in (1) the preparation of multipurpose policy plans, (2) a continuous planning and review process, (3) a decentralized planning function located inside the planning area, (4) short-range time horizons, and (5) flexible planning units based on the resource, users, or problem.

The traditional approach is primarily concerned with costs and efficiency while the new approach is primarily concerned with benefits and effectiveness. The new approach is more quantitative in method and qualitative in its ends than the traditional approach. It relies on the use of sophisticated research methods, gaming simulation, systems analysis, program budgeting, and advocacy planning to develop policy alternatives that can be translated into action programs.

While the traditional approach might have been adequate for dealing with the problems of the past, it is inadequate to cope with the problems of the present and future. Recreation planning is in transition between the accepted methods of the past and untested methods of the future. Most current planning efforts include aspects of both approaches. However, the traditional approach is still dominant because most consultants or public agencies do not have the time, money, or expertise to change.

Ingredients and Criteria

Regardless of what approach is taken to the planning process, there are some important ingredients and criteria that condition the scope, direction, and products of this process. A serious consideration of these at the beginning of a planning effort should increase its effectiveness.

PERFORMANCE CRITERIA These criteria outline what should be expected of the planning process. They can also be used to give planners, decision makers, and citizens guidelines for evaluating the products of the process.

1 The scope of the planning process should be as broad as the concerns of the client or government it serves.

2 The scope and sophistication of the planning effort should be related to available tools and resources to implement proposals.

3 Plans should provide the decision maker with internally consistent policy recommendations that can be implemented over time.

4 Plans should assess the probable consequences, costs, and benefits of alternative courses of action.

5 The process should be balanced in all five stages in terms of the professional and citizen effort devoted to each stage.

6 Planning is a way to encourage more orderly urban development and rational public or private decisions. It is one means to these ends and not an end in itself.

7 Planning will be effective only to the extent it is understood and supported by citizens who have been realistically involved in every step of the process.

8 Planning is a continuous process dealing with changing opportunities, problems, and issues that require constant monitoring, evaluation, and feedback by citizen participation.

9 Controversy and compromise are normal dimensions of the planning process which should be expected by all concerned with any planning effort.

10 The planning process and products will be no better than the resources committed to this effort.

Precedent and Practice

There is no formula for the planning process, only precedent and practice. Each situation may require or create a different approach to fit the needs of the client, planning area, and times. If many plans are inadequate, it is because they are products of people, politics, and the times. They reflect the state of an evolving art.

There are no absolutes in the planning process. However, there is a growing body of experience that points toward the success or failure of the planning process based on these ingredients:

COMMUNITY SUPPORT   Special interest groups recognize the need for a plan and for being actively involved in the process. The establishment of citizen advisory committees to provide information and serve as a sounding board for political feasibility is essential.

TECHNICAL SUPPORT   Administrative organization, technical expertise, cooperation, and support of the planning effort by all public agencies is as important as citizen participation. Technical advisory committees of professionals to collaborate in the planning process and resolve the institutionalized biases of different agencies or professional groups is fundamental to any planning effort.

WORK PROGRAM   A detailed program to establish the timing and responsibility for each task is essential. The problem, planning area, planning period, and methods of data collection, analysis, or reporting, should be established in advance and agreed to by all involved in the planning effort (Figure 1.17).

GOAL FORMULATION   Early establishment of initial goals and policies is imperative to provide direction to the planning effort. Tentative goals should be formulated to stimulate the process of citizen and staff involvement at the beginning of the planning process. These goals should remain flexible and subject to change during the planning process.

DATA COLLECTION   Systematic data collection and analysis are the foundation of a sound planning program. Alternatives cannot be developed or considered without the facts. The planning process must have a credible data base to provide a context for resolving issues.

POLITICAL COMPROMISE   Facts should provide an objective basis for the development of alternatives that can be considered in the decision process. The ultimate choice may be a matter of value instead of fact.

DEVELOPING ALTERNATIVES   The development, selection, and testing of alternatives is the most difficult part of the planning process. Achieving consensus on which alternative best reflects the preliminary goals and policies is crucial to the success of any planning effort.

FUTURE PERSPECTIVE   A bold, imaginative view of the foreseeable future based on the best available facts or interpretation of near-certain trends is essential. The planning process and plan should be future-oriented.

2 | CONCEPTS AND PRINCIPLES

The nature of cities and recreation requires an understanding of basic terms, relationships, and issues before applying the methods of recreation planning. There is no consensus on all concepts because of the rapidly changing nature of recreation planning and cities. However, precedent and practice suggest these concepts as a place to begin in most communities.

The basic planning task is to understand the significant relationships between people, cities, leisure, recreation, open space, and urban form. The detailed planning task is to relate time (leisure), activity (behavior), and space to a geographic area (the city). Both tasks will require value judgments, calculated risk decisions, and additional research. Both will require demonstration to find out what will work best in situations ranging from the inner city to the suburb.

BASIC DEFINITIONS

Many recreation planning efforts are not effective because of the ambiguous terms used to describe recreation. While no definitions can meet all needs, there is a general acceptance of these terms and those listed in the glossary:

Leisure Any portion of an individual's time not occupied by employment or in pursuit of essential activities.

Recreation Any leisure time activity which is pursued for its own sake, or what happens to a person as a result of a recreation experience.

Outdoor Recreation Leisure time activities which utilize an outdoor public or private space.

Park Any area of public or private land set aside for aesthetic, educational, recreational, or cultural use.

Recreation Planning A process that relates people to leisure time and space. The use of information for the allocation of resources to accommodate the current and future leisure needs of a population and planning area. The emphasis is at the macroscale and systems level.

Recreation Design A process that relates people to the form and function of a recreation resource. The use of information to create designs that relate to the existing or potential users of a recreation space or population of a planning area. The emphasis is at the microscale and site or project level.

Glossaries and interpretation of these terms are available in many texts and government documents. Because some terms have different philosophical or pragmatic meanings in different communities and high levels of citizen participation are needed to prepare a recreation plan, it is *essential* to establish a working set of definitions at the *beginning* of any planning effort.

The meaning given to words conveys a set of values and establishes the level of sophistication in the planning process. These meanings can change over time, as the symbolic or philosophical interpretation of a term changes. Defining terms is an important aspect of any planning effort because it will prompt people and professionals to consider their values or understanding of the problem. Definitions can condition the scope or emphasis of the planning process. They can also play a vital role in helping to clarify issues, encourage communication, and minimize the ambiguity associated with most recreation planning efforts.

SIGNIFICANT RELATIONSHIPS

The relationships between people, cities, leisure, outdoor recreation, open space, and urban form are the essence of recreation planning and design. This overview can be used as a justification for the provision of recreation space and services in cities.

People and the City

Our reliance on the city for a livelihood, social interaction, food, shelter, and services has made it the focus of American life. Most Americans meet their major needs, desires, and ambitions in a metropolitan area. Family life, employment, education, culture, and leisure activities take place essentially in an urban setting. Instead of viewing the city or suburb as a place to escape from, during leisure, it should be considered a recreation resource with great potential. We can build cities in parks instead of parks in cities (Figure 2.1).

People and Leisure

The prospect of leisure has become an end in itself for many people engaged in dull or meaningless work. Leisure also provides the time and means for human development in a technological, work-oriented society. A major problem for growing numbers of people is how and where to utilize increasing amounts of leisure time. How we solve this problem may influence our culture and society. Leisure can be the blessing or the curse of an urban society.

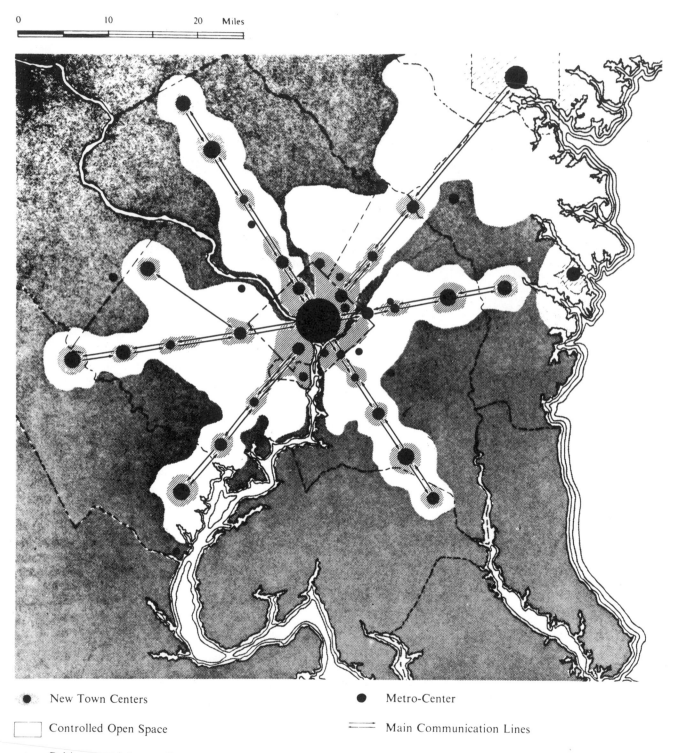

0   10   20   Miles

New Town Centers

Controlled Open Space

Baltimore and Annapolis

Metro-Center

Main Communication Lines

FIGURE 2.1 Washington radial corridor plan/Maryland National Capital Park and Planning Commission.

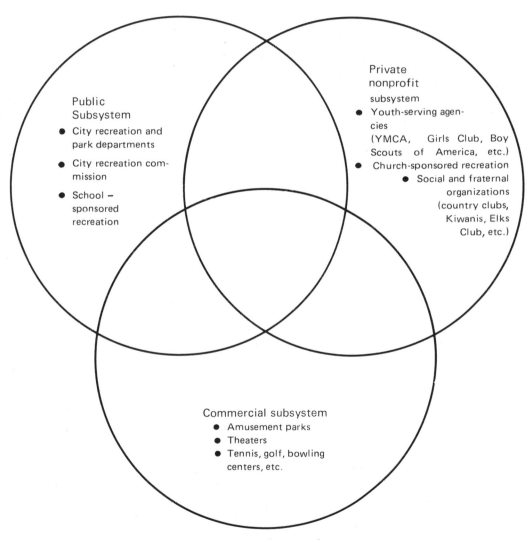

FIGURE 2.2 Community recreation system.
*(James F. Murphy and Dennis R. Howard,
Delivery of Community Leisure Services,
Lea & Febiger, Philadelphia, 1977.)*

FIGURE 2.3 Urban parks with a natural character/Central Park, New York.

Leisure and Recreation

Leisure and recreation are related, but different things. While leisure has commonly been thought of as a period of time or state of mind and recreation as an activity in space, the contemporary view is much broader and more humanistic. This view sees leisure as a context for pleasure and self-expression, and recreation as what happens to people as a direct result of activities or experiences. Recreation is not a point in time or space; it is an emotional condition independent of activity, leisure, or social acceptance.

Recreation is what happens to people in terms of self-image, achievement, or satisfaction and can occur at any time and in many places. By this definition, the requirements for an effective recreation experience in cities go far beyond traditional public spaces and programs. They

include any aspect of a city where an individual can experience freedom, diversity, self-expression, challenge, or enrichment (Figure 2.2).

Outdoor Recreation and Open Space

The relationship of outdoor recreation to open space is based on a biological need to retain some association with the natural environment in an urban setting and a psychological need for contrast and change in spacial surroundings and activities that most indoor environments do not provide. When these needs are linked with the routine indoor jobs of most people and the sterile or stressful outdoor environments of many cities and suburbs, they generate strong desires for escape to open space, especially those with a natural character.

This desire is why many people seek recreation opportunities in regional parks or travel long distances to public wilderness areas or private resorts. The desire to experience open space also explains why many large urban parks with a natural character are heavily used and essential to those without the means to leave cities for this type of recreation experience (Figure 2.3). The same holds true at the neighborhood scale, except the desire is more for visual contrast to the surrounding area, simple outdoor recreation activities, or social focus in a landscaped setting.

Open Space and Urban Form

Open space can be the structural framework of a city to produce edges, focuses, nodes, districts, and regions of different size, scale, and character (Figure 2.4). The opportunity to experience an architectural element from the vantage point of open space is a unique visual quality. No single element can better shape and compliment urban form than well-placed open space. Its ability to differentiate, integrate, or buffer different types of land use or activities is unsurpassed. Sensitively designed open space can give people a sense of identity and territoriality. It can define urban form and limit the physical size, shape, or density of a city or neighborhood (Figure 2.5).

REALITY CHECKS

Relationships and definitions change over time and are conditioned by values. The process or products of recreation planning relate to facts, trends, and changing

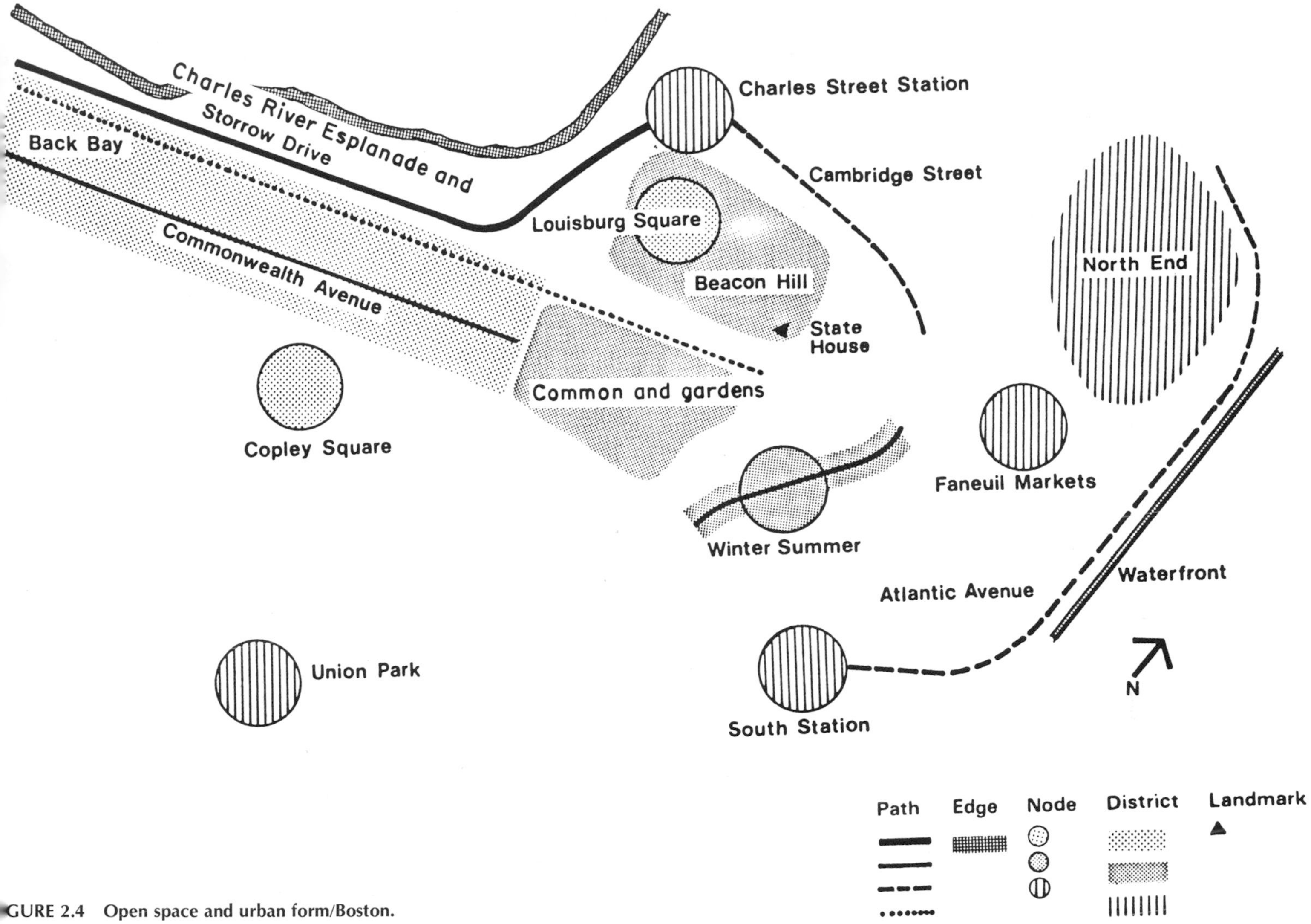
Charles River Esplanade and
Storrow Drive
Back Bay
Commonwealth Avenue
Charles Street Station
Cambridge Street
Louisburg Square
Beacon Hill
State House
North End
Common and gardens
Copley Square
Faneuil Markets
Winter Summer
Atlantic Avenue
Waterfront
Union Park
South Station
N
Path
Edge
Node
District
Landmark

GURE 2.4 **Open space and urban form/Boston.**

perspectives about life and leisure in America. This overview provides the factual and issue context for other chapters. It also provides a reality check to help measure the effectiveness of planning techniques detailed in other parts of this book.

Facts and Trends

A perspective on the time, space, and municipal budgets devoted to providing public leisure services in Urban America includes these important facts and trends that should be considered in preparing recreation plans:

USE PATTERNS Most urban parks are underutilized or unused by a majority of the population they were intended to serve. The phenomena of nonuse is common in both urban and suburban areas. Neighborhood type public parks accommodate only a small proportion (5 percent) of the total population and accommodate an insignificant portion of the average leisure time budget (0.1 hour per day). Both the number of users, and the time they spend in neighborhood parks, is decreasing relative to their total time budget for leisure and the amount of leisure time spent in nonurban and private recreation places.

SPACE The amount of space devoted to urban recreation is approximately 10 million acres. This space represents an estimated investment, or replacement value, of $100 billion at a cost of $10,000 per acre for land, development, and maintenance in most metropolitan areas.

ACCESS TO REGIONAL PARKS The amount of time people spend traveling to a day-use regional area generally equals the amount of time they spend onsite. For example, a two-hour picnic implies an hour of travel each way and an estimated round trip of 50 to 100 miles in most urban areas. Reduced speed limits to conserve energy, increasing levels of traffic congestion, and the termination of freeway construction programs will discourage convenient automobile access to remote regional parks.

DEMAND Decreasing levels of disposable income, increasing unemployment, and inflation will lessen the

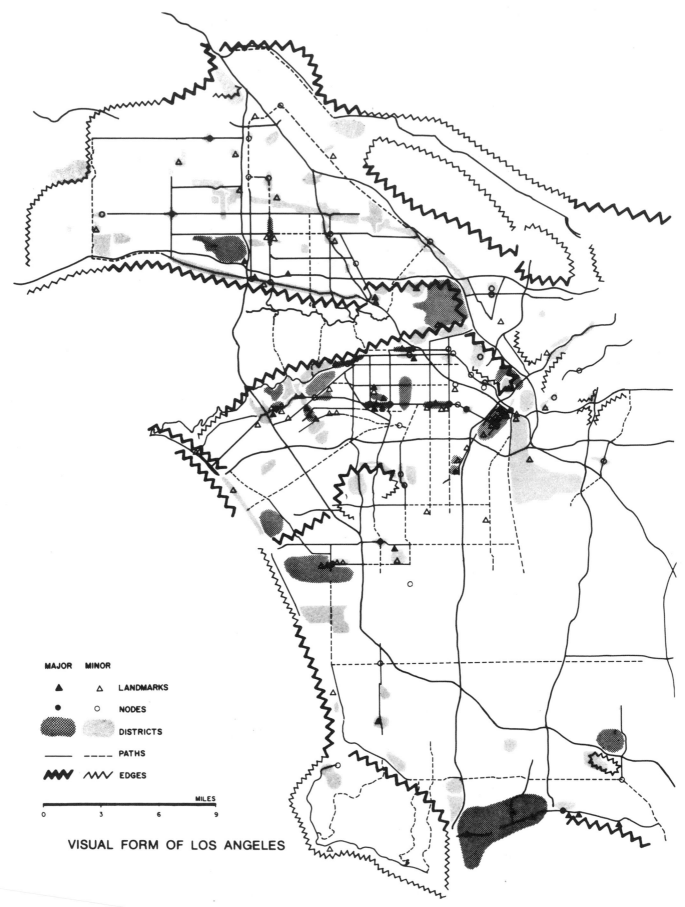

MAJOR MINOR

▲ △ LANDMARKS

● ○ NODES

DISTRICTS

PATHS

EDGES

MILES

0   3   6   9

VISUAL FORM OF LOS ANGELES

FIGURE 2.5   Open space and urban form/Los Angeles.

demand for high-cost activities, e.g., power boating, resorts, skiing. Conversely, it will increase the demand for simple, low-cost activities, e.g., walking, bicycling, swimming, canoeing.

ENERGY CONSERVATION The increased cost of gasoline or the prospect of fuel rationing may force many people to change their priorities and seek energy-conserving ways to spend their leisure time in or near cities. The option of personal transportation will be replaced with mass transit, bicycle, or pedestrian access to local recreation opportunities (Figure 2.6).

URBANIZATION By 1980, over 80 percent of all Americans will live in 150 metropolitan areas with populations of 250,000. Unless significant changes are made in the quantity and quality of the urban and suburban parks and residential environments in these areas, there will be a continuing demand to leave these areas during leisure period.

PUBLIC TRANSPORTATION Because adequate public transportation is not available to most regional and community parks, approximately 30 percent of the urban population who cannot drive or do not own cars must rely on local parks for recreation opportunities.

CULTURAL RESOURCES Some of the nation's finest leisure resources, e.g., art museums, libraries, are close to low-income, central-city residents, yet are comparatively little used by them. Conversely, many potential suburban users of these regional facilities do not use them because of the travel distance or their lack of convenient access to the central city where most of these facilities are located.

FUNDING Municipal austerity programs have had a profound effect on the maintenance, development, and redevelopment of urban parks. These park systems would be unable to accommodate increased use levels which could result from a prolonged energy crisis or recession without substantial increases in funding. Deferred development and maintenance of existing parks and declining municipal budgets for parks and recreation has made it difficult to accommodate normal use levels without imposing fees and charges or curtailing levels of development and management.

Problems and Issues

The problems and issues related to urban parks and recreation have been the focus of several national studies and the *Nationwide Recreation Plan*. These studies describe important differences between the quality and quantity of opportunities provided by individual cities, and major differences between the inner city and the suburbs of most metropolitan areas. However, there is a common set of problems and issues that should be considered for recreation planning at the city and regional level. An abstract of these problems and issues follows:

DISTRIBUTION OF RECREATION RESOURCES Most Americans live in urban areas. The resources for outdoor recreation are not where most people live. Severe inequities exist in the distribution of recreational opportunities and are getting worse.

RURAL BIAS Federal policy and expenditures for recreation favor nonurban areas which are accessible only to families with automobiles and used primarily for summer vacations.

TRADITION Public outdoor recreation policies and programs have not changed with the speed of social

FIGURE 2.6 **Mass transit and bicycle access to regional parks/East Bay Regional Park District, California.**

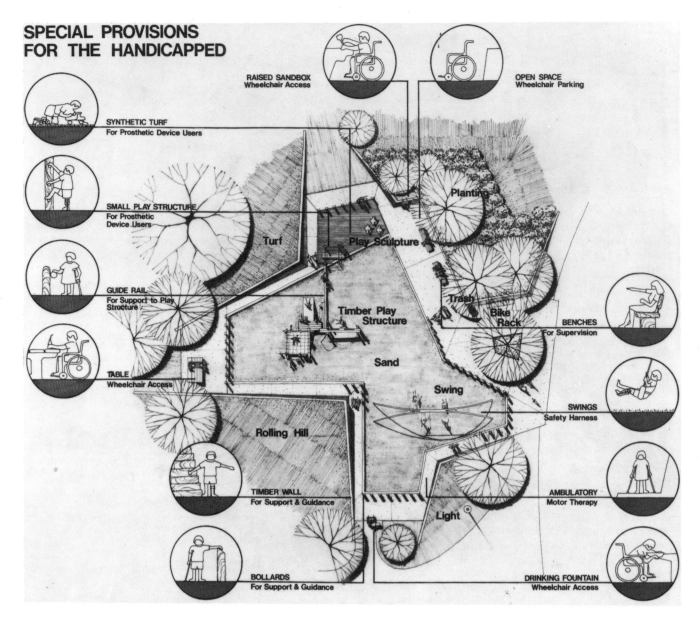

SPECIAL PROVISIONS FOR THE HANDICAPPED

RAISED SANDBOX
Wheelchair Access

OPEN SPACE
Wheelchair Parking

SYNTHETIC TURF
For Prosthetic Device Users

SMALL PLAY STRUCTURE
For Prosthetic Device Users

GUIDE RAIL
For Support to Play Structure

TABLE
Wheelchair Access

TIMBER WALL
For Support & Guidance

BOLLARDS
For Support & Guidance

Turf

Planting

Play Sculpture

Timber Play Structure

Trash

Bike Rack

Sand

Swing

Rolling Hill

Light

BENCHES
For Supervision

SWINGS
Safety Harness

AMBULATORY
Motor Therapy

DRINKING FOUNTAIN
Wheelchair Access

RALSTON CREEK PARK PLAYGROUND
EDAW inc.
Environmental Planning Urban Design Landscape Architecture
San Francisco Newport Beach Honolulu Minneapolis Ft. Collins
211 West Oak Street Ft. Collins CO 80521 (303) 484-6073

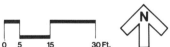
0   5   15   30 Ft.

N

FIGURE 2.7   Special playground provisions for the handicapped/Arvada, Colorado.

change and are not meeting the challenge. Most cities continue to develop park and recreation facilities of a traditional type with few innovations in design or construction.

RESEARCH AND TECHNICAL ASSISTANCE   There is a serious lack of research and evaluation in urban recreation. The federal government has not provided adequate support to states and metropolitan areas for research and technical assistance.

OPEN SPACE PRESERVATION   There is a critical lack of open space in central cities and a need for natural areas within metropolitan areas.

MAINTENANCE AND OPERATION FUNDS   Existing recreation opportunities in urban areas suffer severely from a shortage of operation and maintenance funds.

PUBLIC SAFETY AND VANDALISM   Preventing vandalism and protecting the safety of park users and staff members has become a serious problem in most major cities.

COORDINATION AND COOPERATION   In most cities, no concerted effort has been made to coordinate public and voluntary or private recreation services.

NONUSE   Many urban parks and playgrounds are

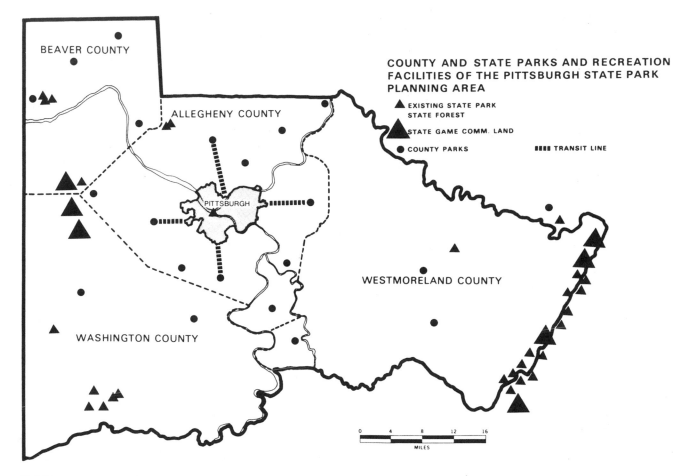

COUNTY AND STATE PARKS AND RECREATION
FACILITIES OF THE PITTSBURGH STATE PARK
PLANNING AREA

▲ EXISTING STATE PARK
   STATE FOREST

▲ STATE GAME COMM. LAND

● COUNTY PARKS   ▪▪▪▪ TRANSIT LINE

0   4   8   12   16
MILES

FIGURE 2.8   Mass-transit access to regional parks/Pittsburgh.

empty. Inadequate design, maintenance, and program prevent them from fulfilling their potential.

SPECIAL POPULATIONS   Most urban leisure spaces and services do not adequately serve the needs of racial or ethnic minorities, children, the elderly, the poor, and the handicapped (Figure 2.7).

Nationwide studies of these problems in the central cities (HUD, 1974) and metropolitan areas (HCRS, 1978) of Urban America are summarized below and in Appendix A. Although there are exceptions to some of these findings, they provide a typical profile of the present situation:

LOCATION AND ACCESS   Location of parks and recreation facilities is a primary factor affecting the success of recreation programs. Consideration must be given to population density and the availability of public transportation in the location of new facilities. The acquisition of large tracts in outlying areas will not meet the recreation needs of the great majority of city residents. Emphasis must be placed on neighborhood facilities (Figure 2.8).

FEDERAL AND STATE ASSISTANCE   In spite of a commitment to increased recreation programs and opportunities, cities do not have the financial capability to sustain expanded recreation programs. Cities must look to

state and federal governments for financial assistance to sustain existing recreation programs.

POTENTIAL RECREATION RESOURCES   Optimum utilization of potential recreation resources is not being achieved in most of the nation's cities. Publicly owned facilities with existing recreation capabilities are being underused. School facilities, even in jurisdictions having city-school recreation agreements, are not being utilized effectively. Cities must expand the multiple use of facilities, establish park-school complexes, and employ imaginative designs and new construction techniques.

COMMUNICATION   Lack of communication among city, county, and private agencies is a major problem preventing the optimum utilization of existing recreational facilities and programs. Coordination is inadequate between city and county recreation departments and semipublic organizations carrying on recreation activities. Communication between recreation departments and the citizen is frequently inadequate. Citizens must be not only informed of the availability of the various programs but also convinced that participation and utilization are worthwhile.

SPECIAL POPULATIONS   Cities must take into consideration the recreation needs of special segments of the population in developing priorities. In most cities, the

37

FIGURE 2.9 Programs for special populations/East Bay Regional Park District, Oakland, California.

needs of all population groups are not being adequately met. Only in recent years have cities begun to recognize an obligation to provide recreation for the handicapped and deprived.

POVERTY   Residents of deprived urban neighborhoods are almost entirely dependent upon public recreation facilities. Residents of more affluent neighborhoods have a wide range of recreational alternatives. Adequate recreation programs and facilities are considered a high-priority item among the deprived (Figure 2.9).

CITIZEN PARTICIPATION   Residents of inner-city neighborhoods believe too much effort is directed toward park and recreation facilities for the middle- and upper-income groups and that recreation planning is done by persons having no real knowledge of their needs. Planners should encourage citizen participation in the planning process. Recreation programs must be what people want, not what the recreation department believes is best for people.

Changing Perspectives

Although it is difficult to rationalize leisure or recreation as significant problems when this country is burdened with problems of inflation, unemployment, poverty, energy, and environmental quality, there are significant relationships between the provision of urban parks and recreation and these problems. There is hope that park and recreation services or places can play a role in helping solve these problems and enrich the quality of community life.

The past role of public parks and recreation in contributing to the quality of life and environment in Urban America is clear, but its future is not. The survival of many urban park and recreation systems is at stake in a projected era of scarce resources and competing needs for public support. It is time to question past and present assumptions, concepts, and techniques used to plan, design, and manage urban parks and consider alternatives, if the urban park is not to become an endangered species.

Philosophical and pragmatic changes in American society, the Park and Recreation Movements, and evolving public policy project many changes for the delivery of leisure services in cities. These changing perspectives can provide a dynamic context for recreation planning:

QUALITY OF LIFE   A cultural revolution is taking place in American thought about the environment, leisure, work, and the sense of community. This revolution places a high value on self-development, humanism, and process. It is concerned with the consumer, physical health, and the quality of life.

RATIONAL USE   An era of limits is being defined in politics, science, government, and industry that says small is beautiful, less is more, we have reached the limits of unqualified growth and must make more rational use of existing resources. It is economics as if people mattered, based on a lowered set of expectations and conservation of human and natural resources.

ENERGY CRISIS   The energy crisis is beginning to have an impact on disposable income, mobility patterns, and life-style. The choice of work or leisure patterns in many places is being conditioned by the price of fuel for transportation and heating.

EQUALITY   Advocacy and pluralism are becoming expected dimensions of the planning and decision-making process. The rights of individuals, neighborhoods, and communities, for self-determination and respect for social values are being addressed by consumers, the handicapped, and racial and ethnic minorities. It is no longer enough for government to do many things for some people and exclude special populations. It must do appropriate things for and with all people and be able to rationalize this effort in human terms (Figure 2.10).

INFLATION Local governments are experiencing a cost-revenue crisis that will not diminish in a steady-state economy coupled with rapid inflation. Cities cannot expect needed financial help from the federal government, states, or counties for the same reasons. Drastic cuts in municipal services will be necessary just to keep pace with inflation.

COST-EFFECTIVENESS Taxpayers faced with a decline in real income are not likely to approve bond issues or tax increases for local parks. They will also develop a serious interest in the effectiveness of leisure services to obtain the best value for their dollar. Parks and recreation must compete as never before for budget. The days of rationalizing public budgets with rhetoric, instead of facts, are gone.

HUMAN DEVELOPMENT Professionals have begun to redefine recreation in terms of human development. In the emerging view, it is not activities, facilities, or programs that are central; it is what happens to people. Recreation is not a specific event, point in time, or place in space. It is a dimension in life or self-development that may have little to do with activity or social acceptance.

RECYCLING The existing system of recreation spaces in most communities will be all they can afford to operate and maintain. Local funds will not be available for new spaces, which implies making the best use of existing spaces that need renewal. Many community and especially neighborhood parks no longer meet the needs of changing populations. The facilities and landscaping are obsolete and the programs may be irrelevant to the needs of special populations, e.g., racial or ethnic minorities.

PRIORITIES The traditional priorities of public land acquisition, development, and programs are being reversed in some cities that are beginning to sense the city as a recreation place in which voluntary program leadership and private opportunities are alternatives to extensive public investments in land, facilities, or program. The philosophy of alternative, noncompetitive, or self-generated recreation programs is being tried in many communities.

SELF-HELP A new spirit of self-help, community involvement, and volunteerism is emerging in many

places. This spirit recognizes the limits of government in solving many human problems. It senses a degree of commitment, responsibility, and resourcefulness that can be used by people to help design, develop, and maintain urban parks. The ideas of self-generated and self-maintained urban parks are being tested in some communities (Figure 2.11). The expectation of government doing everything may be passé, if not fiscally impossible, or may not serve the best interests of people.

LIFE-STYLE The idea that urban parks are for all people and are established for the pleasurable use of leisure time is in contradiction with the life-styles and leisure behavior of a growing number of people. Many types of leisure behavior are labeled "deviant" because of outmoded laws, arbitrary policies, and conventional thinking. Urban parks are one reflection of reality in a plastic world. The notion they should be used only by "normal" people for the "constructive use of their leisure time" is not necessarily in accord with the social emphasis that characterized the establishment of the Park and Recreation Movement in America.

CONSOLIDATION A consolidation of government services is combining the traditional park and recreation department with other social services or departments of

FIGURE 2.10 Environmental education programs for racial and ethnic minorities/East Bay Regional Park District, Oakland, California.

Want List:

MATERIALS, EQUIPMENT AND SKILLS

Almost everything is useful, but here are some suggestions:

If you can help, check the appropriate box; then fold this form in half and send to the address on overleaf:

MATERIALS

☐ Plastic piping and fittings
☐ Steel piping and fittings
☐ Spray heads, valves, remote controls, etc.
☐ Heavy duty electric cable—100s of feet plus fittings and flood lights
☐ Asphalt—dozens of tons
☐ Sand, cement and ballast for construction—many tons

☐ Soil conditioner—100s of yards
☐ Broken stone and brick for construction of walls and paths, etc.
☐ Blocks of stone—dozens
☐ Large rocks, beautiful ones for habitats—big enough not to be moved—many different kinds
☐ Lumber of all shapes and sizes, particularly: 4″x4″, 2″x4″, 2″x6″, 2″x8″, 2″x10″, 3″x6″, 3″x10″, etc., 10,000s of feet, large baulks, e.g., 12″x12″ and larger, etc., 100s of feet. Exterior quality plywood, 100s of square feet, 8′x4′ sheets
☐ Telephone poles—dozens
☐ Driftwood—loads
☐ Railroad ties—100s
☐ Lengths of tree trunk—100s of feet
☐ Old tree trunks, stumps—dozens
☐ Prunings from campus and city—truck loads
☐ Steel piping (1″ dia. up to 6′0″?)—100s of feet
☐ Sheet steel, various thicknesses
☐ 50 gallon drums (no end, one end, both ends)—dozens
☐ Swing seats and shackles
☐ Rope (1″ dia. up)—100s of feet —plus pulleys, shackles and fittings

☐ Steel cable (½″ up)—100s of feet—plus pulleys, shackles and fittings
☐ Nails 3½″-6″ (standards, heavy duty)—100s of lbs.
☐ Carriage bolts—4½″-12″—100s
☐ Machine bolts—4½″-10″—100s
☐ Lag bolts—4½″-10″—100s
☐ Burlap sacks filled with a weak concrete mix
☐ Reinforcing bars—100s of feet —and cutter
☐ "Bentonite," prop. sealing compound—100s of tons
☐ Huge blocks of sponge plastic
☐ Huge pieces of any interesting material
☐ PAINT—100s of gallons of all types, especially primary colors
☐ Paint brushes, all sizes—dozens
☐ Tin cans for paint
☐ Paint thinner—dozens of gallons

☐ Strong cable spools of all shapes and sizes
☐ Old tires of all shapes and sizes
☐ Concrete pipes of all shapes and sizes—dozens (especially 3′-4′ diameter and 18″-48″ high for planters)
☐ Broken china for murals and mosaics—several loads
☐ Tri-ply cardboard—100s of sheets
☐ Rolls of newsprint—dozens of rolls
☐ Cotton and synthetic materials for flags, tie-dye, etc.—100s of yards

AN ENDLESS ARRAY OF SCRAP STUFF, CASTOFFS AND READY-MADES. KEEP ON THE LOOK-OUT IN INDUSTRIAL AREAS, DOWN BY THE BAY, ON CONSTRUCTION AND DEMOLITION SITES, AND SO ON!

EQUIPMENT AND TOOLS:

☐ D6 bulldozer and operator
☐ Heavy truck
☐ Front bucket loader
☐ Trencher
☐ Grader
☐ Cultivator
☐ Winch and hauling tackle
☐ Stake truck with sides
☐ Pickup trucks
☐ Jackhammers and compressor
☐ Post-hole borer
☐ Power saws
☐ Welding set and supplies
☐ Pipe wrench and cutter
☐ Paint brushes, all sizes—dozens
☐ Shovels
☐ Spades
☐ Pickaxes
☐ Crowbars
☐ Rakes
☐ Sledgehammers
☐ Wheelbarrows

☐ Circular saws
☐ Drills
☐ Planers
☐ Bits and extensions
☐ Extension cords
☐ Chisels
☐ Saws
☐ Wrench sets
☐ Tape measures
☐ Trowels
☐ Carpenters' horses

LIVING THINGS:

☐ Trees and bushes
☐ Flowers
☐ Bulbs
☐ "Weeds"
☐ Grasses
☐ Seeds of all kinds
☐ Succulents
☐ Cacti
☐ Ivy
☐ Brambles
☐ Water plants
☐ Pampas grass

☐ Bamboo, etc.
☐ Lizards
☐ Fish
☐ Insects
☐ Spiders, etc.

Check your back yard for stuff, or the nearest vacant lot! Just bring 'em when you think there is a habitat available!

☐ Money: Contributions are tax deductible.

We can always use people with specific skills or expertise to offer. Just make contact.

Our phone numbers are:
Washington School (415) 644-6310
Project WEY (415) 845-4536

FIGURE 2.11 Self-generated parks: Washington Environmental Yard/Berkeley, California.

environmental planning and management. In both cases, the traditional "fun and games" or "housekeeper" images of these departments is broadened toward life enrichment or human development and environmental change or improvement (Figure 2.12).

These changing perspectives represent dramatic opportunities for the provision of leisure services. They indicate a growing awareness that the use of leisure time has important implications for community development, mental and physical health, the conservation of resources, the local economy, and the quality of life. In a planning context, these changes imply it is necessary to move beyond a narrow focus on recreation activities, buildings, and parks toward improving the quality of urban life and environment. At the policy or operational level of local government, these perspectives place parks and recreation in the broader context of a human service and environmental management system. They recognize the relationship of leisure spaces and services to the social and physical environment of cities.

CONCEPTS AND PRINCIPLES

If one accepts these relationships and realities as a context for recreation planning and design, the next step is to translate them into concepts and principles that can be applied to different situations. Human service becomes the framework for developing common principles and applying the methods and techniques of recreation planning.

Human Service Orientation

The use of leisure time has important implications for human development, community development, resource conservation, and the quality of human exis-

tence. These implications mean planners and designers must accept the consequences of what they do in terms of making people and communities better. They emphasize a humanistic approach to professional practice based on these concepts. Park and recreation agencies should:

1 Emphasize human development, social welfare, and community integration. Services should be defined in terms of human experiences rather than activities, programs, and buildings.

2 Provide for the needs of special groups and integrate their efforts with other social services (Figure 2.13).

3 Shift their philosophy of service to environmental beautification, open space planning, and a concern for all aspects of the living environment.

4 Seek a common ground with environmental and consumer groups who are also concerned with improving community life and environment.

5 Plan with, instead of for, people and be held accountable for their actions.

Planning Principles

There are some common principles of recreation planning that apply to a wide range of typical and extreme situations. These principles should be considered basic to the success of any planning effort and can be used to monitor the quality of the planning process:

1 All people should have access to activities and facilities, regardless of interest, age, sex, income, cultural background, housing environment, or handicap (Figure 2.14).

2 Public recreation should be coordinated with other community recreation opportunities to avoid duplication and encourage innovation.

3 Public recreation should be integrated with other public services, such as education, health, and transportation.

4 Facilities should be adaptable to future requirements.

FIGURE 2.12 Consolidation of government services.

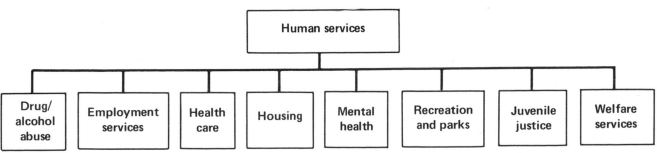

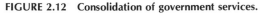

FIGURE 2.13 Touch and see nature trail for the blind/National Arboretum, Washington, D.C.

FIGURE 2.14 Recreation program for the physically handicapped/Los Angeles.

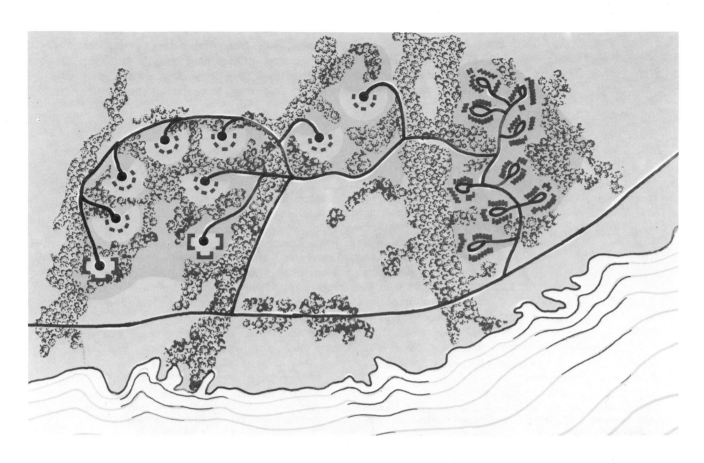

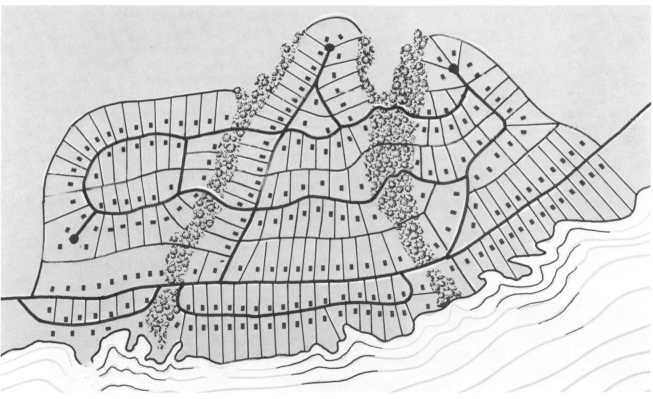

FIGURE 2.15 Cluster development concept of housing to preserve open space/Outdoor Recreation Resources Review Commission Report.

5 Facilities and programs should be financially feasible at all stages of development. Operation and maintenance places a greater financial burden on the municipality than the initial capital cost.

6 Citizens should be involved in the planning process throughout all stages.

7 Planning should be a continuous process, requiring constant review and evaluation of the recommendations or projects.

8 Local and regional plans should be integrated.

9 Land should be acquired prior to urban development and dedicated to park and recreation uses.

10 Facilities should make the most efficient use of land, be designed and managed to provide for the convenience, health, safety, and pleasure of intended users, and represent positive examples of design, energy conservation, and a concern for people (Figure 2.15).

Design Strategies

At the project level, there are some common design strategies that apply in most cases. These strategies are the results of many case studies. They represent a basic approach to many situations:

1 Most people do not necessarily share a designer's values. They often care more about social than physical factors. Their use of the space depends more on who is there rather than what is there.

2 People involved in the design process will contribute information vital to the designer's success. Their knowledge of the planning area, activity preferences, and social needs can only be known by their active involvement in the design process.

3 People learn the benefits of self-determination by involvement in the design process. If denied this opportunity, they may oppose any proposal because it does not respect their right to be involved.

4 The application of social factors to the design of spaces results in successful spaces that acknowledge the factors of territoriality, status, conflict, cooperation, comfort, class, and life-style, which are important in urban parks.

5 People involved in the design process like the results better than people who are not involved. They will use and respect the space in proportion to their identity with it.

Translating Concepts into Practice

The only way to test these concepts and principles of recreation planning is by demonstration and practice. Until this field has a more vigorous experimental dimension to develop new products and services, the best way to find out what works is to try them in a demonstration situation. The case studies or techniques described in the following chapters represent successful applications of these concepts to show what is possible in practice.

3 | METHODS AND TECHNIQUES

The methods and techniques of urban recreation planning have focused on the application of space and facility standards to a population or planning area. Although these standards are commonly called "guidelines," they often become absolutes, regardless of significant differences in the population, density, leisure patterns, climate, or economic base of a community.

The problems and implications of a standards approach to urban recreation planning are described in many sources. To perpetuate this approach in most communities will magnify the problems described in Chapter 1. What is necessary and possible is a more sensitive and systematic approach to the needs of people living in urban and suburban environments.

The planning task is to inventory, analyze, and project information that relates people (behavior), time (leisure), and activity (recreation) to space (resources) and a geographic area (planning unit), using criteria or measures (performance standards/social indicators) that are sensitive to the changing physical character, social needs, and political priorities of a community. This information can be used to identify deficiencies by planning unit and population subgroups for specific activities or spaces. It can also be used to establish regional, citywide, and neighborhood policies and programs.

This chapter describes the basic approaches and methods of recreation planning. Other chapters in the book will detail these. The emphasis here is on conceptual relationships, definition of problems, and the range of possible techniques that apply to these problems.

APPROACHES TO RECREATION PLANNING

Recreation planning can be approached in four different ways. These are commonly referred to as the resource, activity, economic, and behavioral approaches to recreation planning. The approach used conditions the planning process, research methods, and character of facilities or services. It can also have a positive or negative impact on the community's attitude or awareness of these opportunities and their support of the planning process or recreation plan.

The approach should be appropriate to the physical or social character, values, and planning capability of a community. In most cases, the physical and social factors of a planning area will determine which approach is best. For example, it would be illogical to adopt a resource-oriented approach, instead of a behavioral approach, to the central city where man-made features (housing and density) and social factors (poverty and unemployment) may be most important.

Likewise, it would be illogical to apply the activity instead of the economic or resource approach to a tourist-oriented community where the major factors may be transient populations and superlative scenery. Each approach is described here and will be illustrated with examples in other chapters.

Resource Approach

Physical or natural resources determine the types and amounts of recreation opportunities. Supply limits the demand or use to the human or natural carrying capacity of the resource. Expressed demand is more important than latent demand, which encourages duplication instead of diversification of existing facilities. Supplier or management values are usually dominant in the planning process.

Natural factors are ranked over social factors. Environmental considerations determine the acquisition and preservation of open space, regardless of people's expressed needs or the fiscal resources to pay for this space. The emphasis is on the resource instead of the user. The planning process is conditioned by ecological determinism instead of advocacy or pluralism (Figure 3.1).

This approach emphasizes supply instead of demand and minimizes the importance of social or political factors. It is most effective in nonurban, resource planning such as water reservoirs, national forest preserves, and national parks. It also has much utility for private tourist development, new communities, or military installations, where there is a well-defined resource to protect and centralized control of the planning and decision process (Figure 3.2).

The resource approach to recreation planning is associated with the work of Lewis (1961) and McHarg (1969). Their methods provided a systematic way of describing the natural resource base needed to support different types of recreation activities. Their most important contribution was the criteria and classification methods for regional open space systems in metropolitan areas, detailed in Chapter 8.

Activity Approach

Past participation in selected activities is used to determine what opportunities should be provided in the future. Supply creates demand. The public preference or

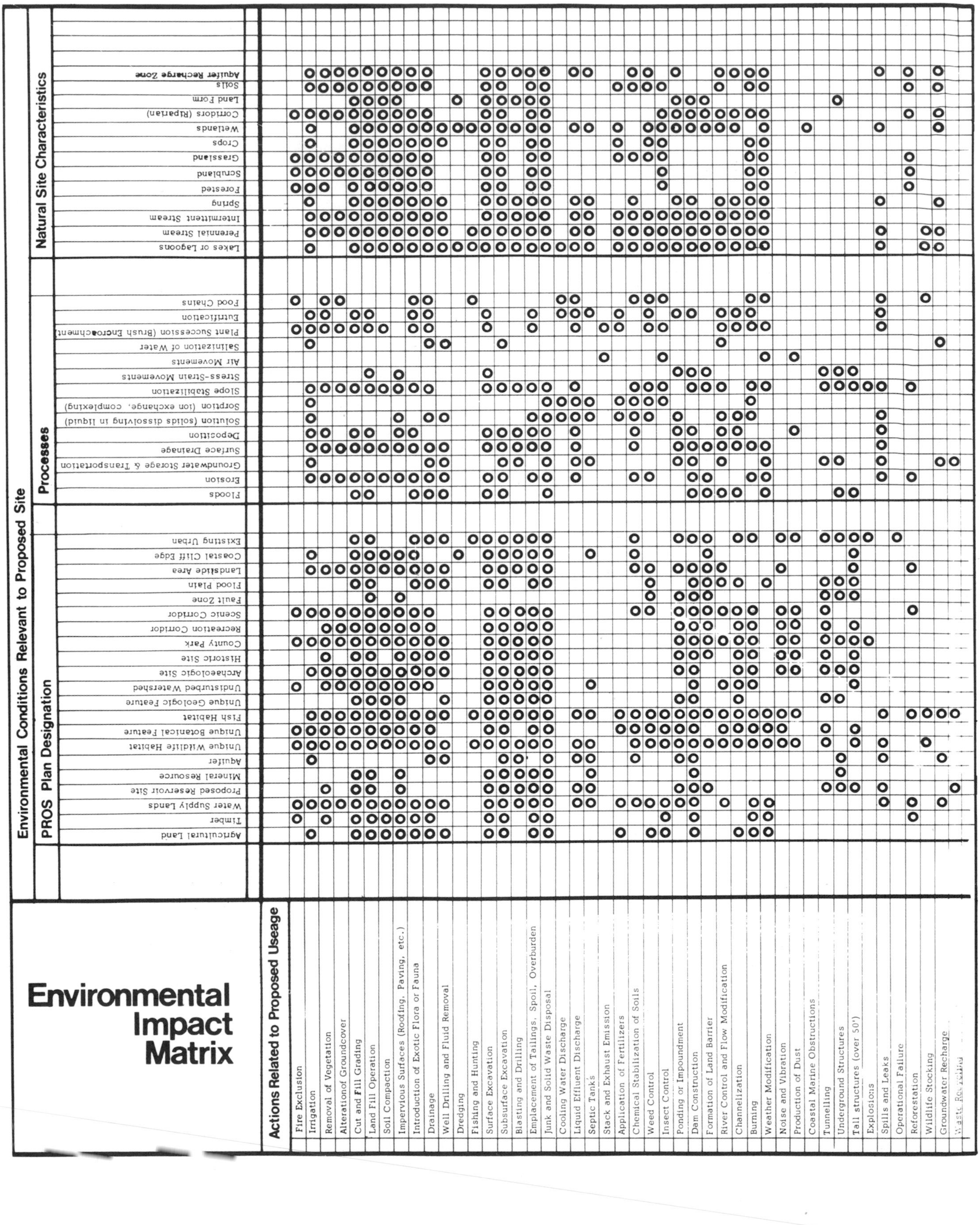

Environmental Impact Matrix

Environmental Conditions Relevant to Proposed Site

Natural Site Characteristics

- Aquifer Recharge Zone
- Soils
- Land Form
- Corridors (Riparian)
- Wetlands
- Crops
- Grassland
- Scrubland
- Forested
- Spring
- Intermittent Stream
- Perennial Stream
- Lakes or Lagoons

Processes

- Food Chains
- Eutrification
- Plant Succession (Brush Encroachment)
- Salinization of Water
- Air Movements
- Stress-Strain Movements
- Slope Stabilization
- Sorption (ion exchange, complexing)
- Solution (solids dissolving in liquid)
- Deposition
- Surface Drainage
- Groundwater Storage & Transportation
- Erosion
- Floods

PROS Plan Designation

- Existing Urban
- Coastal Cliff Edge
- Landslide Area
- Flood Plain
- Fault Zone
- Scenic Corridor
- Recreation Corridor
- County Park
- Historic Site
- Archaeologic Site
- Undisturbed Watershed
- Unique Geologic Feature
- Fish Habitat
- Unique Botanical Feature
- Unique Wildlife Habitat
- Aquifer
- Mineral Resource
- Proposed Reservoir Site
- Water Supply Lands
- Timber
- Agricultural Land

Actions Related to Proposed Useage

- Fire Exclusion
- Irrigation
- Removal of Vegetation
- Alteration of Groundcover
- Cut and Fill Grading
- Land Fill Operation
- Soil Compaction
- Impervious Surfaces (Roofing, Paving, etc.)
- Introduction of Exotic Flora or Fauna
- Drainage
- Well Drilling and Fluid Removal
- Dredging
- Fishing and Hunting
- Surface Excavation
- Subsurface Excavation
- Blasting and Drilling
- Emplacement of Tailings, Spoil, Overburden
- Junk and Solid Waste Disposal
- Cooling Water Discharge
- Liquid Effluent Discharge
- Septic Tanks
- Stack and Exhaust Emission
- Application of Fertilizers
- Chemical Stabilization of Soils
- Weed Control
- Insect Control
- Ponding or Impoundment
- Dam Construction
- Formation of Land Barrier
- River Control and Flow Modification
- Channelization
- Burning
- Weather Modification
- Noise and Vibration
- Production of Dust
- Coastal Marine Obstructions
- Tunnelling
- Underground Structures
- Tall structures (over 50')
- Explosions
- Spills and Leaks
- Operational Failure
- Reforestation
- Wildlife Stocking
- Groundwater Recharge
- Waste Recycling

FIGURE 3.1 Environmental impact matrix/Santa Cruz County, California.

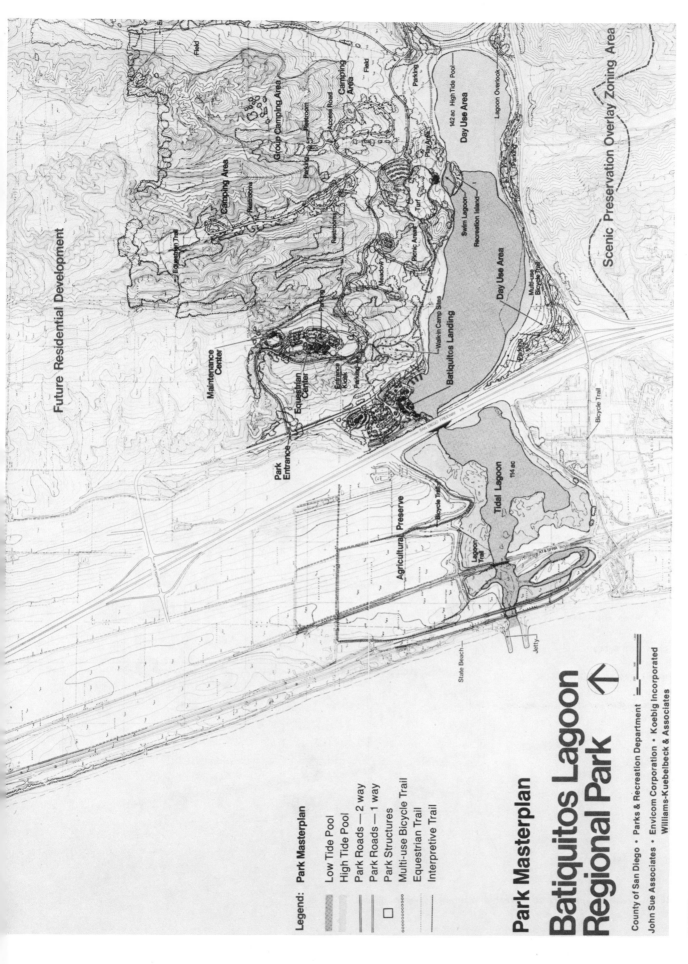

Park Masterplan
Batiquitos Lagoon Regional Park ↑

County of San Diego • Parks & Recreation Department
John Sue Associates • Envicom Corporation • Koebig Incorporated
Williams-Kuebelbeck & Associates

Legend: Park Masterplan

Low Tide Pool
High Tide Pool
Park Roads —2 way
Park Roads —1 way
Park Structures
Multi-use Bicycle Trail
Equestrian Trail
Interpretive Trail

Future Residential Development

Scenic Preservation Overlay Zoning Area

Field
Field
Group Camping Area
Camping Area
Parking
Access Road
Camping Area
Restroom
Parking
Parking
Equestrian Trail
Restrooms
Restrooms
Meadow
Picnic Area
Turf
Play Area
142 ac High Tide Pool
Day Use Area
Lagoon Overlook
Maintenance Center
Equestrian Center
Entrance Kiosk
Parking
Swim Lagoon·
Recreation Island
Day Use Area
Multi-use Bicycle Trail
Walk-in Camp Sites
Batiquitos Landing
Parking
Patio
Park Entrance
SAN DIEGO FREEWAY I-5
Bicycle Trail
Agricultural Preserve
Bicycle Trail
Tidal Lagoon
114 ac
Lagoon Trail
State Beach
Jetty
I-5 PATH

FIGURE 3.2   Resource approach to recreation planning/Batiquitos Lagoon Regional Park, San Diego County, California.

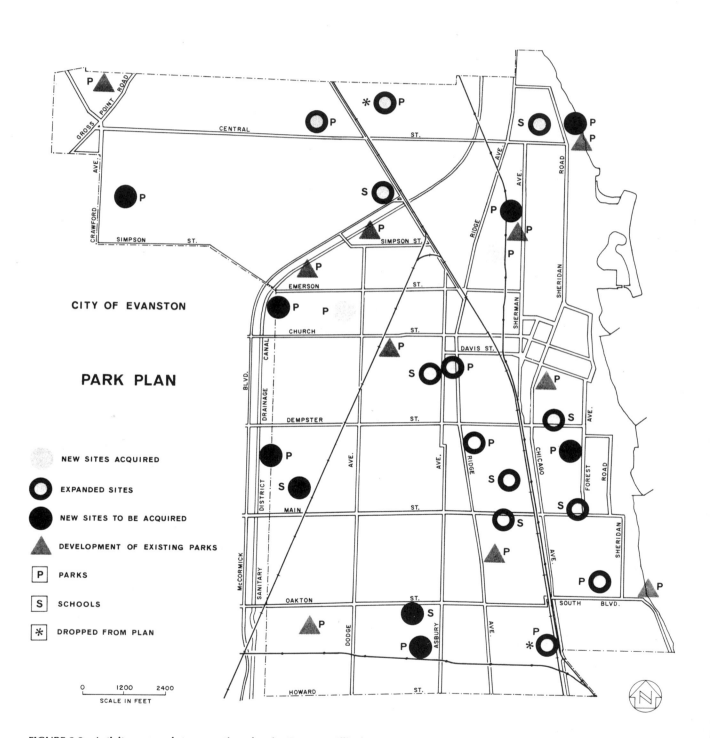

FIGURE 3.3 Activity approach to recreation planning/Evanston, Illinois.

demand for opportunities is based on participation rates or attendance, which usually projects more of the same type of opportunities. Because only expressed demand or use is measured, the focus is on providing more program leadership instead of self-directed activities. Nonuse, or the latent demand for opportunities, is not seriously considered. The values of users and the supplier are dominant in the planning process.

Social factors are ranked over natural factors. Use of public facilities is projected to rationalize more public facilities and programs. The emphasis is on users and the supplier of existing public recreation opportunities. The planning process is often influenced by the values of well-organized special interest groups.

This approach emphasizes expressed demand and is often distorted by political factors that may not reflect the public interest. Because of a heavy emphasis on the past, this approach may not respond well to accommodating the needs of nonusers or future trends. It also places too much emphasis on the public sector, organized sports, and program leadership when alternatives may be needed and possible. It has been favored in most recreation plans prepared prior to 1975 (Figure 3.3).

The activity approach works best when applied to a homogenous population by a public agency with a limited scope. It has been effective in small suburbs or special districts, but it has limited value in cities over 50,000 and is not appropriate to planning for the central city or metropolitan areas because it is not responsive to diverse populations and life-styles.

This approach is associated with the ideas of Butler (1962, 1967) and Bannon (1976), who reinforce the activity standards of NRPA (1971). Their approach to design for existing recreation activities encouraged the development of national standards and elaborate ways to classify existing recreational activities. It recognized what people do in public urban space and developed space and facility requirements for various activities.

Economic Approach

The economic base or fiscal resources of a community are used to determine the amount, type, and location of recreation opportunities. Investment and responsibility for providing land, facilities, or program are conditioned by measurable costs and benefits or the self-supporting nature of activities. Fees and charges are commonly required for many opportunities. The supply and demand

for activities is manipulated by price. User and supplier objectives are balanced in the planning process.

Economic factors are more important than social or natural factors. The emphasis is on market demand and pricing of opportunities. Attention is focused on questions of fees and charges, government vs. private responsibility for appropriate facilities, capital investment, and evaluating alternatives in terms of economic benefits and costs. Both latent and expressed demand are projected to rationalize the use of public resources or private alternatives. The planning process is influenced by politics and special interests. Quantity outweighs quality, and problem solving is limited to political jurisdictions which may not parallel the problems of access, tax base, or efficient management of local and regional parks.

This approach emphasizes sophisticated statistical techniques to analyze alternatives. It lends rigor and objectivity to the planning or decision process and is useful for large jurisdictions with diverse populations. The economic approach has great value for analyzing the questions of welfare economics, user charges, and private investment opportunities at the metropolitan or regional level. It can also provide the facts needed to help rationalize the cost-effectiveness of public park and recreation facilities in cities.

The economic approach is commonly associated with the writings of Clawson and Knetsch (1966), who apply economic methods to projecting recreation demand and introduce the ideas of benefit-cost analysis of alternatives. These ideas are conspicuous in many of the state and federal recreation plans of the 1960s that projected the activity patterns of the 1950s. The most important contribution of this approach is a recognition of costs and benefits not common in other approaches (Figure 3.4).

Behavioral Approach

Human behavior and events in leisure settings influence the choice of how, where, and when people use their free time. Time budgets of individuals and social groups are translated into public and private opportunities that require land, facilities, and program (Figure 3.5). The focus is on recreation as an experience, why a person participates, what activities are preferred, and what happens to the person as a result of this activity. User preference and satisfaction condition the planning process.

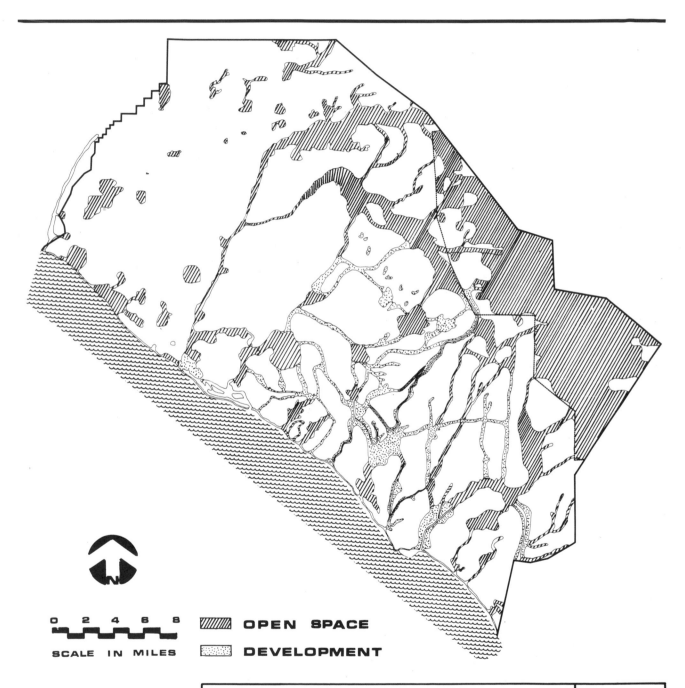

SCALE IN MILES

OPEN SPACE

DEVELOPMENT

AREAS OF OPEN SPACE AND
ALLOWABLE DEVELOPMENT
WITHIN THE CONCEPT PLAN

FIGURE 3.4 Economic approach to recreation planning/Orange County, California.

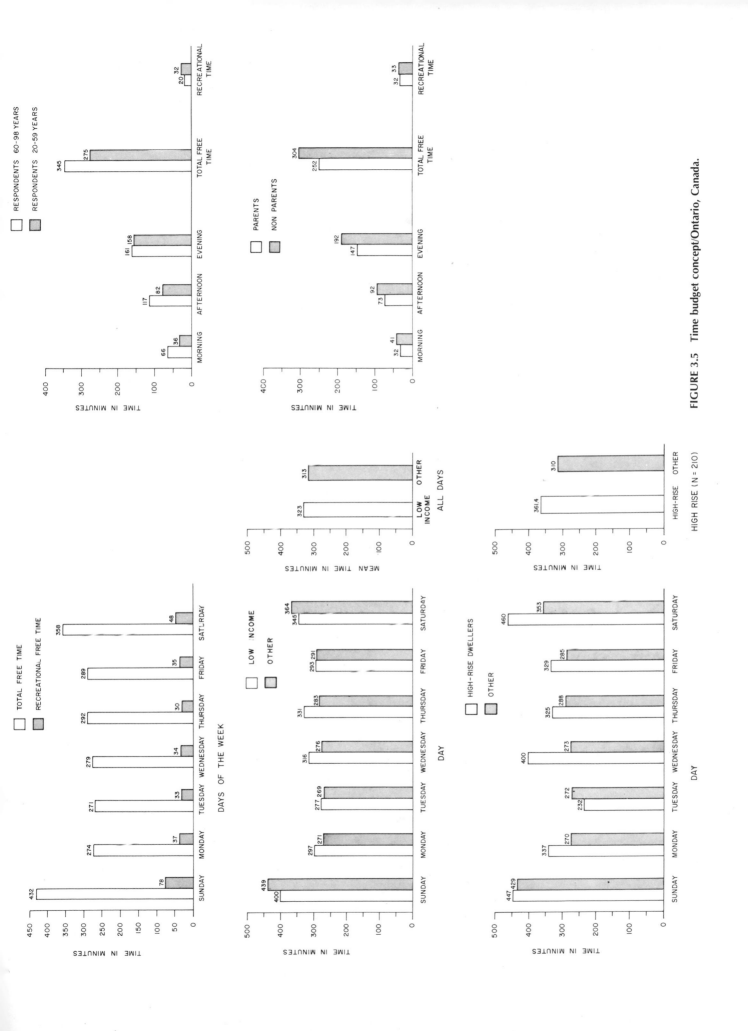

FIGURE 3.5 Time budget concept/Ontario, Canada.

Advocacy and pluralism are expected dimensions of the planning, design, and management process. User and nonuser objectives are dominant, and satisfying experiences are the expected product.

This approach is concerned with accommodating latent and expressed demand. It relates demand to supply to develop indicators of social need. These needs can be met in leisure settings that combine physical environment (space) and behavior (activity). Leisure settings can include a wide range of public and private opportunities in cities beyond traditional public parks (Figure 3.6).

The behavioral approach is most conspicuous in the ideas of Driver (1970), Gold (1973), Hester (1975), and Check, Field, and Burdge (1976). Their emphasis on the merits of citizen participation, user and nonuser surveys, and the relationship of people to space challenges many traditional methods or space standards.

The nature of the problems described in Chapter 2 suggest the behavioral approach as the best way to understand and provide for the recreation needs of urban populations. This approach is more complex and controversial than the other approaches because it requires value judgments, the development of credible measures, and high levels of citizen participation. It has great utility for analyzing nonuse, latent demand, future trends, and the needs of special populations at the neighborhood level. This approach compliments the advocacy and pluralism of most communities and the trend toward a more humanistic view of leisure services in cities.

Combined Approach

A combination of the above approaches uses the positive aspects of each and is balanced to reflect the requirements of the user and resource. This approach was developed for use in the *California Outdoor Recreation Plan* and called the User Resource Planning Method (National Advisory Council, 1959). Aspects of this approach have been tried in several statewide recreation plans, but there is no known application of this complete approach. Because it has never been tested, it is premature to evaluate its utility for urban or regional recreation planning. This approach holds much promise for especially regional recreation planning.

The combined approach has the basic relationships shown in Figure 3.7. These relationships are linked in a planning process that (1) inventories and evaluates existing and potential recreation resources, (2) identifies user groups and their characteristics, (3) estimates the recreation supply and demand in terms of potential resource

types and user group requirements, and (4) translates these requirements with planning guides, design studies, landscape interpretation, and benefit-cost analysis into a recreation plan. This approach is based on these concepts:

1 All potential recreation participants can be consolidated into user groups according to the nature and quality of the recreation experience that each user desires.

2 Each user group can be described by social and economic characteristics from census data and surveys to estimate the size and distribution of their present and future recreation requirements.

3 Each user group requires certain types and amounts of resources in order to provide needed opportunities.

4 The amount of space allocated for each type of recreation experience is determined by physical as well as psychological requirements.

5 The recreation planning area can be described in terms of existing landscape characteristics.

6 The environmental characteristics of each landscape type have a measurable potential for recreation use.

7 Each recreation resource type in the planning area has a maximum carrying capacity. When used beyond this capacity, the quality of the resource and recreation experience is impaired.

8 The accessibility, distribution, and information about recreation areas have an influence on their potential use.

9 Natural resource capability and design studies can determine the most suitable and allowable kind, amount and arrangement of recreation development at each potential site.

10 Recreation experiences have both tangible and intangible values. These values include direct-dollar expenditures, user satisfaction, and social benefits.

Some unique aspects of this approach are (1) classifying people into user groups that require certain environmental characteristics which can be described and measured, (2) dividing each planning area into resource types by its environmental characteristics, (3) relating the desired recreation experience to resource types, and (4) developing planning and management guidelines based on an analysis of user and resource requirements. These concepts represent a dramatic departure from, and synthesis of, other approaches.

SUPPLY AND DEMAND ANALYSIS

The methodological challenge of supply and demand analysis is to relate existing and future recreation be-

FIGURE 3.6   Behavioral approach to recreation planning/Robson Square, Vancouver, British Columbia, Canada.

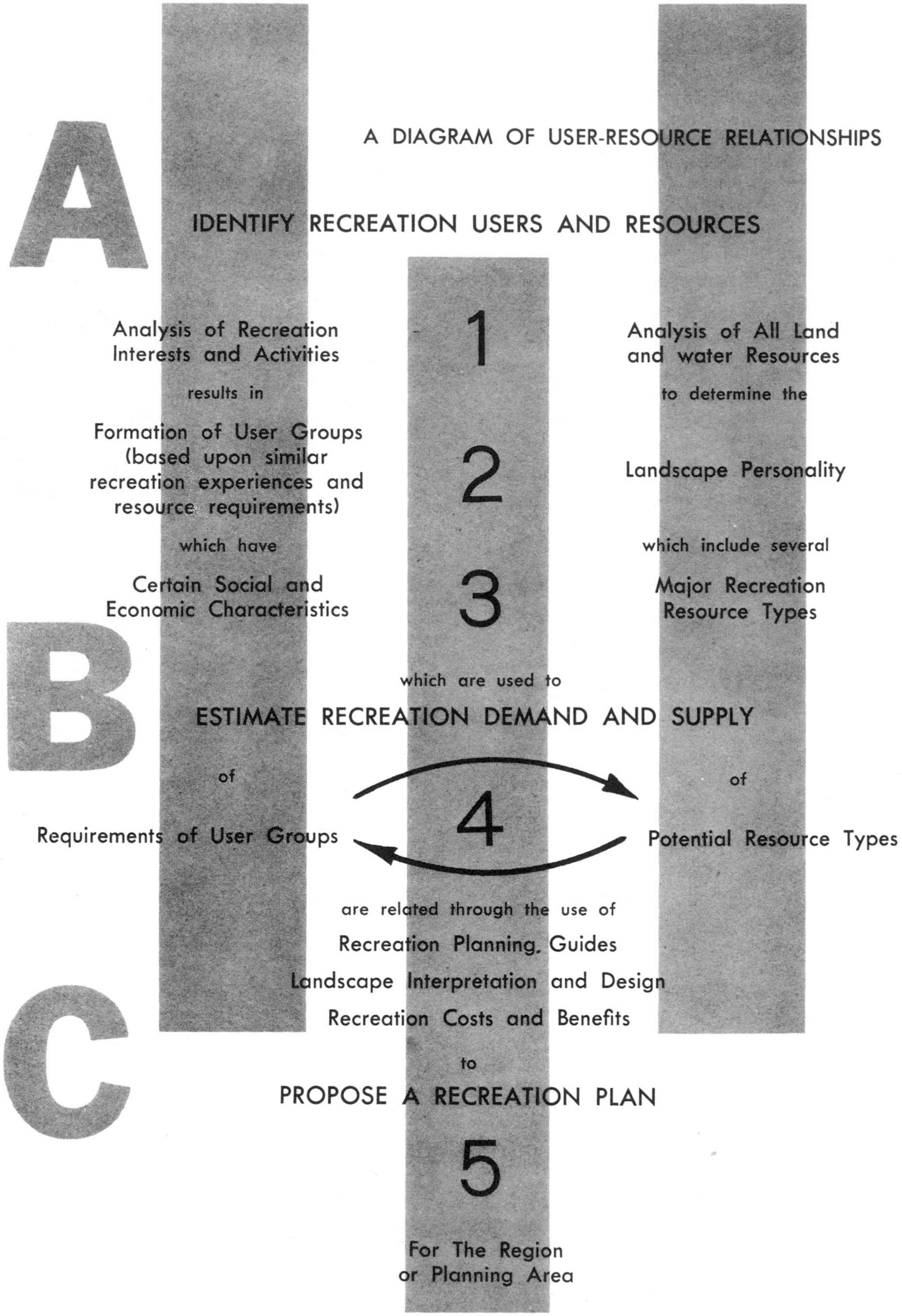

A DIAGRAM OF USER-RESOURCE RELATIONSHIPS

A — IDENTIFY RECREATION USERS AND RESOURCES

Analysis of Recreation Interests and Activities	Analysis of All Land and water Resources
results in	to determine the
Formation of User Groups (based upon similar recreation experiences and resource requirements)	Landscape Personality
which have	which include several
Certain Social and Economic Characteristics	Major Recreation Resource Types

1
2
3

which are used to

B — ESTIMATE RECREATION DEMAND AND SUPPLY

of	of
Requirements of User Groups	Potential Resource Types

4

are related through the use of
Recreation Planning, Guides
Landscape Interpretation and Design
Recreation Costs and Benefits

to

C — PROPOSE A RECREATION PLAN

5

For The Region or Planning Area

FIGURE 3.7 Combined approach to recreation planning.

havior (demand) to existing opportunities (supply) with a measure (standard) that indicates need (deficiency). The conceptual challenge is to develop sensitive classification systems to describe space, facilities, and services (supply) and recreation activities or experiences (demand) that can be aggregated at the neighborhood, city, and county level. Both demand and supply can be related in terms of effectiveness (quality) for general and special populations.

The identification of relative need (deficiency or surplus) should be based on criteria or standards other than the traditional National Recreation and Park Association (NRPA) standards. If NRPA standards are used, they should be *adapted* to the special requirements of each planning unit. Any measures used to determine relative need and deficiency should be:

1 Based on the latent and expressed recreation demand of the general and special populations of a planning area.

2 Attainable in the planning period by a combination of public and private action or alternatives provided.

3 Understood and supported by the public or their elected representatives.

4 Based on the leisure behavior, environment, and social values of the planning areas.

5 Measures of quality, performance, or effectiveness for a given time period, population group, and planning area.

Basic Methods

Ten basic methods of supply and demand analysis are in current use. Each method is outlined here and detailed in other chapters or books listed in the bibliography. The best aspects of each can be incorporated into an approach that fits the special needs and levels of planning expertise in a community.

INNOVATIVE APPROACH Based on user goals, preference, and incremental implementation. It results in a social indicator that reflects only the needs of a neighborhood at a given time. It translates values into space and money (Gold, 1973).

MEASURES OF EFFECTIVENESS Based on sensitive measures of use, accessibility, preference, and satisfaction for existing facilities, which are developed into a needs index for planning future facilities (Hatry and Dunn, 1971).

LEVEL OF SERVICE APPROACH Based on qualitative measures of effectiveness for a given set of facilities. An acceptable level of service is one that satisfies a given set of values (MNCPPC, 1977).

NEEDS-RESOURCES INDEX Based on the concept that different neighborhoods have different needs and resources which can be ranked in a comparative need index. It uses indicators, e.g., income, poverty level, population density, youth population, and crime levels, to calculate comparative needs (Staley, 1969).

RECREATION EXPERIENCE COMPONENTS CONCEPT Performance standards that describe the type of experience and similar activities that support this experience and translate this into space and design requirements (Christiansen, 1975).

POPULATION RATIO METHOD Specific ratios of acres, facilities, or program leadership for a general population (Buechner, 1971).

AREA PERCENTAGE METHOD Specific percentage of the planning area for public recreational uses (Buechner, 1971).

CARRYING-CAPACITY APPROACH Based on the concept that space or facilities have minimum, desirable, and optimum levels of human and natural carrying capacity and these can be translated into space with standards (Hendee, 1974).

SYSTEMS MODEL APPROACH Describes and projects existing supply and expressed demand based on participation rates for selected activities and relates this to time-distance impacts on facilities (PARIS, 1966).

USER RESOURCE PLANNING METHOD Based on classifying people into user groups that require certain environmental characteristics, dividing each planning area into resource types, relating the desired recreation experience to the resource, and developing planning guidelines based on an analysis of user and resource requirements (National Advisory Council, 1959).

Regardless of the method used, the development of measures, criteria, or performance standards for recreation land, facilities, and program should be based on *objective* factors instead of arbitrary judgments. The

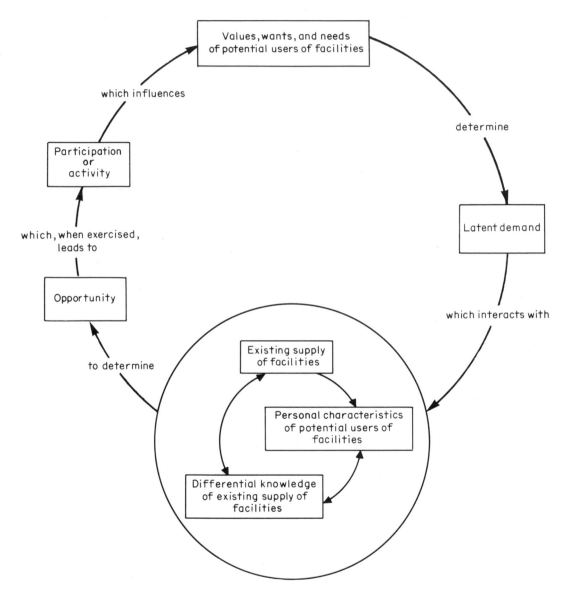

FIGURE 3.8 Supply and demand process.

methodology should view supply and demand as the process shown in Figure 3.8, with an emphasis on the quality or *effectiveness* of opportunities. The question of how *good* is as important as how *much* because space does not constitute service. In many communities, less space with better design and management is the most constructive solution to meeting recreation needs (Figure 3.9).

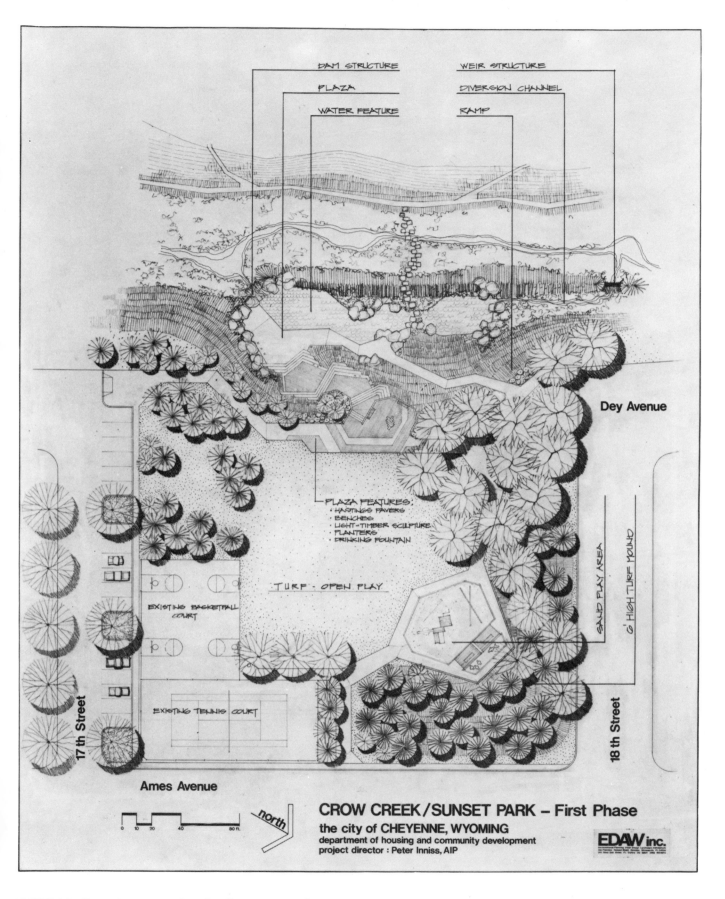

Labels within the illustration:

DAM STRUCTURE

WEIR STRUCTURE

PLAZA

DIVERSION CHANNEL

WATER FEATURE

RAMP

Dey Avenue

PLAZA FEATURES:
• HASTINGS PAVERS
• BENCHES
• LIGHT-TIMBER SCULPTURE
• PLANTERS
• DRINKING FOUNTAIN

TURF - OPEN PLAY

SAND PLAY AREA

6' HIGH TURF MOUND

EXISTING BASKETBALL COURT

EXISTING TENNIS COURT

17th Street

18th Street

Ames Avenue

north

0 10 20 40 80 ft.

CROW CREEK / SUNSET PARK – First Phase
the city of CHEYENNE, WYOMING
department of housing and community development
project director : Peter Inniss, AIP

EDAW inc.

FIGURE 3.9 Recreation space and service/Cheyenne, Wyoming.

4 | PARK AND RECREATION PLANS

The park and recreation plan is an expression of a community's objectives, needs, and priorities for leisure space, service, and facilities. It should provide a guide for public policy and private decisions related to the scope, quality, and location of leisure opportunities to meet the needs of residents and visitors. The plan should be a required element of the comprehensive plan that details recreation needs and the implementation program to meet these needs.

SCOPE AND EMPHASIS

The park and recreation plan should be a long-range, comprehensive, and policy-oriented document that (1) describes alternatives, recommendations, and guidelines for decisions related to the use and preservation of open space for recreation, and (2) makes recommendations on the acquisition, development, and management of both public and private recreation spaces or facilities.

The plan should acknowledge the past leisure patterns of the population, describe the present use of facilities, and project future needs with words, graphics, or data that communicate the facts, outline alternatives, propose new ideas, and motivate action. The plan should outline what is possible, who can best provide these opportunities, and project the benefits and costs of alternative opportunities in a time-phased program (Figure 4.1).

The planning process for this type of park and recreation plan requires a high degree of citizen involvement and understanding of public opinion of all stages. There is no substitute for effective citizen involvement at the neighborhood and community scale.

Although most plans have focused on the public sector, outdoor space, and organized program, the trend is toward a balanced emphasis of the public and private sector, indoor and outdoor opportunities, and the integration of recreation space, services, and facilities with other community services. (Figure 4.2).

Plans should also meet the federal and state requirements for assistance programs such as the Land and Water Conservation Fund administered by the Heritage Conservation and Recreation Service. Appendix B contains an abstract of the federal guidelines and format for a recreation plan.

CHARACTERISTICS OF THE PLAN

The park and recreation plan should emphasize those aspects of land use, circulation, conservation, and community facilities that detail how and where people use their leisure time in cities. Most communities will also have a separate conservation and open space element of the comprehensive plan with a broader set of objectives such as growth management, managed resource production, or public safety, as shown in Table 4.1 and Figure 4.3. The open space element will also detail the methods, benefits, and costs of preserving open space, which are described in Chapter 15, Tables 15.1 and 15.2. Many communities are now combining the parks, recreation, and open space elements into single element of the comprehensive plan (Figure 4.4).

Note that parks and recreation represents only one possible use of open space. Although parks and recreation can be a multipurpose use of all lands designated as

TABLE 4.1 | FUNCTIONS AND CLASSIFICATION OF OPEN SPACE

Managed Resource Production
Agricultural production
Mineral production
Forest production
Energy production

Environment and Ecological Balance

Fish and wildlife refuges
Watershed areas
Significant geological features
Visual corridors and viewpoints

Public Health and Safety

Flood control and water supply
Waste disposal areas
Airshed quality improvement
Geological hazard zones
Fire hazard zones
Airport flight path zones
Hazardous storage zones

Community Development and Social Welfare

Parks and recreation areas
Historic preservation districts
Cultural and archaeological sites
Public and institutional building sites
Land use buffers

Urban Form

Growth control
Circulation corridors
Utility corridors
Future expansion reserves

FIGURE 4.1 Implementation matrix/Lake Tahoe, California.

PLAN ELEMENT		TRPA Funding Aquisition Fee Simple	TRPA Funding Aquisition Other	TRPA Planning	TRPA Coordination	TRPA Management (Programs)	TRPA Control	FEDERAL Funding Aquisition Fee Simple	FEDERAL Funding Aquisition Other	FEDERAL Planning	FEDERAL Coordination	FEDERAL Management (Programs)	FEDERAL Control	STATE Funding Aquisition Fee Simple	STATE Funding Aquisition Other	STATE Planning	STATE Coordination	STATE Management (Programs)	STATE Control	COUNTY Funding Aquisition Fee Simple	COUNTY Funding Aquisition Other	COUNTY Planning	COUNTY Coordination	COUNTY Management (Programs)	COUNTY Control	CITY Funding Aquisition Fee Simple	CITY Funding Aquisition Other	CITY Planning	CITY Coordination	CITY Management (Programs)	CITY Control	OTHER Special Districts	OTHER Private Enterprise	OTHER Foundations/Donations	OTHER Public Support
CONSERVATION	Land	o	o	M	M	S	M	M	S	M	S	M	M	M	S	S	S	M	S	S	S	M	M	S	M	S	S	M	M	S	M	S	S	M	M
	Water	o	o	M	M	S	M	M	S	M	S	M	M	M	S	S	S	M	M	S	S	S	M	S	M	S	S	S	M	S	M	S	S	S	M
RECREATION	Summer	o	o	M	M	S	M	M	o	M	S	M	M	M	o	M	S	M	S	M	S	M	S	S	M	M	S	M	S	S	M	M	M	S	M
	Winter	o	o	M	M	S	M	M	o	M	S	M	M	M	o	M	S	M	S	M	S	M	S	S	M	M	S	M	S	S	M	M	M	S	M
OPEN SPACE		o	o	M	M	S	M	M	M	M	M	M	M	M	M	M	M	S	S	S	S	M	M	S	M	S	S	M	M	S	M	S	S	M	M

RESPONSIBILITY CORRELATION:

M MAJOR
S SHARED
o MINOR OR NONE

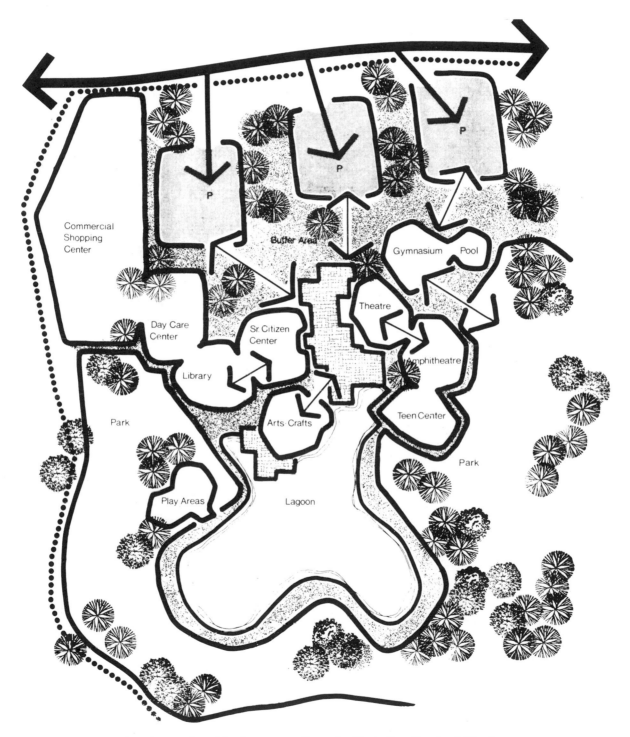

Commercial Shopping Center

P

P

P

Buffer Area

Gymnasium   Pool

Day Care Center

Sr. Citizen Center

Theatre

Library

Amphitheatre

Park

Arts·Crafts

Teen Center

Play Areas

Lagoon

Park

FIGURE 4.2   Integration of recreation with other community services/Santa Cruz County, California.

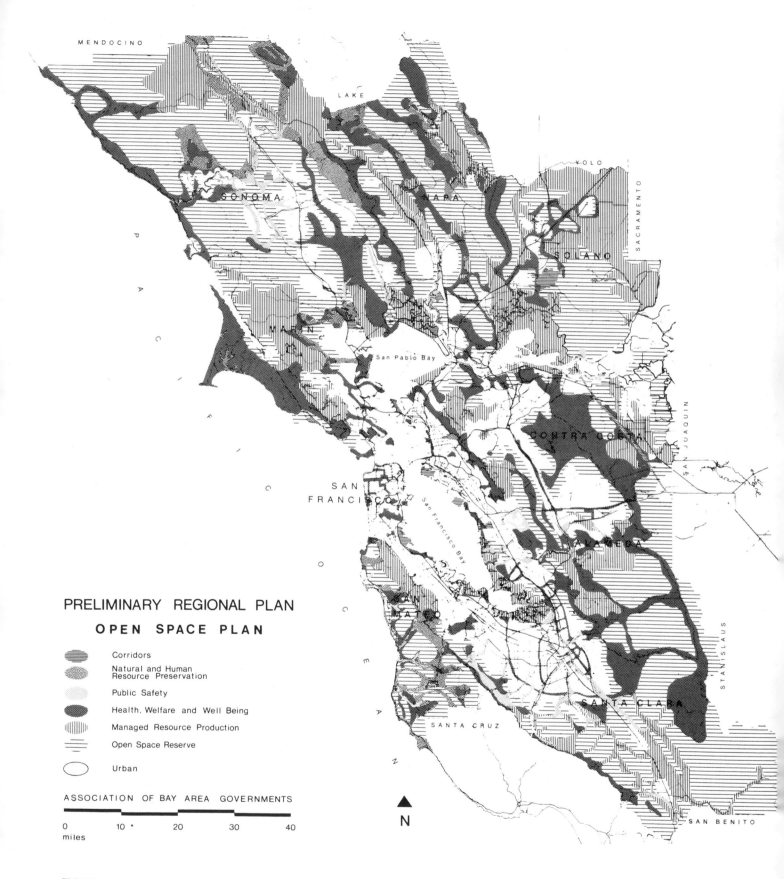

PRELIMINARY REGIONAL PLAN

OPEN SPACE PLAN

- Corridors
- Natural and Human Resource Preservation
- Public Safety
- Health, Welfare and Well Being
- Managed Resource Production
- Open Space Reserve
- Urban

ASSOCIATION OF BAY AREA GOVERNMENTS

0   10   20   30   40
miles

N

FIGURE 4.3   Open space element of a comprehensive regional plan/San Francisco.

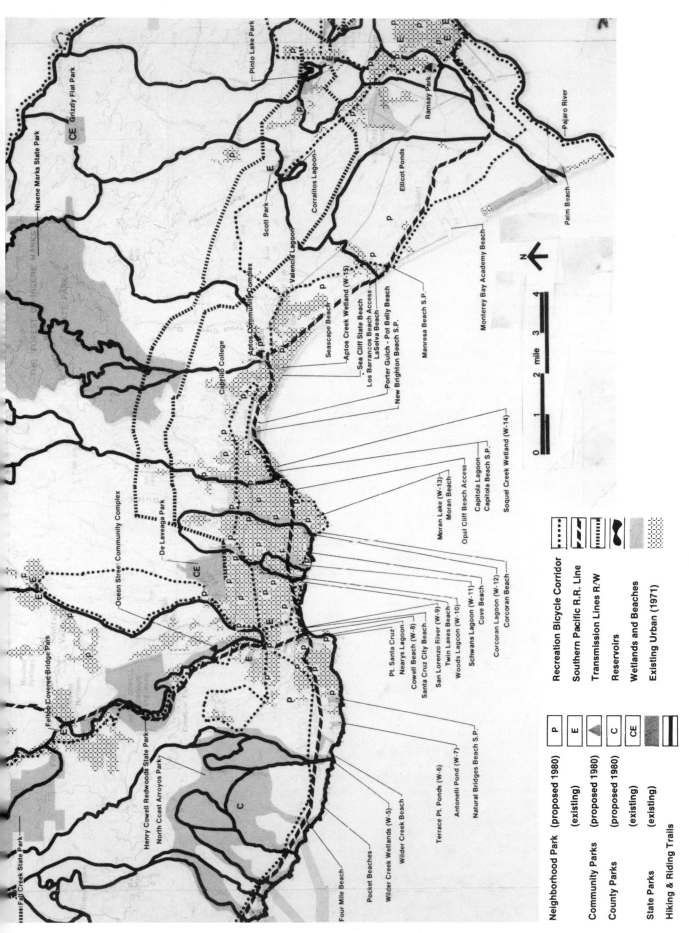

Neighborhood Park (proposed 1980) P

(existing) E

Community Parks (proposed 1980)

County Parks (proposed 1980) C

(existing) CE

State Parks (existing)

Hiking & Riding Trails

Recreation Bicycle Corridor

Southern Pacific R.R. Line

Transmission Lines R/W

Reservoirs

Wetlands and Beaches

Existing Urban (1971)

FIGURE 4.4 Park, recreation, and open space plan/Santa Cruz County, California.

63

open space in the comprehensive plan, these lands should *not* be considered as a substitute in the requirements and allocation of user-oriented recreation spaces unless they are used primarily for recreation purposes.

This distinction is not to discourage the multiple use concept of open space, but to recognize that certain types of recreation opportunities have special requirements. For example, airport flight paths, freeway buffers, and utility corridors with open-space designations on a land use map may have multipurpose recreation potentials, but these areas are *not* the equivalent of lands normally considered for *primary* recreational purposes. There may also be serious questions of public health and safety associated with recreational facilities in transportation corridors or near high-voltage transmission lines.

The plan should be (1) balanced to meet present deficiencies and future needs, (2) oriented to the projected population and economic base of a community, and (3) in scale with a community's fiscal resources or expected federal or state assistance programs to help implement the plan.

An effective plan will (1) identify problems, (2) present information on the social and physical implications of these problems in measurable human terms, (3) develop problem-solving alternatives, (4) describe the expected results of each alternative in terms of environmental and social impact on the planning area, and (5) rank or recommend alternatives in terms of economic, social, and political feasibility

PLANNING PERIOD

The time horizon for the park and recreation plan should parallel the comprehensive plan. In most communities, this will be a 20-year projection of trends with four 5-year increments that parallel the capital improvement budget cycle. Because leisure patterns are very subject to changes in life-style, the economy, and technology, it is important to project future trends with the best available information and revise or update the plan at least every five years.

Long-range (more than 20 years) park and recreation plans without incremental revision are difficult for the general public to understand and support and for planners to update. Political officials are often reluctant to support long-range plans because tangible results are not evident to potential voters. Rapidly changing federal and state assistance programs also make long-range plans more difficult to revise than short-range plans.

The short-range (five-year) time horizon is most appropriate for recreation planning in the inner and central city of metropolitan areas with a high concentration of special populations. Flexibility and results are the measures of success for recreation planning in the inner city. A commitment of money for land, development, and program at intervals encourages demonstration and continuing public involvement. It allows people to change their preferences or priorities and focuses planning at a human or neighborhood scale.

Coping with Change

At the community scale, the planning period should be able to cope with a broader spectrum of change. The planner needs a way to organize information that parallels the range of expected change. This "hierarchy of uncertainty" is one way to categorize degrees of change and consider them in the planning process:

STABLE FEATURES Physical features, natural phenomena, or events unlikely to be changed or change, such as mountains, flood plains, utilities, railroads, prevailing winds, and major holidays.

NEAR-CERTAIN TRENDS Physical features, natural phenomena, or events certain to change in the short-range future, such as freeway proposals, revenue-sharing formulas, water tables, levels of urban growth, local economy, tax rates, crime levels, energy shortages, and birth rates.

LIKELY TRENDS Physical features, natural phenomena, or conditions likely to change in the long-range future, such as metropolitan government, levels of air pollution, traffic congestion, mass transit, energy depletion, housing styles, and work patterns.

ALTERNATIVES Conditions dependent on events or inventions which have not taken place, such as natural disasters, technological breakthroughs, new legislation, or economic depression.

DESIRABLE CHANGE Ideas or proposals to complement or improve physical features or social patterns such as historic preservation, urban renewal, leisure counseling, or the elimination of poverty.

The preparation of a comprehensive, long-range park and recreation plan should consider all degrees of uncertainty because the physical, social, and economic diversity of a city is not equal in predictability. Conversely, the design for a neighborhood park may require only one or two levels of uncertainty because of the relatively homogeneous nature of a neighborhood with a high degree of predictability.

These differences should be conspicuous in the planning process to develop policies for solving long-range and immediate problems. This hierarchy provides a framework for assigning priorities in data collection, goal formulation, implementation, and performance budgeting. It also forces the planning process to be responsive to the present and future at different scales.

PLANNING AREA

Because of the relative mobility of most users and the specialized nature of many urban park and recreation opportunities, a problem-shed approach should be used to determine the planning study area. This approach prompts the solution of problems in terms of cause and effect. It describes how and where urban populations will use existing or potential recreation opportunities and has important advantages in distributing the cost of specialized facilities, e.g., a zoological park or arboretum, over a broader tax base.

The problem-shed approach also has important advantages in seeing how people perceive different types of recreation opportunities. There are several perceptual scales people can relate to, but most people's image of the city is limited to their particular living or working environments (Figure 4.5).

Recreation planners and designers should pay particular attention to the perceptual, problem-shed, and taxing units before defining the planning area for a recreation project or plan. In many cases, the normal or arbitrary political and census boundaries may not apply. Figure 4.6 shows a typical situation where the service area of a neighborhood park may not respect normal physical, political, or census boundaries, but may relate to the way people perceive and use these parks.

The problem shed may differ according to a city's demographic character, density, degree of development, and economic base. The planning area or problem shed is dramatically different for a tourist-oriented city with a natural resource focus than it is for a resident-oriented community with a cosmopolitan urban character.

A parks, recreation, and open space system could consist of the components shown in Figure 4.7. In an area with relatively few natural resources, man-made

recreation resources would be dominant. For example, the components of wildlife and vegetation for a suburban community might be substituted or supplemented by components of street life and architecture in the central city.

A comprehensive plan could include the widest range of components that can contribute to a recreation experience in an urban setting. It should include those places traditionally considered as public park and recreation opportunities. But, it can also include facilities such as shopping center, amusement parks, theaters, bars, restaurants, libraries, museums, airports, farmers' and flea markets, private yacht and sport clubs, community colleges, historic districts, hotel and motel districts, waterfront districts, and pedestrian malls and plazas (Figure 4.8).

This approach views the entire city as a recreation space instead of a set of isolated spaces and experiences. It integrates space and services, public and private, and indoor and outdoor opportunities where appropriate and possible. It considers any place where people can experience pleasure or enrichment as a potential leisure resource (Figures 4.9 and 4.10).

COMPONENTS AND WORK PROGRAM

The detailed requirements for the park and recreation element of a comprehensive plan are described in federal and state guidelines, which should be consulted before a work program is established by a consultant or public agency. However, these general requirements can be used to define the components and work program of the plan:

- *Introduction*
  Describe objectives and scope of plan.
  Define legal authority for federal/state programs.
  Define agency responsible for preparation of plan.
  Describe previous and future studies related to plan.
  State assumptions and qualifications of plan.

- *Existing Conditions*
  Describe regional context of planning area.
  Describe leisure behavior patterns of population.
  Describe environmental characteristics of planning area.
  Describe recreation problems and potentials by planning unit.
  Describe general character of planning units.

- *Recreation Resources*
  Classify resources and opportunities.
  Inventory existing land, facilities, and program.
  Evaluate opportunities by planning unit.
  Describe potential recreation resources/programs.
  Evaluate design, access, and public safety.

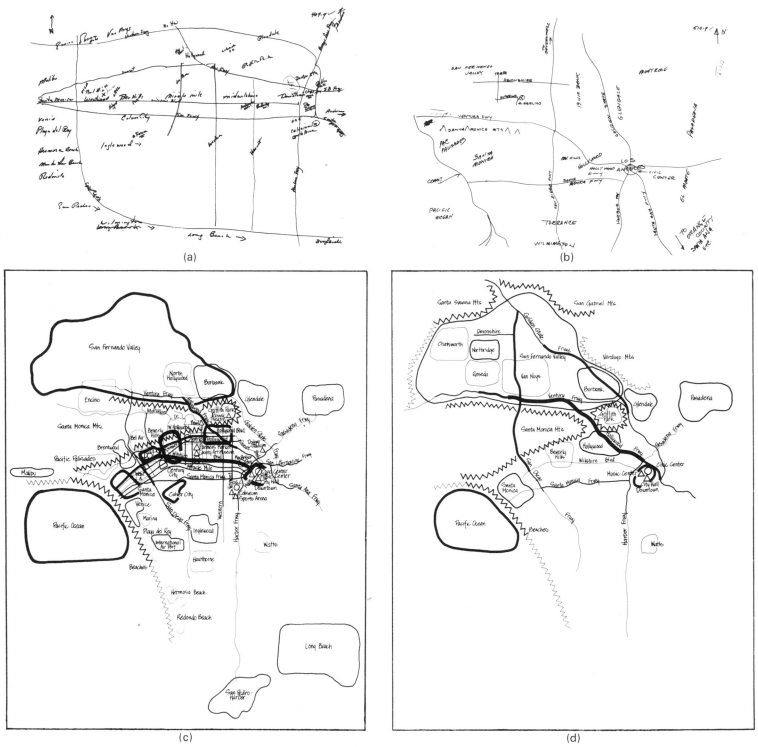

FIGURE 4.5 Perceptual scale of urban residents/Los Angeles. *(a)* Actual citizen's map, Westwood; *(b)* composite citizen's image, Westwood; *(c)* actual citizen's map, Northridge; *(d)* composite citizen's image, Northridge.

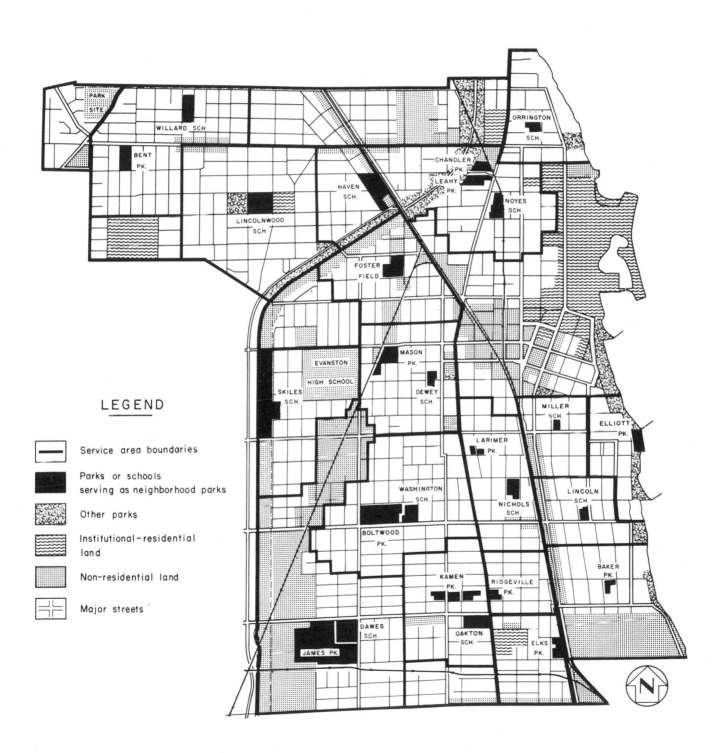

LEGEND

Service area boundaries

Parks or schools
serving as neighborhood parks

Other parks

Institutional-residential
land

Non-residential land

Major streets

SCALE IN FEET
0   1200   2400

FIGURE 4.6 Neighborhood park service areas/Evanston, Illinois.

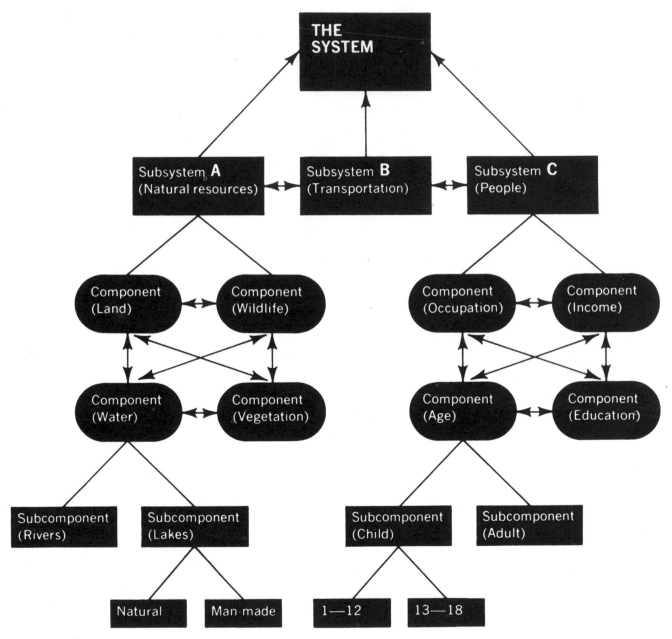

FIGURE 4.7 Model of a park and recreation system.

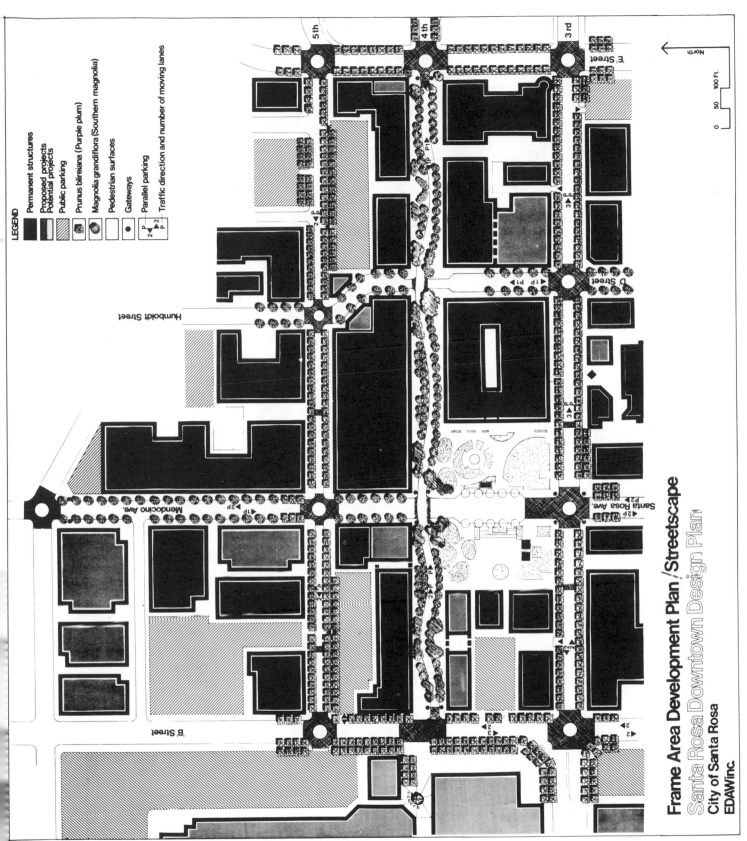

LEGEND

- Permanent structures
- Proposed projects
- Potential projects
- Public parking
- Prunus blireiana (Purple plum)
- Magnolia grandiflora (Southern magnolia)
- Pedestrian surfaces
- Gateways
- Parallel parking
- Traffic direction and number of moving lanes

North

0   50   100 Ft.

5th
4th
3rd
'E' Street
D Street
Humboldt Street
Mendocino Ave.
Santa Rosa Ave.
'B' Street

Frame Area Development Plan / Streetscape
Santa Rosa Downtown Design Plan
City of Santa Rosa
EDAWinc.

FIGURE 4.8   Downtown design plan/Santa Rosa, California.

**Los Angeles
Central City**

**PROPOSED
PLAN**

DEPARTMENT OF CITY PLANNING □ LOS ANGELES, CALIFORNIA

FIGURE 4.9 Central city as a recreation place/Los Angeles.

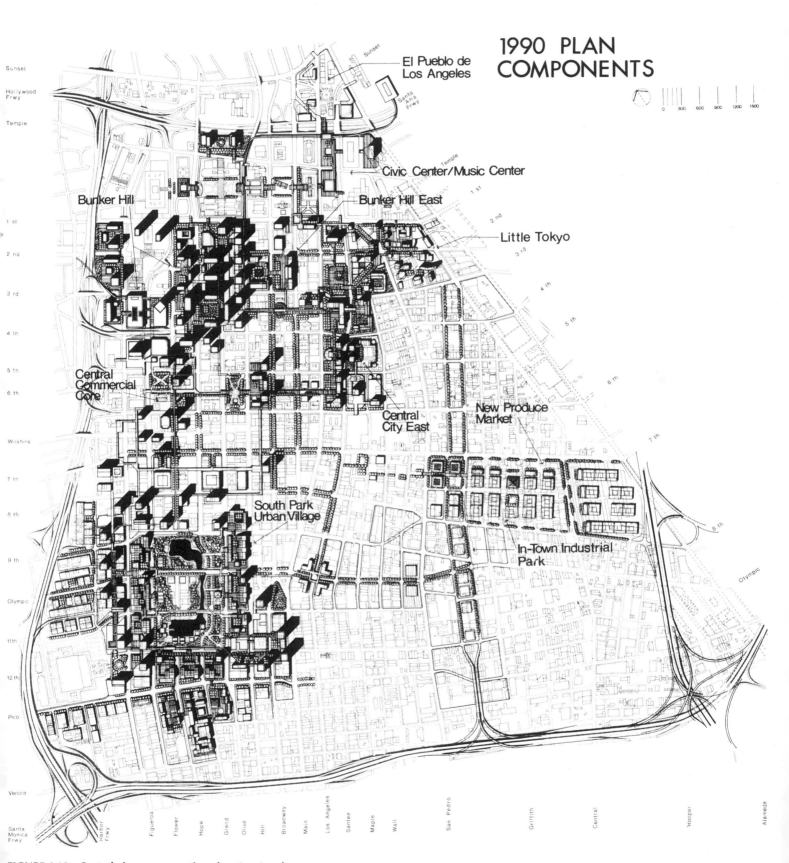

1990 PLAN
COMPONENTS

El Pueblo de
Los Angeles

Civic Center/Music Center

Bunker Hill

Bunker Hill East

Little Tokyo

Central
Commercial
Core

Central
City East

New Produce
Market

South Park
Urban Village

In-Town Industrial
Park

FIGURE 4.10   Central city as a recreation place/Los Angeles.

- *Demand and Use Patterns*
  Inventory time budgets of population.
  Analyze recreation use patterns by demographic groups.
  Describe user perference/satisfaction.
  Analyze causes for nonuse of existing opportunities.
  Describe problems of special populations.
  Assess impact of nonresidents/tourists.
  Assess impact of fees and charges on demand patterns.
  Assess impact of access on use of facilities.

- *Needs Analysis*
  Analyze demand-supply relationships.
  Develop use concepts, principles, and design criteria.
  Develop space, development, and program standards.
  Describe deficiencies by planning unit.
  Project needs by planning period and planning unit.
  Describe public/private potentials to accommodate needs.

- *Goals, Policies, and Alternatives*
  Describe existing goals, objectives, and policies.
  Describe desirable goals, objectives, and policies.
  Analyze alternative ways to achieve desirable goals.
  Describe the implications of each alternative.
  Recommend an alternative.
  Describe social/environmental impact of the alternative.

- *Implementation*
  Describe public/private actions by project/planning unit.
  Schedule actions by time, planning unit, and responsibility.
  Estimate benefits and costs of each project or program.
  Relate costs to general and capital improvement budgets.
  Describe needed financing and sources.
  Describe needed legislation or responsibility.
  Describe public participation to implement plan.
  Describe how and when the plan will be revised.

- *Appendix*
  Background studies.
  Data and methodology.
  Bibliography and sources.
  Acknowledgments and credits.

RELATIONSHIP TO COMPREHENSIVE PLAN

The comprehensive plan is a general guide to the future character and development of a community. It identifies significant areas to be preserved or changed to achieve social, economic, or environmental goals. The park and recreation plan uses the information, policies, and recommendations of the comprehensive plan to develop detailed policies, standards, design or management criteria, and a capital improvement program to achieve the leisure objectives of residents and visitors.

The comprehensive plan focuses on the relationship of open space and leisure services to land use and the quality of urban life and environment. The parks and recreation plan details these relationships and translates them into systemwide and site-specific proposals or projects to acquire or develop over time. It also details policies, practices, or criteria related to the design and management of these leisure spaces and services. Both the comprehensive and the park and recreation plan can be considered as a system with the inputs and outputs shown in Figure 4.11.

The comprehensive plan provides the basis for a community's recreation plan and should be completed first. It provides general concepts and goals for the social and physical development of a city. The recreation plan details a community's recreation needs with specific recommendations for land acquisition, facility development, operations, maintenance, and financing that are not normally part of the comprehensive plan. If properly done, both the comprehensive plan and the recreation plan will complement each other and satisfy requirements for federal and state assistance.

The preparation of a park and recreation plan is normally the joint responsibility of the planning and recreation agencies. Figure 4.12 shows the subdivision of responsibilities. Note that while the planning agency has the prime responsibility during the preparation of a comprehensive plan, these roles gradually reverse as a community prepares and implements its park and recreation plan.

THE USE OF CONSULTANTS

The nature of most park and recreation plans and relative lack of professionals with specialized training in recreation planning prompts many public agencies to use private consultants for all or part of the work program. The procedures for selecting and using consultants are detailed in publications by professional societies such as ASLA, APA, AIA, and NRPA. Appendix C contains a recommended procedure for selecting a professional planning consultant and sample agreements for the preparation of a park master plan and community recreation study.

The decision of when, where, and how to use consultants or agency staff to prepare or revise a comprehensive recreation plan or design should be based on these basic factors or questions:

Consultant's Role

1 The professional ability, technical competence, and design ability of a firm is easy to gauge by a review of completed projects.

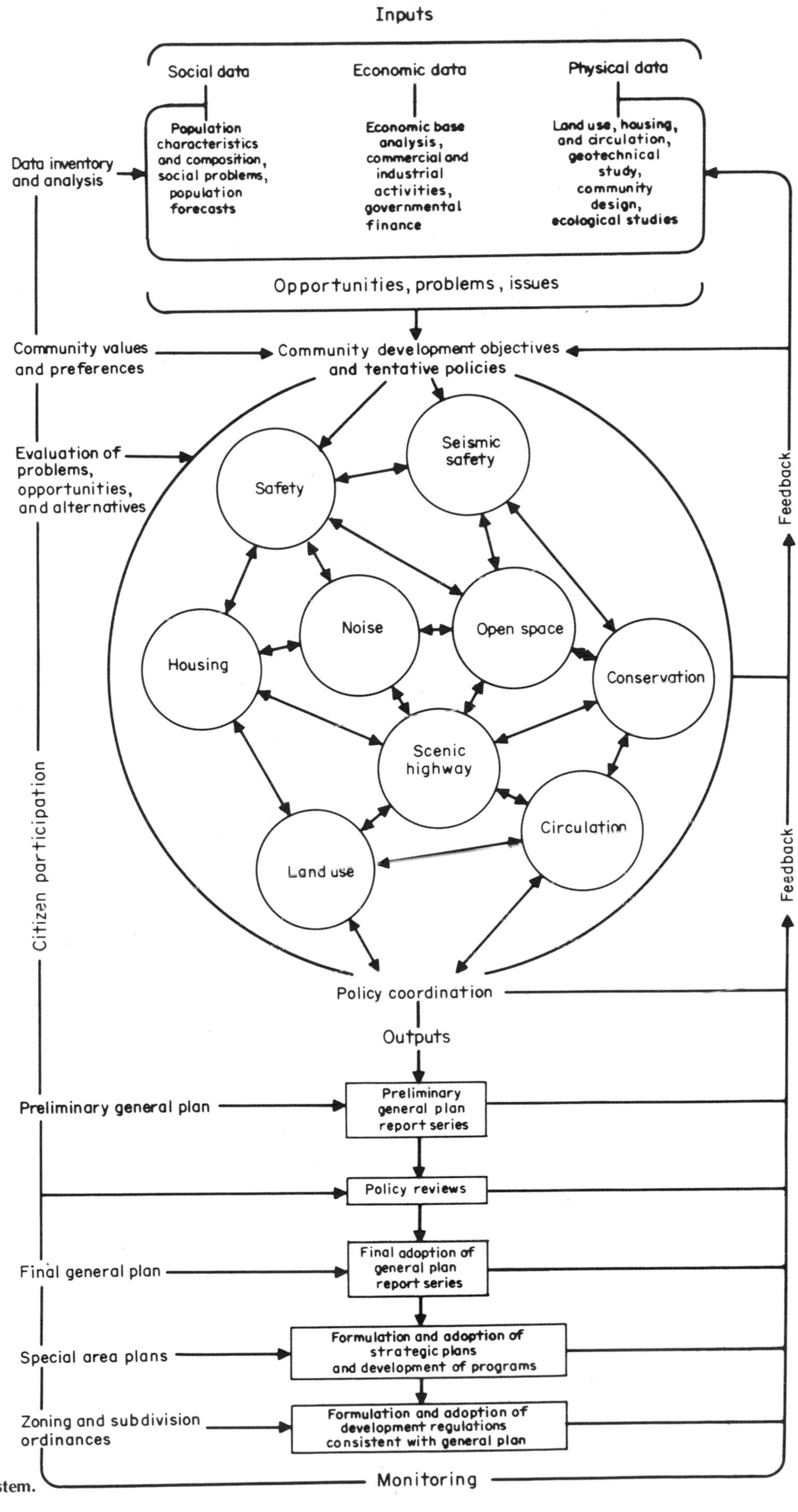

Inputs

Social data

Population characteristics and composition, social problems, population forecasts

Economic data

Economic base analysis, commercial and industrial activities, governmental finance

Physical data

Land use, housing, and circulation, geotechnical study, community design, ecological studies

Data inventory and analysis

Opportunities, problems, issues

Community values and preferences

Community development objectives and tentative policies

Evaluation of problems, opportunities, and alternatives

Safety

Seismic safety

Noise

Open space

Housing

Conservation

Scenic highway

Land use

Circulation

Citizen participation

Feedback

Feedback

Policy coordination

Outputs

Preliminary general plan

Preliminary general plan report series

Policy reviews

Final general plan

Final adoption of general plan report series

Special area plans

Formulation and adoption of strategic plans and development of programs

Zoning and subdivision ordinances

Formulation and adoption of development regulations consistent with general plan

Monitoring

FIGURE 4.11   The general plan system.

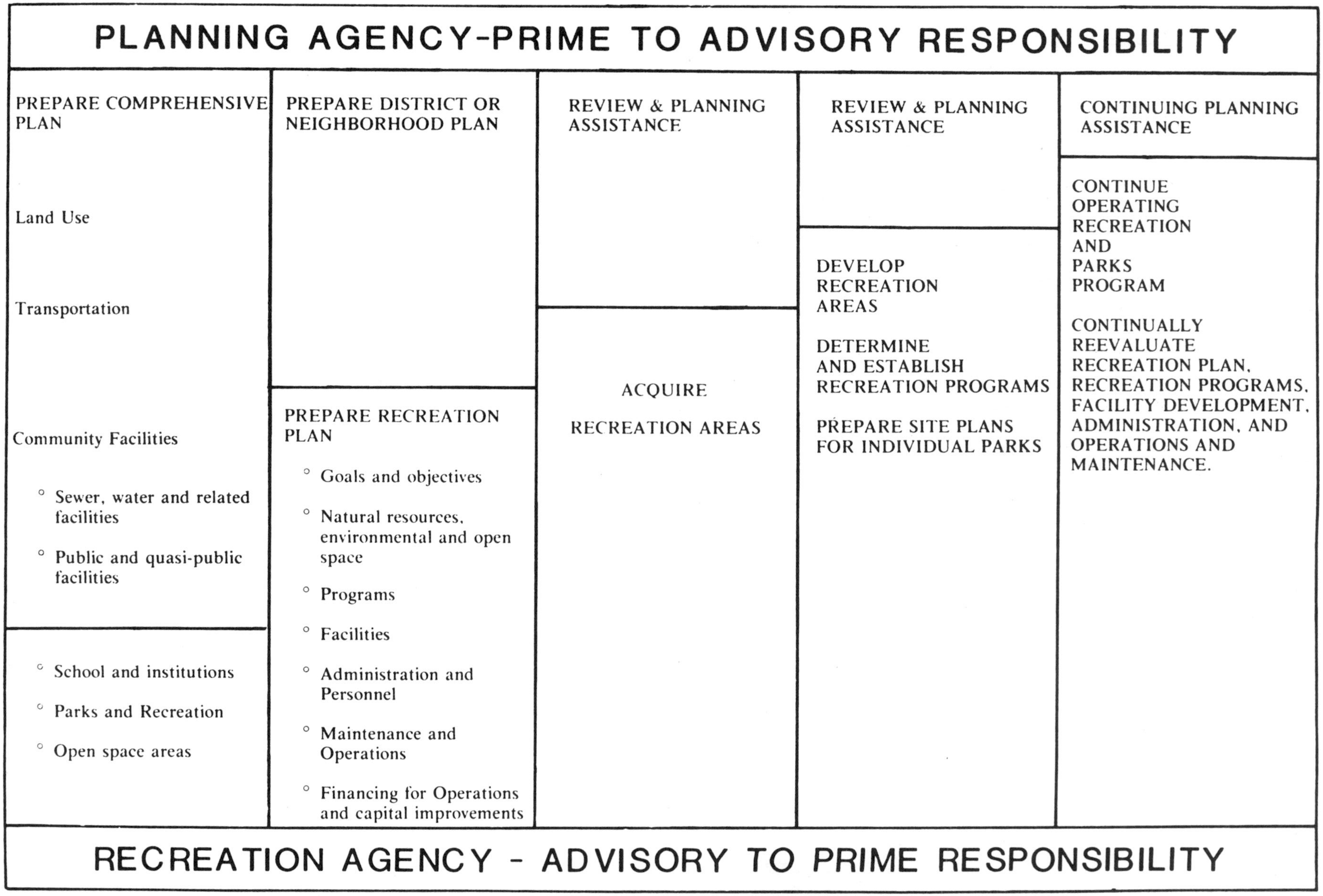

PLANNING AGENCY—PRIME TO ADVISORY RESPONSIBILITY

PREPARE COMPREHENSIVE PLAN	PREPARE DISTRICT OR NEIGHBORHOOD PLAN	REVIEW & PLANNING ASSISTANCE	REVIEW & PLANNING ASSISTANCE	CONTINUING PLANNING ASSISTANCE

Land Use
 	
Transportation
 	
Community Facilities
  ○ Sewer, water and related facilities
  ○ Public and quasi-public facilities
  ○ School and institutions
  ○ Parks and Recreation
  ○ Open space areas
	PREPARE RECREATION PLAN
	  ○ Goals and objectives
	  ○ Natural resources, environmental and open space
	  ○ Programs
	  ○ Facilities
	  ○ Administration and Personnel
	  ○ Maintenance and Operations
	  ○ Financing for Operations and capital improvements
		ACQUIRE RECREATION AREAS	DEVELOP RECREATION AREAS
			
			DETERMINE AND ESTABLISH RECREATION PROGRAMS
			
			PREPARE SITE PLANS FOR INDIVIDUAL PARKS
				CONTINUE OPERATING RECREATION AND PARKS PROGRAM
				
				CONTINUALLY REEVALUATE RECREATION PLAN, RECREATION PROGRAMS, FACILITY DEVELOPMENT, ADMINISTRATION, AND OPERATIONS AND MAINTENANCE.

RECREATION AGENCY – ADVISORY TO PRIME RESPONSIBILITY

FIGURE 4.12 Agency responsibilities for recreation planning/State of Maryland.

2 Their ability to perform and render services can be evaluated by references from previous clients.

3 Consultants can provide a planning team with adequate staff, background, experience, and know-how to deal with a project and complete it within a given time period.

4 Because consultant firms represent private enterprise, their flexible employment policies allow hiring of personnel as needed to keep up with work loads.

5 Consultant firms normally have a backlog of experience, tools, and know-how directly related to a variety of situations and projects. Liaison has been established with specialists and experts from other disciplines to provide a team best suited for a project.

6 A consultant firm has political separation from the client without the direct emotional involvement which may detract from ability to perform professionally in an objective sense.

7 Most consultants work on fee schedules which have been developed to provide equitable profit. In general, there is no room in competitive private enterprise for inefficient operation or excessive profits.

Staff Role

1 What is the relative level of competence necessary? Are there methods other than a review of completed work to judge the design competence of any professional?

2 Will people added to the staff have adequate experience and technical ability to cover all the skills necessary for the successful conclusion of current or future projects? If so, will the salary offered attract personnel with the skills required? If these skills are available in one individual, what should his or her salary be?

3 Will new staff have the performance capability and time available to meet immediate demands?

4 Will supporting staff have the abilities and attitudes to help a new staff member meet time schedules?

5 Will the efforts of a new staff member be reviewed by superiors with the same set of professional values expected of a consultant?

6 Will a new staff member have the ability to relate to the special interests of pressure groups? Would a person on staff be emotionally too close to the client and task to be objective?

7 Have the real costs of the added personnel including basic salary, fringe benefits, overhead, and cost of carrying personnel over nonproductive periods been considered?

In an era of public austerity, the best way to compliment existing staff may be with competent consultants. This could be the most cost-effective and expedient option. It demands that extra care be devoted to the selection and supervision of qualified consultants with a demonstrated ability to engage in recreation planning and design. The results of this joint effort could be beneficial to public agencies and consultants to improve the state of the art and provide the public with the best value.

5 | INFORMATION SOURCES

An effective recreation plan translates data into information that citizens and decision makers can consider. The professional's primary role in the planning process is to collect, organize, analyze, interpret, and present information that provides a systematic basis for describing alternatives or making recommendations. This requires an understanding of (1) what information is needed, (2) why it is important, (3) where it can be obtained, (4) how it can be analyzed and presented, and (5) where it fits in the planning process.

DATA AND INFORMATION

Most plans do not make a careful distinction between data and information. They do not define terms, describe why certain items were included or omitted, explain what is significant, or outline how this information can be used. The reader of most plans is confronted with a maze of statistics that often complicate instead of clarify the situation.

Statistics become part of the problem instead of the solution. Citizens and professionals become mired in semantic or statistical ambiguity instead of focusing on the meaning of the information. They are expected to understand and act on a set of numbers or symbols that may not describe the problem, alternatives, and solutions in understandable terms. A definition of terms and understanding of how to use data will give credibility to the planning process.

Types of Data

Data is a set of unassociated or unrelated facts to describe the physical, social, or institutional characteristics of the resource or the user. *Information* is facts arranged in a way that can be useful in the planning and decision-making process. The facts should provide an *objective* description of the behavior, values, and de-

mographic, environmental, or institutional variables of a planning area, unit, or project.

The types of data collected can include any combination of the categories shown in Table 5.1. A basic distinction is the difference between site-specific and system-oriented data. *Site-specific* data focuses on the relationships between a single space and people that are classified as users or nonusers of an area. *System-oriented* data focuses on the relationships between many spaces and people that are classified as users or nonusers of the system or any part of it.

Both site-specific and system-oriented data can be obtained before or after a project or system is completed in *preconstruction* or *postconstruction* evaluation studies. These studies will be concerned with information commonly found in the four combinations shown in Table 5.2 (Hester, 1975). A study of nonusers will normally double this combination of information.

Data can also be classified as reference or primary. *Reference* data is generally obtained from secondary sources, e.g., the U.S. Census or a local school census. Normally, it is information collected for purposes other than recreation planning. *Primary* data is generally original information collected for a specific purpose. It is usually unknown information collected as part of the recreation planning process. Most plans use a combination of reference and primary data.

For example, the task of describing recreation demand or use patterns for a given site or system requires a demographic profile of users or nonusers (reference data) and a leisure behavior profile (primary data). In most cases, the reference data is known and available while the primary data is unknown and must be collected in the field.

A common shortcoming of many plans is to use reference data as a substitute for primary data to save time or money. This often results in facts that may be impressive, but are of little value in formulating public policy or giving physical form to social values. This practice can

TABLE 5.1 | RECREATION PLANNING DATA MATRIX. Types and Use of Data

| Factors | Types | | Scale | | Primary use | | | | | |
	Primary	Secondary	Site	System	Reference	Analysis	Planning	Design	Management	Evaluation
Physical										
Social										
Institutional										

Source: Reprinted, with permission, from *Neighborhood Space*, by Randolph T. Hester, Jr., © 1975 by Dowden, Hutchinson & Ross, Inc., Stroudsburg, Pa.

TABLE 5.2 | COMBINATIONS OF RECREATION PLANNING INFORMATION

Known to planner	Unknown to planner
Known to user	Known to user
Known to planner	Unknown to planner
Unknown to user	Unknown to user

Source: Reprinted, with permission, from *Neighborhood Space,* by Randolph T. Hester, Jr., © 1975 by Dowden, Hutchinson & Ross, Inc., Stroudsburg, Pa.

also result in a historical bias instead of a current or futurisitc dimension to the planning process because most reference data is collected at five- or ten-year intervals.

An explanation of the way data is collected, analyzed, and interpreted is essential, if a plan is to have credibility. Many efforts are misunderstood because both the planner and client do not understand the statistical meaning of information. One way to avoid difficulties is to begin with these basic definitions:

Validity What the data measures in terms of how statistically sound the results are and can be explained with standard tests.

Reliability The accuracy and predictibility of data in terms of how generalizable it would be for a similar set of variables.

Significance The statistical meaning of data relative to similar sets of data and the problem.

Every effort should be made to reduce bias in the way the data is collected and interpreted. The best ways to do this are to (1) use proven statistical techniques, (2) obtain a second opinion from a qualified person before a particular statistical method is used, and (3) hold in-process, critical reviews of the measures and methods being used.

If the data is obtained as part of a survey, there are qualifications which should be used in interpretation. Serious errors in judgment and embarrassment to the public officials or consultant can occur, if statistical and pragmatic caution is not used to interpret the results of a survey. These qualifications apply to the surveys described in this chapter and Chapter 7:

1 Beware of opinion polls on complex issues about which citizens lack information.

2 Beware of responses reflecting short-run considerations and neglecting long-term problems.

3 Beware of surveys taken during election campaigns or closely associated with referendums.

4 Beware of using surveys to hide from controversy and responsibility.

5 Beware of the wording of questions; what is said or not said can be misleading.

6 Beware of sensitive issues and questions that seem to elicit silence or misleading answers.

7 Beware of unrepresentative results; inadequate survey procedures may have been used.

8 Beware of antagonizing citizens who consider interviews an invasion of privacy.

9 Beware that survey findings may raise false expectations among citizens.

10 Beware that the results are only one expression of public opinion or a measure of leisure behavior at one point in time in response to existing conditions.

These qualifications are detailed with many examples in several texts (Hatry, 1977). The object here is to establish the concept of qualifications for using or interpreting data that can condition both the approach used to collect data and the products of the planning process.

Beyond the qualification of data, it is desirable to establish a checklist of questions professionals and citizens can use to evaluate the statistical significance of findings. These questions can also be used by those conducting surveys or in the review of proposals by consultants or public agencies to conduct a survey. No general format will fit all situations, but this illustrative list of questions can provide a guide for many studies used in recreation planning:

1 What population are the findings meant to represent?

2 What sampling frame was used and how was the sample actually selected?

3 How and when was the data collected, and were the methods used appropriate to the population being sampled?

4 How were specific variables measured in the sample and analyzed to achieve the objectives of the survey?

5 How strong are the associations or relationships among the variables being measured, and are these associations realistic in terms of the population sample or problem being studied?

6 Has the researcher adequately explained the logic of these associations, tested for possible distortions, and presented alternative explanations for all findings?

7 Do the empirical relationships suggest further analyses that the researcher or client has not considered?

8 Could another researcher or client replicate this survey on the basis of information in the report or proposal?

Approaches to Data Collection

The typical approach to data collection is to gather as many facts as possible. The premise is that more is better or that some data is better than none, regardless of how useless it may be. This commonly results in too much data that overwhelms everyone involved in the planning process. It also diverts professional efforts toward processing superfluous data instead of applying the results to problem solving. One way to avoid this problem is to follow these steps:

1 Evaluate previous and current methods used to collect data to establish a recreation planning information system for the community.

2 Compare these to similar cities and the state of the art described in the literature.

3 Determine what types of data are essential and unique for recreation planning in this community.

4 Determine how this essential data can interface with other government functions and what data other levels of government, public agencies, or the private sector can provide.

5 Establish chronological benchmarks for the collection, projection, and revision of data.

6 Ask these questions: (a) What decisions are currently being made? (b) What decisions need to be made? and (c) What information is essential to help make these decisions?

7 Design an information system to answer the above questions.

8 Test, evaluate, and refine this information system.

9 Keep the system current.

10 Communicate significant meanings of information to the widest possible audience in ways they can understand to solve problems.

This approach makes information an essential ingredient of the planning process instead of an artifact with a limited purpose. Information collected in this way conditions both the process and the product. It views (1) landscape architecture, urban planning, and park administration as professions which provide space and services for people, (2) design, planning, and management as the processes by which this takes place, and (3) design and planning as a process that provides information to facilitate decision making. This approach to data collection provides objective and relevant information to:

1 Increase the level of professional sophistication in the planning process.

2 Encourage people to participate in the planning process.

3 Allow public officials to make rational decisions based on authoritative findings.

4 Justify complex projects in human, environmental, or economic terms.

5 Reduce the levels of bias, distortion, and controversy commonly associated with the planning process.

SOURCES OF INFORMATION

The value of using credible information in the recreation planning process is well established in practice. However, many potential information sources are not known or used when appropriate and possible. This oversight commonly results in extra time and expense gathering data that is already available from other sources, or using only limited information from a single source. Figures 5.1–5.5 show the scope and process for data collection used in planning for the Golden Gate National Recreation Area in San Francisco.

One way to avoid distortion and inaccurate information is to use several sources for comparison, correlations, and checking the validity of any single source. This is best accomplished by using any combination of the conventional and unconventional sources.

Conventional Sources

Conventional types of data can be classified as demographic, environmental, and institutional. *Demographic* data describes the social characteristics of users or nonusers of recreation opportunities. *Environmental* data describes the physical characteristics of the planning area or site. *Institutional data* describes the program, budget, or management characteristics of a recreation site or a system of public or private opportunities. Figures 5.1–5.3 show typical examples of demographic, environmental, and institutional data. Some conventional sources of data are catalogued below. Tables 5.3 and 5.4 describe the relationship and orientation of these four important sources:

U.S. CENSUS   The U.S. Department of Commerce Census of Population contains statistics on sex, age, marital status, ethnic origin, race, employment, educational level, family income, and years of residence down to the block or census tract level. Special census data for selected cities contains statistics on items such as means of transportation, handicapped populations, and housing conditions. Much of the data is comparable back to 1950. The 1980 census will ask specific questions on the quality of life and environment that should have a direct bearing on the provision of urban leisure services. (Figures 5.6 and 5.7).

EROS DATA   In 1970, the National Aeronautics and Space Administration (NASA) initiated the Earth Resources Observation Systems (EROS) program. This

DATA SEARCH

Figure 5.1 — NATURAL RESOURCES

KEY:
- ◆ Data Available In-House (Mapped Data)
- ● Data Partially Available (Mapped Data)
- ○ Data Unavailable

GEOGRAPHIC UNIT	GEOMORPHOLOGY Topography	Soil	Geology/Seismology	Hydrology	Hazards	ENVIRONMENTAL QUALITY Climate	Air Quality	Water Quality	Acoustics	Visual Quality	BIOTIC PROCESS Vegetation	Wildlife	Oceanography/Marine Biology
GGNRA South Unit	◆	◆	◆	◆	◆	◆	◆	◆	●	●	◆	●	●
Alcatraz	●	◆	◆	◆	●	○	●	◆	○	●	●	○	●
Aquatic Park	●	●	●	◆	●	●	●	◆	●	●	●	○	●
Fort Mason	●	◆	◆	◆	●	○	●	◆	●	●	●	○	●
Marina	●	●	●	◆	●	●	●	◆	○	●	●	○	●
Presidio	◆	◆	◆	◆	●	○	●	◆	●	●	◆	●	●
Fort Point	●	●	●	◆	●	○	●	◆	●	●	●	○	●
San Francisco Headlands	●	◆	◆	◆	●	○	●	◆	○	●	●	○	●
Land's End/Sutro Point	●	◆	◆	◆	●	○	●	◆	●	●	●	●	●
Ocean Beach	●	●	●	◆	●	○	●	◆	○	●	●	○	●
Fort Funston	●	●	●	◆	●	○	●	◆	○	●	●	○	●

FIGURE 5.1 Natural resources data search chart/Golden Gate National Recreation Area, San Francisco.

Figure 5.2 — RECREATION

KEY:
- ◆ Data Available In-House (Mapped Data)
- ● Data Partially Available (Mapped Data)
- ○ Data Unavailable

GEOGRAPHIC UNIT	FACILITIES List & Description	Total Acreage Park/Rec	Special Facilities	Environmental Characteristics	PROGRAMS Types of Events and Programs	User-Groups Served	Number of Participants	PLANNING User Surveys	Demand/Deficiencies	Trends	Park & Rec Policies	Park & Rec Standards	Park & Rec Plans & Proposals
GGNRA South Unit	◆	◆	●	●	●	◆	◆	○	○	●	◆	◆	◆
National	●	●	●	●	●	●	●	●	●	●	●	◆	◆
State	●	◆	●	●	●	●	●	◆	◆	◆	●	●	●
Regional	●	◆	●	●	●	●	●	●	●	●	◆	◆	◆
Alameda Co.	●	◆	●	●	●	●	●	●	●	●	◆	◆	◆
Cities in Alameda Co.	●	◆	●	●	●	●	●	●	●	●	●	●	●
Alameda Quasi-Public	●	●	●	●	●	●	●	○	●	○	●	●	○
San Francisco City & Co.	●	◆	●	●	●	◆	●	●	●	●	●	●	●
San Francisco Quasi-Public	●	●	●	●	●	●	●	●	●	○	●	●	○
San Mateo Co.	●	●	●	●	●	◆	●	●	●	●	●	●	●
Cities in San Mateo Co.	●	●	●	●	●	●	●	○	○	○	●	●	●
San Mateo Quasi-Public	●	●	●	●	●	●	●	●	●	●	●	●	●
Santa Clara Co.	◆	◆	●	●	●	◆	●	●	◆	●	◆	◆	◆
Cities in Santa Clara Co.	◆	◆	●	●	●	●	●	●	●	●	●	●	●
Santa Clara Quasi-Public	●	●	●	●	◆	●	●	○	●	○	○	●	○

FIGURE 5.2 Recreation data search chart/Golden Gate National Recreation Area, San Francisco.

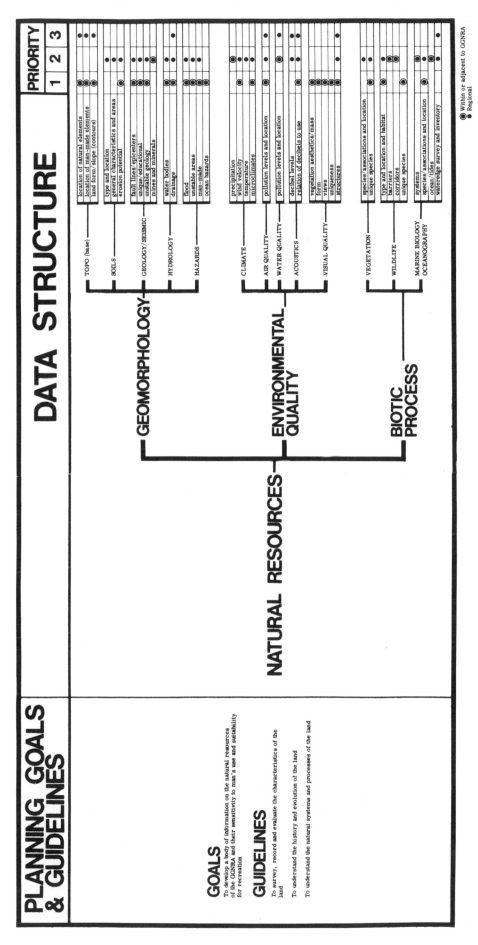

FIGURE 5.3   Natural resources data structure chart/Golden Gate National Recreation Area, San Francisco.

81

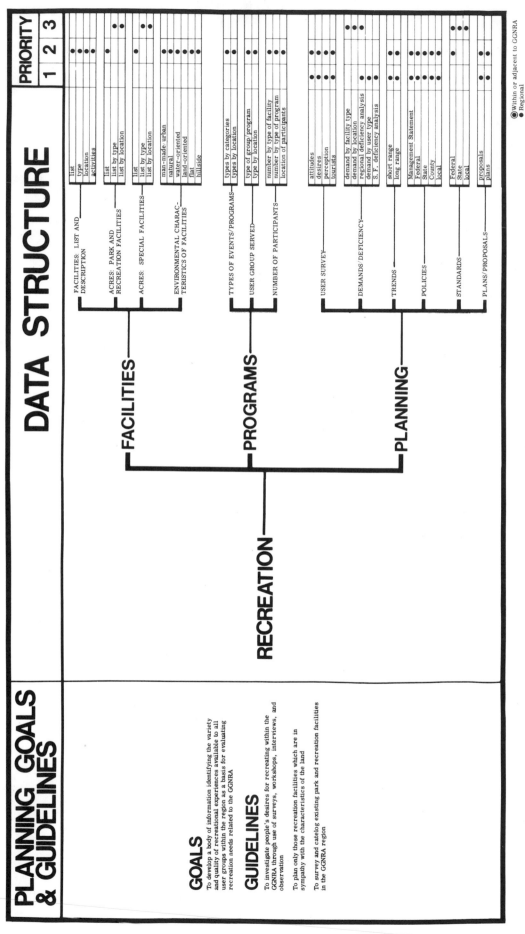

FIGURE 5.4 Recreation data structure chart/Golden Gate National Recreation Area, San Francisco.

82

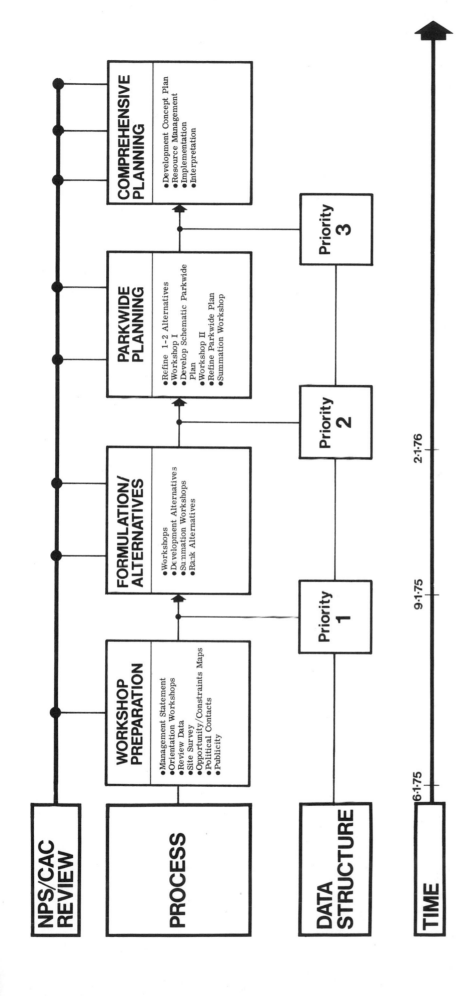

FIGURE 5.5 Project flowchart/Golden Gate National Recreation Area, San Francisco.

TABLE 5.3 | INFORMATION SOURCES FOR
RECREATION PLANNING

Unit of analysis	U.S. census of population	EROS photographs	NRPA yearbook	Urban leisure needs study
United States	X		X	
Individual states	X		X	
Selected cities	X	X	X	X
Census tracts	X	X		
Recreation areas		X		X

program uses remote sensing to monitor urban land use changes for 28 U.S. cities. It identifies changes in geographic features, transportation linkages, urban growth, and other environmental characteristics useful for recreation planning. For example, it can be used to identify vegetation patterns, recreation use patterns of selected areas, and the presence of home swimming pools or gardens. It can also be used to identify vacant land, concentrations of leisure activities, or the environmental impact of air and water pollution on existing or potential recreation resources.

PARK AND RECREATION YEARBOOK   Since 1950, the National Recreation and Park Association has published a yearbook of federal, state, and local statistics at five-year intervals. The data focuses on finances, facilities, space, personnel, programs, and the management of primarily public recreation, park, and leisure services. This document is an authoritative inventory and comparison of the quantitative aspects of park systems for cities of comparable size. It has great utility for evaluating the amount of land, facilities, or program a community provides in comparison to similar communities. It can also be used to describe the types, levels, and proportions of recreation opportunities provided in a planning jurisdiction.

URBAN NEEDS STUDY   In 1970, the National Recreation and Park Association conducted a study of 25 selected cities with populations over 250,000. This study focused on the supply, demand, and effectiveness of public park and recreation opportunities in selected core area census tracts of the country's largest cities. It presents a candid analysis of urban parks with an emphasis on effectiveness, citizen participation, nonuse, and the nature of public recreation opportunities in the inner city.

Other important conventional sources of information include the following:

NATIONAL AND STATE PARK RECREATION PLANS   The *Nationwide Recreation Plans* (BOR, 1973; HCRS, 1979), the *National Urban Recreation Study* (HCRS, 1978), and the *Statewide Comprehensive Outdoor Recreation Plans* provide information which can be used to establish benchmarks for projection or comparison at the local level. They present the most authoritative and detailed information available at the metropolitan scale. However, caution should be used in applying this information to communities or suburbs that may not be typical of the large metropolitan areas sampled in these studies.

GOVERNMENT DOCUMENTS AND PRIVATE STUDIES   Additional sources include (1) a wide range of government documents published by federal, state, and local park and planning agencies, (2) studies by planning and design consultants, utility companies, or chambers of commerce, (3) reports by environmental, consumer, cultural, or other special interest organizations, (4) research or extension publications by local or state universities, and (5) reports by leisure-oriented businesses or industries, the local building industry, or local newspapers.

For example, an analysis of patterns of utility consumption, building permits, unemployment levels, newspaper subscriptions, and sales tax receipts can reveal useful data about how or where people use their leisure time, social or employment trends, urban growth, and changing neighborhoods. Data from these secondary sources will have to be supplemented by original data on items such as leisure behavior, user preference and satisfaction, nonuse, tourism, fees and charges, ac-

TABLE 5.4 | RECREATION PLANNING INFORMATION SOURCES: LEVEL AND ORIENTATION

Level	Orientation	U.S. census of population	EROS photographs	NRPA yearbook	Urban leisure needs study
Micro	Social	X			X
	Physical				X
	Institutional				X
Macro	Social	X			X
	Physical		X	X	X
	Institutional			X	

KEY:
☐ GOVERNMENTAL UNITS
⬭ STATISTICAL UNITS

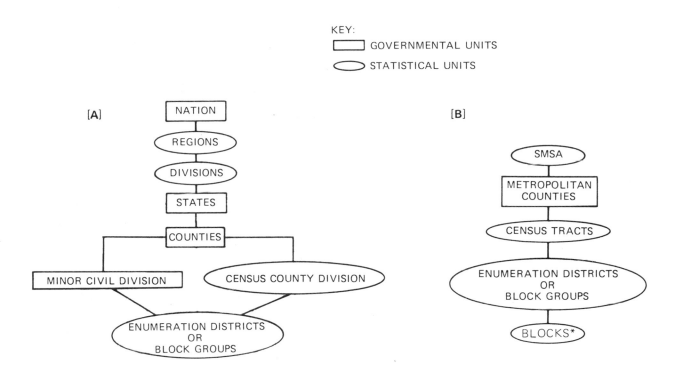

[A]

NATION
REGIONS
DIVISIONS
STATES
COUNTIES
MINOR CIVIL DIVISION
CENSUS COUNTY DIVISION
ENUMERATION DISTRICTS OR BLOCK GROUPS

[B]

SMSA
METROPOLITAN COUNTIES
CENSUS TRACTS
ENUMERATION DISTRICTS OR BLOCK GROUPS
BLOCKS*

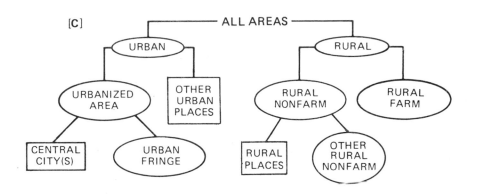

[C]

ALL AREAS
URBAN
RURAL
URBANIZED AREA
OTHER URBAN PLACES
RURAL NONFARM
RURAL FARM
CENTRAL CITY(S)
URBAN FRINGE
RURAL PLACES
OTHER RURAL NONFARM

*Blocks do not cover the entire SMSA, only the urbanized part.

FIGURE 5.6 Census geographical units.

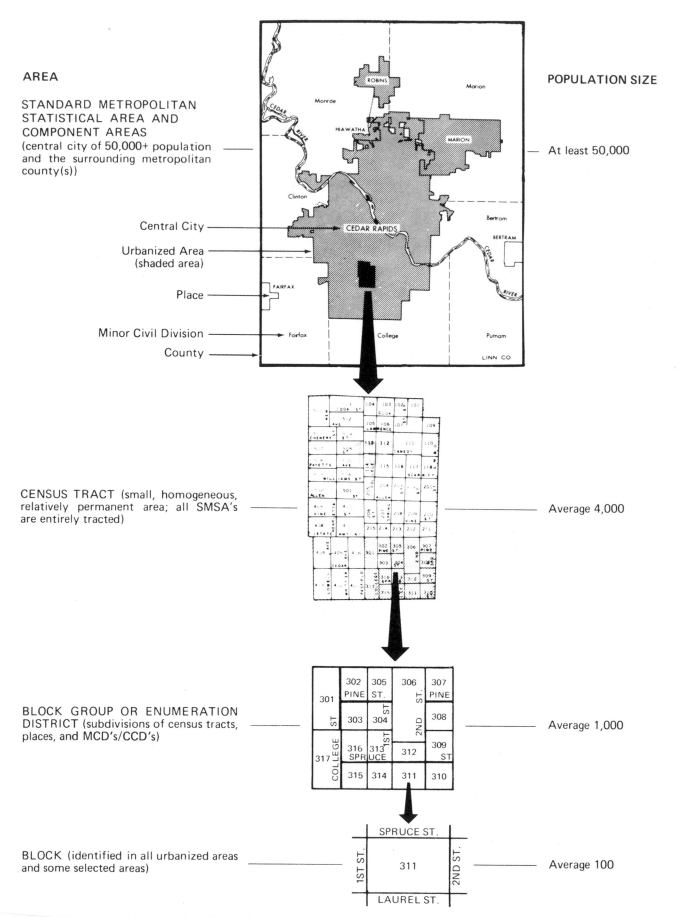

FIGURE 5.7 Geographic subdivisions of a standard metropolitan statistical area.

cess, and the needs of special populations. This data can be collected with these techniques:

QUESTIONNAIRES AND INTERVIEWS   A wide range of survey research methods and information sources is described in Chapter 7. In all cases, both users and nonusers of especially public facilities should be included in the survey. The sample should be representative and generalizable or it will not be credible.

TIME BUDGET STUDIES   How people use their time is one measure of individual choice and can provide a basis for studying their leisure values and priorities. It can also provide information about the demand for recreation facilities and measure (1) the amount of time allocated to leisure activities by time of day, day of week, or season, (2) participation rates for selected activities, and (3) patterns of typical activities for different population groups. The common way of collecting this information is a diary or interview which records what a person does during a selected 24-hour period or series of days. Figure 5.8 shows a typical time budget log.

OBSERVATION   At the microscale, systematic observation of how people interact with each other and the environment can provide important information about leisure behavior patterns, preferences, and needs. Photography or simple observation can be used to measure and map (1) activity patterns, (2) use levels, (3) size and types of user groups, (4) time, space, or energy associated with selected activities, and (5) design or management constraints or inducements to expected use patterns. The techniques of time-lapse photography and behavioral mapping have been used in many case studies (Whyte, 1974; Hester, 1975) to describe user needs for neighborhood parks or downtown open spaces.

Unconventional Sources

Unconventional data can be classified in the same way as conventional data, but it must be used with caution because many of the methods of collection and analysis need refinement. These sources are commonly used to obtain primary or secondary data: (1) physical and behavioral traces, (2) archives, (3) gaming simulation, (4) public meetings, and (5) content analysis. Each source is outlined here and detailed in other chapters.

PHYSICAL AND BEHAVIORAL TRACES   Systematic field studies and observations of both the site and the users can reveal important information about recreation use patterns, preference, and satisfaction. Physical and behavioral traces in the landscape can be described with measures of wear, erosion, accretion, change, or vandalism. For example, the wear on picnic benches or erosion of trails is a good indication of use. Litter or trash accumulation in selected sites is also a sign of use and can be related to time periods and group size. The movement and grouping of picnic tables can help to describe personal space, user density, and group size. The level and type of vandalism can be a direct or indirect reflection of user satisfaction with the site or the experience.

ARCHIVES   A wide range of public and private records can be used as indicators of leisure trends or behavior patterns. These can include (1) actuarial records of births, marriage, or death, (2) political and judicial records of voting patterns, tax assessment, or court decisions, and (3) government records of weather, crime levels, and economic trends. Other records can include (1) media programming or subscriptions, (2) utility consumption, and (3) sales tax receipts, consumer credit, productivity levels, employee absenteeism, membership in private recreation clubs, or use levels of commercial recreation facilities. In most cases, this information is a matter of public record or available on request.

GAMING SIMULATION   A game is a model of reality in which the players express preferences or make choices to arrive at some outcome. It is a way to represent and study a system in terms of components, relationships, inputs, and outputs. Gaming can be used as a planning or decision-making device that allows people to play roles and study the consequences of their actions. It has been successfully used in recreation planning to (1) analyze the impact of policies, (2) compress time and scale, (3) identify actors and conflict in the planning process, (4) analyze institutional change, and (5) teach students, professionals, or citizens different methods or approaches to problem solving.

PUBLIC MEETINGS   Many variations of the public meeting have been successfully used to obtain information for recreation planning. Common vehicles include the neighborhood forum, public hearing, panel discussions, and debates. All require skilled leadership, advance notice, careful organization, and a written or taped record. There is no substitute for the candid information on citizen values and priorities expressed in these meetings. Because of the random attendance and emotional

KINDS OF ACTIVITIES YOU MAY DO DURING THE DAY

(but please use your own words to describe what you are doing)

TRAVEL: All the trips you make, both at home and at work.

WORK: Actual work; work breaks; delays or sitting around at work; work meetings or instruction periods; meals at work; overtime; work brought home.

HOUSEWORK: Preparing meals and snacks; doing dishes; arranging and straightening things; laundry and mending; cleaning house (inside and outside); care of yard and animals; repairs.

CHILD CARE: Baby care; dressing; helping with homework; reading to; playing with; supervising; medical care.

SHOPPING: Groceries, clothes, appliances, or home furnishings; repair shops; other services (for example: barber, hairdresser, doctor, post office).

PERSONAL LIFE: Eating meals and snacks; dressing; care of health or appearance; helping neighbors or friends; sleep or naps.

EDUCATION: Attending classes or lectures; training and correspondence courses; homework; reading for the job.

ORGANIZATIONS: Club meetings or activity; volunteer work; going to church services; other church work.

GOING OUT: Visiting (or dinner with) friends, neighbors or relatives; parties, dances, nightclubs or bars; sports events and fairs; concerts, movies, plays, or museums.

ACTIVE LEISURE: Sports or exercise; playing cards or other games; pleasure trips and walking; hobbies, knitting, painting, or playing music.

PASSIVE LEISURE: Conversations; radio, TV, records; reading books, magazines or newspapers; writing letters; planning, thinking or relaxing.

What you did from 9 in the morning until 5 in the afternoon

Time	What did you do?	Time Began	Time Ended	Where	With Whom	Doing Anything Else?	Remarks
9 AM							
10 AM							
11 AM							
Noon							
1 PM							
2 PM							
3 PM							
4 PM							

FIGURE 5.8 Time budget log/Survey Research Center, University of Michigan.

FIGURE 5.9 Public meeting/Decatur, Illinois.

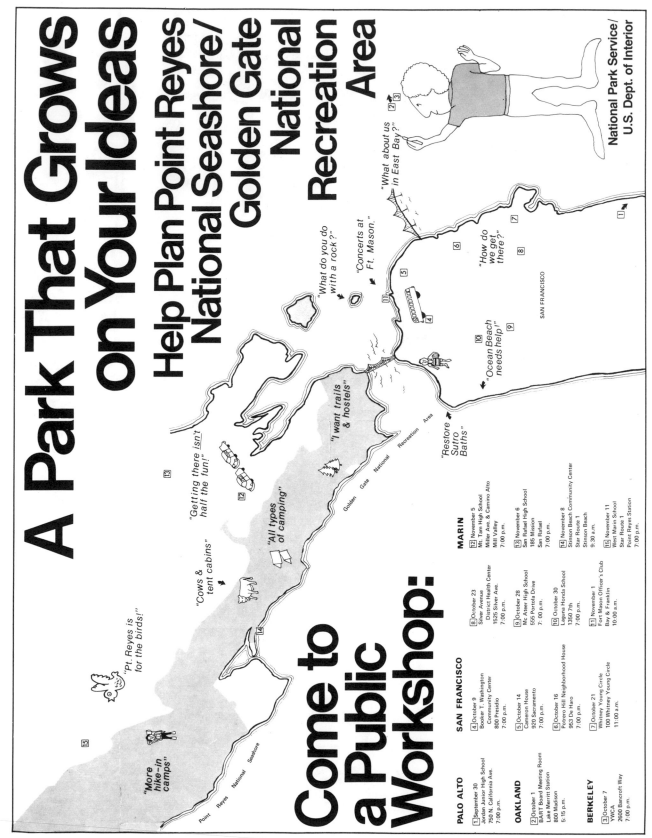

FIGURE 5.10 Public workshop/Golden Gate National Recreation Area, San Francisco.

nature of most public meetings, the information may not be objective, but it can often reveal more than a systematic sample of public opinion. Public meetings are an essential ingredient of recreation planning, especially at the neighborhood or project planning level (Figures 5.9 and 5.10).

CONTENT ANALYSIS A systematic evaluation of the way selected words are used to describe recreation issues can be used to document public opinion. Content analysis can be used to analyze user or nonuser perception or preference for recreation opportunities. It can also identify deficiencies, problems, or conflicts in the use of existing facilities. The best sources of information include local newspapers, radio and television talk shows, public meetings, and complaints or suggestions to public officials. This technique is most effective at the systems or regional level.

6 | RECREATION MEASURES

The preparation of recreation plans requires the development and application of a wide range of measures to describe the user and the resource. Traditionally, measurement has been dismissed as unnecessary or not possible because of the intangible nature of many aspects of recreation. However, this attitude is changing with the development of new measurement techniques, requirements of federal or state funding programs, and the need for local government to rationalize the performance of parks, recreation, and open space.

This chapter describes selected types of existing and developing measures. The definitions and concepts outlined here are detailed and applied in Chapters 8–12. One cannot consider topics such as leisure behavior surveys, demand, or need without an understanding of what measures are possible and why it is important to use them.

TYPES OF RECREATION MEASURES

A serious effort should be made to define, develop, and qualify the measures used in the planning process. No set of measures will fit all situations. Most existing or developing techniques have shortcomings. However, the state of the art is rapidly improving, and there is no reason to continue using arbitrary or conventional measures.

Recreation measures are objective indicators that can be used to relate people to leisure time and space. They should measure the quantity and quality of user-resource relationships in terms that can be used to formulate public policy, allocate resources, rationalize programs, and assess the effectiveness of the recreation experience or environment.

Quantitative Measures

The traditional approach to recreation planning uses quantitative measures of land, development, or program that describe the site or experience in terms of how *much*, instead of how *good*. Inventories of the amount of recreation land and facilities or attendance records do not necessarily describe effectiveness. They often present meaningless numbers and do more to obfuscate than solve problems. These numbers are difficult to translate into public policy because they commonly lack qualitative or social dimensions that relate to human needs.

The dominant measures in recreation planning are the types shown in Table 6.1. Chapter 11 will critique the conceptual and pragmatic shortcomings of these recreation standards. Other quantitative recreation measures commonly used by federal, state, and local recreation or planning agencies to report recreation use include those listed in Table 6.2.

Note, these measures do not necessarily assume the qualitative aspects of leisure behavior such as user satisfaction, mood, perception of the resource, or human development. These units also do not describe or measure a recreation experience in terms of relative need, opportunities available, cost, energy consumption, ac-

TABLE 6.1 | CLASSIFICATION OF QUANTITATIVE RECREATION MEASURES

Orientation	Specific type	Measurement units	Examples
Use	Population ratio Recreation demand Percent of area	Area/population Area/user group Area/planning unit	1 ac neighborhood park/1000 pop. 1 ac playground/600 children 10% of planning unit area
Development	Facility to site Facility placement Facility to activity Facility size	Units/acre Distance between units Units/user group Area/facility	16 picnic tables/acre Picnic tables 50 ft apart 1 softball diamond/10,000 pop. 3–5 ac neighborhood playground
Capacity	User to resource User to time	Users/site Users/time/site	400 people/mile of trail/hr 50 people/mile of trail/hr
Program	Activity to population Leadership requirements	Activity/population Leaders/activity	1 arboretum/10,000 pop. 2 leaders/100 children
Management	Supervision to users Maintenance to site	Staff/population Degree/area	1 supervisor/1000 users 1 laborer/10 ac playground

TABLE 6.2 | COMMONLY USED QUANTITATIVE RECREATION MEASURES

Recreation visitor-hour The presence for recreation purposes of one or more persons for continuous, intermittent, or simultaneous periods of time aggregating 60 minutes.

Recreation activity-hour A recreation visitor-hour attributable to specific recreation activity.

Recreation visit The entry of any person into a site or area of land or water for recreation purposes.

Recreation-day A visit by one individual to a recreation development or area for recreation purposes during a reasonable portion (or all) of a 24-hour period.

Design load The proportion of annual visitation in recreation days which will be accommodated by public use facilities.

Visit The entry of any person into a site, or area of land or water, generally recognized as providing outdoor recreation. Visits may occur either as recreation visits or as nonrecreation visits.

Access capacity A factor which considers the extent to which a resource is available, e.g., number of boat moorings or boat ramps.

Turnover rate The number of times a resource or facility can provide an opportunity for recreation in a 24-hour period.

Season length The average number of days per year during which the activity can be enjoyed.

Instantaneous capacity The number of recreational opportunities provided at any given instant by the facility or resource.

Daily capacity The instantaneous capacity multiplied by the turnover rate.

Yearly capacity The daily capacity multiplied by the season length.

cess or experience levels, actual or perceived levels of public safety, crowdedness, diversity, and a host of other factors that are significant in recreation planning.

Most quantitative recreation measures assume a positive experience when this may not be the case. They assume levels of preference and satisfaction that may not be realistic. These measures normally omit the concepts of resource and use quality described in Chapter 7.

Qualitative Measures

The qualitative measures described in Table 6.3 have been used with limited success. Refinement of these measures will probably take a decade of research and demonstration. However, there is evidence in the literature and practice to suggest these qualitative measures can provide an alternative or balance to existing measurement techniques.

These measures assume an actual or perceived dimension of quality that relates to the recreation experience, site, and community. They describe or imply fac-

tors that can be objectively measured to describe leisure behavior or the environment. These measures are far from perfect and should be used with qualification. However, they are no worse than most existing measures and offer great promise.

Measurement Criteria

The development, testing, and revision of measures for recreation planning in each community will require different levels of precision. For example, measures at the neighborhood scale should be fine enough to reflect the social and physical diversity of that area while these units can be aggregated at the regional scale.

The measures should consider both inputs and outputs. The traditional focus of most park and recreation agencies has been to measure *inputs* of land, development, or programs in terms of cost. While this is important, the mission of the agency is to provide *outputs* of human service, community development, or environmental beautification. This concept is fundamental to the development of any set of quantitative or qualitative recreation measures for a community.

Beyond a balanced emphasis on inputs and outputs that can be translated into costs and benefits, it is important to evaluate all measures prior to applying them in the planning process. The following criteria can be used to assess the practicality of any recreation measure. All recreation measures should be:

- *Objective* in the way they are developed and applied.
- *Generalizable* to similar populations, planning units, or areas.
- *Feasible* and realistic to the political, economic, or social dimensions of the planning area.
- *Simple* to apply, revise, and project in the planning and decision process.
- *Understood* by the public or their elected officials.
- *Attainable* in the planning period or time-phased to future periods.
- *People-oriented* instead of supplied-oriented.
- *Relevant* to the leisure behavior and environment of the planning area.

Reasons for Measurement

Although the techniques for developing and applying recreation measures are well established in practice, the reasons for measurement are still not apparent to many practitioners. Most park and recreation agencies do not collect data on a systematic basis and do not have an integrated set of measures useful for planning and decision making.

The major reason most agencies have not developed a sophisticated measurement system is they had no reason to do so. However, this situation will change rapidly as local units of government begin to justify park and recreation budgets in an era of competing needs for limited public resources. The prospect of measurement is no longer a token exercise in many communities. Local agencies must now justify parks and recreation as never before, if they are to survive.

MONITORING CHANGE Measures can be developed to describe the nature, rate, and magnitude of changes in the design or management of recreation areas or programs. These measures can highlight problems, potentials, or the need for additional study. They can also be used to evaluate agency performance and provide comparisons between different service areas. Table 6.4 shows an example of monitoring change for selected recreation opportunities in Washington, D.C. Figure 6.1 illustrates how measurements can be summarized to provide comparisons between service areas.

BUDGETING Measures of effectiveness or performance are essential in justifying budgets, describing needs, or rationalizing the elimination of programs. Benefit-cost analysis can (1) provide comparisons between facilities and departments, (2) assign priorities to specific programs and services, (3) provide guidelines for

TABLE 6.3 | CLASSIFICATION OF QUALITATIVE RECREATION MEASURES

General orientation	Specific type	Measurement units	Illustrative examples
Recreation use	Special populations Population income Population mobility User behavior Accessibility	Percent served Levels served Levels served Percent preference Time/distance ratios	80% of retarded 60% of poverty level 40% of population 50% of possible users 5 minutes on foot
Recreation development	Aesthetics Facility comparison Energy conservation	Adjectives Adjectives Calories saved	Beautiful/ugly park Best/worst facilities R-19 insulation value
Recreation program	Program diversity Program participation Ethnic orientation	Options/facility Percent use/nonuse Proportion/population	Percent of programs 40% accommodation 80% of population
Recreation management	Facility maintenance Hours of operation Public safety	Level of cleanliness Convenient hours/day Surveillance/day	Clean/dirty parks 50% night programs 50% onsite police patrol

NEIGHBOURHOOD TYPE 1

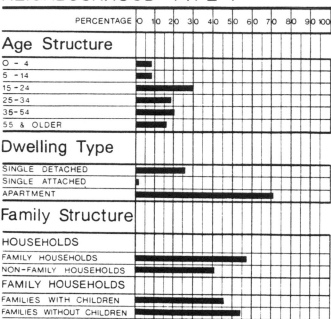

NEIGHBOURHOOD TYPE 3

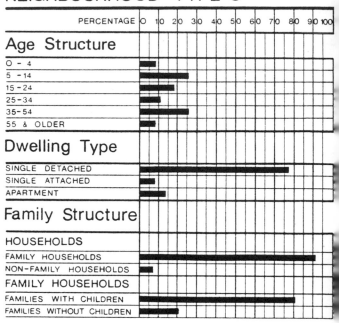

NEIGHBOURHOOD TYPE 2

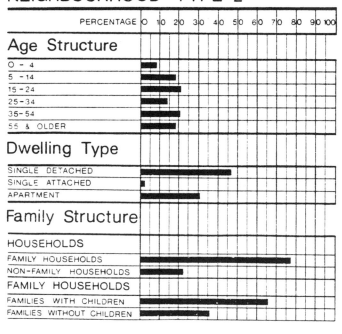

NEIGHBOURHOOD TYPE 4

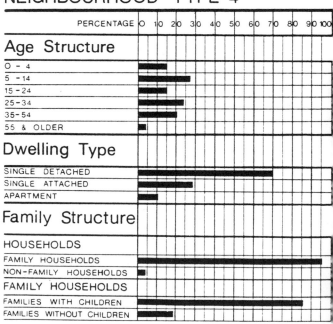

FIGURE 6.1   Measures to compare service area population characteristics/Edmonton, Alberta, Canada.

management decisions, (4) assist in evaluating agency objectives and procedures, and (5) identify high- and low-cost programs and services.

PROGRAM OR SITE EVALUATION   Measures are available to describe what is "right" or "wrong" with recreation programs or sites. Questions of use or nonuse can be described and the reasons categorized into those (1) potentially within government control, or (2) probably beyond government control, as shown in Table 6.5.

Other approaches to program and site evaluation are detailed in this chapter and Chapters 7, 8, and 12.

COMMON MEASUREMENT TECHNIQUES

The recreation measures described in Table 6.1 have conditioned most recreation planning efforts of the 1960s and 1970s. They represent the state of the art. In most cases, these measures have concentrated on the

TABLE 6.4 | MEASURES TO MONITOR CHANGE

| | | Year | |
Measurements	1972	1971	1970
1 Overall citizen rating			
Percent rating very good	16%	15%	12%
Percent rating poor	12%	13%	15%
2 Overall user rating			
Percent rating very good	31%	35%	30%
Percent rating poor	1%	2%	1%
3 Crowdedness			
Percent users rating poor	4%	6%	5%
4 Facility upkeep			
Percent users rating cleanliness poor	5%	3%	2%
Percent users rating maintenance poor	8%	5%	6%
5 Helpfulness–attitude of staff			
Percent users rating poor	2%	2%	3%
6 Hours of operation			
Percent users rating poor	2%	3%	4%
7 Safety			
Percent users rating poor	5%	4%	3%
Serious accidents per 1 million hours	0.17	0.19	0.22
Deaths per 10 million hours	0	0	0
8 Participation			
Percent using one or more times	41%	46%	39%
9 Attendance—total	11,305,000	12,124,000	11,116,000
10 Hours of attendance—total	33,011,000	38,600,000	34,234,000
11 Physical accessibility			
Percent within 1/2 mile of facility	76%	76%	76%
12 Variety			
Average number of programs per facility	5.2	5.3	5.5

Source: Citizen Survey, Washington, D.C., 1972, conducted by Urban Institute (Dunn and Hatry, 1973).

TABLE 6.5 | REASONS FOR NONUSE OF FACILITIES*

	Rockford	St. Petersburg	Washington, D.C.
Causes Potentially within Government Control			
Facility unknown	10	12	26
Too far away	13	5	10
Activities not interesting	3	13	5
Too dangerous	4	4	3
Too crowded	5	2	2
Inconvenient hours	3	1	1
Not attractive	2	0	1
Costs too much	1	1	0
Total	41	38	48
Causes Probably beyond Government Control†			
Too busy	21	20	18
Poor personal health	1		6
Too old	3	19	5
Don't like other users	4	2	2
Total	29	41	31
No opinion—Won't say	31	21	21

*Responses in percentages.
†An additional category not used in these surveys could be "Satisifed with nongovernmental recreation facilities."

Source: Statistics compiled from citizen surveys in Washington, D.C., (June 1972); Rockford, Illinois (August 1972); and St. Petersburg, Florida (September 1973).

user and are site-specific. They measure a selected range of activities in terms of participation and imply that more is better, which may not be true. These techniques essentially measure participation and the existing supply of land, development, or program. They do not measure items such as:

- *Motivation* of users to pursue various activities.
- *Physical fitness* necessary to pursue various activities or use selected areas.
- *Cost* necessary to participate in a given opportunity or visit an area.
- *Proximity* of the resource or opportunity to the user.
- *Uniqueness* of the recreation opportunity or area.

These items are not mutually exclusive and should be integrated in an analysis of supply and demand. The point here is not to suggest measuring everything, but establishing the limits of most common measures and the logic of developing alternative measures.

Measures of Participation

Measures of participation have evolved from simple attendance counts to the concept of a visitor-day, visitor-hour, and recreation activity-hour. The logic of time and activity-specific measures is to prevent double counting users who may participate in several activities onsite and relate participation levels to the time budgets of different user groups.

The traditional way of expressing measures of participation is the participation rate or the participation-days for a given set of activities or site. The participation rate is multiplied by the participation-days to yield an annual number of recreation occasions for a given time period, usually one year. This is commonly shown as activities or spaces which are most or least popular (Figure 6.2).

Measures of Site/System Features

The primary approach is to inventory existing land, development, and program. A second approach is to describe either use or the site in terms of design load specifications for the capacity of facilities (Figure 6.3). Both approaches are oriented to physical instead of social factors. They assume ratios of facilities for the average user or assume what exists provides a satisfactory recreation opportunity.

This approach to measurement is common in extensive inventories of recreation play apparatus which may not be used, or provide little satisfaction to users. Similar examples include inventories of picnic tables, tennis courts, or the square footage of indoor recreation centers. Table 6.6 shows a typical example of this type of inventory. Beyond describing items of public property, this type of inventory has little value. It does not assess the condition of facilities, use levels, hours of operation, and levels of public safety, supervision, or maintenance.

If an inventory approach is used, it should be quantitative and qualitative in terms of both the user and supplier. To measure just the physical existence of facilities or a landscape without establishing their use or condition has little value for planning or decision making. More important, it can lead others to equate levels of recreation opportunity with facilities or space that may not provide these opportunities.

TABLE 6.6 | TYPICAL INVENTORY OF SITE FEATURES

Site no.	Facility name/location	Apparatus	Spray pool	Volleyball ct.	Tennis court	Basketball ct.	Boccie ct.	Shuffleboard	Horseshoe ct.	Handball ct.	Little league field	Softball field	Baseball field	Football field	Soccer field	1/4 Mile track	Swimming pool	Pond	Benches	Picnic tables	Bubbler	Shelter house
South Planning District																						
49	Joseph Williams Field	2									1		1									
50	Tim O'Neil				11						2					1						
51	Roger Williams Park	3				1½													X	X	X	X
52	Columbia Park	5				1½													X		X	X
Annex Planning District																						
53	Merino Park Playfield	5	1										2						X	X	X	X
54	Perry Jr. High																1					
55	Laurel Hill Ave.	5	1			1					1	1	1	1							X	X
56	Neutaconkanut Hill										1	2	1	1		1			X	X		
57	Neutaconkanut and King Parks	4	1																		X	X
58	Daniel Ave.	5			1																X	X
59	Clarence St.	4				1															X	X
60	Wallace St.	2																				

Source: *Master Plan for Public Recreation and Conservation*, City Plan Commission, Providence, R.I., 1966, p. 43.

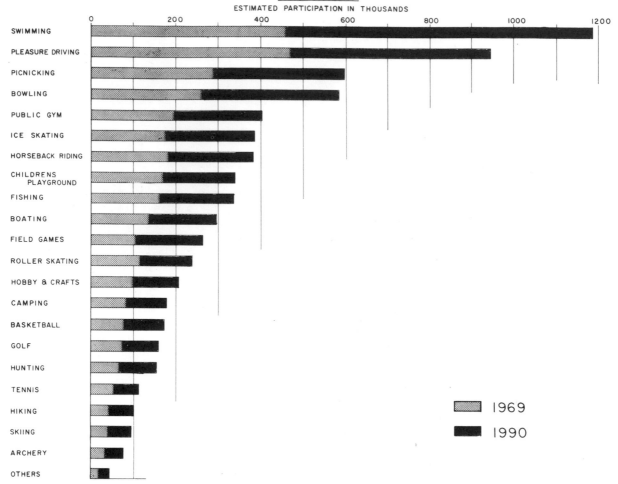

JACKSON COUNTY
ESTIMATED PARTICIPATION IN THOUSANDS

1969
1990

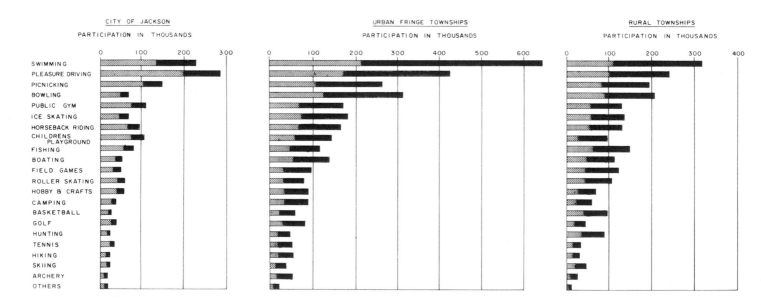

CITY OF JACKSON
PARTICIPATION IN THOUSANDS

URBAN FRINGE TOWNSHIPS
PARTICIPATION IN THOUSANDS

RURAL TOWNSHIPS
PARTICIPATION IN THOUSANDS

JACKSON METROPOLITAN AREA
REGIONAL PLANNING COMMISSION

HARLAND BARTHOLOMEW AND ASSOCIATES
CITY PLANNERS-CIVIL ENGINEERS-LANDSCAPE ARCHITECTS

FIGURE 6.2 Measures of participation/Jackson County, Michigan.

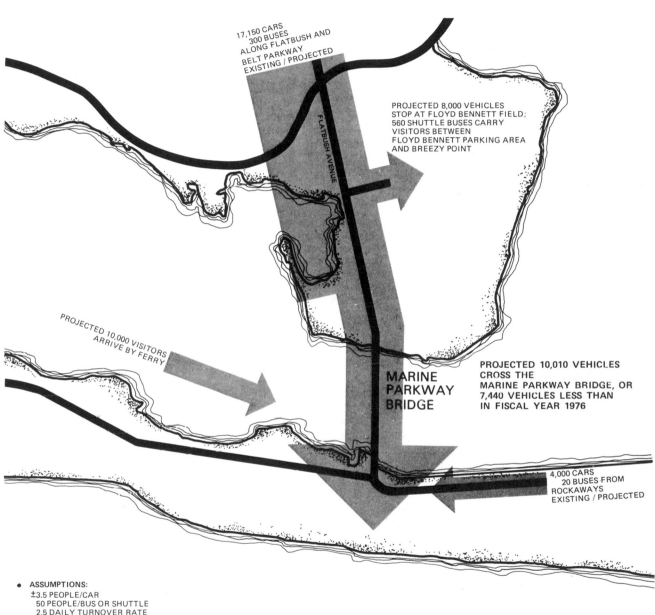

17,150 CARS
300 BUSES
ALONG FLATBUSH AND
BELT PARKWAY
EXISTING / PROJECTED

FLATBUSH AVENUE

PROJECTED 8,000 VEHICLES
STOP AT FLOYD BENNETT FIELD;
560 SHUTTLE BUSES CARRY
VISITORS BETWEEN
FLOYD BENNETT PARKING AREA
AND BREEZY POINT

PROJECTED 10,000 VISITORS
ARRIVE BY FERRY

MARINE
PARKWAY
BRIDGE

PROJECTED 10,010 VEHICLES
CROSS THE
MARINE PARKWAY BRIDGE, OR
7,440 VEHICLES LESS THAN
IN FISCAL YEAR 1976

4,000 CARS
20 BUSES FROM
ROCKAWAYS
EXISTING / PROJECTED

- ASSUMPTIONS:
  ±3.5 PEOPLE/CAR
  50 PEOPLE/BUS OR SHUTTLE
  2.5 DAILY TURNOVER RATE

- BREEZY POINT FY 1976
  PEAK-DAY VISITATION-90,000

- PROJECTED PEAK-DAY VISITATION-100,000
  DUE TO FERRY SERVICE

**PEAK-DAY TRAFFIC ON MARINE
PARKWAY BRIDGE-FY 1976
AND PROJECTED FOR STAGE I**

GATEWAY NATIONAL RECREATION AREA
UNITED STATES DEPARTMENT OF THE INTERIOR / NATIONAL PARK SERVICE

FIGURE 6.3   Design load of recreation facilities/Gateway National Recreation Area, New York.

Figure 6.4 shows the landscape profile of three typical neighborhood parks in Sacramento, California. Any traditional inventory of these spaces would record them as "equal" in terms of opportunity. However, field studies indicate significant differences in use and satisfaction levels for these parks (Gold, 1977).

DEVELOPING MEASUREMENT TECHNIQUES

Most common recreation measures have deficiencies because they lack a qualitative dimension, are normally supplier oriented, and measure inputs instead of outputs. Alternative measures are possible and have been tried with limited success in several case studies. Three approaches to measurement are described here to illustrate what is possible.

Each approach is described in only enough detail to establish major concepts. These measurements need testing and development over time in many situations. They do not meet all the criteria for recreation measures. However, if used with qualification, they can provide the prototype for measures appropriate for recreation planning in the 1980s and beyond.

Measures of Effectiveness

Measuring the effectiveness of existing services can help (1) provide current information on how recreation services are meeting public needs, (2) provide a baseline from which future progress can be measured, (3) estimate the future effectiveness of current types of recreation programs, (4) determine budgets for recreation-related programs, (5) prepare capital improvement requests, (6) provide annual reports of the effectiveness of community services, and (7) consider public issues.

Traditional recreation measurements have focused on quantifiable factors such as acreage, numbers of facilities, and personnel. These statistics represent inputs (resources) instead of outputs (satisfaction), which are the true measures of recreation effectiveness that meet the needs of people. Measurements in common use include:

1 Number of acres, areas, or individual facilities of various types often expressed as so many per thousand population.

2 Amount of recreation staff time spent on individual programs or services.

3 Attendance records or number of visits to recreation facilities or activities.

4 Number of classes, meetings, or organized programs.

5 Number of participant-hours for selected activities.

6 Number of persons so many minutes or miles from specific types of recreation facilities.

7 Attendance and participation categorized by sex and age group.

8 Amount of recreation opportunities available at various time periods.

Measuring the effectiveness of recreation services is difficult because of the subjective nature of recreation, but it is possible and can provide a useful data source for the planning, design, and management of recreation services. Data can be gathered for (1) a specific facility or activity, (2) recreation services provided by government and the private sector, or (3) a geographic area such as a neighborhood, census tract, planning district, or political unit. Illustrative measures can include those shown in Table 6.7.

These measures have been applied in several cities with reasonable success. The trend towards public accountability, professional management of leisure services, and an urgent need to assess the social impact of government services, suggest the use of measures of effectiveness in most communities on a continuing basis. They can provide the manager and public with an objective way to evaluate the use of public funds.

Measures of Physical Accessibility

No measure of effectiveness is more important than physical accessibility, because all other factors are irrelevant if people do not have access to the recreation opportunity. The technique of drawing arbitrary circles around a recreation resource to measure service area population has been radically improved in a demonstration study of access to swimming pools in Washington, D.C. (Urban Institute, 1972). The key elements of this technique are the measures of accessibility shown in Table 6.7, items 16–20. The procedure for mapping these relationships is shown in Figure 6.5 and is summarized as follows:

Step 1 *Obtain base maps.* Use U.S. Census maps to key population statistics to the tract, block group, and block numbers on these maps. Place calibration marks on each base map to align the map overlays described in succeeding steps.

Step 2 *Identify physical access barriers.* Note physical barriers such as freeways, railways, industrial zones, and rivers on the base maps. Major thoroughfares, discontinuous sidewalks, poorly lighted or dangerous local streets, and walkways should also be noted.

PORTAL PARK

N   E

S   W

TAHOE PARK

N   E

S   W

HENSCHEL PARK

N   E

S   W

FIGURE 6.4 Landscape character of neighborhood parks/Sacramento, California.

TABLE 6.7 | EFFECTIVENESS MEASURES FOR RECREATION SERVICES
Overall Objective: To provide for all citizens a variety of enjoyable leisure opportunities that are accessible, safe, physically attractive, and uncrowded.

Objective	Quality characteristic		Specific measure*	Data collection procedure
Enjoyableness	Citizen satisfaction	1	Percentage of households rating neighborhood park and recreation opportunities as satisfactory.	General citizen survey
	User satisfaction	2	Percentage of those households using community park or recreation facilities who rate them as satisfactory.	General citizen survey or survey of users (of particular facilities)
	Usage—participation rates	3	Percentage of community households using (or not using) a community park or recreation facility at least once over a specific past period, such as three months. (For nonusers, provide the percentage not using facilities for various reasons, and distinguish reasons that can be at least partly controlled by the government from those that cannot.)	General citizen survey
	Usage—attendance	4	Number of visits at recreation sites.	Attendance statistics; estimates from general citizen survey
Avoidance of crowdedness	User satisfaction	5	Percentage of user households rating crowdedness of community facilities as unsatisfactory.	General citizen survey or survey of users (of particular facilities)
	Nonuser satisfaction	6	Percentage of nonuser households giving crowded conditions as a reason for nonuse of facilities.	General citizen survey
	Crowding factor	7	Average peak-hour attendance divided by capacity.	Attendance statistics and estimates of carrying capacity
Physical attractiveness	User satisfaction	8	Percentage of user households rating physical attractiveness as satisfactory.	General citizen survey or survey of users (of particular facilities)
	Nonuser satisfaction	9	Percentage of nonuser households giving lack of physical attractiveness as reason for nonuse.	General citizen survey
	Facility cleanliness	10	Percentage of user households rating cleanliness as satisfactory.	General citizen survey or survey of users
	Equipment condition	11	Percentage of user households rating condition of equipment as satisfactory.	General citizen survey or survey of users
Safety	Injuries to participants resulting from accidents	12	Number of serious injuries (for example, those requiring hospitalization) per 10,000 visits.	Accident and attendance statistics

*Many of the measures inquire into percentages of citizens or users who find conditions "satisfactory." Local officials may wish in some instances to focus more directly on the amount of *dissatisfaction*, in which case the word "satisfactory" would be changed to "unsatisfactory."

Source: Reprinted with permission from Harry Hatry et al., *How Effective Are Your Community Services?* The Urban Institute, Washington, D.C., 1977, pp. 42–43.

Objective	Quality characteristic		Specific measure*	Data collection procedure
	Criminal incidents	13	Number of criminal incidents per 10,000 visits.	Criminal incident statistics of some park and recreation agencies and most municipal police forces; attendance statistics
	User satisfaction	14	Percentage of user households rating safety of facilities as satisfactory.	General citizen survey or survey of users
	Nonuser satisfaction	15	Percentage of nonuser households giving lack of safety as a reason for nonuse of municipal facilities.	General citizen survey
Accessibility	Physical accessibility	16	Percentage of citizens living within (or not within) 15 to 30 minutes' travel time of a community park or recreation facility distinguished by type of facility and principal relevant mode of transportation.	Counts from mapping latest census tract population figures against location of facilities, with appropriate travel-time radius drawn around each facility
	Physical accessibility— user satisfaction	17	Percentage of user households rating physical accessibility as satisfactory.	General citizen survey or survey of users
	Physical accessibility— nonuser satisfaction	18	Percentage of nonuser households giving poor physical accessibility as a reason for nonuse.	General citizen survey
	Hours/days of operation— user satisfaction	19	Percentage of user households rating hours of operation as satisfactory.	General citizen survey or survey of users
	Hours/days of operation— nonuser satisfaction	20	Percentage of nonuser households giving unsatisfactory operating hours as a reason for nonuse.	General citizen survey
Variety of interesting activities	User satisfaction	21	Percentage of user households rating the variety of program activities as satisfactory.	General citizen survey or survey of users
	Nonuser satisfaction	22	Percentage of nonuser households giving lack of program variety as a reason for nonuse.	General citizen survey
Helpfulness of staff	Staff helpfulness—user satisfaction	23	Percentage of user households rating helpfulness or attitude of staff as satisfactory.	General citizen survey or survey of users
	Staff helpfulness—non-user satisfaction	24	Percentage of nonuser households giving poor staff attitude as a reason for nonuse.	General citizen survey

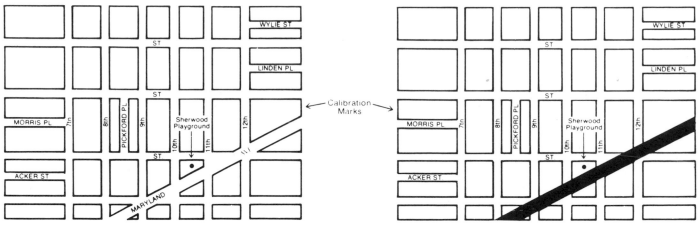

Step 1. Obtain base map.

Step 2. Identify and mark physical barriers on base map.

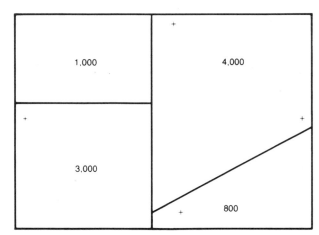

Step 3. Tabulate population; plot on map overlay.

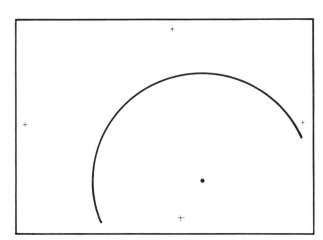

Step 4. Plot facility and activity locations on map overlay.
Step 5. Draw physical accessibility circles around each location.

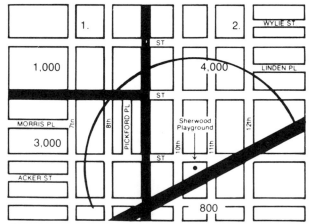

Step 6. Assemble overlays on base map. (For clarity, only overlays for population by block groups and facility are shown.)

FIGURE 6.5 Mapping technique for measuring physical accessibility.

Step 3 *Tabulate population on map overlays.* Plot demographic data by census tract on map overlays. Where the accessibility circle bisects census units, make proportionate adjustments.

Step 4 *Plot facility and activity locations.* For each type of recreation activity, plot the location of facilities on an overlay.

Step 5 *Draw accessibility circles.* Draw accessibility circles on the facility location overlay around each plotted facility. These circles should not pass through physical barriers on the base map to account for these constraints to safe, convenient access.

Step 6 *Draw city administrative boundaries.* Mark administrative or service area boundaries on the base map. Where possible, these should parallel neighborhood boundaries.

Step 7 *Plot demographic information.* Display social and economic data such as median family income, car ownership, ethnic origin, and family composition for each census tract on different colored overlays.

Step 8 *Assemble overlays on base map.* Align overlays to grapically measure and analyze accessiblity for each facility or activity.

Step 9 *Calculations.* Estimate the number and percent of people living within the accessibility circles.

Step 10 *Translate data to tables or graphics.* Describe each service area, and the entire city, with comparative tables, or translate these numbers to symbols or colors to indicate major differences between service areas.

Measures of Benefit-Cost

The techniques of economic analysis have traditionally been used to justify nonurban, resource-oriented recreation opportunities, e.g., Corps of Engineers reservoirs. They are also commonly used to justify many social programs. These techniques are now being applied to measure the cost-effectiveness of urban recreation opportunities. Several sophisticated and costly techniques are available, but the technique used in Eugene, Oregon, shows what is possible with a limited amount of resources (Figure 6.6).

This technique is based on two measures: (1) *attendance* or the number of persons, and (2) *participation* or the amount of time per visit. Both measures are the basis for a measure called the participation-hour (PH). Procedures for gathering attendance and participation data use standard techniques that measure all users or a rep-

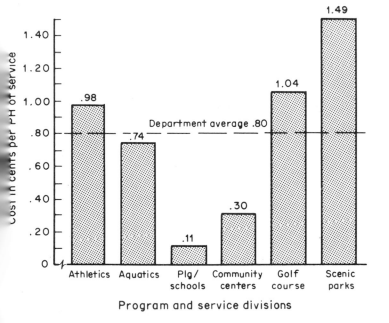

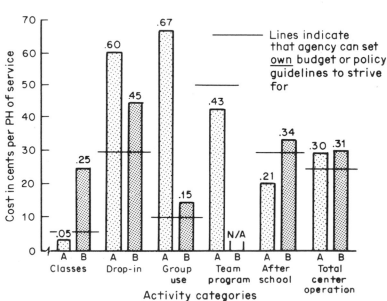

FIGURE 6.6 Participation-hour (PH) technique/Eugene, Oregon.

resentative sample of users. For example, these PH calculations could apply to these activities.

Swimming. 1500 swimmers (counted by pool turnstile) 2 hours average visit (determined by interviews) = 1500 swimmers × 2 hours = 3000 PH per activity day.

Similarly, the PH for a crafts class in a community center could be calculated in this manner:

Crafts class. 75 participants in crafts class × 2 days per week, 2 hours per class = 75 participants × 2 days × 2 hours = 300 PH for the week.

The PH for a wilderness camping trip sponsored by the parks and recreation department could be calculated this way:

Wilderness camping program. 30 campers × 10 days, 24 hours per day = 30 campers × 10 days × 24 hours per day = 7200 PH per trip.

PH can also be calculated for a passive, unsupervised neighborhood park. The basic task is to survey a representative sample of users that is generalizable to the total service area population. In all calculations, *benefits* are measured in participant-hours. *Cost* equals the total expenditure in dollars, while *net cost* equals the expenditures minus any fees collected. This technique can yield information for planning and management such as:

1. An evaluation of maintenance cost per amount of service rendered:

$$\frac{\text{Cost}}{\text{Benefit}} = \frac{\text{maintenance dollars}}{\text{participant-hours}}$$

2. An evaluation of leadership costs per amount of service rendered:

$$\frac{\text{Cost}}{\text{Benefit}} = \frac{\text{leadership dollars}}{\text{participant-hours}}$$

3. An evaluation of administration costs per amount of service rendered:

$$\frac{\text{Cost}}{\text{Benefit}} = \frac{\text{administration dollars}}{\text{participant-hours}}$$

This information can be used to help answer questions about inputs (cost) or outputs (service) related to parks and recreation. This technique can be used to describe:

- Gross cost per PH of service
- Net cost per PH
- Leadership cost per PH
- Administrative support cost per PH
- Maintenance support cost per PH
- Equipment and suppliers cost per PH

These costs and service levels can be related to (1) total department operations, (2) comparison between different types of facilities, such as community centers vs. pools, (3) comparisons between specific activity categories, such as sports vs. nature study, and (4) specific age, sex, income categories, or special populations, such as the handicapped vs. senior citizens to specific programs and services. It can provide valuable information to help justify budgets and establish guidelines for the planning and management of urban park systems.

SUPPLY AND
DEMAND ANALYSIS

7 LEISURE BEHAVIOR SURVEYS

The behavioral approach to recreation planning described in Chapter 3 is detailed here to show how levels of user preference and satisfaction can be measured. Successful techniques are illustrated to develop an awareness of the techniques, potentials, and qualifications of leisure behavior surveys.

The objective of leisure behavior surveys is to provide systematic information to planners and decision makers. This information should condition the planning process and be seriously considered in developing alternatives. The place to begin is with an understanding of the recreation experience, concepts of quality, and a logical classification of recreation activities and spaces that relate to existing or potential users. Once these concepts are established, a wide range of survey research techniques can be used to measure preference for and satisfaction with existing or potential recreation opportunities. If carefully done, these surveys can be used to establish the levels of demand, participation rates, and needs of representative groups in the population.

USER PREFERENCE AND SATISFACTION

A consideration of user preference and satisfaction is fundamental to the provision of urban recreation space, services, or facilities. It should be based on (1) a concept of quality, (2) a recreation activity classification system, (3) a recreation space classification system, (4) recreation resource inventories, (5) leisure behavior surveys, and (6) measures of effectiveness that can provide systematic information to planners and decision makers.

Concepts of Quality

Two concepts are fundamental to the urban park experience and all measures of user preference and satisfaction associated with this experience. Both concepts are based on the premise that people (1) expect a *pleasurable* experience in an urban park, (2) appreciate a range of *choice* in how and where they use their leisure, and (3) have social/psychological *needs* that can be accommodated as part of a park experience. These basic concepts are commonly expressed as:

Resource Quality Objective measures of factors or conditions a visitor views as part of the permanent, natural, and man-made physical elements or facilities of an area, e.g., scenery, vegetation, water, toilets, tables, trails (Figures 7.1 and 7.2).

Use Quality Objective measures of factors or conditions visitors view as constraints (negative) or inducements (positive)

to their expectations and satisfaction during a visit to an area, e.g., overcrowding, waiting, noise, conflict, fear, embarrassment, danger, or program leadership, interpretation, information, law enforcement, or food service (Figures 7.3 and 7.4).

Recreation Desires

The concept of quality is based on a behavioral approach to the recreation experience which translates basic human needs into three desires that condition user preference and satisfaction for a given area or activity:

Resource-Directed Contact with a natural resource, e.g., sun, sand, surf, wildlife. The degree of satisfaction depends on the quality and access to the resource (Figure 7.5).

Image-Directed The fulfillment of a desirable image, e.g., jogger, sailor, or tennis player. The degree of satisfaction depends, not on the resource, but on they way others may view the resource, activity, or user (Figure 7.6).

Leisure-Directed A pleasurable way to use leisure time, e.g., Sunday drive, window shopping, television, movies. The degree of satisfaction does not depend on the resource or others, but on how effectively the place or activity consumes leisure time (Figure 7.7).

User preference and satisfaction for a recreation experience can be described with the definitions below and the model of recreation choice shown in Figure 7.8. This model was developed by the National Academy of Sciences (1975). It suggests three factors that condition an individual decision to participate in a recreation activity: (1) individual characteristics, e.g., demographic characteristics, (2) social relationships, e.g., family or ethnic group, and (3) availability of recreation opportunities, e.g., access, cost, and information.

User Preference The voluntary choice of an activity or area to fulfill a desire.

User Satisfaction The fulfillment of a desire and a preference which is normally conditioned by the user's preconceived ideas about the area, activities available, natural setting, man-made facilities, and management of the area.

The Recreation Experience

The recreation experience has five phases which can be used to measure user preference and satisfaction for urban parks. These phases are commonly labeled anticipation, travel to, onsite, travel back, and recollection. Although most planners, designers, or managers are concerned with the onsite phase of the recreation experience, user satisfaction is affected by all phases of this experience.

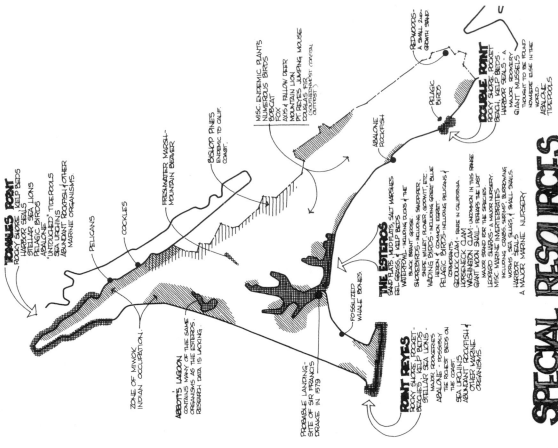

SPECIAL RESOURCES

TOMALES POINT
ROCKY SHORE, KELP BEDS
HARBOR SEALS
STELLAR SEA LIONS
PELAGIC BIRDS
ABALONE
"UNTOUCHED" TIDEPOOLS
SEA URCHINS
ABUNDANT ROCKFISH & OTHER MARINE ORGANISMS

PELICANS

COCKLES

FRESHWATER MARSH—
MOUNTAIN BEAVER

BISHOP PINES—
ENDEMIC TO CALIF. COAST

MISC. ENDEMIC PLANTS
NUMEROUS BIRDS
BOBCAT
FOX
AXIS & FALLOW DEER
MOUNTAIN LION
PT. REYES JUMPING MOUSE
DOUGLAS FIR
(SOUTHERNMOST COASTAL OUTPOST)

REDWOODS—
A SMALL 2ND-
GROWTH STAND

PELAGIC BIRDS

ABALONE
ROCKFISH

ZONE OF MIWOK
INDIAN OCCUPATION.

ABBOTTS LAGOON
CONTAINS MANY OF THE SAME
ORGANISMS AS THE ESTEROS.
RESEARCH DATA IS LACKING.

FOSSILIZED
WHALE BONES

DOUBLE POINT
ROCKY SHORE POCKET
BEACH, KELP BEDS
HARBOR SEALS - A
MAJOR ROOKERY
GIANT MUSSELS
THOUGHT TO BE FOUND
NOWHERE ELSE IN THE
WORLD
ABALONE
TIDEPOOLS

THE ESTEROS
SAND FLATS, MUDFLATS, SALT MARSHES
EEL GRASS, KELP BEDS
WATERFOWL - INCLUDING DUCKS & THE
BLACK BRANT GOOSE
SHOREBIRDS - INCLUDING SANDPIPER,
SNIPE, WILLET, PLOVER, GODWIT, ETC.
WADING BIRDS - INCLUDING GREAT BLUE
HERON & COMMON EGRET
PELAGIC BIRDS - INCLUDING PELICANS &
CORMORANTS
GEODUCK CLAM - RARE IN CALIFORNIA
HORSENECK CLAM - UNCOMMON IN THIS RANGE
WASHINGTON CLAM
GIANT WOOD SNAIL - PERHAPS THE LAST
MAJOR STAND FOR THE SPECIES
LEOPARD SHARKS - A MAJOR NURSERY
MISC. MARINE INVERTEBRATES
INCLUDING CRABS, SHRIMP, BURROWING
WORMS, SEA SLUGS, SMALL SNAILS
HARBOR SEALS
A MAJOR MARINE NURSERY

POINT REYES
ROCKY SHORE POCKET
BEACHES, KELP BEDS
STELLAR SEA LIONS
ABALONE - POSSIBLY
THE RICHEST BEDS ON
THE COAST
SEA URCHINS
ABUNDANT ROCKFISH &
OTHER MARINE
ORGANISMS

PROBABLE LANDING-
SITE OF SIR FRANCIS
DRAKE IN 1579

FIGURE 7.2 Resource quality: special resources/Pt. Reyes National Seashore, California.

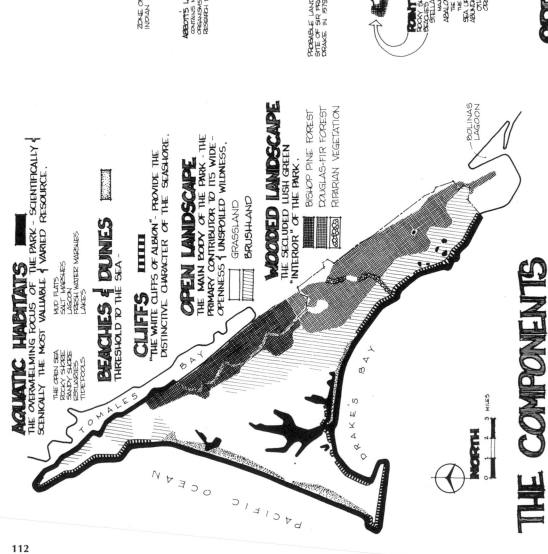

THE COMPONENTS

AQUATIC HABITATS ▬
THE OVERWHELMING FOCUS OF THE PARK - SCIENTIFICALLY &
SCENICALLY THE MOST VALUABLE & VARIED RESOURCE.

THE OPEN SEA   MUD FLATS
ROCKY SHORE   SALT MARSHES
SANDY SHORE   LAGOON
ESTUARIES   FRESH WATER MARSHES
TIDEPOOLS   LAKES

BEACHES & DUNES ▨
THRESHOLD TO THE SEA -

CLIFFS ▥
"THE WHITE CLIFFS OF ALBION" - PROVIDE THE
DISTINCTIVE CHARACTER OF THE SEASHORE.

OPEN LANDSCAPE
THE MAIN BODY OF THE PARK - THE
PRIMARY CONTRIBUTOR TO ITS WIDE-
OPENNESS & UNSPOILED WILDNESS.

▨ GRASSLAND
▥ BRUSHLAND

WOODED LANDSCAPE
THE SECLUDED LUSH GREEN
"INTERIOR" OF THE PARK.

▦ BISHOP PINE FOREST
▨ DOUGLAS-FIR FOREST
▧ RIPARIAN VEGETATION

TOMALES BAY

PACIFIC OCEAN

DRAKE'S BAY

BOLINAS LAGOON

NORTH
0 1 2 3 MILES

FIGURE 7.1 Resource quality: components/Pt. Reyes National Seashore, California.

112

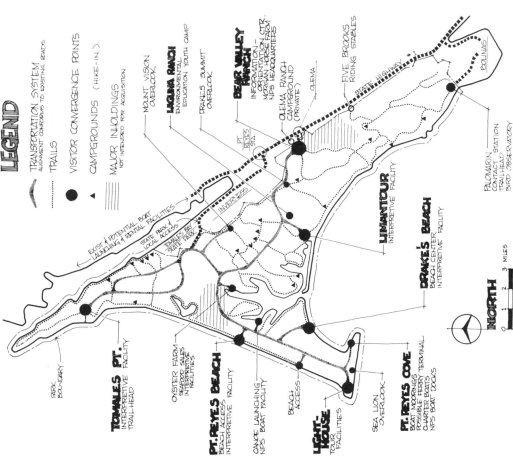

LEGEND

- TRANSPORTATION SYSTEM
  ALIGNMENT CONFORMS TO EXISTING ROADS
- TRAILS
- ● VISITOR CONVERGENCE POINTS
- ▲ CAMPGROUNDS (HIKE-IN)
- MAJOR INHOLDINGS
  NOT INTENDED FOR ACQUISITION

MOUNT VISION OVERLOOK

LAGUNA RANCH
ENVIRONMENTAL EDUCATION YOUTH CAMP

DRAKE'S SUMMIT OVERLOOK

BEAR VALLEY RANCH
INFORMATION-ORIENTATION CTR.
MORGAN HORSE FARM
NPS HEADQUARTERS

OLEMA RANCH CAMPGROUND (PRIVATE)

OLEMA

FIVE BROOKS RIDING STABLES

STATE HIGHWAY

BOLINAS

PT. REYES STA.

INVERNESS

EXIST & POTENTIAL BOAT
LAUNCHING & RENTAL FACILITIES

STATE PARK LOCAL ACCESS

TOMALES BAY STATE PARK

PALOMARIN
CONTACT STATION
TRAILHEAD
BIRD OBSERVATORY

LIMANTOUR
INTERPRETIVE FACILITY

DRAKE'S BEACH
BEACH CENTER
INTERPRETIVE FACILITY

PARK BOUNDARY

TOMALES PT.
INTERPRETIVE TRAIL HEAD

OYSTER FARM
SEAFOOD SALES
INTERPRETIVE FACILITIES

PT. REYES BEACH
BEACH ACCESS
INTERPRETIVE FACILITY

CANOE LAUNCHING
NPS BOAT FACILITY

BEACH ACCESS

LIGHT-HOUSE
TOUR FACILITIES

SEA LION OVERLOOK

PT. REYES COVE
BOAT MOORINGS
POSSIBLE FERRY TERMINAL
CHARTER BOATS
NPS BOAT DOCKS

NORTH
0 1 2 3 MILES

GENERAL DEVELOPMENT

FIGURE 7.4 Use quality: general development/Pt. Reyes National Seashore, California.

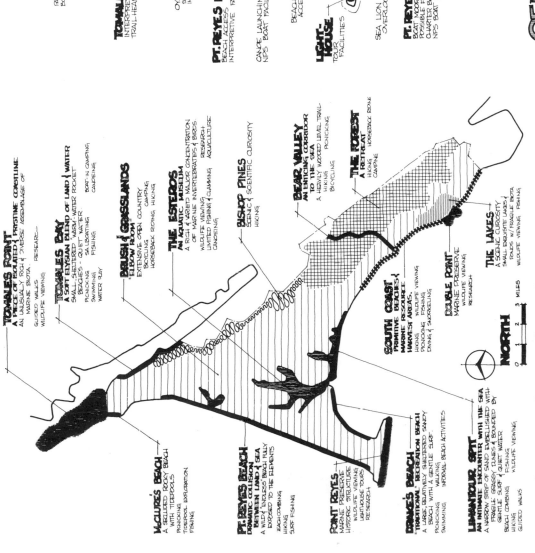

TOMALES POINT
A PIECE OF ISOLATED & PRISTINE COASTLINE
AN UNUSUALLY RICH & DIVERSE ASSEMBLAGE OF
MARINE BIOTA.
- GUIDED WALKS   RESEARCH
- WILDLIFE VIEWING

TOMALES BAY
A SOFT ELYSIAN BLEND OF LAND & WATER
SMALL SHELTERED "WARM" WATER POCKET
BEACHES - QUIET WATER.
- PICNICKING   SAILBOATING   BOAT-IN CAMPING,
- SWIMMING   FISHING   CANOEING
- WATER PLAY

BRUSH & GRASSLANDS
"ELBOW ROOM"
EXTENSIVE OPEN COUNTRY
- BICYCLING   CAMPING
- HORSEBACK RIDING   HIKING

THE ESTEROS
AN AQUATIC MUSEUM
A RICH & VARIED MAJOR CONCENTRATION
OF MARINE INVERTEBRATES & BIRDS
- WILDLIFE VIEWING   RESEARCH
- LIMITED FISHING & CLAMMING
- CANOEING

BISHOP PINES
SCENIC & SCIENTIFIC CURIOSITY
- HIKING

BEAR VALLEY
AN ENTICING CORRIDOR
TO THE SEA
A HEAVILY WOODED LEVEL TRAIL
- HIKING   PICNICKING
- BICYCLING

THE FOREST
A RETREAT
- HIKING   HORSEBACK RIDING
- CAMPING

THE LAKES
A SCENIC CURIOSITY
SMALL EXQUISITE LAKES &
PONDS w/ FRAGILE BIOTA
- WILDLIFE VIEWING   FISHING

DOUBLE POINT
MARINE PRESERVE
- WILDLIFE VIEWING
- RESEARCH

SOUTH COAST
PRIMITIVE BEACHES &
MARINE RESOURCE
HARVEST AREAS.
- HIKING   WILDLIFE VIEWING
- PICNICKING   FISHING
- DIVING & SKINDIVING

McCLURE'S BEACH
A SECLUDED ROCKY BEACH
WITH TIDEPOOLS
- PICNICKING
- TIDEPOOL EXPLORATION
- FISHING

PT. REYES BEACH
DRAMATIC COLLISION
BETWEEN LAND & SEA
A WILD & ENDLESS BEACH FULLY
EXPOSED TO THE ELEMENTS
- BEACHCOMBING
- HIKING
- SURF FISHING

POINT REYES
MARINE PRESERVE
HISTORIC STRUCTURE
- WILDLIFE VIEWING
- LIGHTHOUSE TOURS
- RESEARCH

DRAKE'S BEACH
"TRADITIONAL" RECREATION BEACH
A LARGE, RELATIVELY SHELTERED SANDY
BEACH WITH A GENTLE SURF.
- PICNICKING
- WALKING
- SWIMMING
- INFORMAL BEACH ACTIVITIES

LIMANTOUR SPIT
AN INTIMATE ENCOUNTER WITH THE SEA
A NARROW STRIP OF SAND EMBELLISHED WITH
FRAGILE GRASSY DUNES & BOUNDED BY
GENTLE SURF & QUIET WATER
- BEACH COMBING   FISHING
- HIKING   WILDLIFE VIEWING
- GUIDED WALKS

NORTH
0 1 2 3 MILES

CONCEPTS of USE

FIGURE 7.3 Use quality: concepts of use/Pt. Reyes National Seashore, California.

113

More attention should be given to what happens offsite by providing better information about what to expect in parks, how to get there, what to bring, and what to do. Much of this information can be furnished by environmental education or interpretative programs in the schools and community colleges. It can also be provided by public information programs proposed in the recreation plan.

Although the onsite phase of the recreation experience is usually activity-oriented, some people prefer to do "nothing" and come to urban parks simply to "get away from it all." Planners and designers can give more attention to this leisure desire by providing spaces where people can do "nothing" and not be disturbed by others doing "something." The concept of creating open spaces in cities and filling them with activities or development that does not allow people to do "nothing" may be in contradiction with the preferences of some people. Conversely, many people view the urban park as a place to do "something" or watch others doing something. Both concepts are valid and can be accommodated by sensitive design and management.

Recreation Activity Classification

The wide range of leisure activities in cities can be classified in a way that acknowledges the concepts of quality and is useful for the planning and management of urban recreation spaces. The problem is to analyze existing recreation spaces asking, What do people *expect* in terms of a recreation experience? and What did they *receive* in terms of satisfaction based on the concepts of resource and use quality?

The primary task is to classify and aggregate recreation activities into categories that reflect similar components of experience and resources. A secondary task is to analyze the relationships between different activities (multiple use), environmental impact (carrying capacity), space requirements (standards), and support elements (management) required for each category. Most activities can be classified into these four categories of recreation experience:

- *Physical recreation*, which requires exertion or physical effort as the major experience of the activity.

- *Social recreation*, which involves social interaction as the major experience of the activity.

FIGURE 7.5   Resource-directed desire.

FIGURE 7.6   Image-directed desire.

FIGURE 7.7   Leisure-directed desire.

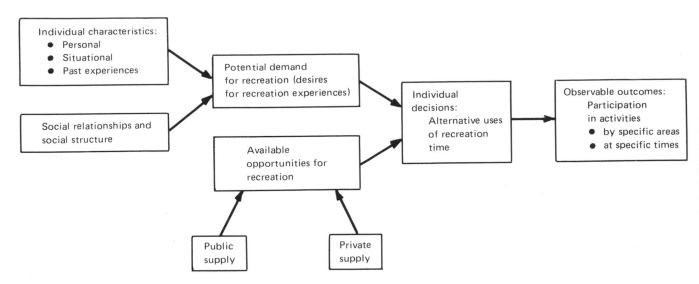

FIGURE 7.8 Model of recreation choice.

- *Cognitive recreation*, which includes cultural, educational, and creative or aesthetic activities.
- *Environment-related recreation*, which requires use of a natural resource such as water, trees, scenery, or wildlife to provide the setting, or focus, for an activity.

Because the total recreation system is not outdoor-based, both indoor and outdoor experiences are considered. Within each of these four experience categories, there are activity clusters which represent similar types of activities. These activities generally require the same types of resources to allow for greater flexibility in the application of standards. Table 7.1 shows possible activity clusters and examples of activities for two recreation experience categories.

In a similar manner, data related to user satisfaction can be classified in terms of *use quality* and *resource quality* and related to each planning unit. This results in classification systems that are generalizable to existing parks or new parks, and can be analyzed for relationships between the user and resource. These relationships can provide a *behavioral* basis for the planning or management of each park and the entire system.

Recreation Space Classification

The range of existing or potential recreation spaces in a city can be classified in a way that (1) acknowledges different scales or service areas, (2) relates to travel time–

distance or access criteria, (3) provides for different levels of design and management, and (4) relates to the natural or human carrying capacity and design load of the area.

The classification of a space should also match the functional use and design potentials of a given area. For example, to designate an area a playground, but not have this space designed or managed to accommodate the behavioral needs of children, is absurd. Likewise, an area designated as a downtown plaza for office workers requires an appropriate commitment of design and development, or a different classification.

One common flaw of leisure behavior surveys is to not orient the survey to the *use* and design *potentials* of a given area. A symbolic or actual classification system is not apparent to the person being surveyed. This can result in distortions or false expectations of users who expect more of the space than may be realistic.

The classification of an area in the planning process implies the commitment of resources to develop and manage it to an adequate level. It also implies a level of use and satisfaction that can be used in projecting needs. The classification of recreation spaces should be approached seriously, or the plan will lack credibility.

Recreation spaces can be classified by (1) function or dominant use, (2) ownership, (3) degree of use density or development, and (4) planning unit orientation. The planning unit orientation is most appropriate at the

TABLE 7.1 | RECREATION ACTIVITY CATEGORIES

Recreation experience	Activity cluster	Examples of activities
Physical Recreation		
Outdoor	Free play and self-generated activities	Jumping, climbing, swinging, sliding, skateboarding, jogging
	Organized turf and hard-surface court games	Volleyball, tetherball, basketball, tennis, hopscotch
	Turf games	Croquet, badminton, golf, lawn bowling
	Field sports	Baseball, rugby, soccer, football, field hockey
	Organized sports	League baseball, football, soccer
Indoor	Self-generated	Basketball, volleyball, handball, squash
	Organized sports	Basketball, bowling, tennis, wrestling, gymnastics, squash
Social Recreation		
Outdoor	Participants	Picnicking, dances, fairs, restaurants, flea markets
	Spectators	Watching sports, drama, listening to music
Indoor	Participants	Meetings, crafts, bazaars, dances, table games
	Spectators	Watching sports, movies, drama, television

Source: Adapted from *Application of a Recreation-Experience Components Concept for a Comprehensive Recreation Planning* by Monty Christiansen, Pennsylvania State University, 1975.

community or metropolitan scale because it best relates to use patterns, public recreation, and private recreation opportunities. The following categories include most recreation spaces and provide logical planning service areas:

HOME-ORIENTED SPACE Most leisure time (90 percent) is spent in or around the home in private spaces. This type of open space is frequently ignored in most plans and can be made more effective by changes in the zoning ordinance, subdivision regulations, or subdivision planning that acknowledge the potentials of the home as a leisure environment.

NEIGHBORHOOD SPACE These spaces are generally associated with an elementary school, are pedestrian-

oriented, and normally serve a population of 5000 people. They should provide a range of active and passive recreation opportunities oriented to the changing needs of a neighborhood.

COMMUNITY SPACE These spaces usually serve three to six neighborhoods, are pedestrian- or mass-transit-oriented, and normally serve a population of 20,000 people. They are normally associated with a junior high or high school complex and shopping or community center. They provide a range of specialized facilities not possible in neighborhood parks to serve the diverse needs of a planning district.

CITYWIDE SPACE These spaces serve the entire community, are auto- or mass-transit-oriented, and normally serve a population of 100,000 people or more. They provide a range of intensive and extensive activities and highly specialized facilities not possible in community-oriented spaces.

REGIONAL SPACE These spaces are commonly resource-oriented areas that serve metropolitan needs with the types of passive, extensive activities not possible or appropriate in citywide parks. Access is by private or public transportation.

Examples of types of activities, facilities, and service areas in each category are described in Appendix D Part 1. A logical extension of this list could include any of the cultural facilities, commercial recreation enterprises, and special districts, events, or spaces described in Chapter 1.

LEISURE BEHAVIOR SURVEYS

The best way to study the leisure behavior of a community is to initiate a continuing program of survey research to measure (1) user preference and satisfaction for recreation activities and spaces, (2) levels of participation or nonuse, and (3) latent demand. Survey research techniques can also be used to assess the recreation needs of special populations, identify major problems and potentials, describe public opinion, and determine the effectiveness of existing facilities or programs.

Types of Surveys

Two types of surveys are required to prepare and revise park and recreation plans: (1) communitywide surveys of leisure patterns describing expressed and latent demand, participation rates and people's perception of recreation opportunities, and (2) preconstruction and postconstruction evaluation surveys of specific projects describing user and nonuser response to these projects. Both types of surveys should include a probability sample of users and nonusers and surveys taken onsite and in the home.

Constraints of time and money make it difficult or unnecessary to survey the entire population. Most surveys use a sample of people to represent the entire population. From this representative group, planners can make projections to the total population. This is called a probability sample.

There are many probability sampling techniques, but all are based on the concept of random selection, which implies every member of a population has an equal chance of being surveyed. This technique minimizes bias and allows the planner to use statistical techniques to measure the accuracy of the survey, project the results to the total population, and estimate the size of error.

The merits of using survey research as a planning tool are well established in practice and described in many sources. If a planning agency does not have the time, funds, or expertise to undertake recreation surveys, it can use a combination of consultants and volunteers for many aspects of the survey effort.

Survey Methods

These five survey methods are commonly used to study leisure behavior: (1) mail questionnaires, (2) self-administered questionnaires, (3) personal interviews, (4) telephone interviews, and (5) field observations. Each method is briefly described here and compared in Table 7.2.

MAIL QUESTIONNAIRES The mail questionnaire is the least credible survey method because it is difficult to ensure who responds and to collect the questionnaires. It offers the most privacy and convenience to those being surveyed, is easy to administer, and can reach a large population in a short time at a minimum cost. Two variations of this method are questionnaires inserted with the utility bill or in the local newspaper.

SELF-ADMINISTERED QUESTIONNAIRES These are similar to the mail questionnaire except for some personal contact with an interviewer who hands out and collects the completed questionnaire. Personal contact usually allows the interviewer to select a representative sample, give instructions, and obtain a higher rate of return. Both mail and self-administered surveys require a fair degree of literacy and are most appropriate where the population is highly motivated to respond.

PERSONAL INTERVIEWS Major advantages of this method are credibility, high return rate, and the possibility of using visual material. The personal interview yields the best sample because technically it can reach everyone in the population. However, the disadvantages of high cost, logistics, interviewer bias, and intrusion of privacy should be considered before using this method in many urban areas. This method has great value in surveying special populations such as ethnic minorities or the handicapped.

TABLE 7.2 | LEISURE BEHAVIOR SURVEY METHODS*

Major factors	Survey methods				
	Mail questionnaire	Self-administered	Personal interview	Telephone interview	Field observation
Cost	L	M	H	M	H
Administration	L	M	H	M	H
Privacy/anonymity	H	M	L	M	L
Sample size/coverage	H	M	L	H	L
Nonresponse bias	H	M	L	M	L
Follow-up required	H	M	M	M	L
Time required	H	M	M	M	H
Depth/detail	L	L	H	H	H
Personal contact	L	M	H	M	L
Flexibility	L	L	H	M	L
Interviewer bias	L	L	H	M	H
Use of visual material	L	L	H	L	L
Logistics/travel	L	H	H	L	H

*Summary of relative advantages and disadvantages for typical situation expressed in terms of high (H), medium (M), or low (L), based on criteria described in *Survey Research for Community Recreation Services*, Michigan State University, Experiment Station Research Report No. 291, February 1976, p. 9.

TELEPHONE INTERVIEWS The telephone interview is increasingly used because of its relatively low cost, ease of administration, and ability to conveniently reach most of the population. It has significant advantages in allowing flexibility, relative privacy, and a good return in a short time with a minimum effort. Volunteers or clerical staff can be trained to take these surveys. Random-dialing techniques or weighting can ensure that a representative sample reaches or accounts for people without phones or unlisted numbers. Telephone surveys have great utility in large cities with special populations, where a relatively large sample is required in a short time at a minimum cost (Table 7.3).

FIELD OBSERVATIONS This method is primarily used to measure the effectiveness of existing facilities to show differences between user and supplier or designer objectives. Systematic field observation is most useful to evaluate the expressed demand or preference for various spaces or services. It has serious limitations in terms of cost, sample size, objectivity, and logistics. However, it may be a more realistic measure of preference or de-

mand than revealed in the other methods because there is a difference between what people say they want to do and what they actually do. Field observation can be a valuable check on the validity of other methods. It can also be used in pilot studies to establish the scope and detail of other survey research methods.

There are many additional sophisticated techniques available, including time-lapse photography, behavioral trace measurement, and aerial photography. However, personal observation is the most direct and revealing technique. This simple method of field observation has been used in many studies:

1 Divide the park into functional areas designated or implied by the designer/manager.

2 Think of each designed element in the landscape as a "message" from the designer/manager to the user about what is hoped to happen there. Evaluate each message to see whether it is ambiguous or clear, weak or strong. Consider these as symbolic messages from the designer/manager to potential users that can have a positive or negative influence on user behavior.

3 Observe actual behavior systematically at different times and survey behavioral traces, e.g., litter, shortcuts, or vandalism.

TABLE 7.3 | INTERVIEW COMPLETION RATES FOR GENERAL CITIZEN TELEPHONE SURVEYS ON RECREATION IN ST. PETERSBURG, WASHINGTON, D.C., ROCKFORD, AND NASHVILLE

Category	St. Petersburg Random sample of telephone directory		Washington Random sample of all telephone numbers		Rockford Random sample of telephone directory		Nashville Random sample of city directory	
	Number	Percent	Number	Percent	Number	Percent	Number	Percent
Completed usable interviews	384	48	836	58	415	58	402	50
Interview rejections	138	17	139	10	116	16	106	13
Bad telephone numbers*	164	21	307	21	80	11	152	19
Lost forms	54	7	31	2	0	0	16	2
No answer†	58	7	107	8	102	15	128	16
Unusable interview forms	2	—	17	1	0	0	0	0
Total numbers dialed	800	100	1,437	100	713	100	804	100
Nonrefusal Rate: Completed as a percentage of total households answering call: $\dfrac{a}{(a + b)}$	$\dfrac{384}{522} =$	74	$\dfrac{836}{975} =$	86	$\dfrac{415}{533} =$	78	$\dfrac{402}{508} =$	79
Completion Rate: Completed as a percentage of "good" numbers attempted: $\dfrac{a}{(a + b + e)}$	$\dfrac{384}{580} =$	66	$\dfrac{836}{1,082} =$	77	$\dfrac{415}{633} =$	66	$\dfrac{402}{636} =$	63

*This category includes nonworking or disconnected numbers, business numbers, address changes, telephone number changes, and respondent on vacation.

†As many as six call-backs were made in St. Petersburg, Washington, D.C., and Rockford. In Nashville, as many as nine call-backs were made.

Source: St. Petersburg, Florida, September 1973 survey; Nashville, Tennessee, November 1973 survey.

4 Identify discrepancies between what the designers/managers of the space were trying to communicate about expected behavior and what was actually observed happening.

5 Analyze the effectiveness of the park. Make recommendations for redesigning the space to accommodate desired activities that are possible in this type of park.

This approach provides an objective evaluation of effectivensss that describes differences between design/management values and user behavior. It recommends constructive changes based on fact instead of intuition. Field observation forces the observer to answer the questions (1) How does it *look?* and (2) How does it *work?* in terms of user objectives.

Survey Procedures

The steps described in Figure 7.9 are common to all leisure behavior survey methods. Appendix E shows examples of survey questions and formats. Before starting a survey, one should carefully review the literature and refine previous efforts. In all cases, a consultant, or third party, and pilot studies should be used to minimize ambiguity and increase the credibility and usefulness of the data.

Poorly done surveys can distort the planning process and diminish the value of all future planning and design efforts. They can be worse than no surveys at all. Conversely, well-conceived leisure behavior surveys are an essential aspect of recreation planning. They provide a systematic way to describe, evaluate, and project a community's leisure patterns and needs. They can also establish baselines to monitor the effectiveness of existing programs, measure change, and describe the need for future facilities or programs.

USING VOLUNTEERS The use of volunteers from local schools, service groups, businesses, or the media to conduct recreation surveys can help to popularize the survey effort, increase its credibility, and reduce costs. Successful surveys can be the collaborative effort of volunteers, consultants, media, and public agencies. This division of responsibility has been successful in many communities:

- *Public Agency's Role*
  Arrange and coordinate necessary meetings
  Promote and coordinate cooperation of community
  Act as liaison between local groups and consultant
  Make local physical arrangements

- *Consultant's Role*
  Consult with local staff
  Meet with local organizations
  Prepare questionnaires
  Prepare documentation
  Provide overall direction
  Evaluate results and prepare final report

- *Volunteer's Role*
  Distribute and collect questionnaires
  Analyze data
  Distribute results
  Serve as continuous feedback vehicle

- *News Media*
  Advance stories
  Publish actual survey in newspaper
  Promotional announcements on radio and television
  Interim progress stories to stimulate public interest
  Radio or television talk shows as vehicles

ILLUSTRATIVE COSTS The costs of user surveys will vary with the sample size, type of community, and staff, consultants, or volunteers available to conduct the survey. Tables 7.4–7.7 show illustrative costs for different types of surveys in typical cities. User surveys are a very cost-effective way to approach the planning, design, or management of public recreation opportunities. They have no substitute in these times. To use cost as a reason for not attempting user surveys is to perpetuate the problems described in Chapter 1.

TRANSLATING THE RESULTS A major shortcoming of many survey efforts is the token attention given to trans-

FIGURE 7.9 Steps in the survey process.

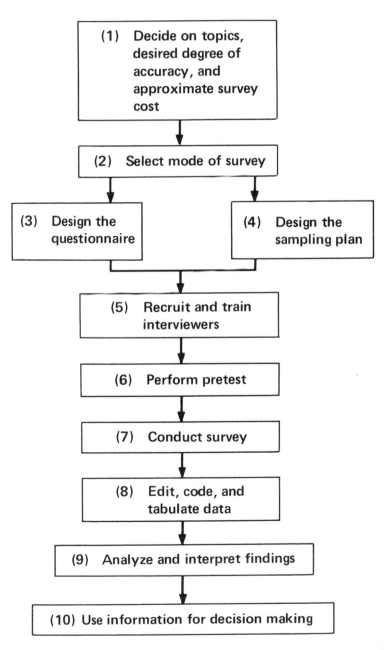

TABLE 7.4 | STAFFING AND DOLLAR EXPENDITURES, 1973 RECREATION TELEPHONE SURVEY—ST. PETERSBURG AND NASHVILLE

Survey elements	St. Petersburg (average interview = 8 minutes)			Nashville (average interview = 15 minutes)		
	Calendar time in weeks	Dollars expended	Person-weeks expended	Calendar time, in weeks	Dollars expended	Person-weeks expended
Set up—Get Ready						
Design questionnaire	4		2	6		4
Select random sample	3		2	4		4
Prepare survey material	4		12	4		15
Printing		50			100	
Postage		100			100	
Conduct Survey						
Train interviewers	2		14	2		20
Conduct survey	2		14	2		20
Professional trainer		150			200	
Tabulation and Analysis						
Check and code data				2		7
Tabulate data	2		4	3		
Prepare report	1		2	3		3
Keypunch					200	
Computer runs					300	
Total	13*	300	36	18*	900	53

*Some of the survey elements overlap so the total calendar time required is less than the sum of the individual elements.

Source: St. Petersburg, Florida, September 1973 survey; Nashville, Tennessee, November 1973 survey.

TABLE 7.5 | ESTIMATED TIME REQUIREMENTS FOR USER SURVEY (for 100 interviews at each of 10 facilities open 10 hours per day for one week)

Task	Time required	
	Elapsed calendar time, in weeks	Person-weeks
1 Select topics, specify accuracy, and design management plan	½	½
2 Design and pretest questionnaire	1	1
3 Design sampling plan and prepare material	1	1
4 Recruit and train interviewers	½	½
5 Conduct survey	1	15
6 Edit, code, keypunch, and tabulate	2	2
7 Analyze and prepare written findings	4	4
Total	8*	24

*Because some survey elements overlap, the total time required is less than the sum of individual elements.

TABLE 7.6 | ESTIMATED COST OF ESTABLISHING AND OPERATING A RECREATION EFFECTIVENESS MEASUREMENT SYSTEM, MEDIUM-SIZE CITY. (250,000 population; 100 full-time recreational employees, medium level of measurement)

Measurement Tool or technique	First year		Subsequent years	
	Person-hours	Cost, $	Person-hours	Cost, $
Data Collection				
General citizen survey One survey per year* (400 households)	1,400	12,500	1,200	6,250
User survey One survey per year (15 recreation sites)	950	5,250	725	3,650
Other measurements				
Physical accessibility	300	2,000	150	700
Attendance	100	500	50	250
Safety	50	250	25	100
Crowdedness	100	750	25	100
Subtotal	2,900	21,250	2,175	11,050
Data Analysis				
Subtotal	1,100	18,750	825	13,950
Total collection and analysis	4,000	40,000	3,000	25,000

*Actual out-of-pocket expenditures can be reduced significantly if current government personnel undertake certain tasks, such as interviewing. Costs also can be reduced if survey designers adopt the options discussed in the text, such as avoiding the requirement for interviewers to identify the nearest community recreation facilities for each respondent, or including a more limited set of questions on a multiservice survey.

Source: Adapted from U.S. Bureau of Outdoor Recreation, *How Effective Are Your Outdoor Recreation Services?* Exhibit 32, p. 75, with revisions based on 1974-75 experiences in Nashville and St. Petersburg. Cost estimates are based on 1975 salary levels.

TABLE 7.7 | ESTIMATED ANNUAL RECURRING COST OF A RECREATION EFFECTIVENESS MEASURFMENT SYSTEM (three city sizes and three measurement levels*)

Classification	Recreation agency size			Classification	Recreation agency size		
	Small	Medium	Large		Small	Medium	Large
Population	Fewer than 100,000	Approx. 250,000	More than 500,000	Number of user surveys per year	1	1	1
Agency operating budget	$500,000	$1,000,000	$10,000,000	Total staff-years of effort	0.75	1.5	2.0
Number of full-time employees	40	100	500	Total yearly cost	$15,000	$25,000	$30,000
Low Budget				Percentage of operating budget	3%	2.5%	.03%
Update of measurements	Annual	Annual	Annual	**High Budget**			
Number of user surveys per year	1	1	1	Update of measurements	Monthly	Monthly	Monthly
Total staff-years of effort	0.5	0.75	1.0	Number of user surveys per year	2	2	2
Total yearly cost	$10,000	$15,000	$20,000	Total staff-years of effort	1.0	2.0	2.5
Percentage of operating budget	2%	1.5%	.02%	Total yearly cost	$20,000	$30,000	$40,000
Medium Budget				Percentage of operating budget	4%	3%	.04%
Update of measurements	Seasonal	Seasonal	Seasonal				

*All options shown include a general citizen recreation survey. Actual out-of-pocket expenditures can be reduced significantly if current government personnel undertake certain tasks, such as interviewing. Costs also can be reduced if survey designers adopt the options presented in the text, such as avoiding the requirement for interviewers to identify the nearest community recreation facilities for each respondent, or including a more limited set of questions on a multiservice survey.

Source: Adapated from U.S. Bureau of Outdoor Recreation, *How Effective Are Your Outdoor Recreation Services?*, Exhibit 31, p. 74, with revisions based on 1973-74 experiences in Nashville and St. Petersburg.

TABLE 7.8 | EXAMPLE OF USER SURVEY RESULTS

Neighborhood Characteristics

Kirkpatrick is located on South 9th Street on 7.75 acres in East Nashville. The J. A. Cayce Homes, public housing for low-income persons, are located behind the center. The Community Center has a gym, two club rooms, a game room, and a kitchen. The Community Center Director has determined that this center should serve the immediate neighborhood bordered on the west by South 7th Street, to the east by South 15th, Lenore Street to the south, and Woodland Street to the north. The areas served by Kirkpatrick and East Community Centers correspond to Census Tracts 120, 123, and 124. These Census Tracts reported a racial composition (1970) of 14 percent nonwhites, 86 percent whites. In age distribution there were 36 percent children to 18 years, 51 percent adults to 64 years, and 13 percent 65 and older. Forty-seven percent of the population is male, 53 percent female. The median family income (the average of three medians) is $4,819.

User Characteristics (1973)

The characteristics of users from the December 1973 sample were as follows, based on the 47 persons filling out forms: 66 percent of those stated their race was black, and 33 percent white; 58 percent of users were male and 42 percent female. In age composition, 38 percent were from ages 6 to 12, 45 percent 13 to 17, 14 percent 18 to 34, and 2 percent 35 to 59. That is, 83 percent were children and teen-agers and 16 percent were adults. No elderly persons were users that week. The predominant mode of transportation of Community Center users was walking (62 percent), although 30 percent did use a car to get there. For the majority of users, time spent traveling to the center was ten minutes or less (74 percent). For those traveling by car, length of travel time ranged from five to thirty minutes.

Day of the week and hour of arrival were also sampled. Users were sampled from Monday through Thursday only; no data were collected on Friday and Saturday, which were identified as the least frequented days. About 43 percent of users arrived between 6:30 and 10:00 p.m. The average length of stay was about 3½ hours. The attendance was higher on Tuesday and Thursday because of league basketball games.

Users' Ratings

Users' favorite activities were basketball for both boys and girls; only 28 percent of the males and 44 percent of the females listed other activities. Among things respondents liked about the center were "basketball," "everything," and "the staff." Most people said they disliked "nothing" about the center. A few complained that the center closed too early and had too many league basketball games. Forty-five percent of the users learned about the Community Center through friends, relatives, or neighbors.

The center received the following satisfactory ratings, listed in order from best to worst ratings:

	Percentage of satisfactory ratings	
	Center ratings	Average all centers
Helpfulness and attitude of staff	96	81
Amount of supervision	93	78
Cleanliness	89	68
Conditions and safety of equipment	86	71
Feeling of security	74	70
Amount of space	72	64
Convenience to your home	68	73
Hours and days open	67	74
Variety of programs and activities	63	73

In summary, the center received high ratings for staff, supervision, and cleanliness. The lowest ratings were for convenience, hours and days open, and the variety of programs.

Park Users

The random sample telephone survey included only two household members who had used Kirkpatrick Park; therefore, there are no results to report.

Conclusions and Recommendations

The neighborhood surrounding the center is a low-income one, 86 percent whites and 14 percent blacks. Thirty-six percent of the population are children (to 18), 51 percent are adults (to 64 years), and 13 percent over 65. Among the users, 83 percent were children (to 17 years), 16 percent were adults (to 59 years), and there were no elderly. *It is concluded that the center is not meeting the needs of its adult and elderly populations.* The center is serving a high proportion of females (42 percent), although these are mainly teen-age blacks who come more as spectators than participants.

It is recommended that more programs should be offered for the adults and the elderly population. It is also recommended that more of a variety of programs and activities should be offered to the eighteen-and-under age groups because of the low "variety" rating the center received in the users' survey. In order to facilitate the development of more programs for the elderly, some type of transportation is needed. They live a few blocks from the center and there is a perceived and actual danger involved in walking because of muggers and other street crime. Another possibility is to initiate a recreation program within apartment dwellings in community rooms. A number of adult and elderly men have expressed interest in playing croquet on the outdoor area provided in the park, if a shade or cover is added to provide protection from the sun.

Source: Based on the 1974 Nashville Users Survey and Nashville-Urban Observatory, *Leisure Services: The Measurement of Program Performance,* June 1974, pp. 73–77.

Tables 7.4–7.8 reprinted with permission from Harry P. Hatry et al., *How Effective Are Your Community Services?* Washington, D.C.: The Urban Institute, 1977, pp. 57–64.

1. QUESTION

Where do you play?

RESULTS

At your friends's house	62%
In your backyard	48
In the street	45
In the school playground	35
In the park	30

Scale: 0 · · · · 50 · 70%

Most younger children play close to home, generally within the neighborhood.

2. QUESTION

In the City of Orange, which parks do you use?

RESULTS

Eisenhower	59%
Hart	43
Shaffer	21
Yorba	10
El Modena	9
Sycamore	7
La Veta	6

Scale: 0 · · · · 50 · 70%

Younger children tend to use those city parks which are less specialized and more typically "park-like."

3. QUESTION

If you do not use the a park, why not?

RESULTS

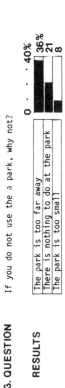

The park is too far away	36%
There is nothing to do at the park	21
The park is too small	8

Scale: 0 · · · · 40%

Most children do not use the parks because of the distance from home and the absence of adult supervision.

4. QUESTION

What would you like to do at your neighborhood park?

RESULTS

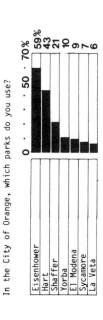

Go sack riding	50%
Wade in the water	49
Play softball/baseball	49
Build a tree house	46
Play tennis	45
Play volleyball	32
Play frisbee	31
Make arts and crafts	30
Meet new friends	29
Find wildflowers	20
Go for a walk	19

Scale: 0 · · · · 60%

Active, self-motivated activities are preferred by children.

5. QUESTION

Do you go outside of Orange for your recreation?

RESULTS

YES	NO
29%	59%

6. QUESTION

How do you get where you want to go?

RESULTS

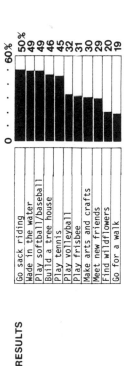

By bicycle	71%
By car	55
By foot	55
By hitchhiking	6
By motorcycle	5
By bus	5

Scale: 0 · · · · 50 · 80%

Handwritten notes:

keep Dogs in parks! PLEASE

clean up Eisenhower lake

go Kart racing trails

More bicycle paths

Put pools in parks for children

Have a recreation program in the summer.

Put more fish in lakes

We need Go-cart trails so we can have practice learning how to race!!!! Only two races

Keep strong bums out of parks

FIGURE 7.10 Local park user survey, elementary school repsondents/Orange, California.

lating the results in a format that can be understood by citizens and decision makers. The challenge is to translate data into useful information for the preparation of recreation plans, project designs, or management practices at the systems and site levels.

This can be effectively done with words and graphics which convey the meaning of statistics. Table 7.8 shows a concise summary of survey results that clearly describes the problems and potentials of a community center and park. Figure 7.10 shows the results of a user survey at the local scale in graphics.

8 | RECREATION RESOURCE INVENTORIES

A basic task of recreation planning is to classify and inventory the quantity, quality, and location of recreation resources. This inventory should include existing and potential public and private resources with the capability of providing recreation opportunities. The value of this inventory can be increased by using the strategies, classification systems, and techniques described in this chapter.

INVENTORY AND CLASSIFICATION PROCESS

The normal approach to this task is to inventory public areas and facilities by type, amount, and location. The private sector is given token attention and the emphasis is on land and development. The *qualitative* aspects of the recreation experience or site described in Chapters 6 and 7 are generally omitted. There is no description of space or experience related to outputs or *performance* criteria. This approach commonly results in much effort with little utility because the inventory lacks a logical classification system and technical credibility.

Basic Strategies

The way to approach recreation resource inventories is to first establish a context and definitions that describe how, where, and when this information can be used in the planning and design process. No context or definition can fit all situations because of significant differences in scale, jurisdiction, resource capability, and the level of planning expertise or budget for a resource inventory.

Figure 8.1 shows a typical approach applied to a relatively complex planning area: the Lake Tahoe region in California and Nevada. Note how the planning process (1) integrates plan elements for two types of related land use (conservation and recreation), (2) includes a comprehensive range of resources in terms of their appropriateness (capability and suitability), and (3) classifies these elements by orientation (land or water), season (summer and winter), and objectives (resource management or public safety).

Many other combinations are possible, but the basic approach of using land capability and suitability to link plan elements and condition the type of classification system is a logical way to approach the problem especially in ecologically sensitive areas such as Lake Tahoe. A simplified version of this approach, adaptable to most urbanized areas, is shown in Figure 8.2. Most elaborate

classification systems are difficult to understand or apply, if there is no common set of meanings for the words used to describe things or relationships. The following definitions are suggested:

Recreation Resources Land and water areas and facilities that provide opportunities for recreation.

Recreation Site A specific tract of land or water within a recreation area used for particular recreation activities.

Recreation Supply The quantity and quality of recreation resources available for use at a given time.

Recreation Facilities Man-made improvements of a recreation site provided to facilitate recreation use.

Recreation Complex An area containing a variety of resources and facilities providing different types of recreation.

Carrying Capacity The capability of natural resources to withstand use for a desired quality of recreation experience.

Establishing the meanings of terms at the beginning of the inventory process will foster an understanding of the user-resource relationships. It will also reduce levels of ambiguity for public officials and citizens as they participate in the planning process. The initial step of defining terms will help to make all other steps in the inventory process mores systematic and cost-effective.

Types of Recreation Resources

Recreation requires the use of a wide range of resources in varying combinations of location, accessibility, function, development, carrying capacity, and ownership. No universal system exists or is proposed for classifying the wide range of recreation resources. There is no "order of parks" similar to the classifications of plants and animals. However, several systems are in common use. They emphasize different factors and apply to different situations and scales.

For example, Table 8.1 shows a common classification of areas by dominant use and ownership. This system is currently the basis of most local recreation plans. Table 8.2 classifies recreation land by levels of use density and development. It is the system used by most federal and state agencies. This system has great value because it is based on the human and natural carrying capacity of a resource for a given type of experience.

A third system for classifying types of recreation resources is under development by the Heritage Conservation Recreation Service for use in the 1980 Nationwide Recreation Plan. This system is computer-oriented and classifies recreation resources by (1) land use and cover

CONSERVATION/RECREATION/OPEN SPACE PROCESS CHART

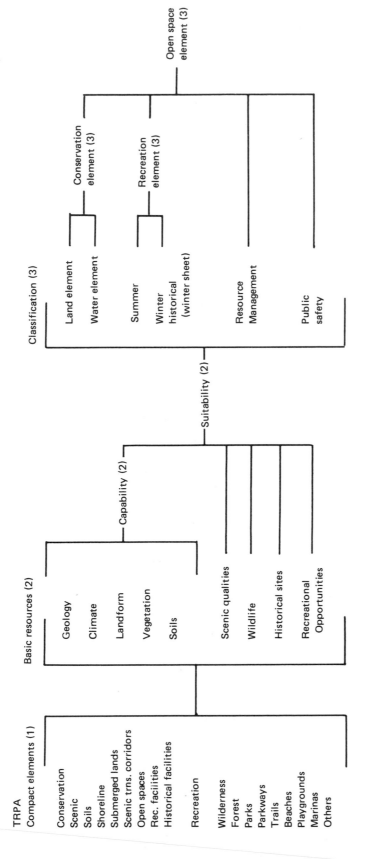

(1) Public Law 91-148, 91st Congress S118, Dec. 18, 1969.
(2) Prepared by the Forest Service, U.S. Department of Agriculture.
(3) Prepared by EDAW Inc.

FIGURE 8.1 Regional recreation resource inventory/Lake Tahoe, California.

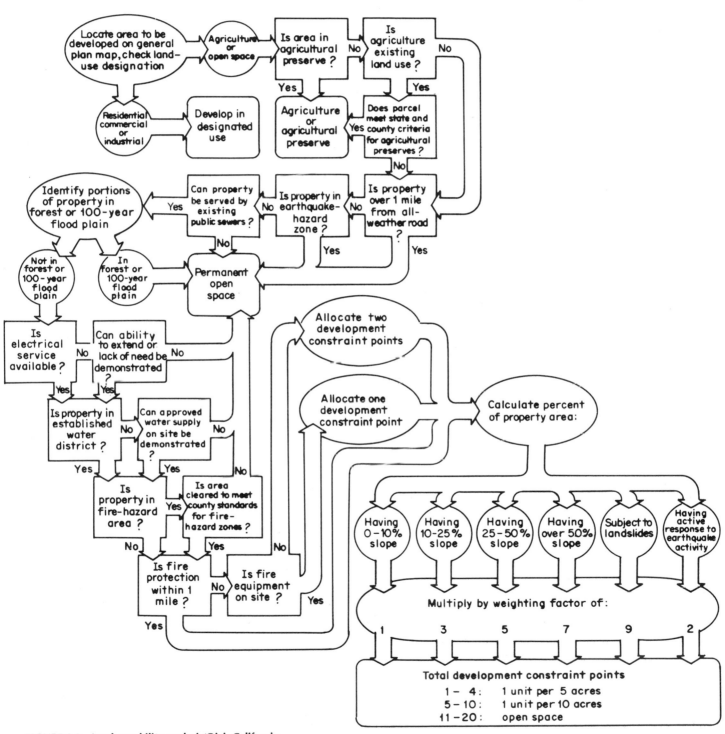

FIGURE 8.2 Land capability analysis/Ojai, California.

TABLE 8.1 | AREA CLASSIFICATION BY USE AND OWNERSHIP

Scientific Areas

Areas with scientific or historical values.
Park system includes outstanding/representative examples.
Value of areas does not depend on convenient access.
Preservation of values is paramount.

Scenic Areas

Preservation of aesthetic values is primary.
Park system includes outstanding/representative examples.
Access is not important.
Preservation of values dominates management.

Strategic Areas to Serve Residents/Tourists

Located to serve population concentrations.
Access is most important factor.
Recreation services are paramount.
Man-made developments may dominate the scenery.

Private Recreation Areas

Tourist accommodations
Organized camps/club membership
Resorts/commercial facilities

Semiprivate Recreation Areas

Facilities operated by community organizations.

Local Recreation Areas (Cities, Districts, Counties)

Street parks	Playfields
Playlots	Community centers
Playgrounds	Parkways
Neighborhood parks	Streets
County parks	Metropolitan parks
Special areas	Reservations

State Recreation Areas

Forests	Parkways
Regional parks	Monuments
Preserves	Fishing sites
Beaches	Scenic sites
Waysides	Wildlife areas

Federal Recreation Areas

National parks	Bureau of Reclamation
National monuments	Bureau of Land Management
National parkways	Fish and Wildlife Service
National seashores	Tennessee Valley Authority
National capital parks	Indian reservations
National forests	Military reservations

TABLE 8.2 | RECREATION LAND CLASSIFICATION SYSTEM

Class	Physical-environmental characteristics	Developments
I Intensive use density and development	High person-per-acre use. Generally but not always small in size due to space limitations. Setting may be either natural or man-made.	High level of facilities development which often requires large investment. Management primarily for recreation. May include recreation-related commercial facilities.
II Intermediate use density and development	Topographic features may be important. Sizes are variable. Attractive natural environment generally desirable, but may also be man-made. Environmental controls present but generally not overriding.	Median degree of development. Generally managed primarily for recreation. May include complementary commercial facilities such as luxury hotels, lodges, stores, ski-areas, dude ranches.
III Low use density and and development	Very low person-per-acre use. Attractive, neat-natural setting is of primary importance. Topographic features usually important. Varied and interest-landforms which are aesthetically pleasing.	Minimum developments and facilities for recreation. Area may be managed for recreation and other purposes. These lands often adjoin, surround, or are surrounded by other classes, thus serving as a buffer. May also serve compatible nonrecreation activities such as grazing, lumbering.

Source: U.S. Bureau of Outdoor Recreation, *Nationwide Outdoor Recreation Plan* (first draft), February 1973, chap. 12, p. 41.

type for use with remote sensing techniques, (2) resource management objectives and gross acres of ownership for use in the management of areas or systems, (3) administrative jurisdiction, for use in describing responsibility or authority, (4) user accessibility, social needs, and special significance for use in describing demand or mobility, (5) recreation activity classification for use in describing participation patterns, and (6) facilities to support activities for use in describing the design load of areas.

Criteria for Open Space Preservation

Most park and recreation areas are associated with a regional or local open space system. Chapter 4 describes the functions and classification of open space. These classifications can be rationalized with criteria to describe areas of critical importance for open space preservation. The following criteria or questions can be used to develop policy alternatives and coordinate public or private efforts to preserve open space:

- *Safety*

1 Is the area or site subject to natural or man-made hazards that would be detrimental to life and property if they were developed to urban uses?

2 Does the area present existing or potential hazards such as (a) earth slippage or subsidence or other geological hazards, (b) flooding from storm runoff or tidal conditions, (c) fire in brush or timber, and (d) proximity to airport runways, military bases, storage of explosives, or other man-made hazards?

- *Health and Social Welfare*

1 Does the proposed area enhance and protect the health and social welfare of the public?

2 Does the site provide open space opportunity within built-up urban places, especially disadvantaged minority and low-income areas?

3 Does the proposed site correct deficiencies in park and recreation needs?

4 Does the site or area provide a buffer between incompatible land uses?

- *Ecological Balance*

1 Will the area preserve or protect ecological balance?

2 Areas that generally satisfy this criterion are water recharge areas; estuaries, marshes, and tidal pools; beaches, rivers, and stream beds; watershed areas; soil erosion control areas; wildlife refuges; and land for sewage treatment/solid waste disposal.

- *Unique Site*

Does the area include a site which is unique or nonreplaceable, such as a scenic area, historic site, cultural and archaeological site, or site with unique geological formations?

- *Recreation Area*

Does the area have potential for recreational activities related to natural resources such as beaches, desert, bodies of water, mountains, or hunting areas?

- *Urban Shaping and Improvement*

1 Does the proposed site or area shape or improve urban development?

2 Does this open space provide for the separation of communities or prevent urban sprawl?

3 Does the open space encourage more economical or desirable urban developement?

4 Does the open space prevent the spread of urban blight?

5 Does the area discourage population growth?

Park Unit Classification System

A classification of units is necessary to inventory existing opportunities in a park and recreation system. This classification establishes a framework for planning, design, and management. It describes what to expect from each type of park in terms of size, facilities, and service levels.

The park unit classification system also allows comparison between similar communities and capital budgeting for the acquisition, development, maintenance, and use of each park type. It can be the basis of standards for managing different types of parks. It can also increase public involvement in the planning process because the use criteria for a site or system should be based on natural factors, user needs, cost-effectiveness, or political values that people can consider.

Several classification systems are in common use. Chapter 7 describes a system oriented to the planning service area or planning unit. Three other systems are outlined here.

NATIONAL RECREATION AND PARK ASSOCIATION

This system spans the urban and regional scale but is most useful at the urban scale. It describes these basic designations for a public park and recreation system:

Playlots Areas of less than one acre serving the special needs of portions of a neighborhood with active and passive activities as space permits.

Neighborhood Parks   Areas of five acres or more, normally adjacent to an elementary school serving the general needs of a neighborhood population for active and passive recreation.

District Parks   Areas of 20 acres or more, normally adjacent to a junior or senior high school serving the general and specialized needs of more than one neighborhood for active and passive recreation.

Metropolitan Parks   Areas of over 100 acres centrally located, if possible, to serve the general and special needs of the entire community or metropolitan area for active and passive recreation.

Regional Parks   Areas of over 250 acres, normally administered by a county or regional park authority serving citywide or metropolitan needs for primarily passive and extensive, or resource-oriented, recreation.

The NRPA classification system also includes a category for special facilities such as parkways, swimming pools, golf courses, marinas, and zoological parks. These facilities are normally associated with one of the above categories, but can stand alone. This system is widely used and typically described with the criteria in Appendix D, Part 2.

MARYLAND NATIONAL CAPITAL PARK AND PLANNING COMMISSION   This system is useful at the urban and regional scale because it is sensitive to both user and resource areas. It also accommodates a wide range of specialized facilities such as historical/cultural parks and details the types of facilities appropriate for each type of park. Table 8.3 and Figure 8.3 summarize the major features of this system.

EAST BAY REGIONAL PARK DISTRICT   This system is useful at the metropolitan scale and is resource-oriented. It accommodates a wide range of specialized facilities in large areas with a natural or scenic character. This system is most useful at the regional scale in areas with superlative or unique natural resources. It also pro-

---

TABLE 8.3 | REGIONAL PARK CLASSIFICATION SYSTEM

COMMUNITY RECREATION AND URBAN BEAUTIFICATION PARK

Neighborhood Parks

Urban Parks.   Small parks serving central business districts, highly urban areas (including new towns), or commercial districts.

Residential Neighborhood Parks.   Small, walk-to parks, providing informal leisure opportunities and recreation in heavily populated residential areas.

Local Parks

Ten ± acre parks that provide ball fields and other programmed and unprogrammed recreation facilities for local residents.

Community Parks

Larger parks (approximately twice the size of local parks) that provide clustered recreation facilities.

REGIONAL USE PARKS

Regional Parks

Large parks of more than 200 acres that provide a large range of recreational opportunities and facilities.

CONSERVATION PARKS

Stream Valley Parks

Interconnected parks along major stream valleys providing conservation and recreation needs.

Conservation Area Parks

Parks that preserve areas of significant value from encroachment by residential or commercial developments and uses.

SPECIAL PARKS

Recreational Parks

Fifty ± acre parks that provide concentrations of athletic facilities for specialized programming for all county residents.

Historic/Cultural Parks

Areas acquired and maintained for their historic or cultural significance, and which vary in size and use.

Other

A miscellaneous category for parks that do not fit other categories.

Source: Maryland National Park and Planning Commission, *Park, Recreation and Open Space Plan,* 1977, p. 84.

FACILITY [1]	TYPE OF PARK								
	COMMUNITY RECREATION & URBAN BEAUTIFICATION				SPECIAL USE		REGIONAL USE	CONSERVATION	
	NEIGHBORHOOD		LOCAL	COMMUNITY	RECREATIONAL	HISTORIC CULTURAL	REGIONAL	STREAM VALLEY [2]	CONSERVATION AREA
	URBAN	RESIDENTIAL							
PLAYGROUND EQUIPMENT	◐	●	●	●	●		●	◐	
TENNIS COURTS		◐	●	●	●		◐		
ENCLOSED TENNIS CTS.				◐	●		◐		
MULTI-USE COURTS	◐	◐	●	●	●		◐		
OTHER SMALL COURTS	◐	◐	◐	◐	●		◐		
PICNIC AREAS	◐	◐	●	●		◐	●	●	◐
BEAUTIFICATION LANDSCAPING	●	◐							
DECORATIVE FOUNTAINS	◐	◐							
SHELTER		◐	◐	◐	◐				
SMALL REC. BUILDING		◐	◐	◐	◐				
COMMUNITY BUILDING [3]				◐	◐				
ATHLETIC FIELDS			●	●	◐		◐		
PLAYFIELD [4]		●	◐	◐					
INTERPRETIVE NATURE CENTERS						●	●	◐	●
HIKER-BIKER TRAILS		◐	◐	◐	◐	●	●	●	●
BRIDLE PATH						◐	●	●	◐
EQUESTRIAN CENTER						◐	◐		◐
PUBLIC SWIMMING POOL				◐	◐		◐		
ICE RINK					◐		◐		
GOLF COURSES					◐		◐	◐	
WATER ORIENTED RECREATION							◐	◐	◐
CHILDRENS ZOO							◐		
MINI TRAIN TROLLEY							◐		
AMPHITHEATER					◐	◐	◐		◐
SITTING AREA	●	●	●	●	●	●	●		●

KEY
◐ Facility may be located in this type of park, if need or interest is shown.
● Facility is generally located in this type of park.
□ Except under unusual circumstances the facility will not be provided in this type of park.

1 Includes M-NCPPC facilities, only school facilities are not contained in matrix.
2 Other facilities may be located on adjacent usable land.
3 Large multi-roomed center, often with a gym.
4 Grassy area, no backstop, non-regulation.

FIGURE 8.3 Proposed park facility matrix/Maryland National Capital Park and Planning Commission.

vides for specialized, user-oriented parks that do not duplicate the responsibilities or park classifications of urban park systems. Appendix D, Part 3 summarizes the major features of this system.

RESOURCE ANALYSIS TECHNIQUES

Resource analysis techniques have been used to establish the suitability of sites or corridors for open space preservation. The potential of open space for recreation use can be described with reasonable precision. Each site can be evaluated in terms of its resource characteristics, landscape character, and ecological capability for different impacts of use, design, and management (Conservation Foundation, 1967).

The techniques described here have essentially the same characteristics, although they were developed by different people for different situations. They all describe the resource base with physical or biological characteristics that can be used in the planning and design process to establish the most suitable use for a specific ecosystem or site.

Although each technique uses a different set of measures or descriptions in a different sequence, all inventory and classify the valuable or irreversible natural and cultural qualities of the environment. The key concepts are human values and environmental quality based on *ecological determinism*. These concepts raise three central questions: (1) how to identify the elements that lend

TABLE 8.4 | RESOURCE DEVELOPMENT APPROACH

1 The total site for analysis is subdivided into smaller units of physiographic differentiation based on a gradient scale of climate and landform features.

2 A possible range of general land uses is determined and physical requirements for each are identified.

3 Use potential is ranked at two area levels under various management conditions and using separate value scales.

   a At the local level: Site types and phases are evaluated for natural groupings of activities related to the features within the unit on the basis of assumed levels of physiographic limits to production according to use capability, suitability, and feasibility.

   b At the community level: Patterns of site types and phases with similar landform characteristics are regrouped into landscape units to provide a basis for comparative evaluation of feasible uses. The following are again ranked before making a recommendation: use capability, use suitability, and use feasibility.

4 The land use activity with the highest feasibility ranking in a landscape unit is recommended as a major or comajor use.

5 Maps are prepared showing recommended multiple major and comajor uses for each landscape unit.

TABLE 8.5 | LANDSCAPE CORRIDOR APPROACH

1 Given a total study area.

2 Uses to be planned for are identified and use criteria are established.

3 A case study area is selected in which:

   a Resources that meet the use criteria are identified.

   b Major resources are inventoried and located on transparent overlays.

   c Patterns of major resources from each overlay are combined.

   d Additional resources are inventoried and located on transparent overlays.

   e A variety of patterns may be identified for special purposes from additional resources.

   f Additional resources are combined into a single pattern.

   g Patterns of major and additional resources are compared and correlated.

4 Major resources are inventoried for the total study area.

5 Additional resources are inventoried for the total study area.

6 Points are assigned to major and additional resources.

7 Points are totaled to identify relative priority areas.

8 Demand for planned uses is established and final priorities and areas are defined.

9 Limitations of each priority area to specific uses are identified and specific uses are assigned.

quality to the physical environment, (2) how to analyze and incorporate these elements into the planning, design, and decision process, and (3) what trade-offs are necessary or desirable in a world of limited resources and competing needs.

The ethical aspects of these questions represent difficult challenges to the planner because the problem transcends the traditional context of resource planning. These challenges require the planner, decision maker, and citizen to develop alternative courses of action and consider the irreversible effects of these actions on both the landscape and society.

Resource Development Approach

In 1961, G. Angus Hills developed a resource mapping system for Canadian lands based on (1) a physiographic classification of land into homogeneous units, and (2) an evaluation of the physiographic classes on the basis of their potential for alternative uses under several management conditions. This system accepts natural processes as a means of achieving human ends. It is oriented to development, instead of preservation, of resources. An outline of this procedure is shown in Table 8.4.

This system has utility to determine the potential productivity of land. It describes the capability, suitability, and feasibility of physiographic land units that can be used for recreation. This technique is useful in assessing the potential of dynamic ecosystems such as lakes or beaches.

Landscape Corridor Approach

In 1963, Philip Lewis developed a technique of resource analysis based on (1) making a detailed inventory and mapping natural and man-made features in the landscape, (2) describing these features or resource patterns in the geographic framework of a corridor, and (3) assigning priorities to specific visual and natural resources with actual or potential use for recreation. This pioneering effort established the concepts of visual quality, diversity, and resource corridors. It also developed the techniques of overlay mapping and resource evaluation by a numerical ranking system.

This system combines the techniques of the natural scientist, planner, and landscape architect to describe the visual, natural, and cultural features of a landscape unit. The landscape unit provides a physical and ecological unit for organizing information that can be used for planning, design, and management. The landscape unit or corridor becomes a perceptual and physical space

TABLE 8.6 | ECOLOGICAL APPROACH

1 Given a total study area.

2 An ecological inventory is prepared and interpreted.

   a Natural and cultural resources are inventoried and mapped.

   b Inventory data is interpreted to reveal dominant prospective land uses for each discrete area in the total study area.

      (1) Data relevant to prospective land uses is interpreted.

      (2) Intrinsic suitability maps are produced.

   c A value is attributed to every land area in the total study area for *all* prospective land uses.

      (1) A system for rating intrinsic resources is established.

      (2) Compatible and incompatible land uses are grouped.

3 Economic inventory is prepared and interpreted.

4 Criteria for visibility are established.

5 Criteria for form and design are established.

6 Powers necessary to realize the plan are acquired.

people identify with and use for a wide range of recreation opportunities. An outline of this procedure is shown in Table 8.5. A typical application of this approach is shown in Figure 8.4.

Ecological Approach

In 1966, Ian McHarg developed an approach to resource analysis based on ecological determinism. He demonstrated that (1) elaborate mapping techniques could be used to identify natural processes, (2) these natural processes had values and relationships, (3) these values and relationships could be described in terms of ecological cause and effect, and (4) these causes and effects could be used to predict the ecological consequences of design alternatives. This technique is summarized in Table 8.6. A typical application of this approach is shown in Figure 8.5.

This approach combines the skills of the ecologist, planner, and landscape architect to focus on natural systems. It uses natural factors and processes to determine which areas are most suitable for urban development or open space preservation. The mapping, analysis, and ranking techniques developed in many applications of this approach represent a very sophisticated approach to recreation resource analysis.

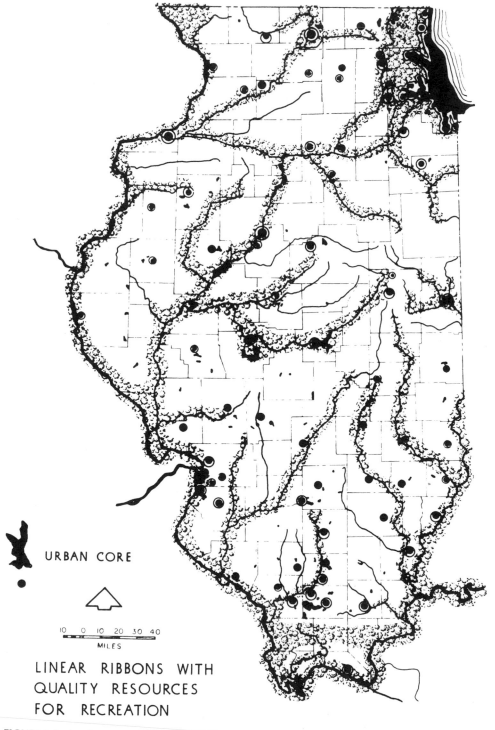

URBAN CORE

10 0 10 20 30 40
MILES

LINEAR RIBBONS WITH
QUALITY RESOURCES
FOR RECREATION

FIGURE 8.4 Landscape corridor approach: application at the state level/Illinois.

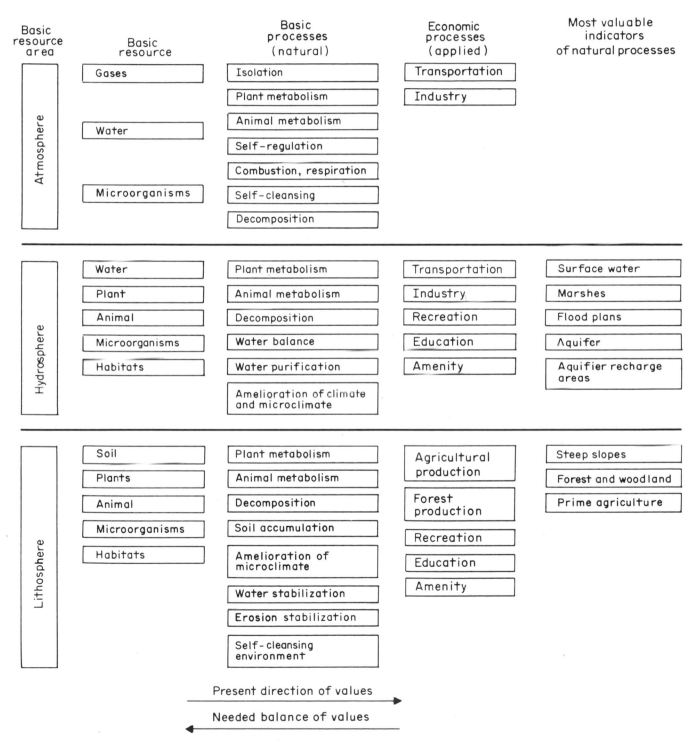

FIGURE 8.5 Ecological approach: application at the metropolitan level/Green Spring and Worthington Valleys of Baltimore County, Maryland.

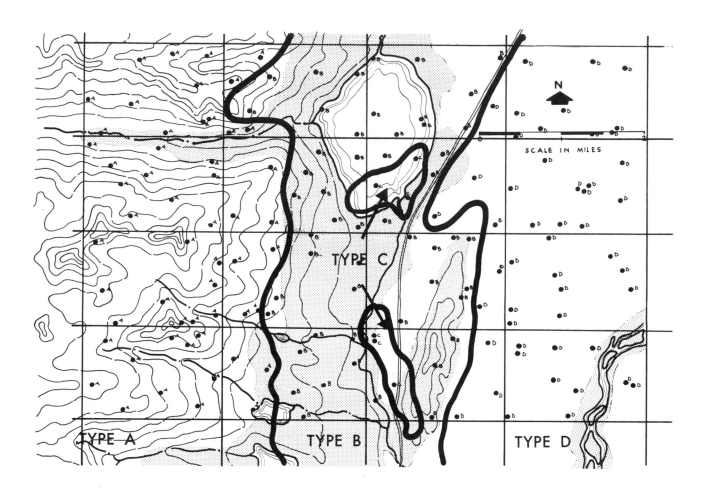

Measuring Recreation Resources by the Random Point Method

Directions:

1. Place a grid (ten random points in each rectangle) over the planning area.
2. Describe the location of each random point by a system of coordinates.
3. Determine the characteristics (slope, land use, scenic quality, etc.) of each random point and enter this data on mechanical tabulation cards.
4. Sort the cards according to the characteristics that define each major recreation resource type (A, B, C, or D).
5. Prepare a map of the major resource types and calculate the area (in acres) of each resource.

FIGURE 8.6   User resource planning method: random point technique.

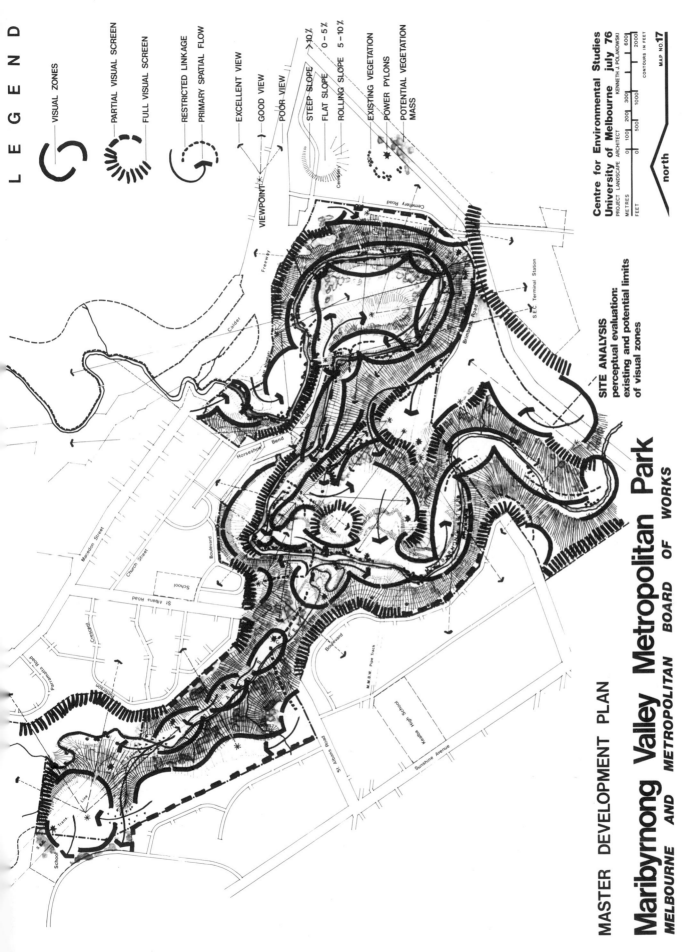

LEGEND

VISUAL ZONES

PARTIAL VISUAL SCREEN

FULL VISUAL SCREEN

RESTRICTED LINKAGE

PRIMARY SPATIAL FLOW

EXCELLENT VIEW

GOOD VIEW

POOR VIEW

VIEWPOINT

STEEP SLOPE   >10%

FLAT SLOPE   0 – 5%

ROLLING SLOPE   5 – 10%

EXISTING VEGETATION

POWER PYLONS

POTENTIAL VEGETATION
MASS

Centre for Environmental Studies
University of Melbourne   july 76
PROJECT LANDSCAPE ARCHITECT   KENNETH J. POLAKOWSKI
METRES   0   100   200   300   600
FEET   0   500   1000   2000
CONTOURS IN FEET

MAP NO.17

north

SITE ANALYSIS
perceptual evaluation:
existing and potential limits
of visual zones

MASTER DEVELOPMENT PLAN

Maribyrnong Valley Metropolitan Park
MELBOURNE AND METROPOLITAN BOARD OF WORKS

FIGURE 8.7   Perceptual site analysis/Melbourne, Australia.

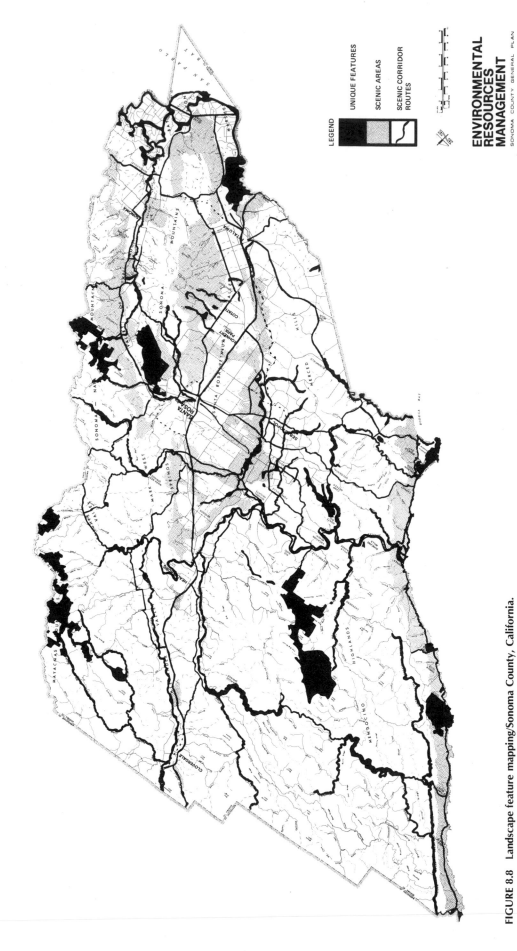

LEGEND

UNIQUE FEATURES

SCENIC AREAS

SCENIC CORRIDOR
ROUTES

ENVIRONMENTAL
RESOURCES
MANAGEMENT
SONOMA COUNTY GENERAL PLAN

FIGURE 8.8 Landscape feature mapping/Sonoma County, California.

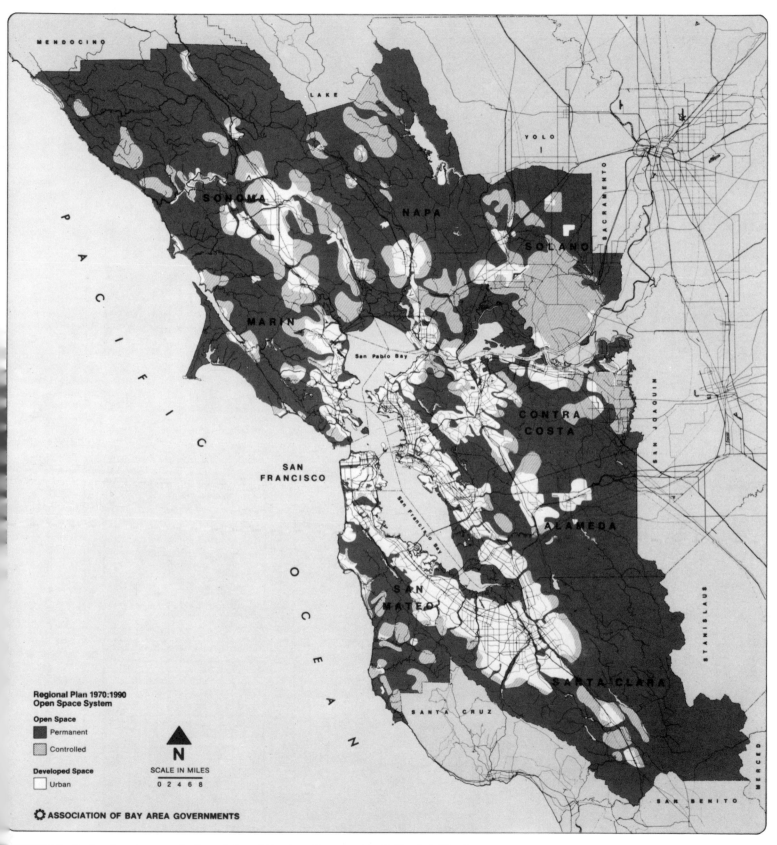

FIGURE 8.9 Regional open space plan/Association of Bay Area Governments, Oakland, California.

OVERLAY

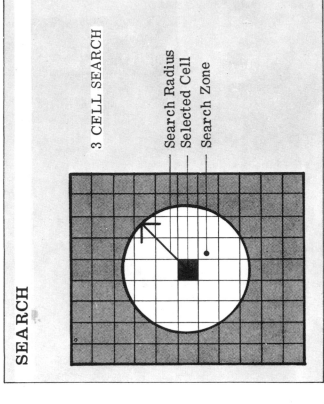

RESCALED DATA MAPS

SUITABILITY MAP

SEARCH

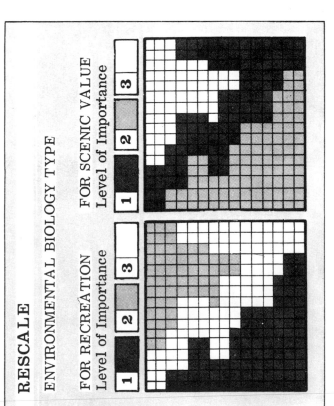

3 CELL SEARCH

Search Radius
Selected Cell
Search Zone

DATA MAPS

ENVIRONMENTAL BIOLOGY TYPE

Horizontal Coordinates

Vertical Coordinate

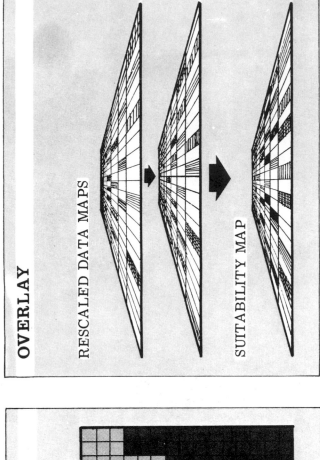

1 Cell

Oak

Chapparel

Grassland

RESCALE

ENVIRONMENTAL BIOLOGY TYPE

FOR RECREATION
Level of Importance

FOR SCENIC VALUE
Level of Importance

1 2 3

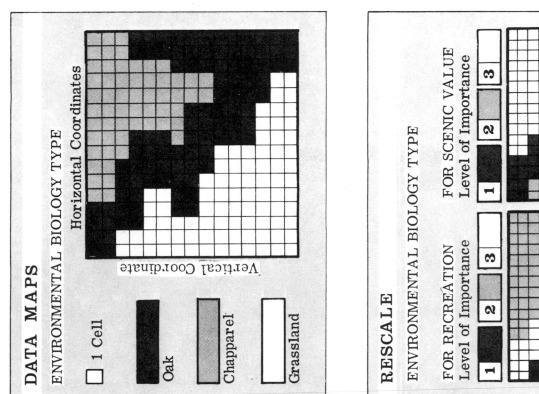

FIGURE 8.10   Recreation suitability mapping data process/Santa Barbara County, California.

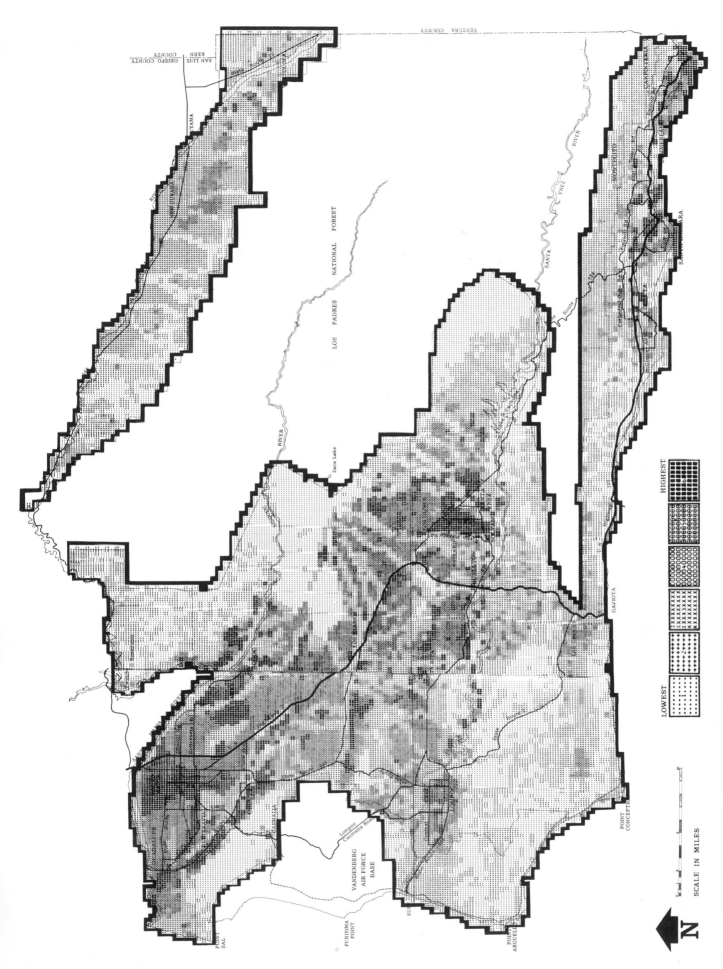

FIGURE 8.11 Recreation suitability map/Santa Barbara County, California.

User Resource Planning Method

The user resource planning method was developed in 1960 for recreation planning in California. Chapter 3 outlines the basic steps and relationships. This chapter summarizes the inventory and classification aspects of this method, which (1) divides each planning area into resource types by environmental characteristics, (2) relates the desired recreation experience to resource types, and (3) develops planning guidelines based on user resource requirements.

Recreation resource types are described with a random point mapping method of landscape characteristics such as slope, topography, climate, flora, fauna, scenic quality, land use, and history. This mapping method assumes any point selected at random represents an area surrounding that point. The characteristics of an area can be assigned to the random points selected to represent the area. The amount of area each random point represents is determined by the number of random points per unit area. This procedure is outlined in Figure 8.6. The result is a map showing major recreation resources in the following categories: natural reservations, natural park areas, developed park areas, urban areas, and open space.

The categories on this map are used to develop planning guides related to the location, environmental characteristics, and carrying capacities of recreation areas. These planning guides are use to (1) assess the landscape personality of a region, and (2) determine the influence of design on these resources. The result is an environmentally sensitive classification system based on a systematic inventory of resource characteristics.

Other Methods

A wide range of other methods that incorporate aspects of the above techniques are in use, including (1) forest landscape description and inventories, developed by the U.S. Forest Service (Litton, 1968), (2) constraint mapping, developed by EDAW, Inc. (Schaal, 1972), (3) visual quality management system, developed by the U.S. Forest Service (1973), and (4) recreation suitability model, developed for Santa Barbara County (Royston, et al., 1974). Although these methods are oriented to large-scale, nonurban landscapes, aspects of each are now being successfully used at the metropolitan or county level in urbanizing areas.

For example, Figure 8.7 shows a perceptual or usual site analysis for a metropolitan park. Figure 8.8 shows an example of landscape mapping at the county scale. Figure 8.9 shows how permanent open space can be designated at the regional scale.

The Santa Barbara County resource evaluation system is an excellent example of computerizing environmental data. This system uses a suitability model to map, classify, and analyze recreation resources. Figures 8.10 and 8.11 show some aspects of this sophisticated technique. Other aspects of this model will be described in Chapter 14.

9 | RECREATION DEMAND

One of the least understood and most abused aspects of recreation planning is the concept of demand. Although recent advances in methodology and sophisticated models have improved the state of the art, the value of these models as a basis for public policy or site-specific design is questionable.

At one extreme, there is growing scepticism about the role of quantitative techniques for public decision making and design. Critics point out the difficulties of attempting to quantify, relate, and project the complex variables of recreation and environment. They assert that the decision and design process must be conditioned by "judgment," and those who believe in quantitative demand models are unrealistic.

At the other extreme, some regard the quantitative aspects of demand as a meaningful reflection of interest or participation in recreation. This school of thought is expressed in interpretations of "demand" as what people will or can do given the opportunity. Proponents assert factors such as the supply or distribution of resources, cost, access, and other factors can be objectively measured and projected for decision making and design. They believe models have qualifications, but are useful in assessing the consequences of alternatives.

In the absence of objective measures of recreation behavior, planners have taken two approaches to the notion of recreation demand. The first is oriented to what planners think people ought to do; the second tries to find out what people want to do. Methodologies have been developed to support both approaches. The gap between attempting to assess what people *want* to do or *ought* to do parallels the extreme viewpoints on demand.

Both themes are common in the literature and practice. This chapter will not reconcile these extreme views. It will describe selected aspects of both views and extend the behavioral framework for recreation planning described in Chapter 7. This approach to demand provides a range of concepts and methods that can apply to many different situations.

LEVELS OF RECREATION DEMAND

Three levels of demand are conspicuous in the planning process. All are related but have different measures, methodologies, and variables. Each level also has related, but different, implications for the planning, design, and management of recreation systems and sites.

National Policy Orientation

Recreation is a social activity. Policies with regard to recreation should be viewed as they affect or are affected by other social and economic policies. Recreation policy decisions not only affect the availability of resources, facilities, and programs for a given set of leisure activities, but can relate to a wide range of important national issues such as population growth, economic development, energy conservation, and cultural change. Until recreation planners have a better understanding of recreation demand, the coordination of especially local recreation policy with national policy issues is a very complex and ambitious objective.

Demand for Alternative Types of Recreation

Between considering recreation as an element of social policy and site-specific development is the identification, measurement, and projection of the demand for alternative types of recreation. This level of demand prompts choices or trade-offs between the types, quantities, and general location or access of opportunities. It requires recreation planners to know or find out what people want, and what opportunities would best satisfy these wants.

This aspect of recreation demand requires decisions on (1) categories of resources, facilities, or programs to be provided (2) strategies for assessing responsibility, cost, and operation, (3) implementation programs or priorities, and (4) the geographic distribution, access, and effectiveness of recreation resources for general and special populations. It is most conspicuous in national and state recreation plans that aggregate and project activities by:

- Goals and activities of the user
- Degree or level of skill needed
- Types of participants for specific activities
- Resource base necessary to support the activity
- Access to the resource by user populations
- Degree of development/management to support the activity
- Uniqueness of a resource to provide recreation opportunities

These factors are commonly determined by (1) using the political process as a barometer of demand, (2) analysis of participation rates for specific activities or populations, and (3) identification of the recreation needs of general and special populations with standards or survey methods.

A major shortcoming of this process is the limited scope of most efforts. Most national and state recreation plans still focus on outdoor, organized, or programmed activities in public recreation areas when a balanced view should include indoor, self-programmed activities in private recreation areas.

Demand for Site-Specific Recreation

The purpose of recreation planning is to create opportunities for people to engage in activities at specific sites. Planning for a specific site requires estimates of demand to help select the best site and provide the most appropriate type or mix or recreation resources, facilities, and programs. Identification of potential users and a detailed consideration of site characteristics are the basis of demand estimates for a specific site, facility, or program.

Each site or alternative site has special constraints and advantages that are assessed in terms of social and physical factors. The service area is established in terms of access time and mode. This aspect of demand requires (1) benefit-cost analysis of each site or feature, (2) analysis of relative demand levels for alternative activities or facilities, (3) on-site and home surveys of users and nonusers to determine levels of preference and satisfaction, and (4) the application of standards to determine the design load, human, or natural carrying capacity and social need for specific opportunities.

This level of recreation demand is most conspicuous in the preconstruction and postconstruction studies of a specific project to site. These studies are commonly associated with the area master plan and environmental impact statement on that plan. They require systematic user surveys, extensive public participation, and a detailed analysis of alternatives.

The site-specific level of recreation demand is the most difficult, time-consuming, and costly because it must translate the concept of demand into reality. This task requires an understanding of user-resource relationships that has not been common in most recreation planning efforts to date.

Types of Demand

There are three types of demand which condition the use, design, and management of recreation resources. The existing and future dimensions of each type of demand should be considered in the preparation of recreation plans or the design of projects.

Latent demand is the recreation demand inherent in the population, but not reflected in the use of existing facilities. Participation can be expected, if adequate facilities, access, and information are provided. This type of demand is based on the model of leisure choice described in Chapter 7. It translates the hierarchy of human needs shown in Figure 9.1 into resource-, image-, or leisure-directed desires that can be described with measures of user preference and satisfaction.

Latent demand is the basis for the argument that supply creates demand. This argument suggests people will use available opportunities if they are provided. The planner's role is to provide a diverse set of opportunities with the expectation of reasonable use. For example, if bicycle or jogging paths are provided in cities, people will use them. The same would be true for social spaces or water features in urban parks (Figure 9.2).

Induced demand is latent demand which can be stimulated by public conditioning through the mass media or the educational process. Induced demand exploits latent demand by encouraging people to change their recreation patterns. Although the media and educational process are commonly thought to be the most effective ways of inducing demand, Table 9.1 shows planning and management methods which can change recreation use patterns.

These methods should be considered in estimating demand. For example, if it were desirable to encourage camping with tents instead of trailers or sailing instead of power boating at a particular site or planning unit, this could be tried by applying some of these methods. The private sector has commonly used these methods to induce demand. It is time for the public sector to apply these methods in the planning process to assess alternatives or change use patterns.

Expressed demand is consumption or participation in terms of existing recreation opportunities. It describes what people do instead of what they would like to do (latent demand) or can be conditioned to do (induced demand). The differences between expressed and latent demand can also be described in terms of participation and preference for selected activities (Figure 9.3).

Expressed demand is often the expression of latent or induced demand but not always. It only indicates participation at prevailing opportunity conditions and normally omits considerations of price, supply, access, skill, or equipment necessary and user satisfaction with the recreation experience.

FIGURE 9.1 Hierarchy of human needs.

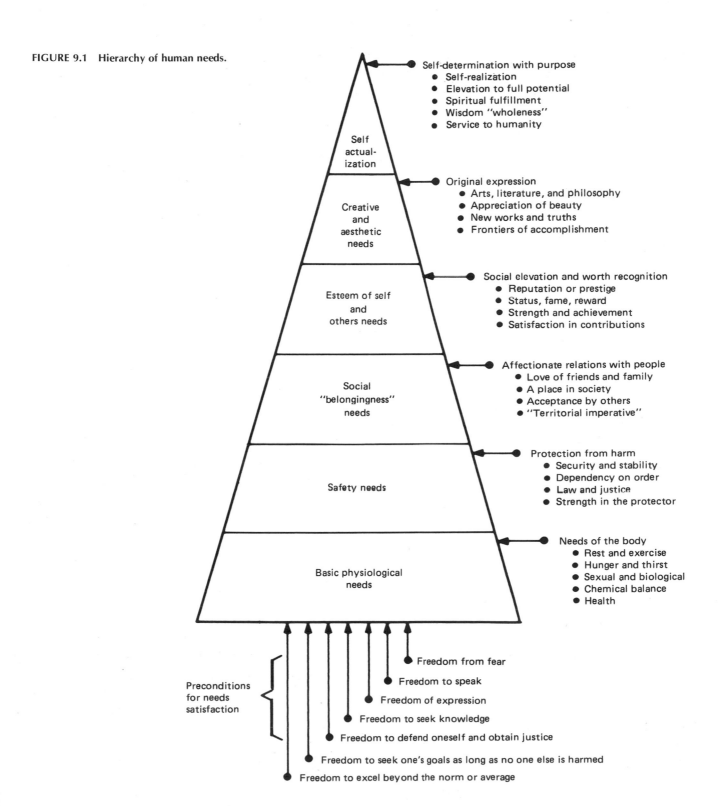

START BY 1 GATHERING INFORMATION.....on the

number & location of cyclists & their current patterns of use, including trip type, purpose, generation rates, length, travel time, origin, destination, time of day, journey times, parking facilities & route preferences. The most effective way of reaching a large user group will be by the conduct of a simple survey directed toward school, university & college students, & administered with the co-operation of local teaching authorities. From this information the need for bikeways in a particular area may be determined, & a map of existing preferred routes prepared.

2 FORMULATE GOALS AND OBJECTIVES

.....within the framework of basic principles of safety, mobility, efficiency & pleasure. Goals for the bikeway should establish the broad aims of the system; objectives should be related to practical & purposeful means of achieving the goals.

3 INVESTIGATE THE PHYSICAL ENVIRONMENT

An inventory of the physical environment should be documented to include topography, public open space, areas of vegetation, community & commercial activity centres, land use characteristics, publicly owned and/or controlled land, pedestrian movement, hierarchy of roads (on an intensity of use basis) & the existing public transport system.

AND 4 LOCATE EXISTING FACILITIES

Take an inventory of existing bicycle facilities & their use. These may include bicycle racks located at schools, swimming pools, and railway stations, velodromes, parks, bicycle hire facilities, paths & trails.

YOU ARE NOW READY TO

5 IDENTIFY OPPORTUNITIES

.....where bikeways may be considered within the community. Physical assets which may be adapted to bikeways should be considered & potential conflicts with pedestrians & vehicular traffic flows noted. The need for grade separation, potential open space links & other issues in structuring the bikeway will be determined.

AND 6 DEVELOP ALTERNATIVE PROPOSALS

.....using the design criteria from Chapter 3. Testing the proposals against the established goals & objectives is then required to enable alternative schemes to be developed with their advantages & disadvantages clearly indicated.

THEN ... *CHECK BACK*

IT IS NOW POSSIBLE TO 7 SELECT BIKEWAY ROUTE

Alternative proposals should be presented to representatives of community groups, council & other relevant bodies for comment, modification & selection of the preferred route. Local cyclists familiar with the area could test the route & report on its effectiveness.

AND 8 IMPLEMENT THE PLAN

Construction of the selected route involves the detailed design, costing & phasing of the bikeway according to an overall policy of finance & management.

FIGURE 9.2   Bicycle paths in cities/New South Wales, Australia.

ACTIVITY	PERCENT OF POPULATION

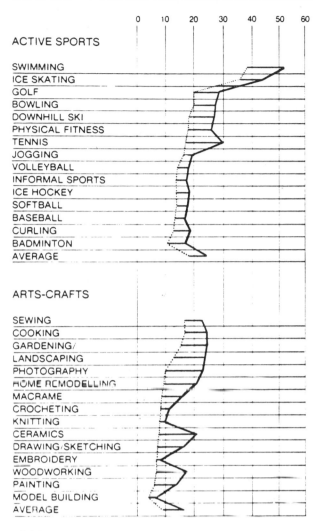

ACTIVE SPORTS

SWIMMING
ICE SKATING
GOLF
BOWLING
DOWNHILL SKI
PHYSICAL FITNESS
TENNIS
JOGGING
VOLLEYBALL
INFORMAL SPORTS
ICE HOCKEY
SOFTBALL
BASEBALL
CURLING
BADMINTON
AVERAGE

ARTS-CRAFTS

SEWING
COOKING
GARDENING/
LANDSCAPING
PHOTOGRAPHY
HOME REMODELLING
MACRAME
CROCHETING
KNITTING
CERAMICS
DRAWING/SKETCHING
EMBROIDERY
WOODWORKING
PAINTING
MODEL BUILDING
AVERAGE

ACTIVITY	PERCENT OF POPULATION

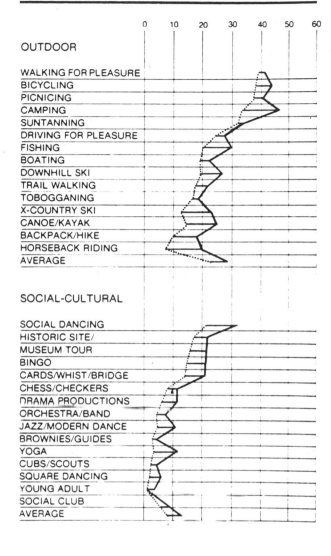

OUTDOOR

WALKING FOR PLEASURE
BICYCLING
PICNICING
CAMPING
SUNTANNING
DRIVING FOR PLEASURE
FISHING
BOATING
DOWNHILL SKI
TRAIL WALKING
TOBOGGANING
X-COUNTRY SKI
CANOE/KAYAK
BACKPACK/HIKE
HORSEBACK RIDING
AVERAGE

SOCIAL-CULTURAL

SOCIAL DANCING
HISTORIC SITE/
MUSEUM TOUR
BINGO
CARDS/WHIST/BRIDGE
CHESS/CHECKERS
DRAMA PRODUCTIONS
ORCHESTRA/BAND
JAZZ/MODERN DANCE
BROWNIES/GUIDES
YOGA
CUBS/SCOUTS
SQUARE DANCING
YOUNG ADULT
SOCIAL CLUB
AVERAGE

LEGEND

.... PARTICIPATION
— — PREFERENCE

FIGURE 9.3 Participation and preference for selected activities/Edmonton, Alberta, Canada. *Participation* indicates that the respondents participated in the activity regularly for a season or more within the preceding three years. *Preference* indicates that the respondents are not currently participating in an activity but desire to. *(Edmonton Parks and Recreation Survey, 1977.)*

TABLE 9.1 | METHODS OF CHANGING RECREATION USE PATTERNS

Methods of Managing the Recreation Resource	Methods of Influencing the Recreation Users
Improve or restrict access	Increase awareness of choice
Extend time use periods	Publicize selected areas
Rehabilitate site to mitigate adverse human impact	Limit size of groups
Decentralize facilities to reduce use concentration	Limit length of stay
Zone by activity, use intensity, and time	Limit types of activities permitted
Increase quality of facilities	Establish use rationing and reservation systems
Improve design of facilities	Establish user fees, permits, and registration
Improve operation of facilities	Provide guided tours and structured experiences
Rotate use areas	Enforce rules and regulations
Remove facilities	Interpret site or experience
Close areas or facilities	Provide supervision and program leadership

Projecting Expressed Demand

The myth persists that planners can multiply population figures by recreation activity participation rates, called "demand," and use these figures to calculate recreation needs. Computers have made this an easy trap to fall into. Most national and state recreation plans over the past decade have reinforced this method of projecting demand, which has these major shortcomings:

COST If the notion of demand is based on price, many activities are relatively free, difficult to assign market values to, underpriced, and subsidized. It is unrealistic not to account for price in assessing the demand for recreation in a market economy.

SUPPLY Expressed demand only indicates quantities or participation at the prevailing opportunity conditions. What people do depends on what is available, or supply generates demand. To assume existing levels of participation as an indication of future demand implies providing more of the same type of opportunities and perpetuating imbalances.

DEMOGRAPHIC DIFFERENCES The notion of describing the recreation participation of an "average" person or geographic area and generalizing this to all people or areas is meaningless. It does not account for significant social, economic, or environmental differences in the population which are critical in forecasting demand or determining need for populations living in diverse metropolitan or suburban areas. To assume significant demographic differences do not exist is politically unrepresentative and statistical nonsense (Figure 9.4).

NONUSE Most studies of expressed demand only measure users in public parks for selected activities. They omit nonusers and private recreation opportunities that constitute a major segment of how and where the majority of people spend their leisure time (Gold, 1972). To describe and project demand in this way is misleading and unrealistic.

EXPERIENCE Recreation behavior is conditioned by previous experience, custom, or awareness. The notion

FIGURE 9.4 Conceptual neighborhood life cycle/Edmonton, Alberta, Canada.

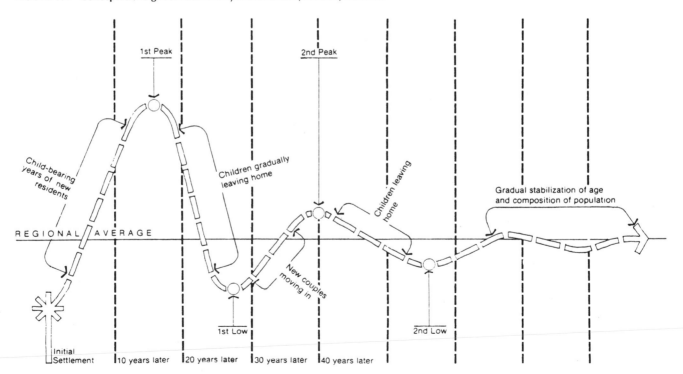

TABLE 9.2 | DEMAND FACTORS FOR A SPECIFIC RECREATION AREA

Factors Relating to the Potential Recreation Users

Total population in the service area

Geographic distribution/density of population

Demographic characteristics of population

Time budgets of population

Leisure customs or habits of population

Experience levels of population for specific activities

Awareness levels of recreation opportunities

Awareness levels of crime or deviant behavior

Factors Relating to the Recreation Area

Attractiveness as judged by the user

Management levels and practices

Availability of alternative sites

Carrying capacity and design load of area

Microclimate of the area

Natural and physical characteristics of area

Factors Relating Potential Users to the Recreation Area

Travel time and distance

Travel mode, cost, and convenience

Cost of supplies or equipment to use area

Cost of fees and charges to use area

Information about area

Status or image of area

Regulations to control behavior

---

of expressed demand generally omits any qualified or weighted analysis of these factors. It assumes no significant change in personal or group values or participation rates due to past or future levels of experience.

Most studies of expressed demand done prior to 1975 have the above shortcomings. They indicate some measure of existing use levels for selected activities, but are generally not a valid source of information for preparing a plan. These studies are even less reliable for forecasting future demand and should be used with great caution.

Factors of Demand

Factors of demand can be classified into the categories shown in Table 9.2 at the site level or into the categories shown in Table 9.3 at the systems level. Both tables show the type and range of factors that generate changes in demand patterns. The weight or importance of any factor might vary for different populations and geographic areas. It also can vary for different ages, life-styles, and social or economic conditions, which is why it is so difficult to forecast the future demand for recreation.

For example, the major factors for increases in recreation demand have been population growth, youth, rising incomes, rising educational levels, and increased mobil-

ity. These positive factors of the 1950s and 1960s may be radically changed in the 1980s and 1990s when population decline, an aging society, decreasing income, and restricted mobility could become a way of life for many Americans.

All factors used to describe or project recreation demand for a given planning period should be critically examined to assess their probable significance in future planning periods. Not to do this using the best available information will create serious distortions in demand projections. These distortions will undermine the credibility of the plan and ultimately the public support needed to implement this plan.

PATTERNS OF RECREATION DEMAND

Recreation demand patterns are conditioned by these variables: (1) seasonable distribution of use, (2) leisure periods or time budgets of people, (3) geographic distribution of users and resources, and (4) participation rates of general and special populations for particular activities. Each variable can be described and projected, with qualification, based on past experience and systematic surveys. Illustrative concepts, methods, and examples are described here to show what is possible to increase the sensitivity of recreation demand estimates.

TABLE 9.3 | CAUSAL FACTORS OF RECREATION DEMAND/CONSUMPTION

Positive*	Negative†
Population increase	Competing activities: television
Leisure time	Complacency
Mobility	Poverty
Income levels	Religious attitudes
Education levels	Generation gap
Age	Discrimination
Health/physical conditioning§	Lack of opportunities§
Urbanization	Physical conditioning
Mass media conditioning	Commuting
Outdoor living	Crime
Easy credit	Racial tensions
Technology and automation	Pollution
Social status	Inflation: competing needs
Work ethic decline	Cultural heritage
Boredom of jobs	Crowding/peak use
Environmental quality of cities	Poor access
Environmental stress	Lack of program
Inflation: low-cost vacations	Deviant behavior
Experience levels	Civil disorder
Habit/custom/heritage	Fees and charges
Early retirement	Energy shortages
Flextime work schedules	Natural disasters
Extended weekends/holidays	Second jobs
	Working wives

*Positive inducements, motivation, or conditions that tend to increase the relative levels of expressed demand for most recreation activities.

†Negative constraints, influences, or conditions that tend to decrease the relative levels of expressed demand for most recreation activities.

§Example of a factor acting in both a positive and negative way for different populations. The current interest in physical fitness is a positive factor. Conversely, the poor physical condition of many Americans is a negative factor for many types of recreation facilities.

Seasonable Distribution

Patterns of use and nonuse should be carefully studied to establish the design load and physical or human carrying capacity of a site or system. It is unrealistic to assume constant levels of use for the planning and design of a system or site when peak use may be the norm. It is possible to describe recreation demand as a "frequency or wave length" with velocity, volume, intensity, and impact on the landscape.

Figure 9.5 shows an example of use patterns that account for such items as seasonal changes in weather, vacation periods, tourism, school schedules, holidays, and habit. These use profiles can be developed for each area, or representative areas, and aggregated at the systems or metropolitan level. They can be helpful in estimating use and management levels for any site or the entire system.

Leisure Periods

The time budget concept of recreation demand is the basis of the behavioral approach to recreation planning described in Chapter 7. In a methodological context, leisure provides the time dimension for recreation. It is discretionary time, or that which remains after all necessary obligations are met. This use of leisure time implies *choice*, including the choice to do nothing. Most interpretations of leisure imply a freedom of time and attitude.

The amount of leisure time varies with each individual and stage of life. Figure 9.6 shows a typical profile of leisure time related to age and sex. Similar profiles can be developed for life-style, marital status, ethnic background, or occupation and used to project relative levels of demand for selected activities or population groups. They can also be used to help formulate public policy on the type, location, and responsibility for providing various types of recreation opportunities.

For example, time budget studies indicate the average working adult has approximately five hours of free time per average day, and of this, only one hour is spent in outdoor leisure. The remaining four hours are spent watching television and in other leisure activities which take place indoors and outside of public parks. Of the 1.4 hours of free time spent in outdoor leisure, an estimated 0.1 hour is spent in local public parks with the remaining time, 1.3 hours, spent in outdoor gardening, walking, reading, and conversation (Converse and Robinson, 1966; Robinson, 1977).

Recreation planners cannot assume people should spend more time in *public* parks. However, they can provide a range of *choice* in public or private opportunities where people can spend their leisure time as they wish. The planner's task is to translate time into space and encourage home-oriented, commercial, private, and public leisure opportunities that can take place in an urban environment. The planner should sense the

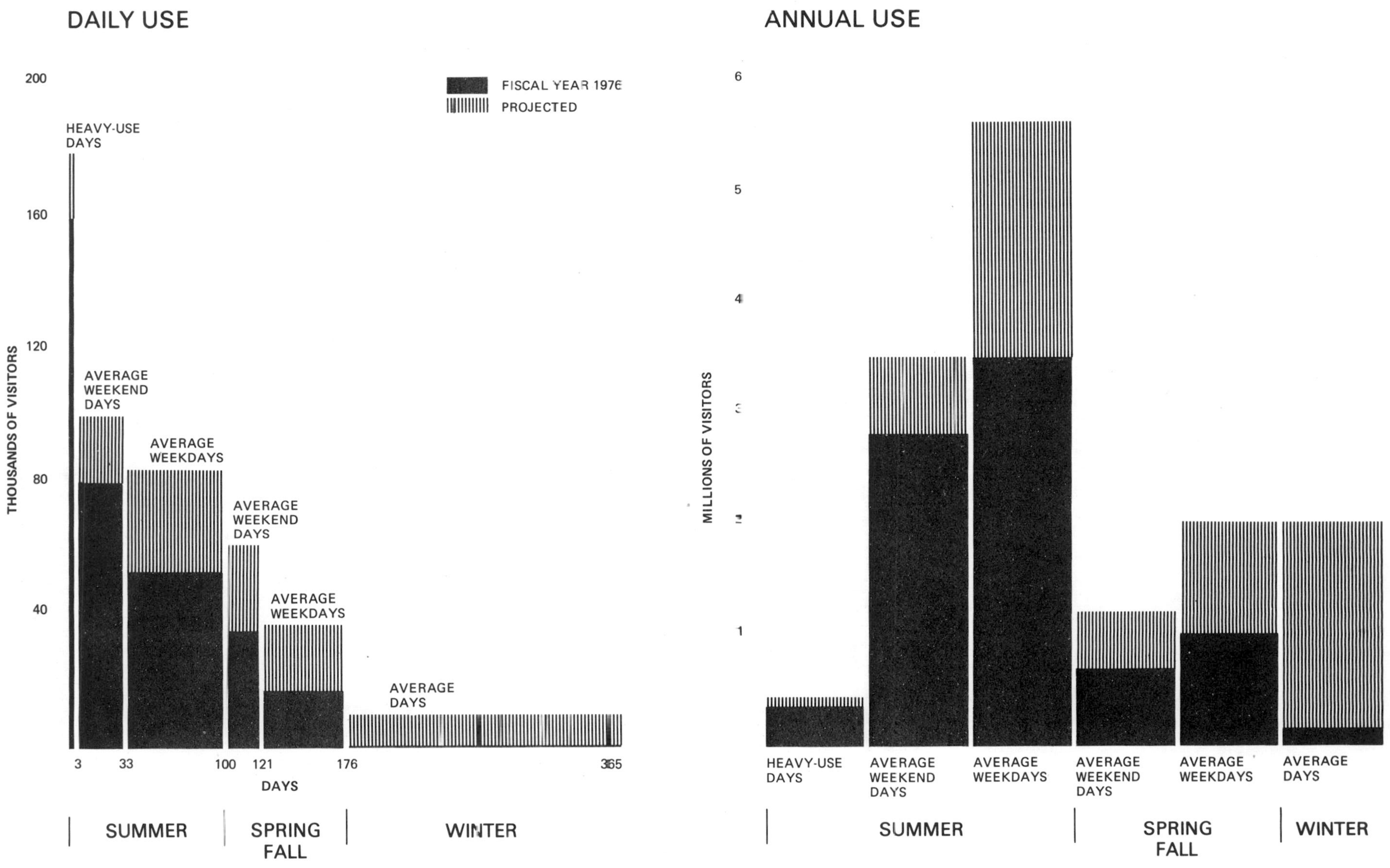

ANNUAL USE

DAILY USE

FISCAL YEAR 1976
PROJECTED

FIGURE 9.5 Recreation use levels and patterns/Gateway National Recreation Area, New York City.

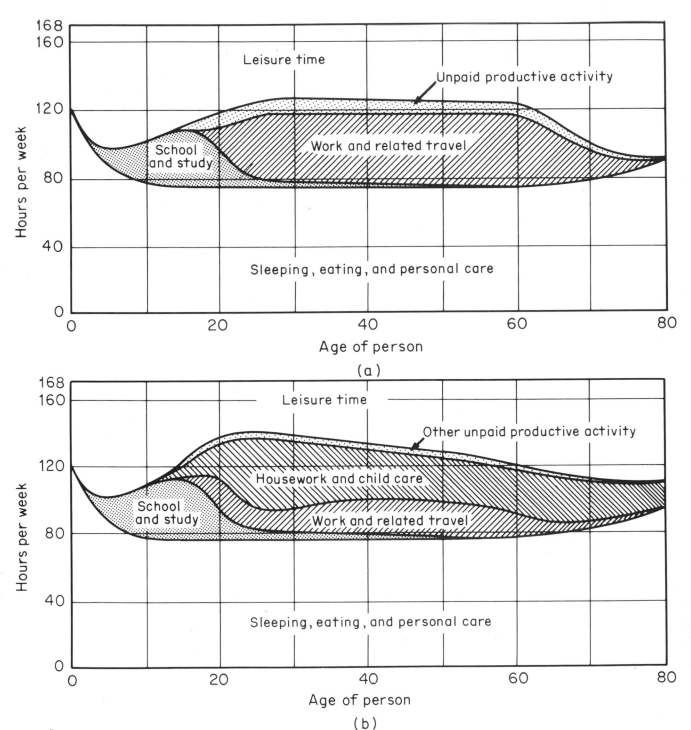

FIGURE 9.6 Profile of leisure time for different groups: how *(a)* an average man and *(b)* an average woman spends time at various ages.

widest range of potential opportunities and design these into the urban environment to provide a range of choice and diversity for leisure time. The city can be designed as a place for work and leisure.

Table 9.4 shows a range of leisure periods that have implications for the planning and design of urban environments. Most items are discretionary and private. However, there are several areas which can be given more attention by the public sector. For example, more effective work-oriented leisure opportunities such as employee picnic areas or exercise rooms can be required in the development review process. Likewise, children's play areas, putting greens, handball courts, and libraries or music rooms can be provided at airports.

The shopping center offers an excellent opportunity to integrate public and private, indoor and outdoor leisure space and program. The multiple use of shopping malls for commercial and community recreation programs has great potential, if this becomes an objective in the planning or site review process. The shopping center can also be integrated with other community services to create a social, commercial, and leisure focus (Figure 9.7).

Geographic Distribution

The geographic distribution of demand is essentially a question of access and service area for a particular site or system of sites. The typical approach is to establish a service radius for each site in terms of time-distance or origin and destination studies. Several techniques are possible.

Figure 9.8 shows the most common technique of establishing a time or distance radius for an area, which assumes all users in the service radius have equal access. Figure 9.9 shows a variation of this technique that determines time-distance contours related to travel routes. A more sophisticated variation of this technique results in travel time zones that classify use by type, time, and distance. This technique is commonly used for statewide planning, but it can be adopted to local and regional plans (Figure 9.10):

- *Zero-to-one-hour travel time zone.* For close-in day-use recreation requiring a maximum of two hours round trip by automobile.
- *One-to-two-hour travel time zone.* Generally for full-day-use recreation requiring a maximum of four hours round trip by automobile.
- *Two-to-four-hour travel time zone.* Generally for weekend or overnight recreation requiring a maximum of eight hours round trip by automobile.

TABLE 9.4 | LEISURE PERIODS BASED ON TIME BUDGET CONCEPT

Retirement	**Sabbaticals**
Unemployment	**Vacations**
Technological	Extended
Seasonal	Normal
Economic recession	Bonus
Illness/handicapped	**Holidays**
Work-oriented leisure	National
Coffee breaks	State
Recreation periods	Local
Flextime schedules	Employer
Compensatory time	**Weekends**
Job sharing	Normal
Disasters/crises	Extended
Natural disasters	**Waiting**
Civil disorder	Air travel
Work stoppages	Services/sales areas
Weather conditions	Mass transit commuting
Energy shortages	Automobile commuting

- *Over four hours travel time zone.* Generally for vacation or extended recreation trips requiring over eight hours round trip by automobile. This zone includes both in-state and out-of-state travel.

This technique results in the travel time zone map shown in Figure 9.11. It assumes the distance people travel to participate in recreation activities should be a major factor in the location of facilities. A computer model allocates the total potential percentage of demand for each activity measured in participation-days to each of the travel time zones. The total potential demand for an activity is estimated by multiplying the number of residents in a planning area (SMSA) by the average per capita participation-day for a given activity.

To estimate the peak demand for facilities at any one time, demand in each travel zone is multiplied by the percent of total participation in recreation activities during the summer months and by the percent of total peak season use. The number of facilities needed for each recreation activity within a travel time zone is determined by dividing the total demand for that activity by the average size of the group using one facility. Figure 9.12 shows the combined steps of this complex process.

FIGURE 9.7 Shopping and leisure center concept for new towns/Australia.

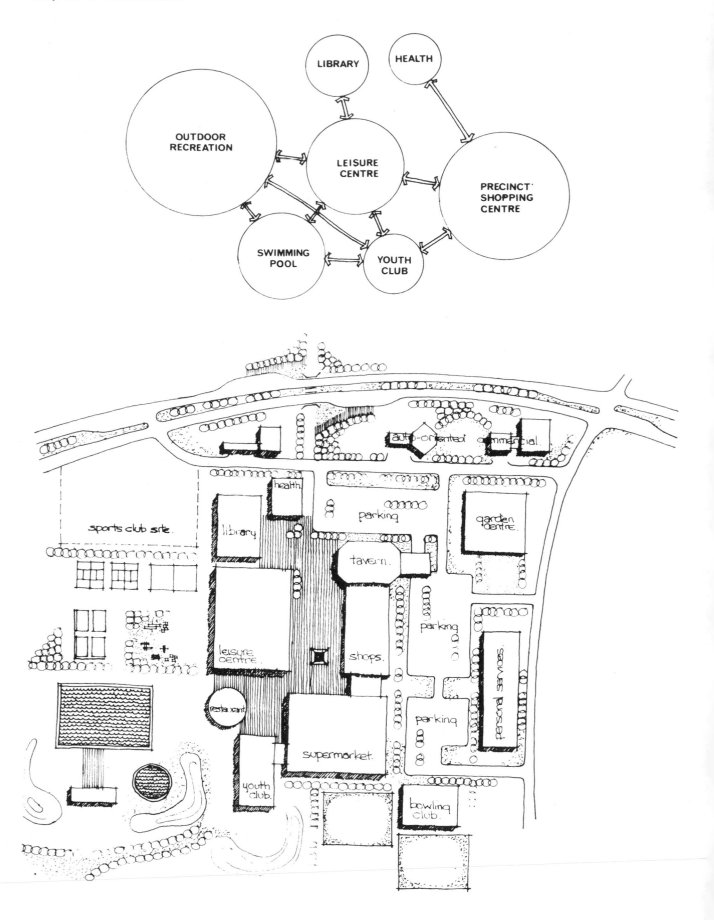

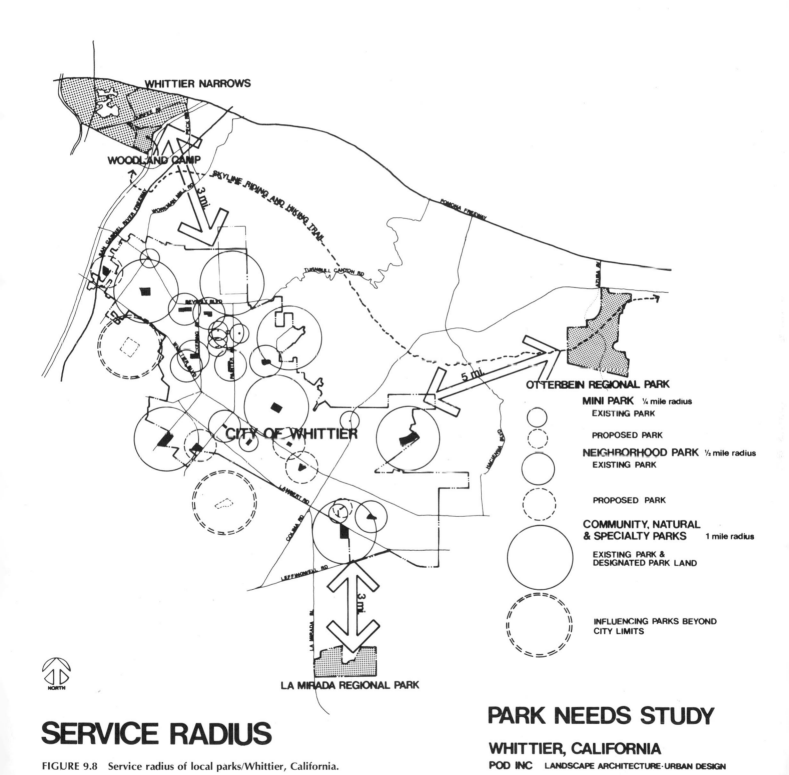

SERVICE RADIUS

FIGURE 9.8   Service radius of local parks/Whittier, California.

PARK NEEDS STUDY

WHITTIER, CALIFORNIA

POD INC   LANDSCAPE ARCHITECTURE·URBAN DESIGN

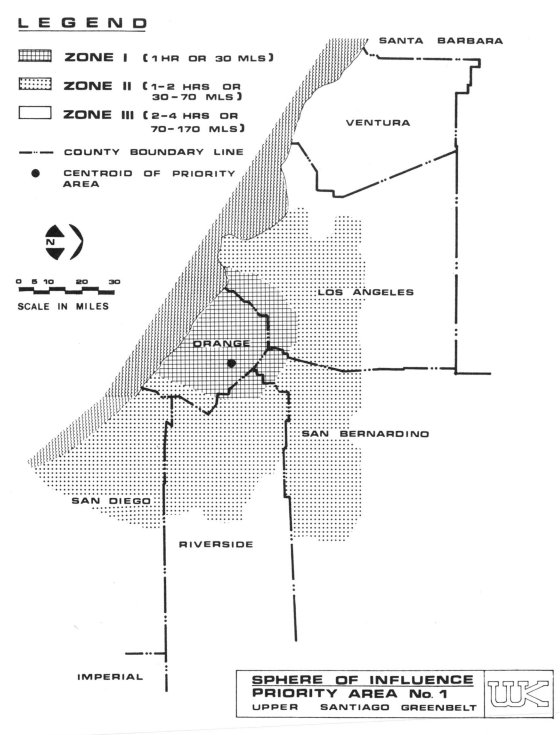

FIGURE 9.9 Recreation travel time–distance contours.

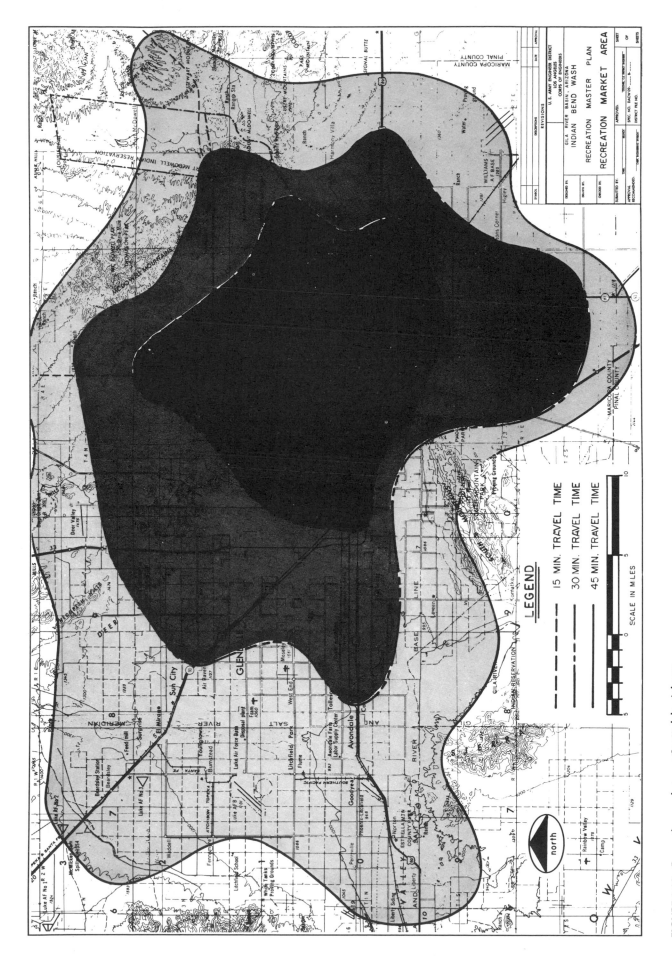

FIGURE 9.10 Recreation market area/Scottsdale, Arizona.

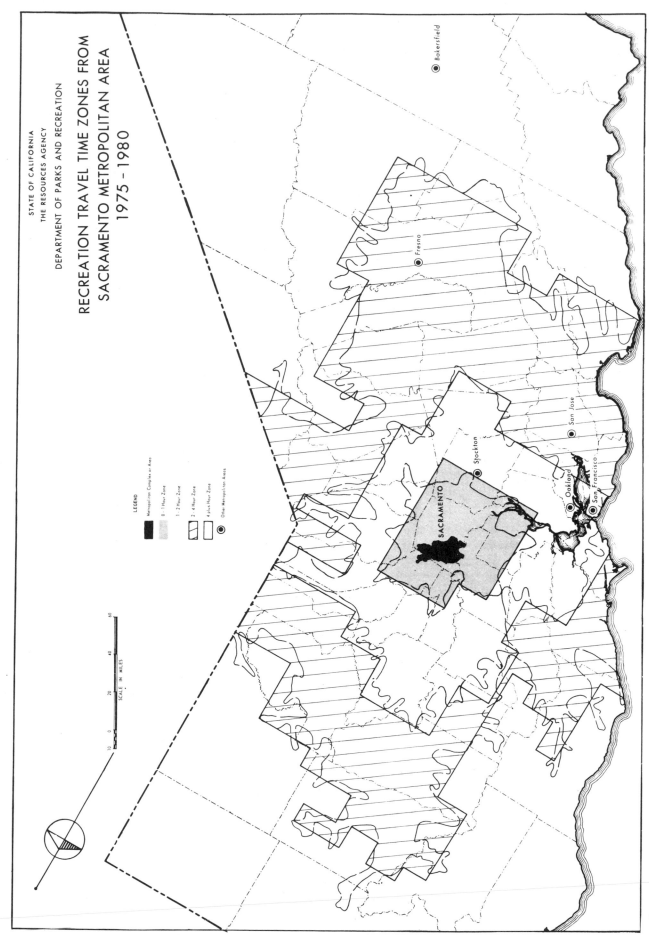

FIGURE 9.11 Recreation travel time zones, 1975–1980/Sacramento, California.

PARK AND RECREATION INFORMATION SYSTEM (PARIS)
DEMAND SUBSYSTEM

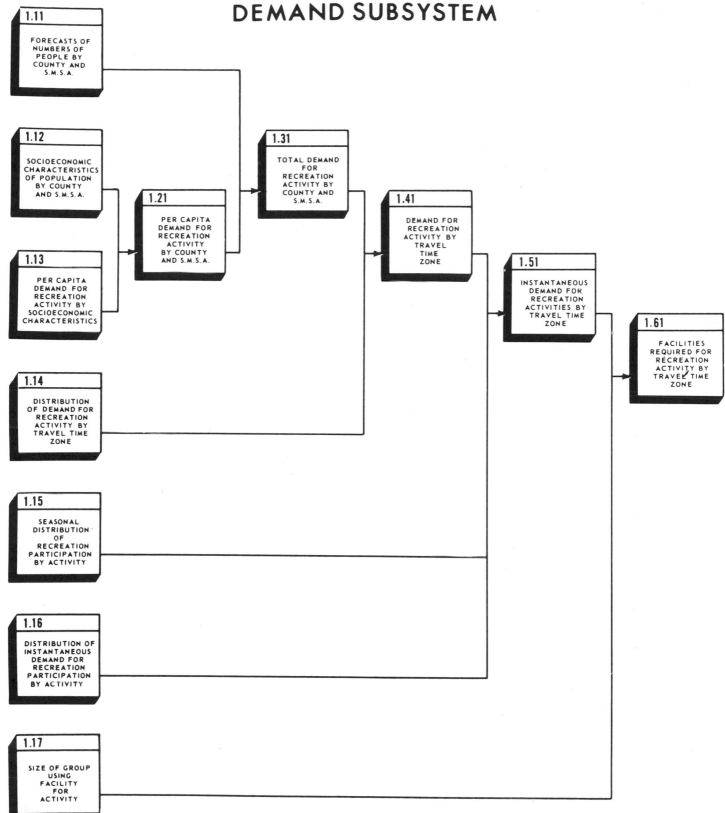

FIGURE 9.12   Recreation demand model: park and recreation information system/California.

161

Participation Rates

The most ambiguous aspect of recreation demand is how to establish credible levels of participation per activity for both general and special populations. Although the participation rate for selected activities is documented in the *Nationwide Recreation Plan* and most state recreation plans, this information is of marginal value for long-range planning because of the reasons given at the beginning of this chapter. The information has historical and comparative value, but it should not be used without qualification and additional studies at the local level.

The only way to establish reliable participation rates at the local level for current or long-range planning is to use the types of leisure behavior surveys described in Chapter 7. These surveys can describe latent and actual participation rates to develop reliable estimates of:

- *Who* is likely to participate in terms of age, income level, educational background, ethnicity, or family composition.

- *When* they are likely to participate. This helps identify peak hours of use during the week, month, and season.

- *What* percentage of the user groups could be expected to participate at any one time. This helps identify the demand at peak use periods to establish the design load for an area or system.

- *Where* they are likely to participate. This helps identify where a facility or program should be located in terms of time-distance from the potential user.

- *Why* they like to participate or not participate in a particular activity or set of activities. The objective is to find out why people behave the way they do rather than measure the behavior itself.

Assessment of participation levels and rates should be a continuous process because of the rapidly changing nature of many neighborhoods and life-styles. A communitywide survey is recommended every five years. If this is not possible, participation rates from the nationwide or state recreation plans can be weighted for significant variations in geography, climate, population, or life-style. Chapters 10 and 12 will illustrate several methods of weighting participation rates to obtain more sensitive forecasts of recreation demand and need.

10 | ESTIMATING DEMAND

Beyond the arguments of demand vs. consumption and the challenge of attempting to forecast the future is the pragmatic task of estimating demand. Arbitrary assumptions about demand are giving way to a behavioral approach to recreation planning. However, much remains to be done, for all methods of estimating demand have serious shortcomings.

COMMON METHODS

All common methods describe or project only expressed demand. These methods have been used in local, state, and nationwide recreation plans over the past decade with limited success. Although there are several variations, these eight methods of estimating demand are commonly used: (1) application of standards, (2) extension of past trends, (3) extension of trends in causal forces, (4) application of the satisfaction principle, (5) estimates of socioeconomic factors, (6) informed judgment, (7) gravity models, and (8) systems models.

Application of Standards

The most popular technique used by public planning agencies or consultants for estimating demand is the application of population-based standards, e.g., 10 acres of park land per 1000 residents. These standards have traditionally been used to determine the relative presence, absence, or "need" for a resource or facility. They arbitrarily establish ratios between the user and the resource, regardless of differences in geography, population characteristics, leisure patterns, or the feasibility of implementing these standards.

Although this technique is easily understood, widely accepted, and administratively expedient, it has serious shortcomings, which are detailed in Chapter 11. However, this technique has some value for comparing similar communities and determining the physical design load of an area for a site-specific activities, e.g., activity-days or -hours per tennis court. With qualifications and field studies, this method also has merit in establishing levels of human or social carrying capacity to avoid physical damage to the site or the detrimental effects of crowding.

Extension of Past Trends

Extension of past recreation use trends has been widely used to forecast demand on a local, state, or national

level. This technique is simple to apply and may provide reasonably accurate use estimates for *short* time periods up to five years. It is most useful where the geographic or service area has a relatively *stable* population and where the supply of recreation opportunities or the participation rate is constant.

Extrapolation of use counts, e.g., visitor-days to predict future demand, assumes a model of the future which omits possible changes in the causal factors of demand. It assumes the factors that operated in the past will continue to operate in the future, which may not be so. For example, this method takes the recreation activities shown in Figure 10.1 and projects them without qualification to the year 2000.

This method ignores the interaction of social or economic conditions, e.g., inflation or an energy crisis. It also provides no information about the value or benefit of providing additional opportunities. It simply assumes that more is better and should be provided, regardless of the tangible benefits or economic feasibility of providing these opportunities. The results of this method are most conspicuous in many federal and state recreation plans prepared in the 1960s.

Great caution should be used in interpreting or applying the demand projections in these plans because they may have no basis in fact. To accept these forecasts without qualification or weighting will result in serious distortions. These projections may have historical value in establishing baselines or studying the limitations of previous methods, but they should not be used to formulate public policy.

Extension of Trends in Causal Factors

Gross estimates of future recreation demand or consumption have been developed using the causal factors shown in Table 9.3 (page 152). This approach assumes changes in levels of consumption for specific activity. It acknowledges past trends, but weights these to reflect forecasts in causal forces such as population growth, increases in leisure time, increased mobility, or more disposable income.

This method has some merit in short-term forecasts. However, a major limitation is that many time-related variables reflect only past growth in recreation consumption. Because a variable, e.g., mobility or income, correlates with recreation consumption in the past does *not* mean it will do so in the future. This approach assumes all factors influencing recreation behavior are known and the relationship between causal factors and recreation

NUMBER OF OCCASIONS OF PARTICIPATION IN OUTDOOR SUMMER RECREATION
1960 COMPARED WITH 1976 AND 2000 (BY MILLIONS)

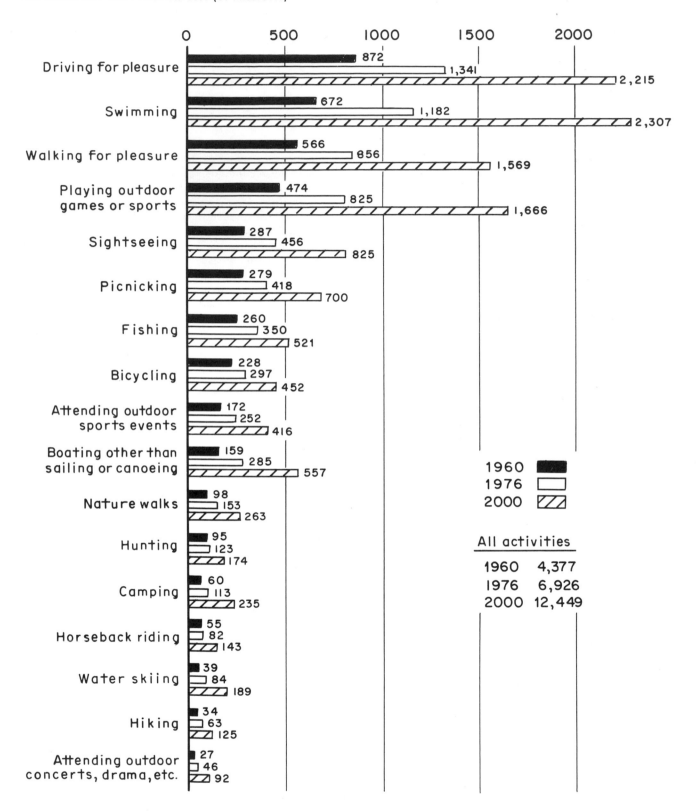

FIGURE 10.1 Extension of past trends/Outdoor Recreation Resources Review Commission.

consumption will remain unchanged in the future.

Although this method is superior to an extension of past trends, it has major shortcomings and should be used with qualifications because (1) demand estimates based on several causal factors do not normally account for the independent effects of each factor, (2) this approach does not incorporate behavioral changes caused by shifts in individual choice or recreation substitutes, and (3) statistical correlation does not necessarily mean causation, especially for time series analysis.

For example, significant changes are projected for the 1980s in the life-style, economy, age distribution, mobility, residence, voting patterns, and leisure behavior of many Americans. To assume the causal patterns of the 1960s and 1970s will remain unchanged is unrealistic in light of the facts.

More important is the need to acknowledge questions of quality or effectiveness which are not accounted for in this method. In historical perspective, despite the limitations of this approach, it may be useful in making short-run projections for areas with relatively stable populations and a limited range of recreation opportunities.

The Satisfaction Principle

No matter how much income and leisure a person has, there are limits to the amount of recreation desired or expressed. These limits apply to specific activities and locations. They also relate to age, leisure periods, and life-style. These limits can be determined by surveys, with reasonable predictability.

For example, there is evidence to suggest participation in many forms of outdoor recreation increases with increased income and education to a point where the demands of some occupations begin to decrease participation levels. Other studies point to saturation levels for particular activities according to social status, region, and family composition. The results are not conclusive, but they do indicate upper limits to the levels of demand for particular activities.

Conservative estimates of the upper limits of demand for particular activities may make it possible to extend participation levels of population groups for selected activities. The dilemma of this approach is (1) we do not really know what the saturation point is for most activities, and (2) to assume the upper limit of all activities is the norm may be unrealistic.

Nevertheless, given the success of market research for many commercial recreation products and services, these same methods could be applied to many public lei-

sure services with predictable success to estimate the upper limits of demand for specific activities or areas. They can be used with reasonable success to establish the maximum possible use of an area or system.

Estimates of Socioeconomic Factors

This method is a refinement of the extension -of the causal factors method which manipulates the variables in sophisticated models. The basic approach is quantitative and lends itself to simulation for planning or decision making. It can be applied to most activities and situations with relative ease and predictability, if the quantity or quality of opportunities does not change.

This method is particularly useful in estimating the demand for remote reservoirs or wilderness areas where the resource is limited and the access controlled. It can also be used with reasonable accuracy to predict short-range changes in participation levels for selected activities (Figure 10.2).

This method must be carefully qualified, however, because it normally (1) gives all factors the same weight, (2) does not take into account the relative quality of the recreation resources or experience, and (3) produces results that are no better than the data to describe complex socioeconomic trends.

This method was commonly used by the Outdoor Recreation Resources Review Commission (ORRRC, 1962) and is the basis of many distortions in local plans that have used this data. Figure 10.3 shows a common projection of this method that is probably too conservative for most activities and very difficult to relate to regional differences of population, geography, and life-style. Without conspicuous qualification and constant updating, it is no better than all previous methods, despite the elegance of sophisticated models.

Informed Judgment

Clawson (1966) describes a method called "informed judgment," which acknowledges the shortcomings of other methods and adds the dimension of professional insight based on experience. This method is based on two concepts: (1) the trend in demand levels for most activities will continue to increase for some time, and (2) the upward trend of the postwar years cannot continue indefinitely because it leads to absurd projections.

The basic dilemma with this approach is lack of agreement on when present trends will peak for what activities, where, and why. Another problem is this ap-

OCCUPATION HAS A CONSIDERABLE INFLUENCE

Activity days per person for 17 outdoor recreation activities
by major occupation, June – August, 1960

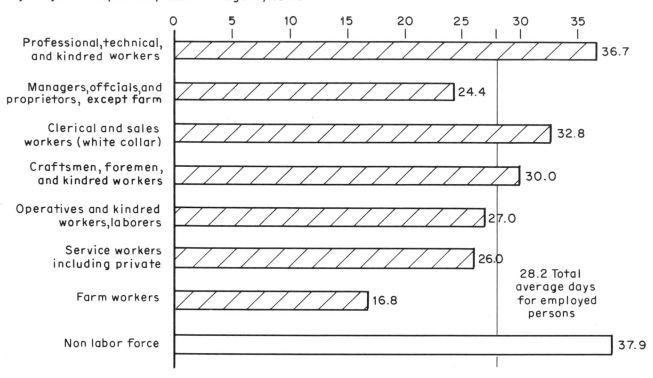

FIGURE 10.2   Estimates of socioeconomic factors/Outdoor Recreation Resources Review Commission.

Estimated Changes In Population, Income, Leisure, and Travel
For the years 1976 and 2000, compared to 1960

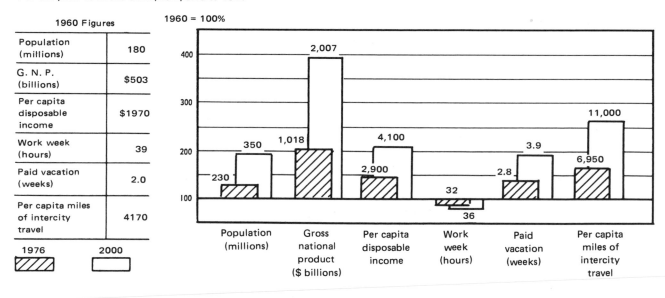

FIGURE 10.3   Projection of socioeconomic trends/Outdoor Recreation Resources Review Commission.

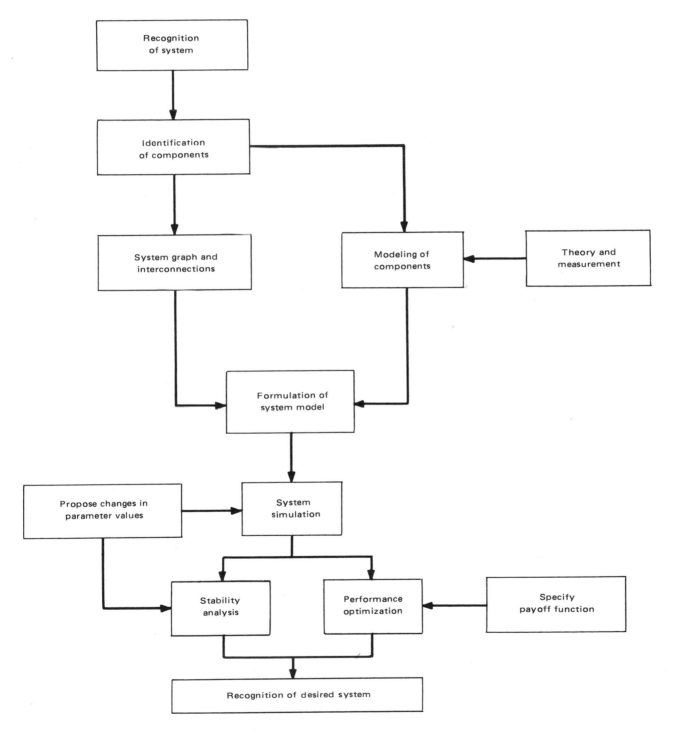

FIGURE 10.4 Conceptual stages of systems analysis. *(Adapted from J. B. Ellis, D. N. Milstein, and H. E. Koenig, "Physical Systems Analysis of Socio-Economic Situations," Oct. 7, 1964.)*

proach is based on (1) historical trends for a particular area or activity, (2) probable future desires of people for a certain area or activity, (3) probable future capability of people to afford the time or money that such recreation will require, and (4) the projected supply of areas in which the desired activity can take place.

Although these are strenuous qualifications, it is possible for professionals who know the history of a particular planning unit and can assess socioeconomic and political trends to make demand estimates with some success. These estimates must be carefully qualified as "informed judgment" and used only for *short-term* decisions.

Gravity Models

The gravity model establishes a mathematical relationship between the relative location of population and the frequency of visits to a given recreation site or system. This model evaluates the use of an area as a function of distance in miles or time traveled from a population center to the recreation area. It suggests that as distance to the recreation area increases, the use of the area decreases.

The procedure involves two steps: First, a demand curve is constructed for the entire recreation experience. The distance traveled from zones surrounding a recreation resource is used as an index to cost. The method assumes distance is the major cost and recreation is priced at near-zero level. A schedule is derived that relates the number of visitors per 1000 base population within a distance zone to travel cost per visit per party. Second, under the assumption that increases in admission prices will influence consumption equally across distance zones, an economic demand curve for the recreation experience is constructed.

Although this method is very systematic, it makes theoretical assumptions which may be the opposite in practice. It also does not account for the suitability of sites, resource quality, and a host of human and institutional factors. It does not respond to dynamic situations or diverse planning units. Its primary use is academic, and great caution should be used in trying to adapt this method to cities.

Systems Models

The systems model approach to forecasting recreation demand for a site, system, or region incorporates many of the complex relationships and problems of the other methods. The systems approach views a recreation system in terms of supply, demand, and access. Origin and destination of users, time-distance-mode of access, population characteristics, and the carrying capacity of resources are combined in a model of the system. Once the model is operational, it can be manipulated to determine the effects of different variables on recreation demand patterns (Figure 10.4).

The use of large-scale predictive models for recreation planning has met with limited success. The PARIS (Park and Recreation Information System) and RECSYS (Recreation System) models developed for the California and Michigan Outdoor Recreation Plans represent state-of-the-art models. Both have been relatively difficult to use and revise because of the expertise, expense, and data base necessary to make them effective planning tools.

Figures 10.5 and 10.6 show an overview of each model. Note the relationships between supply, demand, and travel. In the PARIS model, demand is determined by travel zone and activity compared to the effective supply by travel zone to yield deficiencies by travel time zone. The assumptions and methods of each model are detailed in extensive studies listed in the bibliography.

Although recreation models may be the wave of the future, one should proceed with great caution in the present because of the inherent difficulties associated with them. The time, expertise, and expense necessary to develop a credible model are beyond the needs and resources of most communities.

This does not discount the research value of models or suggest they have no value for nationwide or state planning. However, it does suggest there are more cost-effective ways of estimating demand at the local level than recreation models. The temptation to develop systems models for local recreation planning should be deferred until the state of the art improves or all other methods for estimating demand have been exhausted.

UNCOMMON METHODS

Over the past 20 years, several methods of estimating demand have been developed and applied with limited success. These methods have not been commonly used and may not be generalizable to many situations. However, aspects of each method can apply or be combined with conventional methods for particular situations.

There is no common dimension to these methods except an attempt to be more systematic or less arbitrary in

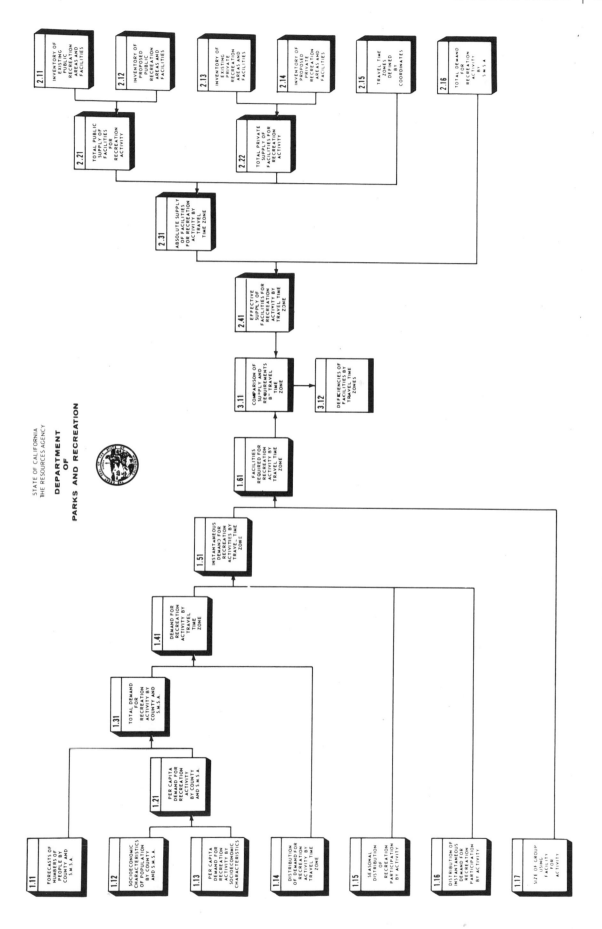

FIGURE 10.5 Park and Recreation Information System Model/California.

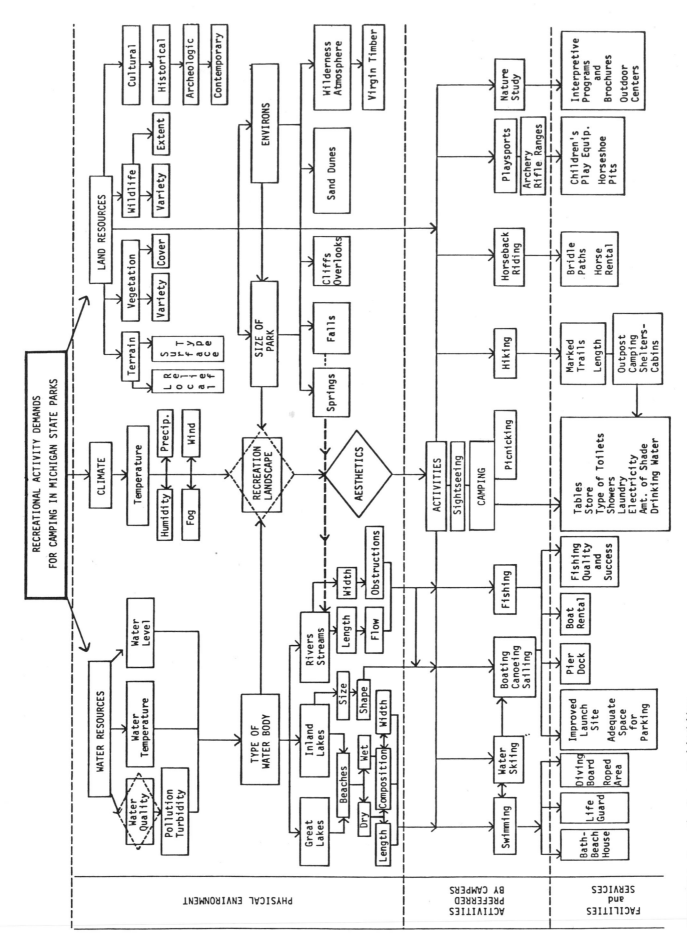

FIGURE 10.6 Recreation System Model/Michigan.

estimating demand patterns for selected activities or areas. In all cases, the shortcomings described for common methods apply here with even greater qualifications because most of these methods have not been tested in enough places over time to be generalizable.

Comparable Project or System

An existing recreation resource is selected to be comparable to the project or system being studied. Expected recreation use at the proposed resource is computed by *analogy* with the existing, comparable project. The analogy involves several steps: (1) Determine the population or travel zones around the proposed park and the existing park use for comparison, (2) determine the per-capita use at the existing area from the total population and attendance figures, (3) establish a ratio using the population and attendance of the existing park, (4) apply this ratio to the proposed park to project attendance, and (5) adjust the figures to account for the influence of existing and proposed recreation developments in the zone of influence.

The reliability of this method depends on the degree of direct comparability between the projects or systems. The use of a comparable area or system has merit only if the natural, social, and institutional factors are essentially the same. For example, it is expedient and cost-effective to apply selected findings of authoritative studies or recreation plans for comparable cities, but this should be qualified with pilot studies to check the degree of comparability.

Bursley's Formula

Bursley's Formula is one method for projecting the day use demand for a nonurban recreation area. This formula was developed by the National Park Service in the 1950s to establish the design load for nonurban parks (Fogg, 1975). This method emphasizes the following items:

1 General attractiveness of the park or area
2 Site in relation to population distribution
3 Economic level of this population
4 Degree of urbanization of this population
5 Influence of areas with similar characteristics

This method assumes there is no area of similar characteristics to influence attendance at the park in question. The average visitation on a Sunday afternoon from a community to the park or recreation area under consideration is derived with this formula:

$$V = \frac{2.5 \times A \times P \times U}{M^x}$$

where V = number of Sunday afternoon visitors
A = general attractiveness of the area
P = population of the service area within $1\frac{1}{2}$ hours driving time of the park
U = coefficient of urbanization in the community
M = road mileage from community to park
X = power dependent upon economic level of the community

Visitor-Day Capacity Method

Most regional parks can be reached only by car. The daily capacity of these parks can be determined by multiplying the number of cars × average turnover rate × number of people per car. A visitor-day usually consists of more than one activity-day. For example, one study describes an average 2.2 activity-days per visitor-day (Pennsylvania State Parks, 1972).

This average was derived from data collected on the number of people per car and average turnover rate shown in Table 10.1. This data can be adjusted on a seasonal or regional basis to estimate the peak or normal day use for a given area. This data should be used with qualification because it is only an illustration of what is possible using this method. The number of people per car or turnover rate for selected activities or areas is subject to wide variation. This approach has some utility for estimating the short-term design load of areas. However, it should not be used for long-range systems planning because it does not account for probable changes in use patterns or the substitutability of areas.

Annual Capacity Method

The annual capacity of a park can be determined by multiplying the daily capacity by the number of capacity days per year (Fogg, 1975). Each area of the country has a different number of capacity days per year per facility. The same might be true on a regional scale for areas with diverse microclimates.

For example, in the Central Atlantic states, a typical park might have 50 capacity days of use determined as follows: 3 days of use per week (40 percent during the week, 20 to 25 percent on Saturday, and 35 to 40 percent on Sunday) × 13 weeks (summer season), + 30 percent off-season use (3 × 13 + 30 percent = 51). In milder areas, there might be as many as 100 capacity days while

TABLE 10.1 | VISITOR-DAY CAPACITY METHOD

Activity	People per car	Turnover rate
Sightseeing	3.2	Variable
Family picnic	3.5–4.0	1–2
Family camping	3.5–4.5	1
Group picnic	4.5	1
Boat ramp	4.5	1
Beach areas	2.5–3.0	1–2
Boat concession	3.5–4.0	2
Overlook	3.0	4
Golf	3.0	2
Restaurant	3.0	4
Stables	4.0	2–3
Fishing	2.5–3.0	Variable
Hiking	4.0	Variable

in colder climates only 40 days. These figures must be adjusted to consider differences in travel time, facilities, and local weather.

The qualifications of the visitor-day capacity method should be applied to this method with more caution because the margin for error increases with the wide variations possible on an annual basis. However, if carefully weighted and validated with onsite user surveys, this method has utility for short-range projections.

Carrying Capacity Method

When a park has a sensitive landscape, the natural capacity of the land to sustain recreation use without deterioration of the resource should be determined by resource analysis and environmental impact studies. The carrying capacity method should be considered for all natural parks in urban areas to establish allowable use levels and management zones.

This method can also be applied to estimating the social or human carrying capacity for a given area or system. Because little is known about the natural and social carrying capacity of especially *urban* or user-oriented park systems, this method is only referenced here as one possible approach to estimating the *limits* of existing or projected demand on a given site.

Figure 10.7 shows how carrying capacity guidelines can be used for the planning, design, and management of areas. Figures 10.8 and 10.9 show an application of carrying capacity concepts to the land classification and resource management strategy of a resource-oriented park in an urban area. Appendix F summarizes general policies for the management of zones defined by the land classification system.

Activity-Day/Responsibility Method

The Pennsylvania Department of Forests and Waters (1973) has developed a method of estimating demand based on the procedure shown in Figure 10.10. This method used the participation rates per activity established by the ORRRC (1962) and adjusted these on a seasonal basis to reflect the possible demand for state parks in Pennsylvania.

The responsibility of the department was determined by relating the existing facilities provided by the department to the total statewide activity-day demand. The total responsibility of the department was obtained by multiplying the percent of responsibility times the number of demand activity-days for that area. Activity standards were applied to activity-days to yield (1) the total required developed acres, and (2) the units required to satisfy the demand for a particular activity.

Activity standards are expressed as either (1) the number of activity-days per developed acre (area standards), or (2) the number of activity-days per unit (unit standards). These standards were developed with this formula: number of units per acre × number of people per unit × turnover factor × number of recreation days per week × number of recreation weeks in summer season equals number of activity-days per developed acre divided by number of units per acre equals number of activity-days per unit.

The number of sites per acre, people per site, the turnover factor, the number of recreation days per week, and weeks per season were based on park records and observations. For example, Table 10.1 shows turnover rates for selected activities. Figure 10.11 shows selected recreation use patterns used in this method.

This method expresses seasonal use in activity-days on a developed acre of park land devoted to a given activity (area standard). If this amount is divided by the number of units per acre, the number of activity-days per unit is obtained (unit standard). By dividing the total number of activity-days the department is responsible for by area standards, the total number of developed acres per activities is obtained. This can be converted to gross acreage for support facilities such as roads. If the

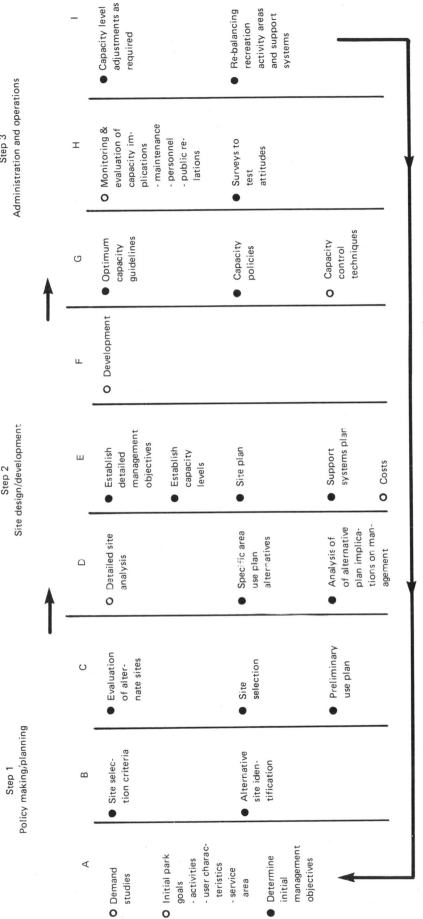

FIGURE 10.7 **Carrying capacity guidelines for recreation planning.** (*U.S. Department of the Interior, Bureau of Outdoor Recreation. 1977. Guidelines for Understanding and Determining Optimum Recreation Carrying Capacity. Prepared by Urban Research and Development Corporation, Bethlehem, Pa., p. III-3.*)

NATURAL ZONE

WILDERNESS SUBZONE
(GGNRA CITIZENS ADVISORY
COMMISSION RECOMMENDATION)

NATURAL/HISTORIC ZONE

DEVELOPMENT ZONE

HISTORIC/DEVELOPMENT ZONE

● HISTORIC ZONE - SPECIFIC SITES

S SPECIAL USE ZONE

P PASTORAL AREA SUBZONE
(LANDS UPON WHICH GRAZING WILL CONTINUE
IN ACCORDANCE WITH POINT REYES ENABLING LEGISLATION)

LAND CLASSIFICATION

POINT REYES National Seashore
GOLDEN GATE National Recreation Area
National Park Service
U.S. Department of the Interior

FIGURE 10.8 Land classification of park resources/Pt. Reyes National Seashore, California.

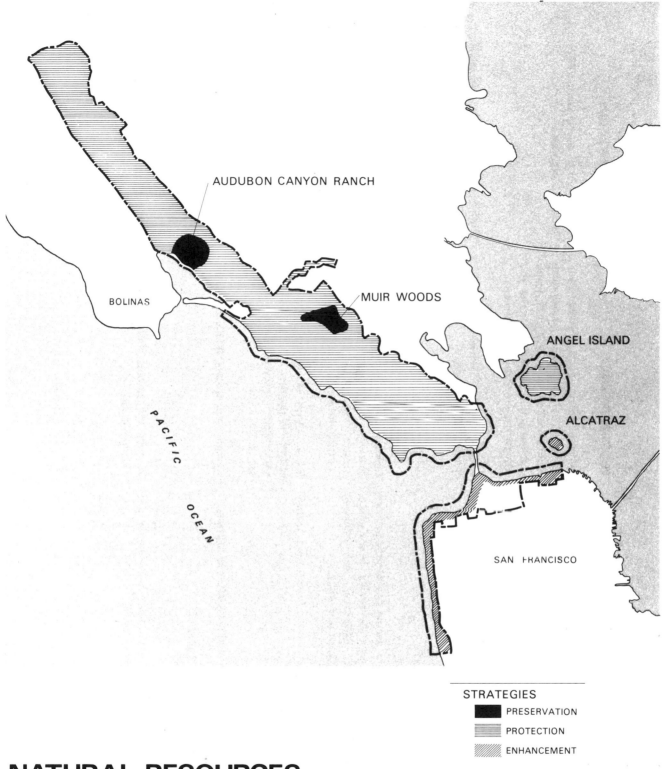

AUDUBON CANYON RANCH

MUIR WOODS

BOLINAS

PACIFIC OCEAN

ANGEL ISLAND

ALCATRAZ

SAN FRANCISCO

STRATEGIES
PRESERVATION
PROTECTION
ENHANCEMENT

NATURAL RESOURCES MANAGEMENT

POINT REYES National Seashore
GOLDEN GATE National Recreation Area
National Park Service
U.S. Department of the Interior

FIGURE 10.9 Natural resource management/Golden Gate National Recreation Area, San Francisco.

FIGURE 10.10 Activity-day responsibility method/Pennsylvania.

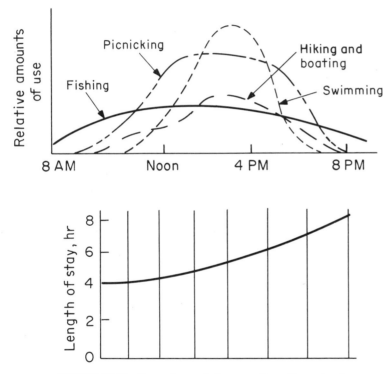

FIGURE 10.11 Recreation activity use patterns/Pennsylvania.

activity-day total is divided by unit standards, the total number of units required to satisfy this activity-day demand will be obtained.

The shortcomings of this method are it fails to account for nonresidents, nonuse, other public or private facilities, and the total range of activities possible in most parks. However, the feature of assigning *responsibility* for selected activities or areas has great merit, especially at the metropolitan level, where several levels of government and the private sector normally provide different recreation opportunities.

Activity Quality Method

The activity quality method is based on an approach to recreation planning developed by Shannon (1975). It divides all activities into (1) activities which the agency now provides, and (2) activities which are not provided by the agency, but should be provided, as determined by surveys. It ranks all activities on the graduated scale shown in Figure 10.12. This scale assumes the more an individual puts into an a activity, the greater satisfaction or "quality" of the activity for the individual.

This approach provides a value judgment and weighting which ranks "creativity" highest and "killing time" lowest. It also establishes "popularity" or possible attendance as one criterion for evaluating the probable success of an activity. These variables (quality and popularity) are used to compute an index value for each activity with this formula:

Popularity percent × quality weighting factor = index value

Popularity is determined by comparing the number of participants in the activity to the total number of participants in the program. This ratio gives the popularity percentage. Quality is determined by comparing the activity to the activity quality scale shown in Figure 10.12. The index value becomes the priority indicator for each activity.

The major shortcomings of this method are value judgments to describe a "quality" recreation experience and omission of nonusers. However, with correction of these deficiencies, it holds some promise for evaluating the relative merits of existing programmed activities of a public agency.

User Resource Planning Method

Chapter 3 described the major concepts of the user resource planning method in the context of an approach to recreation planning that integrates the positive features of other approaches. In estimating demand for specific areas or activities, this method also combines many of the positive aspects of all the methods described here. At the metropolitan scale, it would apply best to regional parks with a natural orientation.

Deficiencies of All Methods

All the methods described in this chapter have deficiencies. Some methods are better for specific purposes than others. However, all are subject to these conditions: (1) the *quality* of the recreation experience associated with a particular level of demand must be considered, and (2) the impact of *technology* on future consumption patterns is difficult to predict with any certainty. The level of *design* and *management* at the site or systems scale can also have a significant impact on both latent and expressed demand.

More research is needed on the *qualitative* aspects of the recreation experience before any of these methods will be effective planning tools. This research should study the role that habit, maintenance, law enforcement, program leadership, supervision, or interpretation play in influencing demand over time. Little is known about these factors, when they may be the most important.

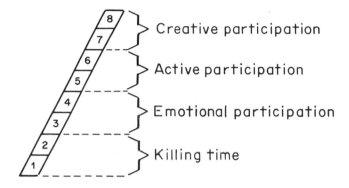

FIGURE 10.12   Activity quality scale.

Although all methods of estimating demand are lacking in some respect, much progress has been made in a short time. Prediction of leisure behavior is still more an art than a science. Developing methods may elevate the state of the art. There is much hope because current research efforts should bear fruit over the next decade. Until this occurs, the task of estimating demand should be approached with caution and humility.

11 | RECREATION STANDARDS

The common technique of applying arbitrary standards to abstract populations to allocate public land, facilities, or program persists, despite serious challenges in the literature and practice of recreation planning. This chapter summarizes the arguments for and against the use of standards, describes some current and developing methods, and places the use or potentials of recreation standards in perspective.

The object is to critique the state of the art, trace the historical development of standards, classify existing standards, and describe what is possible with additional research and demonstration. This chapter extends some of the ideas introduced in Chapters 2, 3, and 6 and establishes a rationale for the needs analysis approach to recreation planning described in Chapter 12.

THE STANDARDS DILEMMA

Despite their methodological problems, there is a pragmatic need to use standards in the planning process. However, these standards do not have to be arbitrary or insensitive to human needs. The dilemma is to acknowledge the shortcomings of conventional standards to establish a rationale for developing alternatives. There is no question that conventional standards have played a positive role in justifying existing recreation opportunities in most cities. To abandon conventional standards without a reasonable alternative is unwise. Conversely, it is difficult to develop needed alternatives without first challenging convention and seeking new or better ways of relating people to space.

Need for Standards

Standards are relative requirements that can serve as guidelines or criteria in the planning and decision process. They should be considered means to help assess the attainment of objectives. Standards can also be used to measure the relative effectiveness of leisure services for similar places or populations or develop a balanced system of public and private recreation opportunities. Some principal uses of standards are:

Systems Planning The preparation of a comprehensive park and recreation plan and integration of public or private land uses at the community scale.

Facility/Site Planning The determination of what types of facilities are desirable or possible on a given site.

Rationalization The justification or priority given to people or political units for the acquisition and development of park and recreation facilities.

Measurement The use of quantitative or qualitative indicators to analyze the performance or effectiveness of a recreation site or park system.

Criteria for Standards

No two communities or neighborhoods need to have the same standard. There is no planning requirement that mandates similar standards for the diverse conditions, populations, and values of Urban America. However, to be effective in any situation, standards should satisfy these criteria.

PEOPLE ORIENTATION They should reflect the needs of people in the area being served. Standards which are agency-, instead of people-serving, are unrealistic and will undermine public support of the recreation plan.

FEASIBILITY They should be attainable in the planning period with existing or projected funds. Standards which are politically, economically, or environmentally unrealistic for a particular planning period and geographic area will be difficult to implement. For example, there is a vast difference between the leisure needs and resources of an affluent suburb, a rural community, and an inner city.

PRACTICALITY They should be simple to apply, revise, or project in the planning decision process. They should be based on sound planning principles and the best available information. Standards that are conditional, romantic, or arbitrary will not be generalizable to similar populations or planning units.

RELEVANCE They should relate to the people and times. To assume a timeless set of standards for most urban areas is to not acknowledge the rapidly changing nature of cities, life-styles, and the economy. There is no reason why most standards cannot have incremental time periods or revision.

The adoption of a set of recreation standards to reflect these criteria is an important aspect of the planning process, to help analyze the existing and projected needs of a community. If properly used, standards can be a guide for estimating (1) the amount of land and facilities required to serve general and special populations, (2) the number of people a recreation area or facility can be designed to serve, and (3) the adequacy of an area or facility to accommodate potential users in a service area.

Conceptual Challenges

Although standards are commonly described as "guidelines," they soon become absolutes few cities change regardless of significant differences in population, climate, leisure patterns, density, or their ability to implement these standards. Most cities and suburbs have essentially the same park, recreation, and open space standards. There are good reasons for this situation.

HISTORICAL PRECEDENT   It is difficult to rationalize the origin, evolution, and almost universal acceptance of conventional standards, except the social reform movement, romanticism, and lack of professionalism that characterized the early Park and Recreation Movement in America. Despite conspicuous warnings against the unqualified use of standards, most cities have adopted NRPA standards without question. Even where standards are impossible to implement, most cities have persistently maintained them. Departing from conventional standards seems unthinkable, despite all logic to the contrary. What began in an arbitrary fashion has become codified by blind acceptance.

The justification for clinging to standards established over a half-century ago is understandable only in the fervor of reform movements. However, this justification is questionable in light of current leisure needs, fiscal realities, and methodological alternatives. It seems irrational to continue to use current NRPA standards (Buechner, 1971) as a measure of adequacy because they have never been qualified, tested, or evaluated in human terms (Gold, 1973).

PROFESSIONAL/POLITICAL EXPEDIENCY   Most standards are absolute and simple. To the busy decision maker or planner, they represent an expedient manner to attain an objective usually established by the supplier. They require no study and can be applied as an instant solution to problems. The standards are established by a national professional organization and are legitimized as expert. Should anyone challenge these standards, most planners defend them by appealing to their authority. National acceptance also gives standards a reference point outside the community and abstracts them from partisan politics or claims of interest groups.

Standards are symbols of community pride and status. They stand for an ideal that few will oppose prior to the allocation of resources. In many instances they become ends rather than means or guidelines. Communities are often evaluated by "how much" rather than "how good"

their facilities are, despite a wide range of demographic variables.

Standards are useful in the community's decision-making process. Although conceived as planning tools or measures, they are commonly used as bargaining points by suppliers to compete with other agencies for the community's resources. Because of their simplicity and authority, standards are used to determine what a community should have. These standards are scaled to persuade decision makers to devote additional resources to recreation to reduce inadequacies.

METHODOLOGICAL AMBIGUITY   Several ambiguities should be clarified before a community adopts traditional standards or considers alternatives.

Degree   The differences between minimum, maximum, desirable, or optimum standards are more than semantic. The issue has significant legal, social, and environmental implications. Most traditional standards do not give rigorous thought to the questions of degree. They are vague and contradictory where they should be explicit.

Time   Time dimensions are seldom attached to conventional standards. The ambiguity of relating a standard to the "ultimate" population of a planning area assumes either infinite wisdom or a stable population. Both assumptions present the paradox of relating an absolute (standard) to a rapidly changing variable (population). For example, many inner-city or suburban neighborhoods are now subject to radical change in a five-year period. To apply an "ultimate" standard to these situations is absurd in concept and marginal in practice without conspicuous qualifications to reflect projected change (see Figure 9.4, page 150).

Scale   The dimension of scale or access is not explicit in conventional standards except for vague references to an arbitrary service radius. At anything but the pedestrian scale, the traditional concepts of community, district, city, or region have a marginal relationship to conventional recreation standards unless they are described with time-distance criteria to include all types of movement by user groups and service radius. To assume an affluent suburban and a poverty-level-inner-city neighborhood have the same service radius or access to a regional park is absurd. Likewise, to assume a teenager and a senior citizen have the same sense of scale for a neighborhood park is unrealistic.

Density The critical dimension of density is normally omitted in conventional standards. At the very least, housing density implies a degree of open space, environmental quality, and recreation opportunity. To assume the same standards for populations living at different densities is irrational. It perpetuates imbalances. For example, if the same standard is used to justify the need for suburban and inner-city open space, this results in a built-in bias for federal assistance. The suburban neighborhood, which needs relatively less open space, obtains more aid, while the inner-city neighborhood, which needs substantially more open space, obtains proportionately less aid. No public purpose is served by this logic or methodology.

In perspective, there is no question that conventional standards were well meant, but ill conceived. They presume judgments about the recreation experience, the city, and public policy which may have no basis in fact or theory. These standards are arbitrary statements of an ideal envisioned by the supplier and legitimized as authoritative by a professional society over time without rigorous testing or qualification. The implications of continuing to accept these standards have been detailed in many sources. The conceptual challenge is to acknowledge the past and develop alternatives instead of continuing to belabor the methological shortcomings of conventional standards.

CURRENT METHODS

The use of conventional standards is the state of the art, despite the above qualifications. Their use is described here for those who (1) accept the advantages of these conventional standards, or (2) accept the disadvantages of these standards and may be seeking an alternative. No evaluation of each standard is made because of the serious qualifications of this approach to recreation planning.

Table 6.1 (page 93) classifies selected types of recreation standards. Space standards are the basis of most public recreation opportunities in cities. These standards are based on three methods recommended by the National Recreation and Park Association. Each method is described and illustrated below.

Population Ratio Method

This is the best-known and most commonly applied park and recreation space standard. It applies essentially to public recreation areas in or near cities. Appendix G contains the recommended NRPA standards and shows typical applications of these standards in Dade County, Florida, and Elmhurst, Illinois. Note the similarity in standards despite differences in these communities and NRPA cautions to adjust recommended standards to local conditions. Figure 11.1 shows a conventional conceptual application of these standards to a community.

A refinement of this method was developed by the California Committee on Planning for Recreation (1956). They recognized the relationship of density, urbanization, service area, and climate to possible recreation needs. They also made a distinction for parks not adjacent to schools and suggested relationships among areas and facilities. Tables 11.1 and 11.2 show a typical application of these standards to a neighborhood park. Appendix G details these standards for a citywide park.

Area Percentage Method

This method recommends what percentage of the total (gross) area of a community should be devoted to public recreation and open space. It applies best to new development or urban renewal and makes no recommendations on how this space is to be used or where it should be located. It does not necessarily relate to density, housing type, or social needs.

This method is commonly used in subdivision ordinances that require the developer to set aside 10 percent of the gross land area for park land or payment (equivalent cost/lot) in lieu of land. Often times this land is not properly located and designed with little value for providing effective parks. For example, Figure 11.2 shows the location options for a typical subdivision in Evanston, Illinois.

Current NRPA standards recommend 25 percent of new towns, planned-unit development, and large subdivisions be devoted to open space. Studies of new communities, urban renewal, and planned-unit development indicate the NRPA standards are very conservative. With good design, it is possible to increase the percentage of total land in open space from 25 to 50 percent or more, as shown in Figure 11.3.

Demand Projection Method

This method projects the participation rates of user groups and translates them into space needs with facility standards. It uses mathematical models to describe and

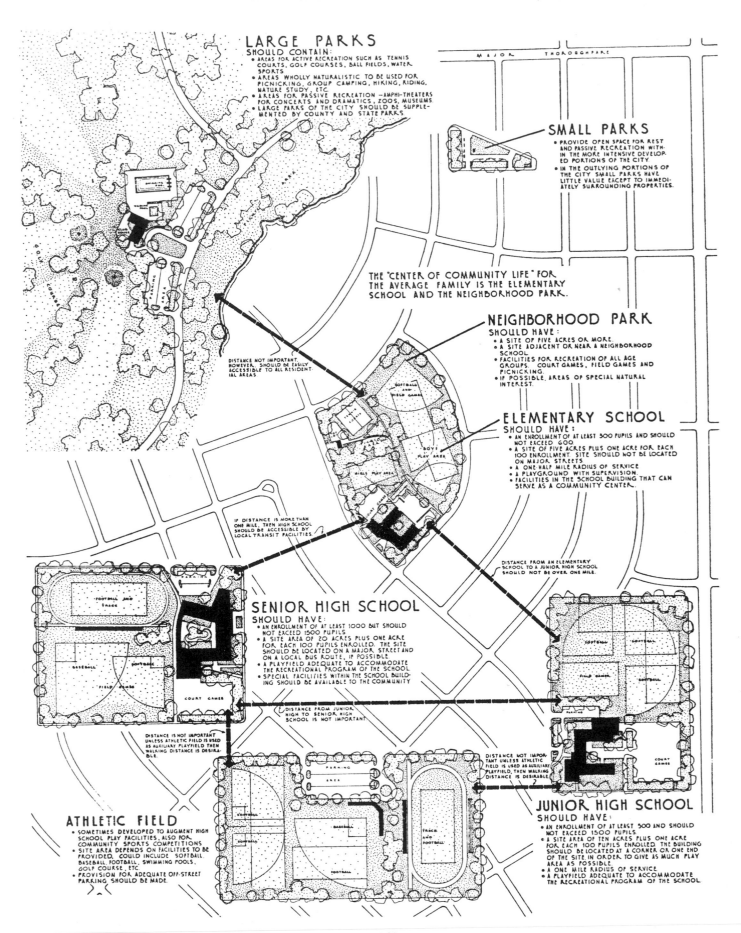

FIGURE 11.1 Recreation standards concept/Jackson County, Michigan.

TABLE 11.1 | RESIDENTIAL DENSITY AND SERVICE AREA OF NEIGHBORHOOD RECREATION CENTERS

	General locations in California	Average family size	Lot size	Predominant building type	Effective service distance	Total net acres excluding streets and public uses	Population within effective service distance
3/8 mile radius / Low density 1 / 15–20 persons per net acre / • = 200 people	Coastal and valley nonmetropolitan mountain	3.5	7000 to 10,000 sq ft	Single-family detached house	1/4 to 3/8 mile	206 ac	2500 to 3000
1/4 mile radius / Low density 2 / 20–30 persons per net acre / • = 200 people	Coastal and valley metropolitan desert	3.3	5000 to 7000 sq ft	Single-family detached house	1/4 mile	91 ac	2000 to 2500
1/4 mile radius / Medium density / 30–50 persons per net acre / • = 200 people	Coastal and valley metropolitan	3.0	Varies	Duplex, row houses, two- and three-story apartments	1/4 mile	91 ac	3500 to 4500
1/6 mile radius / High density / 50–100 persons per net acre / • = 200 people	Coastal and valley metropolitan	2.6	Varies	Multistory apartments	1/8 mile	23 ac	2000 to 4000

Source: Guide for Planning Recreation Parks in California, California Recreation Commission, Sacramento, 1956, p. 45.

TABLE 11.2 | SPACE STANDARDS
FOR NEIGHBORHOOD RECREATION CENTERS

	Facilities	Center adjoining elementary school, in acres	Separate center, in acres
1	Playlot and mothers' area	.35	.35
2	Play area for elementary school-age children	.40	.40
3	Nature and science hobby area	.30	.30
4	Paved area for court games	.75	1.25
5	Field for sports	*	6.00
6	Night lighting (need for acreage depends on design)	—	.25
7	Instructional swimming pool	.25	—
8	Family picnic and barbecue area	1.75	1.75
9	Parklike area for free play	.75	1.50
10	Neighborhood center building	*	.35
11	Quiet area	.50	.50
12	Older people		
	Turfed area	.60	.60
	Paved area	.10	.10
	Building space	.10	.10
13	Off-street parking	.40	.60
14	Landscaping: 30 percent of site in transitional areas and perimeter buffer	1.88	4.22
	Total	8.13	18.27

*Provided by elementary school.

EFFECTIVE SERVICE AREA IN RELATION TO RESIDENTIAL DENSITY

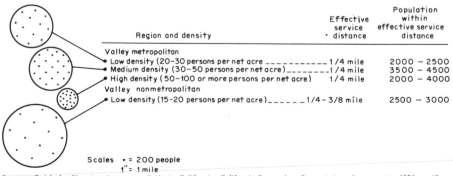

Region and density	Effective service distance	Population within effective service distance
Valley metropolitan		
Low density (20–30 persons per net acre)	1/4 mile	2000 – 2500
Medium density (30–50 persons per net acre)	1/4 mile	3500 – 4500
High density (50–100 or more persons per net acre)	1/4 mile	2000 – 4000
Valley nonmetropolitan		
Low density (15–20 persons per net acre)	1/4 – 3/8 mile	2500 – 3000

Scales • = 200 people
1" = 1 mile

Source: Guide for Planning Recreation Parks in California, California Recreation Commission, Sacramento, 1956, p. 45.

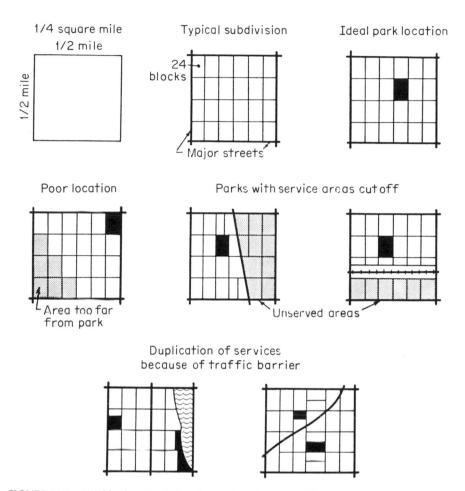

1/4 square mile
1/2 mile
1/2 mile

Typical subdivision
24 blocks
Major streets

Ideal park location

Poor location
Area too far from park

Parks with service areas cut off
Unserved areas

Duplication of services because of traffic barrier

FIGURE 11.2 Neighborhood park location options/Evanston, Illinois.

CONVENTIONAL SUBDIVISION

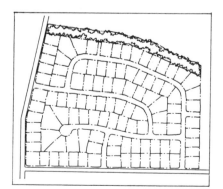

Number of lots: 108
Open space: 10%
Linear feet of streets 5,400
Linear feet of sewer lines 5,400

OPENSPACE SUBDIVISION

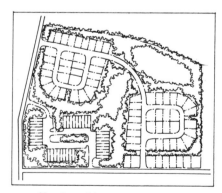

Number of lots: 108
Open space: 50%
Linear feet of streets 4,900
Linear feet of sewer lines 3,900

FIGURE 11.3 Open space vs. conventional subdivision.

project demand on an activity or area basis. Selected aspects of this method are described in Chapters 9 and 10. An illustration of this method used in Maricopa County, Arizona, is shown in Appendix G.

DEVELOPING METHODS

Several approaches to recreation standards methodology show promise. They are described as developing methods because of only limited or hypothetical applications. However, the concepts and methodology can be used for demonstration at this stage with the same degree of success or qualification associated with current methods. Three basic methods are described here as representative of what is possible. Several other methods will be described in Chapter 12 on needs analysis.

Innovative Method

This method was developed as an alternative to the traditional use of standards shown in Table 11.3. The basic concept is summarized here and detailed in Gold (1973). It describes recreation planning at the neighborhood level as an *incremental* process for the determination of opportunities based on the expressed goals and objectives of residents. The allocation of public resources for outdoor recreation is a direct reflection of resident values. These values are expressed in the opportunities, space standards, and priorities selected from *alternatives* by a representative body of the residents or their advocate.

The emphasis is on a short-range, goal-oriented, and advocate planning effort which is adaptable to the inner-city neighborhood. However, the same concepts would apply to most neighborhoods in a suburban setting with minor changes. The concept views government as the advocate of a neighborhood's interests and requires a high level of citizen participation in the planning process. It is based on human needs or values which can be translated into recreation opportunities and results in a recreation standard or indicator that reflects only the objectives or preferences of a given neighborhood at one point in time.

The variables and relationships of this method are shown in Figure 11.4. Resident goals, objectives, and leisure behavior are determined by a wide range of social

research methods. This information is translated into the recreation opportunity alternatives shown in Table 11.4. The index quantifies alternative opportunity levels for a neighborhood park based on (1) the percent of the total possible users that residents would like to have accommodated at any peak hour of use, and (2) the density at which the residents would like this use to be accommodated.

In practice, the use and density scales imply 100 alternatives. Each alternative implies a space requirement and set of activities which can determine the amount of space necessary for a recreation opportunity (activity) or the entire area. Table 11.5 shows the space needs and number of users for selected activities. Table 11.6 translates the recreation opportunity alternatives shown in Table 11.4 into a recreation opportunity index, which results in social indicators and representative space standards.

Table 11.7 shows the major steps of this method. Note that once the amount of area needed is determined, this does not have to be provided at ground level or outdoors. This method encourages the design of recreation environments which can be vertical and indoors to take advantage of rooftops, streets, abandoned buildings, parking lots, air rights over freeways, and similar opportunities in cities.

Recreation Experience Method

This method was developed as a departure from traditional physical standards. The basic concepts are outlined here and detailed in Christiansen (1975). This method parallels and extends the concepts of the innovative method. It applies these concepts to a rural county and suburban neighborhood in Pennsylvania.

The recreation experience method is based on performance standards or criteria that describe the type of experience or opportunity people desire at the neighborhood level. These experiences are selected from alternatives in a cluster of similar activities and translated into space and management requirements to support these activities. The final determination of specific area and facility needs is done by the local community.

The objective of this approach is to provide a recreation experience (output) instead of areas and facilities (input). Standards are means, not ends, in the planning process. They are used to evaluate the relative *quality* of

TABLE 11.3 | TRADITIONAL AND INNOVATIVE USE OF STANDARDS

Approach	Time	Concepts/techniques
Traditional	Past*	Population + A Standard‡ $\longrightarrow$ Allocation
	Present†	Pop. $\longrightarrow$ Demand + A Standard‡ $\longrightarrow$ Allocation
Innovative	Future	Pop. $\longrightarrow$ Demand + Goals§ + Alternative Standards§ $\longrightarrow$ Programs $\longrightarrow$ Allocation $\longrightarrow$ Review $\longrightarrow$ Revision

*Pre-ORRRC Report (1900–1962).
†Post-ORRRC Report (1962–1980).
‡Supplier Standard.
§Resident Goals.

an experience with a quantitative index of activities/ resources and qualitative index of humanistic/support requirements. Both indexes are based on (1) dividing the planning area into the units shown in Figure 11.5, (2) providing alternative activities, and (3) considering public and private opportunities as part of a community leisure service system.

The recreation experience or activity clusters parallel those shown in Table 7.1 (page 117). Appendix G contains examples of the methodology and standards used to determine recreation quality. Since not all opportunities in the system are likely to be provided by one agency, no "standard" park is expected to meet all the requirements of the proposed standard. Each park may have several components which provide recreation opportunities.

QUANTITATIVE INDEX The quantitative index for any recreation experience or activity cluster is determined by (1) a space or unit standard which can be applied to any activity within the cluster, (2) a development norm for that planning unit, and (3) the presence or absence of this opportunity in the hierarchy of planning units.

When specific activities are desired by recreation surveys or public participation in the planning process, these are inserted in the appropriate activity cluster. For example, one battery of tennis courts may be described in the quantitative index, but this could be increased if the people in this planning unit were tennis-oriented. Conversely, if the people expressed a strong desire for

TABLE 11.4 | RECREATION OPPORTUNITY ALTERNATIVES

Percent of users	Users/ acre	Key	General activity*	Specific activitiy*
1	100	A	Passive†	Variable
		B	Passive	
20	200	C	Picknicking‡	Same
		D	Picknicking§	
40	400	E	Area sports	Same
		F	Field games	
60	600	G	Court games	Same
		H	Challenge areas	
80	800	I	Social interaction	Same
100	1000	J	Mass crowds¶	

*Assumed for theoretical purposes. Requires field testing.
†Relative "solitude" in high-density urban area.
‡Family groups.
§Organization groups.
¶Spectator sports, rallies, festivals, public meetings.

TABLE 11.5 | RECREATION SPACE NEEDS*

Leisure activity †	Use dimensions ‡	Space required §	Peak users¶
Archery	50 × 300	15	50
Baseball	300 × 300	90	25
Basketball	60 × 100	60	15
Challenge apparatus	40 × 50	2	100
Football	150 × 300	45	20
Handball	25 × 40	1	8
Horseshoes (4)	40 × 50	2	16
Paddle tennis (5)	100 × 40	4	20
Family picnicking (5)	100 × 100	10	30
Group picnicking (1)	200 × 200	40	200
Shuffleboard (4)	40 × 50	2	16
Soccer	200 × 300	6	25
Softball	200 × 200	4	25
Table tennis (5)	10 × 20	1	25
Tennis (1)	50 × 100	5	8
Volleyball	50 × 60	3	20
Movies/television	200 × 100	20	1000
Combative sports (2)	50 × 50	5	50
Creative skills	100 × 100	1	100
Environment games	100 × 100	10	500

*Adapted from many sources to inner city conditions. Spacial requirements for most activities reduced by approximately 20 to 30 percent. Requires field testing to determine feasibility, safety factors, user satisfaction, etc.
†Selected for their adaptability to inner city conditions. Activity could take place indoors, in several areas or on several levels.
‡Approximate dimensions in feet. Where more than one facility is listed, e.g., horseshoes (4), dimensions are for a battery of four horseshoe pits.
§Space required in thousands of square feet.
¶Peak users implies the maximum number of players or users at a given activity to include spectators, umpires, alternates, etc. Hence, the number is higher than only players for many of the traditional sports. Watching is considered a leisure activity implicit in all others.

TABLE 11.6 | RECREATION OPPORTUNITY INDEX

Benefit value*	Percent of users	U index number†	User density	D index number†	Social indicator†
−	0	0	1000	0	0
	10	1	900	1	1
	20	2	800	2	4
	30	3	700	3	9
	40	4	600	4	16
	50	5	500	5	25
	60	6	400	6	36
	70	7	300	7	49
	80	8	200	8	64
	90	9	100	9	81
+	100	10	0	10	100

*Note that although the index places a higher value on low density, this is to accommodate normal recreation use, which would not take place during the special events or times when high densities would preempt the entire space for a desired community purpose.
†U index number × D index number = social indicator (SI).

TABLE 11.7 | INNOVATIVE METHOD: STEPS AND FORMULA

1. 100 percent of total pop. (TP) = potential users (PU)
2. 20 percent of total pop. (TP) = users/peak hours (U)
3. Users/peak hours (U) = actual users (AU)
5. Activity orientations (AO) = persons/acre = density (D)
4. Goals and objectives (GO) = activity orientations (AO)
6. $\dfrac{U}{D}$ = potential need (PN)
7. Potential need (PN) − supply (S) = actual need (AN)
8. $\dfrac{\frac{AN}{TP}}{1000}$ = standard in acres needed/1000 pop. (STD)
9. U index number × D index number (Table 11.6) = social indicator (SI)
10. Social indicator (SI) = recreation objectives

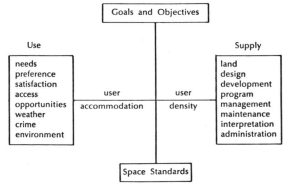

FIGURE 11.4 Innovative method: variables and relationships.

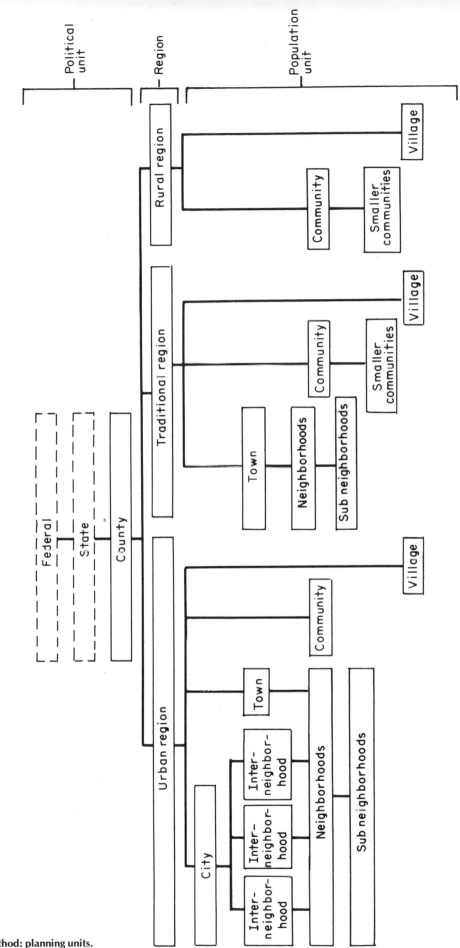

FIGURE 11.5   Recreation experience method: planning units.

Provision Not Recommended in Standards

− Provision Not Recommended due to Specific Local Considerations

SUMMARY EVALUATION

a Adequate   e Expand
i Inadequate   n Need

Existing

Proposed

x Recreation Experience or Humanistic Consideration Provided or Proposed at Site

/ Specific Facility Existing or Proposed to Provide Experience at Site

o Service for Specific Facility Necessary and Provided by Site Facility

LAND AREA

(ACRES)
3 Actual
(3) Approx.

HUMANISTIC & SUPPORT CONSIDERATIONS

Drinking Water
Sanitary Facilities
Refuse Control
Protection from Weather and Climate
Activity Lighting
Safety & Security Lighting
Staffing
   Safety Supervision
   Facility Maintenance
   Activity Leadership & Programming
Transportation/Circulation
Communications
Special Considerations

RECREATION EXPERIENCES

Physical Recreation

Outdoor
   Juvenile Low Organized Games & Free Play
   Hard Surface Court Games
   Recreational Turf Games
   Specialized Individual & Dual Sports
   Older Youth & Adult Field Turf Sports
   Organized Competitive Team Turf Sports

Indoor
   Juvenile through Adult Games & Sports
   Organized Competitive Team Sports

Social Activities
   Outdoor
     Participant Involvement
     Spectator Involvement
   Indoor
     Participant Involvement
     Spectator Involvement

Environment Related Activities
   Outdoor
     Water Activities
     Winter Activities
     Outdoor Education
     Unstructured Quiet Activities
     Outing Sports & Activities
   Indoor

Cultural Educational & Creative Aesthetic Activities
   Outdoor
   Indoor

SITE
Facility

Figure 11.6 Evaluation of recreation opportunitites.

any other activity in that cluster, the specific area or facility requirements could be inserted. This approach provides alternatives and flexibility within the basic recreation experience and activity cluster framework.

QUALITATIVE INDEX   The qualitative index focuses on humanistic/support considerations which relate to activity clusters instead of the planning unit. They relate to the health, safety, and welfare of participants or management of the area to provide these activities. The major elements of this index are:

- Sanitary facilities
- Refuse control
- Drinking water
- Weather protection
- Safety lighting
- Safety supervision
- Fire protection
- Activity programming

- Activity lighting
- Facility maintenance
- Transportation/parking
- Communications
- Interpretation
- Special considerations

Appendix G illustrates standards for each type of recreation experience. Figure 11.6 shows an example of the evaluation format for each site.

Although this method is still experimental, it has promise for rural or suburban areas, where the patterns of recreation demand and supply may not be as concentrated or complex as they are in the central city. The technique of clustering similar activities, evaluating existing opportunities in terms of the recreation experience, and translating this into quantitative and qualitative considerations represents a sensitive approach to recreation planning and the use of standards.

12 | NEEDS ANALYSIS

One of the most important and complex tasks of recreation planning is needs analysis. The techniques for relating demand and supply to describe the relative need for recreation opportunities are shrouded in value judgments, methodological distortion, and theoretical arguments. No aspect of recreation planning is more central to the planning process than needs analysis because it must synthesize the supply and demand components of a plan to develop relative measures of deficiency (or surplus) that can be used to formulate goals, policy, and priorities.

This chapter will not debate the philosophical aspects of recreation need or its relationship to other human needs detailed in many sources. Instead, it will focus on some pragmatic concepts and developing methods of needs analysis that can be applied in practice. The state of the art is still relatively crude compared to other aspects of recreation planning, but it offers much hope for the future.

CONCEPTS AND CRITERIA

Constraints to recreation needs analysis in the past have been a lack of definition, data, methodology, and justification. These constraints have rapidly faded with the developing theoretical foundation provided by researchers (Mercer, 1973; Kaplan, 1975; and Hester, 1975) and extensive documentation of urban recreation needs by the federal government (HCRS, 1978). The fiscal crisis of local government has prompted many cities to give priority attention to needs analysis.

Types of Recreation Need

Recreation need is the difference between current recreation demand and the existing supply of opportunities expressed in terms of land, facilities, or program. In the broadest sense, the concept of recreation need can be placed in the context of quality of life and environment. Its meaning can range from the biological necessities of clean air or water to social desires such as personal safety, fitness, adequate space, quiet, privacy, identity, human scale, choice, diversity, history, and aesthetics. At the community or neighborhood level, this spectrum of needs and values is described in Appendix H. Note the close association of leisure, recreation, and public open space to these needs.

A more direct way of describing recreation need is to categorize it by type and establish which type of need is the primary concern of a recreation planning effort at the community or neighborhood level. One place to begin is the categories of recreation need described in Table 12.1 and Figure 12.1. Note the different definitions, assumptions, and implications of each category. All have a place in the planning process and should be understood before proceeding with a needs analysis.

Objectives of Needs Analysis

The basic objective of needs analysis is to provide information that can be translated into public policy, private initiative, and problem-solving action programs. This information should provide data and conclusions to:

- Describe and project the recreation behavior and needs of residents or visitors in a planning area.
- Describe the levels of participation, user preference, and satisfaction for existing facilities and services provided by all levels of government and the private sector.
- Identify major causes of nonuse of existing facilities and services.
- Describe and project the recreation needs of general and special populations to include the elderly, mentally retarded, physically disabled, low-income, autoless, and racial or ethnic minorities.

In an operational sense, this information should provide the basis of a planning and management information system that can be used to:

- Help identify and rationalize budget priorities.
- Identify and anticipate developing public issues.
- Compare the need for types of leisure services or facilities by planning area and population group.
- Evaluate the quantity and quality of existing services or facilities by planning area and population subgroup.
- Evaluate the impact of existing or proposed assistance by planning area and population subgroup.
- Establish a baseline from which future changes in use levels, community attitudes, or system effectiveness can be measured.
- Project the future impact of proposed facilities or services to identify critical needs, deficiencies, or surpluses.
- Identify areas of possible coordination or cooperation between the public and private sector for the provision of facilities or services.
- Establish levels of public responsibility and performance standards for the provision of facilities and services.
- Answer public questions and provide objective information to public officials that can be used to formulate public policy.

TABLE 12.1 | CATEGORIES OF RECREATION NEED

	Conceptualizations of recreation need	Definitions of recreation	Value assumptions	Research implications
Expressed need	Individuals need for leisure is determined by individual's current leisure activity patterns.	The expression of individual values through participation in freely chosen activities.	Government should be a culturally relative provider. There is a relatively just distribution of recreation resources. Individuals have a relatively easy and equal access to recreation resources. Individuals do not have a similar need for publicly sponsored recreation services. Variation in need is expressed through differences in participation rate.	Determining what people do during leisure: activities participated in, duration, frequency, sequencing, and scheduling.
Comparative need	Need for leisure services of government as systematically related to both supply of leisure resources available to an individual and his or her socio-economic characteristics.	High autonomy in non-work activity which is the prerogative of an elite; a right to pursue happiness which is systematically unequitably distributed.	Government should not be a culturally relative provider. People do not have similar need for public recreation resources. Those with low socio-economic statuses have higher need. There may not be a relatively just distribution of recreation resources. Individuals may have relatively difficult and unequal access to public recreation services.	Studies of participation and nonparticipation and relationship to socioeconomic variables. Studies of relationship of supply of recreation resources to socio-economic status. Case studies examining reasons for participation among various subcultures.
Created need	Leisure need is determined by individual choosing to participate in activity after being taught to value it.	Any activity in which, after sufficient introduction, an individual will freely and pleasurably participate.	Government should not be a culturally relative provider. Individuals often don't know what they want to do during leisure and are happier if given guidance. Leisure activities are substitutable since the individual seeks certain environmental conditions, not specific activities.	Pretesting and posttesting of behavior and attitudes as a result of participation in public recreation services.

Source: Geoffrey Godbey, "Recreation and Park Planning: The Exercise of Values," University of Waterloo, Canada, 1977 (unpublished).

	Conceptualizations of recreation need	Definitions of recreation	Value assumptions	Research implications
			It is legitimate to use recreation to promote the desired goals of the State.	
Normative need	Experts can establish precise, objective standards to establish desirable minimum supply in quantitative terms. Implies physiological need for leisure.	A set of physiologically necessary yet pleasurable activities undertaken during nonwork time which restore and refresh the individual and prepare him or her for work again and otherwise contribute to his or her well-being.	Government should not be a culturally relative provider. Individuals have similar need for public recreation. Certain well-established kinds of recreation resources are inherently in the public interest. Recreation resources should be equally distributed through space.	Testing of assumptions of standards; e.g., accuracy of service radii. Testing relationship between perceived satisfaction, social quality indicators, e.g., crime rate, and having met standards.
Felt need	Individuals need for leisure activity as a function of individual belief, perception, and attitude.	What an individual would choose to do given a minimum of constraints or high autonomy. It is a set of personally ideal activities in the mind of the individual which, given the opportunity, he will undertake.	Government should be a culturally relative provider. Many individuals desire to participate in activities which they currently do not. There may not be a relatively just distribution of recreation resources. Individuals often have legitimate reasons for not using public recreation resources. Individuals may not have relatively easy or equal access to public recreation resources. Individuals will be happier, participating in what they "perceive" they want to do than in what they are currently doing.	Attitudinal research concerning people's desire for recreation experiences and environments and intensity of desire.

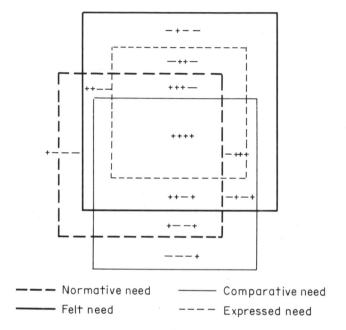

— — — Normative need ———— Comparative need
———— Felt need ---- Expressed need

FIGURE 12.1 A taxonomy of social need.

Planning Criteria

The selection of techniques for needs analysis should relate to the kinds of information desired and the anticipated policies, plans, or designs to emerge from this effort. Abstract models will be of little use in formulating public policy or coping with the urgent problems of most cities. These planning criteria will give needs analysis a pragmatic orientation in most communities.

POLICY RELEVANT   The analysis should focus on what is relevant to the community, not the values of the professionals doing the survey or providing leisure services. Pilot studies to discover latent needs or hidden user groups are as important as formal communitywide studies. A deliberate strategy of asking what kinds of policies, plans, or designs would best provide the levels of opportunity, choice, or satisfaction people desire should be used. A critical evaluation of existing services or spaces should be made by both users and suppliers in terms of effectiveness of these opportunities to serve human needs.

REPRESENTATIVE   The needs of all groups should be studied to include those who may be most deprived or vulnerable to the positive and negative impacts of public actions. A common flaw of many efforts is to slight the needs of a particular group because the definitions or techniques fail to include these needs. For example, to rule mentally retarded or physically handicapped people out of normal programs by definition is to deny their rights and the concept of mainstreaming the disabled in the community.

PRESENT ORIENTATION   Needs analysis should have a present orientation, especially in areas subject to rapid social and physical change such as new suburban neighborhoods or aging inner-city areas. Simulations of long-range future conditions with sketches or models can offer people a range of alternatives, ideas, and hopes, but they are no substitute for accommodating present human needs.

CREDIBLE PROCEDURES   A needs analysis effort should explain why stated group needs are viewed by the community as important and precisely how or why this was determined. Arbitrary or superficial value judgments are no substitute for fact. If an attempt is not made at the onset to establish a credible set of procedures, the effort will inevitably bog down in semantics, politics, or personalities.

MEASURABLE BENEFITS/COSTS   One criterion of relative need is the willingness of the general population, or those directly benefiting, to assume all or part of the cost for providing recreation opportunities. Without this association, needs analysis becomes more a fantasy experience than an exercise in assessing what people really want and are willing to pay for with taxes, fees, or self-help. An association of relative need with the willingness or ability to pay for general or special services is vital to any needs analysis.

PERFORMANCE STANDARDS   Performance standards should be used to establish levels of adequacy and baselines for measuring the attainment of objectives. The standards should be in terms that people can understand and reflect what is cost-effective or realistic. For example, to establish unlimited access to limited facilities such as tennis courts or golf courses is not cost-effective or realistic.

EDUCATION AND DEMONSTRATION   Needs analysis can limit itself to a description of existing needs, or it can stimulate a demand for new needs. It is essential to clarify these options and not raise false expectations. This strategy should be calculated at the beginning of a needs analysis study. Experience suggests a conservative approach in attempting to find out what people want and a more imaginative approach in showing them what is possible to meet these needs, if they are willing to pay for it.

CITIZEN PARTICIPATION   Within the time and cost restraints of a needs analysis survey, citizen participation should be dominant. The more community representation, the better. This is the best stage in the planning process to narrow the value differences between citizens and public officials. Their mutual perception of the problems, understanding of the facts, and willingness to compromise values will improve the credibility of a needs analysis and expedite all following stages of the planning or decision process.

Approach and Methods

Several methods of studying leisure behavior are described in Chapter 7. In the context of needs analysis, a combination of the following methods can be used to obtain facts, values, and insight about community needs.

EXISTING RECORDS   Most communities already have extensive data such as census information, health records, statistics on traffic, energy use, crime, retail sales, newspaper reports, and minutes of public meetings. With careful analysis, these records can reveal a retrospective profile of conditions or needs that relate to recreation needs.

PUBLIC MEETINGS   These are the most direct way of learning about community needs. Public meetings allow people to candidly express their concerns and dramatize their needs. The number of participants depends on the issue, time, and place of the meeting. Since only the most vocal or articulate minority normally express opinions, the needs of the silent majority often do not surface through this technique. Every attempt should be made to encourage the widest range of views in a balanced format. This can be a time-consuming and controversial process, but it is worth the effort and will reveal needs not commonly expressed in surveys or records.

INTERVIEWS/QUESTIONNAIRES   This method offers the most structured way of analyzing needs and can be used in conjunction with group meetings or public hear-

ings. The most rigorous kind of interview is a stratified, random sample of users and nonusers taken in the home by trained interviewers employed by a reliable survey research consultant. If this is not possible, some of the alternatives described in Chapter 7 can be used.

BEHAVIORAL OBSERVATIONS   Observing how people actually use recreation facilities provides many indirect clues to the nature of their needs. People will do what they want to do irrespective of the design of an area, or they will adapt the design to accommodate their needs, e.g., skateboarding where no facilities are provided. To be reliable, behavioral observation should be systematic and use the techniques outlined in Chapter 7.

A major problem of needs analysis is too much information. It is easier to gather information than to interpret it. Since time and cost are the usual constraints, the precise types of information and analysis intended should be outlined at the beginning of the study. Linking expressed needs to policy will be easier, if the analysis incorporates policy options in its framework.

The final phase of need analysis should be as open as possible to involve the entire community. This phase can take the form of public hearings or media presentations with community leaders, politicians, professionals, and the general public. Meetings should be well publicized and accessible to different parts of the community. Information should be clearly presented with the policy implications of choices spelled out. Summaries of the needs analysis should be made available to the entire community.

DEVELOPING METHODS

Several approaches to recreation needs analysis show much promise. All are described as developing methods because of limited applications that must be tested over time. However, these methods can be applied with reasonable success. They are representative of what is possible in a range of typical situations.

Needs-Resources Index

The needs-resources index, developed by Staley (1969), was used in Los Angeles to determine the need for leisure services following the 1965 Watts riots. A refined application of this method was used in San Jose, California in 1974.

Three assumptions are the basis of this method: (1) There are measurable social characteristics and neigh-

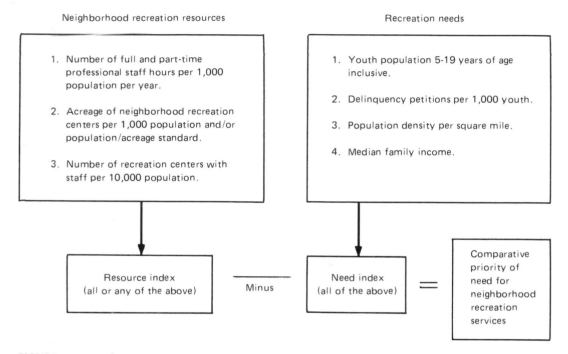

Neighborhood recreation resources

1. Number of full and part-time professional staff hours per 1,000 population per year.

2. Acreage of neighborhood recreation centers per 1,000 population and/or population/acreage standard.

3. Number of recreation centers with staff per 10,000 population.

Recreation needs

1. Youth population 5-19 years of age inclusive.

2. Delinquency petitions per 1,000 youth.

3. Population density per square mile.

4. Median family income.

Resource index (all or any of the above) — Minus — Need index (all of the above) = Comparative priority of need for neighborhood recreation services

FIGURE 12.2   Needs-resource index/San Jose, California.

borhood recreation resources which indicate comparative need for recreation services by neighborhoods in an urban setting, (2) all people have basic needs for recreation services, but because of different socioeconomic characteristics their needs can be met in different ways, and (3) priorities in community-subsidized recreation services should be for those with maximum social problems caused by population density, number of youths, low income, and juvenile crime levels.

The procedure has these four steps: (1) Define logical neighborhood or service areas for planning and capital budgeting, (2) inventory existing neighborhood recreation services and resources, (3) subtract existing resources from needs, and (4) rank all neighborhoods in the city by comparative priority of need for recreation services and facilities.

Figure 12.2 shows the four basic factors used to reflect recreation needs in San Jose. Table 12.2 shows a refinement of these factors used in San Jose. A combination of these and other critical factors such as crime levels, traffic congestion, levels of air or noise pollution, lot size, type of dwelling unit, levels of fitness, unemployment, broken families, and the like would make this technique more sensitive.

To make a comparison between the need and resource indexes, the raw scores for each factor are rank-ordered and converted to relative scores. This statistical technique relates a group of unrelated measurements or data to comparable scales. The score provides a measure of the relative position of each score on a scale of 0–100 with respect to other measures of the same type.

This method results in the comparative priority of recreation need on a citywide scale shown in Table 12.3. A graphic profile of one neighborhood is shown in Figure 12.3. The statistical model and limitations of this method are described in Appendix I. A major problem is all factors are given equal weight, which is not realistic or statistically valid.

Effective Population Method

This method overcomes the shortcomings of the needs-resources method by weighting the needs factors to obtain an "effective population" for each neighborhood. It was developed by John English for the OSCAR (Open Space, Conservation and Recreation) element of the Oakland, California, Comprehensive Plan (1976).

This technique parallels the basic procedure of the

TABLE 12.2 | NEED AND RESOURCE FACTORS

Factors	Indicators
Income	Median family Percent of families below poverty level
Crowdedness	Total population density Average household size
Social disorganization	Juvenile probation referrals/100 population Youth population
Target age group	Age group density Age group as percent of total population
Recreation opportunity	Park acreage/1000 population Park facilities/1000 population School acreage Recreation staff hours

needs-resource method and uses similar factors. However, it differs from this technique by showing how much more deficient one area is than another by *weighting* the existing population based on the factors. This results in an "effective population," which becomes the basis for comparing need on a citywide basis. For example, if an area has a higher than average percentage of young people, poor people, and apartments, its effective population will exceed its actual population. The reverse would be true if a neighborhood had lower percentages of these factors.

The effective population or need index is then compared to (1) the acreage of usable neighborhood and community public park and recreation opportunities as illustrated in Figure 12.4, and (2) the estimated dollar investment in land and facilities. Each neighborhood's resources are then divided by its effective population to yield the investment per capita of effective population as shown in Figure 12.5.

These deficiencies and levels of existing investment are translated into priorities by assuming that the more deficient the area is, compared to other areas, the bigger the allocation it should receive. Each area is assigned an allocation score based on this relationship. For example, if an area now has only a third as much investment per capita as the best-off area, it gets an allocation score of 3.00. Each area's allocation score is then multiplied by its effective population to yield a weighted allocation score.

The weighted scores for all areas are totaled, and each area's score is computed as a percentage of the total. This percentage is this area's implied share of future public investments in neighborhood parks and recreation, as shown in Figure 12.6.

Appendix I illustrates selected aspects and qualifications of this method. This approach to needs analysis requires value judgments that strongly condition the methodology and result. These value judgments could be the opposite in other communities. The advantages of this method are flexibility, sensitivity to community priorities, and a relationship to the capital budgeting process.

TABLE 12.3 | COMPARATIVE PRIORITY OF RECREATION NEED BY NEIGHBORHOOD

Planning area	Need index	Resource index	Comparitive priority
North San Jose	56	0	56
Alum Rock	53	15	38
Alum Rock	71	40	31
Berryessa	49	20	29
South San Jose	53	25	28
Willow Glen	50	25	25
Alum Rock	59	40	19
Alum Rock	74	55	19

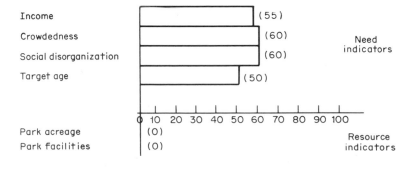

FIGURE 12.3   Recreation need and resource indicators/San Jose, California.

Study Area

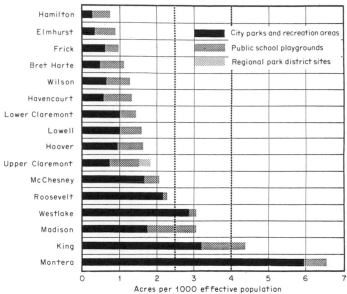

FIGURE 12.4 Usable neighborhood parks/Oakland, California

Study Area

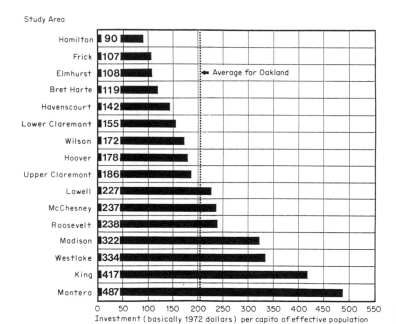

FIGURE 12.5 Investment in public parks by neighborhood/Oakland, California.

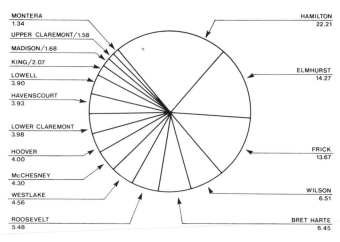

FIGURE 12.6 Future public investments in neighborhood parks/Oakland, California.

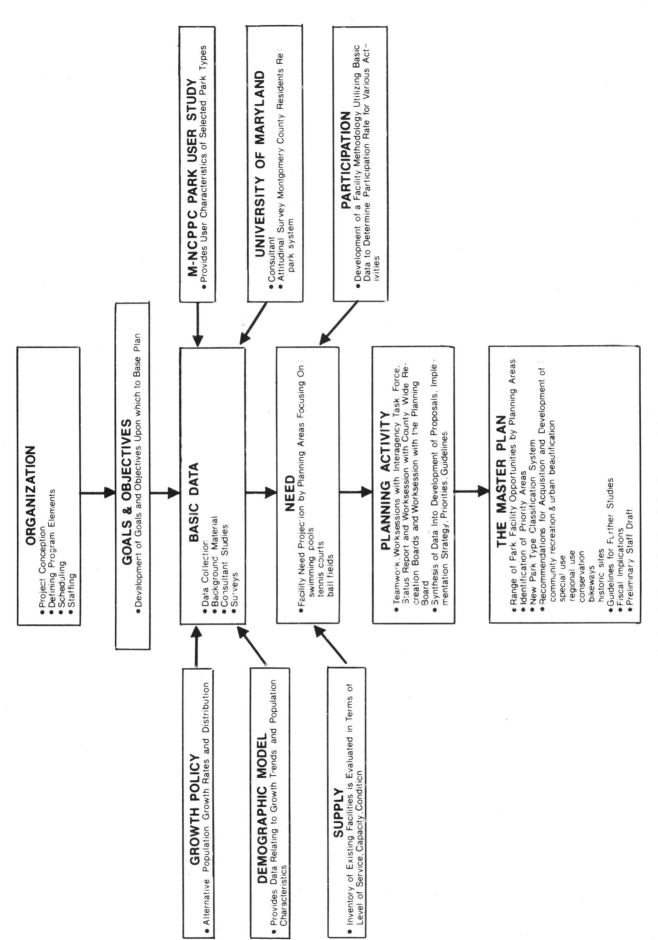

ORGANIZATION
- Project Conception
- Defining Program Elements
- Scheduling
- Staffing

GOALS & OBJECTIVES
- Development of Goals and Objectives Upon which to Base Plan

M-NCPPC PARK USER STUDY
- Provides User Characteristics of Selected Park Types

UNIVERSITY OF MARYLAND
- Consultant
- Attitudinal Survey Montgomery County Residents Re: park system

PARTICIPATION
- Development of a Facility Methodology Utilizing Basic Data to Determine Participation Rate for Various Activities

BASIC DATA
- Data Collection
- Background Material
- Consultant Studies
- Surveys

NEED
- Facility Need Projection by Planning Areas Focusing On:
  swimming pools
  tennis courts
  ball fields

PLANNING ACTIVITY
- Teamwork, Worksessions with Interagency Task Force, Status Report and Worksession with County Wide Recreation Boards and Worksession with the Planning Board
- Synthesis of Data Into Development of Proposals, Implementation Strategy, Priorities, Guidelines

THE MASTER PLAN
- Range of Park Facility Opportunities by Planning Areas
- Identification of Priority Areas
- New Park Type Classification System
- Recommendations for Acquisition and Development of:
  community recreation & urban beautification
  special use
  regional use
  conservation
  bikeways
  historic sites
- Guidelines for Further Studies
- Fiscal Implications
- Preliminary Staff Draft

GROWTH POLICY
- Alternative Population Growth Rates and Distribution

DEMOGRAPHIC MODEL
- Provides Data Relating to Growth Trends and Population Characteristics

SUPPLY
- Inventory of Existing Facilities is Evaluated in Terms of Level of Service, Capacity, Condition

FIGURE 12.7 Level of service method: planning process/Maryland National Capital Park and Planning Commission.

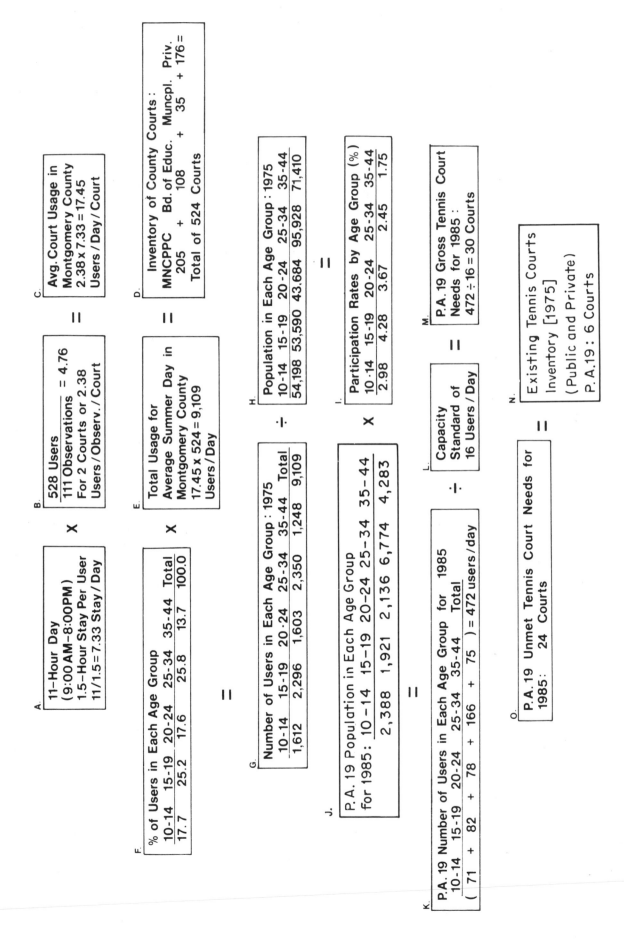

FIGURE 12.8 Tennis court methodology flowchart/Maryland National Capital Park and Planning Commission.

TABLE 12.4 | PARK USERS' AND DESIGNERS' VALUES

Concepts	Rank	
	General Users	Designers
People one wishes to do an activity with or without	1	6
Settings for the activity one wants to do	2	1
Relatedness through interaction with the natural environment	3	4
Safety	4	3
Aesthetic appeal	5	2
Psychological comfort	6	7
Symbolic ownership	7	9
Physical comfort...	8	5
Convenience	9	8
Policy on use	10	12
Cost to use	11	—
Cost of construction	—	10
Definition of space	—	11
Construction methods	—	13

Designers and users frequently do not consider the same factors in planning and using a space. Although designers give careful attention to the cost of construction, the definition of space, and the construction methods, these are almost never considered by users.
Source: Randolph T. Hester, Jr., Neighborhood Space, Dowden, Hutchinson & Ross, Inc., Stroudsburg, Pa., 1975.

TABLE 12.5 | NEEDS AND VALUES OF PARK USER GROUPS

Concepts	Rank				
	Elderly	Middle-Class College Students	Lower-Class College Students	Elementary School Children	Day-Care Children
People one wants to do an activity with or without	1	1	1	1	3
Settings for the activity one wants to do	3	6	4	2	1
Relatedness through interaction with the natural environment	6	2	6	4	2
Safety	2	7	2	5	6
Aesthetic appeal	5	5	5	6	5
Convenience	9	9	10	10	4
Psychological comfort	10	4	3	3	—
Physical comfort...	7	8	7	8	—
Symbolic ownership	4	3	8	7	—
Policy on use	8	10	9	9	—
Cost	11	11	11	11	—

The needs of various users vary according to life-cycle stage and class differences.

Source: Randolph T. Hester, Jr., Neighborhood Space, Dowden, Hutchinson & Ross, Inc., Stroudsburg, Pa., 1975.

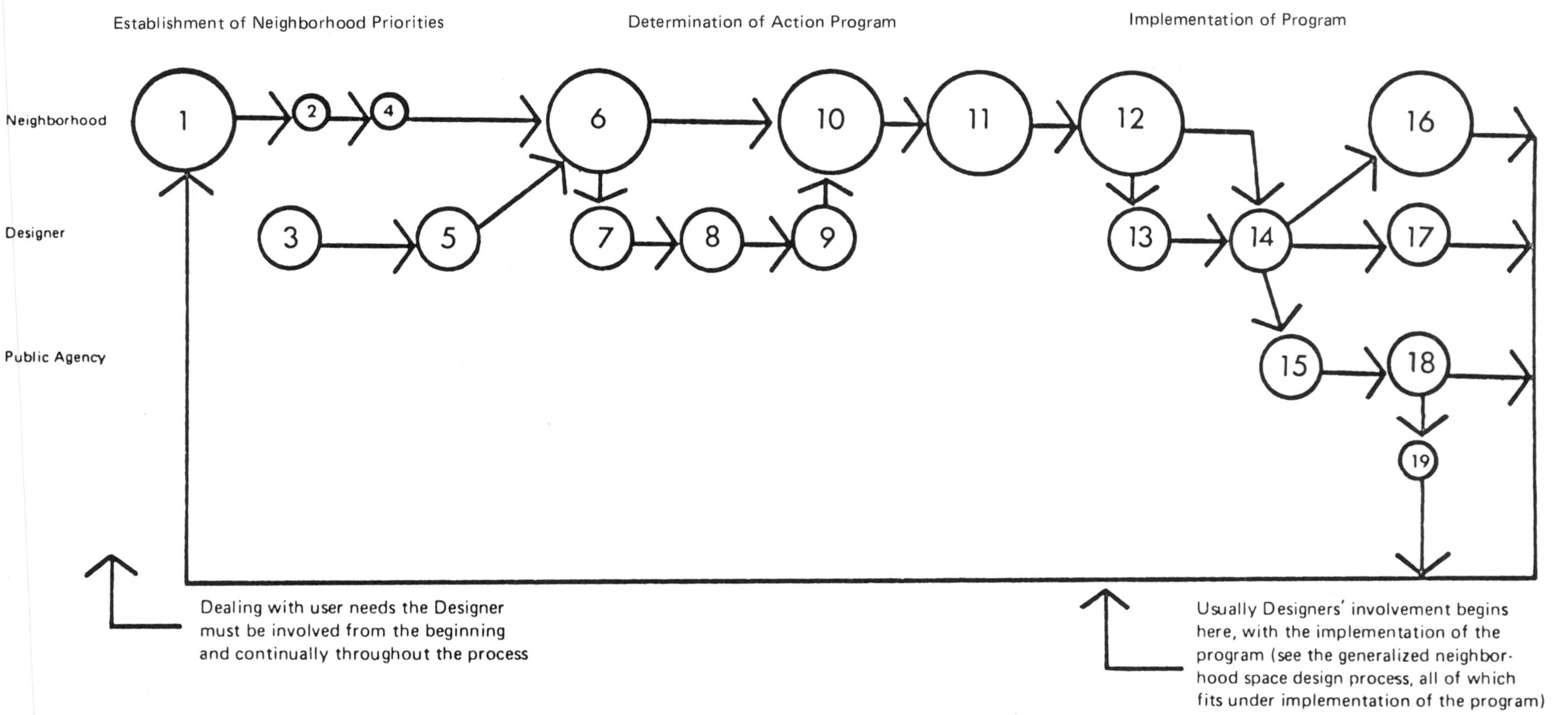

Establishment of Neighborhood Priorities

Determination of Action Program

Implementation of Program

Neighborhood

Designer

Public Agency

Dealing with user needs the Designer must be involved from the beginning and continually throughout the process

Usually Designers' involvement begins here, with the implementation of the program (see the generalized neighborhood space design process, all of which fits under implementation of the program)

1. Neighborhood organizes around problem
2. Neighborhood defines its want needs
3. Neighborhood requests design-planning assistance
4. Neighborhood establishes priorities
5. Designer-planner commits self to problem
6. Neighborhood expands organization
7. Designer-planner inventories priorities
8. Designer-planner makes social analysis
9. Designer-planner makes ecological analysis
10. Designer-planner presents alternatives
11. Neighborhood defines plan of action
12. Neighborhood communicates action
13. Designer-planner determines specific program
14. Designer-planner designs facility
15. Public agency administers plan
16. Neighborhood expands action
17. Designer-planner evaluates action taken
18. Public agency constructs facility
19. Public agency programs facility

FIGURE 12.9 Design process for a neighborhood space. (*Reprinted with permission, from Neighborhood Space, by Randolph T. Hester, Jr.,* © *1975 by Dowden, Hutchinson & Ross, Inc., Stroudsburg, Pa.*)

204

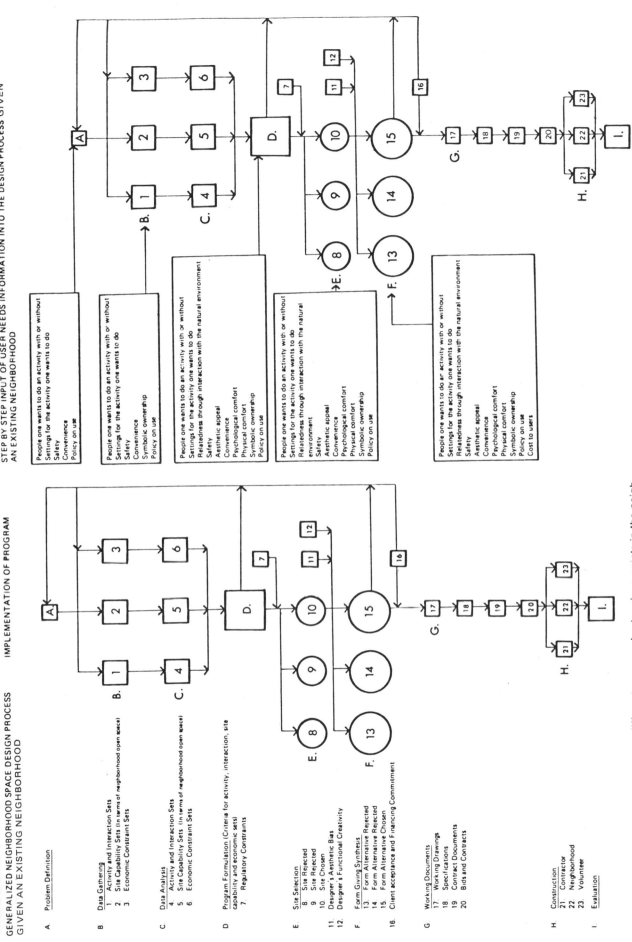

STEP BY STEP INPUT OF USER NEEDS INFORMATION INTO THE DESIGN PROCESS GIVEN AN EXISTING NEIGHBORHOOD

GENERALIZED NEIGHBORHOOD SPACE DESIGN PROCESS GIVEN AN EXISTING NEIGHBORHOOD

IMPLEMENTATION OF PROGRAM

A   Problem Definition

B   Data Gathering
    1   Activity and Interaction Sets
    2   Site Capability Sets (in terms of neighborhood open space)
    3   Economic Constraint Sets

C   Data Analysis
    4   Activity and Interaction Sets
    5   Site Capability Sets (in terms of neighborhood open space)
    6   Economic Constraint Sets

D   Program Formulation (Criteria for activity, interaction, site capability and economic sets)
    7   Regulatory Constraints

E   Site Selection
    8   Site Rejected
    9   Site Rejected
    10 Site Chosen
    11 Designer's Aesthetic Bias
    12 Designer's Functional Creativity

F   Form Giving Synthesis
    13 Form Alternative Rejected
    14 Form Alternative Rejected
    15 Form Alternative Chosen
    16 Client acceptance and Financing Commitment

G   Working Documents
    17 Working Drawings
    18 Specifications
    19 Contract Documents
    20 Bids and Contracts

H   Construction
    21 Contractor
    22 Neighborhood
    23 Volunteer

I   Evaluation

The designer needs information about different user needs at various points in the neighborhood design process.

FIGURE 12.10   Design program for a neighborhood space. *(Reprinted with permission, from Neighborhood Space, by Randolph T. Hester, Jr.,* © *1975 by Dowden, Hutchinson & Ross, Inc., Stroudsburg, Pa.)*

205

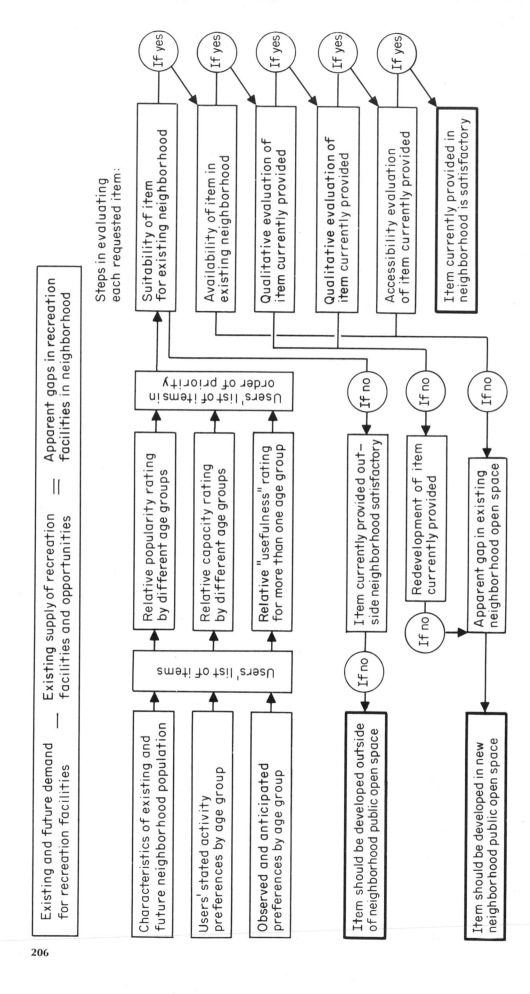

FIGURE 12.11   Model for determining neighborhood recreation needs/Decatur, Illinois.

	TOTAL WEIGHT: OVERALL PRIORITY	TOTAL WEIGHT: Usability[3]	TOTAL WEIGHT: Capacity[2]	TOTAL WEIGHT: Popularity[1]	CAPACITY: TOTAL	CAPACITY: Adults/Elderly	CAPACITY: Teens/Yg.Adults	CAPACITY: Children	POPULARITY: TOTAL	POPULARITY: Adults/Elderly	POPULARITY: Teens/Yg.Adults	POPULARITY: Children
Sandplay	◍	○	◍	◍	◍			◍	◍		○	○
Swinging	◍	○	○	●	○			○	●	◍		●
Sliding & Climbing	●	○	●	●	●			●	●	●		●
Whirling & Riding	◍	○	◍	◍	◍			◍	◍			◍
Balancing	○	○	○	○	○			○	○			○
Game Tables	◍	●	◍	◍	◍	○	○	◍	◍	●	◍	
Tetherball	○	○	○	○	○			○	○			○
Baseball	●	●	●	●	●	◍	◍	●	●		◍	●
Tennis	◍	◍	○	◍	○	○	○		◍		○	○
Football	◍	◍	●	◍	●		●	●	◍		○	○
Basketball	●	◍	●	●	●		◍	●	●		●	◍
Teen's Area	◍	○	●	○	●		●		○		○	
Children's Area	●	◍	●	●	●	○		●	●	●	○	
Area for the Elderly	◍	○	●	◍	●	●			◍	◍		
Bicycle Paths	●	●	●	○	●	●	●	●	○			○
Swimming	●	●	●	●	●	●	●	●	●	●	●	●
Pond Area	●	●	●	●	●	●	●	●	●		●	●
Gymnasium	◍	◍	●	◍	●		●	●	◍	◍	○	
Party rooms	●	●	●	●	●	●	●	●	●		●	
Multi-purpose rooms	●	●	●	●	●	●	●	●	●	●	○	
Vegetable Garden Plots	●	●	○	●	○	○	○	○	●	●		
Flower Garden Plots	◍	◍	○	●	○	○		○	●	●		
Trees, Grass, Flowers	●	●	●	●	●	●	●	●	●	◍		●
Place for Movies	●	●	●	○	●	●	●	●	○	○		
Place for Music	●	◍	●	●	●	●	●		●	◍	●	
Pavilion, Shelter	◍	●	◍	○	◍	◍	◍	◍	○	○		
Picnic Tables	◍	●	○	◍	○	○	○	○	◍			◍
Drinking Fountain	●	●	●	◍	●	●	●	●	◍	○		◍
Restrooms	●	●	●	◍	●	●	●	●	◍	◍		○
Refreshment Stand	●	●	●	●	●	●	●	●	●	○	●	●
Benches/Gliders	●	●	●	●	●	●	●	●	●	●		
Night Lighting	●	●	●	○	●	●	●	●	○	○		

● Relatively High Rating
◍ Moderate Rating
○ Relatively Low Rating

[1] Popularity means relative # of requests for each activity/item listed.
[2] Capacity means the relative # of users each item accomodates at once.
[3] Usability means the relative # of different age groups served by item.

FIGURE 12.12 Setting priorities for activity preferences/Decatur, Illinois.

Concept

·····•••Passing cars·······
·
·
·••Passing pedestrians••••
·
•Parking
Pool entry indirect access
keeping an eye on kids Shallow Pool
watching players Tennis courts watching what older children do from a distance Diving area
keeping an eye on tots parade to concession stand Concession Stand gathering to watch corner action
Splash Pool watching the action buying and ogling
keeping an eye on tots Sitting Area Basketball
people in passing cars

Plan

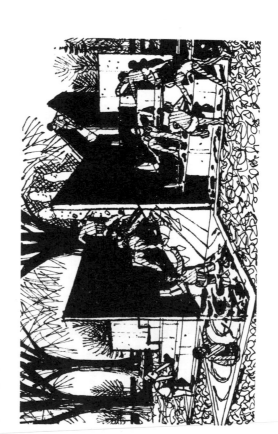

Jasper

Mall
Changing facilities
Parking
Tennis
Pool
Concessions
Sitting area
Spray
Basketball

Proposed Spray Pool

Program

FEATURE CHARACTERISTICS \ USER CHARACTERISTICS	Tots 2–6 yrs	Children 6–13	Teens 12–18	Teens 15–20	Adults 18–34	Adults 30–65	Elderly 60–80	Individuals	Small groups	Family groups	Large groups	Neighbor'hd Use	Community Use	School Use	Organized Use
Active	●	●	●	●	○	○				○	●	○	●	●	●
Passive		○		●	●	●	●		○			○			
Interactive	○	●	●	●	●				●	○	●	○	●	○	○
Competitive		●	●	●							●	○	●	●	●
Manipulative	●	●													
Developmental	○	●	●	●	○				○			○	●	●	●
Nature Interactive															
Culturally Supportive								●	○			●	○	○	●

FIGURE 12.13 Design program for neighborhood pool/Decatur, Illinois.

Level of Service Method

This method was used in the PROS (Park, Recreation and Open Space) plan prepared by the Maryland-National Capital Park and Planning Commission (1977). It is based on the planning process shown in Figure 12.7 and a behavioral approach to recreation planning that assumes *age* is the most reliable variable in determining participation or need. The level of service is a qualitative measure of effectiveness for public service by a given facility or system of facilities. An "acceptable" level of service is the level that satisfies an established set of values.

The methodology is quantitative and facility-oriented. It does not address spatial considerations or the physical characteristics of the planning area. Its purpose is to provide a better means of estimating the future need for specific facilities than traditional NRPA standards. Because the method is based on a demographic model of population that emphasizes age, it can be updated annually to reflect changing population conditions or county policies.

The following application of this method determines the current and future tennis court needs in a hypothetical planning area. The same approach can be used to determine the need for ballfields, swimming pools, and other facilities. The result of this process is a projection of unmet facility needs for the entire county and each planning area, as shown in Figure 12.8. Facility needs were developed with these steps:

1 Current tennis court usage was studied to determine (a) the number and age of participants, and (b) the average length of time played per visit (i.e., turnover rate). The total number of players was calculated by multiplying the average use per court (number of users × turnover rate) times the number of courts.

2 Participation rates for 1975 were derived by calculating the percentage of the general population playing tennis by age. These rates were applied to the projected 1980 and 1985 population by age to yield projected demand in terms of users.

3 Total facility needs were determined by (a) finding an acceptable service capacity of a tennis court in units of hours, days, weeks, months, or season, and (b) dividing the number of projected users by the service capacity. The result is the total number of tennis courts which will be needed.

4 Unmet facility needs or the additional number of tennis courts needed was obtained by (a) compiling an inventory of existing public and private tennis facilities, and (b) subtracting the inventory from the total need.

5 Existing tennis facilities are subtracted from the gross tennis facility need to find net tennis facility needs for each individual planning area.

This facility need is then ranked on a county basis. These facility needs are also related to the capital improvement budget for each planning area and the proposed facility matrix for each park.

This method does not provide the ultimate answer to planning facilities, nor does it yield adequate detail for site selection of parks or facilities since the unit of analysis is the planning area. It also assumes that participants are residents of the area and does not account for mobility of users from outside the county.

However, this method does yield an estimate of facility need in the county by geographic area that is age sensitive and less arbitrary than traditional standards. It is based on a behavioral model of leisure behavior and estimates of design load or turnover for selected activities. It is also related to the budget process and development criteria for each type of park.

User-Needs Checklist Method

This method of describing recreation need is based on performance criteria established for the site or experience. These criteria measure how well an environment responds to the needs of users. Detailed checklists and behavioral mapping techniques are used to determine what and who should be considered in the design process for a specific recreation area. The methodology has evolved from extensive studies of user behavior in neighborhood parks (Hester, 1975).

The technique is essentially qualitative and based on the behavior of existing or potential users of a given site. It relies on high levels of citizen participation, field observation, interviews, and questionnaires to establish relative levels of participation, preference, or priorities for how an area should look and work. Extensive studies of use and nonuse are done to describe how people feel about an area and what they do or would like to do in a public outdoor space.

The recreation behavior of users is studied in terms of items such as social interaction, safety, aesthetics, convenience, comfort, management policies, and cost. These concepts are then compared as they relate to the values of users and designers, or the needs of different user groups as shown in Tables 12.4 and 12.5. The process follows the steps shown in Figure 12.9 and detailed in Figure 12.10.

This method has been used with reasonable success in many cases. One excellent example is the redevelopment plan for an inner-city neighborhood in Decatur, Illinois (Stone and Taylor, 1976). Their studies use procedures shown in Figure 12.11 to develop the types of information shown in Figure 12.12. At the site design level, this information was translated into the design program and concepts shown in Figure 12.13.

THREE

ALTERNATIVES AND ACTION

13 | GOAL FORMULATION

No topic in recreation planning has been given less attention than goals. The lack of definition and application of a goal-oriented approach to recreation planning has resulted in many plans that are difficult to implement. This chapter will concentrate on selected definitions, concepts, and relationships to outline a goal-oriented approach to recreation planning. It applies the concepts and principles outlined in Chapters 1 and 2 to the goal formulation stage of the planning process.

GOAL FORMULATION AND RECREATION PLANNING

The key to a goal-oriented approach to recreation planning is definition, justification, and linkage of goals to problem solving. Abstract efforts will have little credibility. A pragmatic application of the following concepts adapted to fit the timing, scale, and political climate of a community will increase the success of a goal formulation effort.

Justifying Goals and Objectives

Justifying park and recreation budgets with traditional or arbitrary standards has been replaced with an emphasis on performance or effectiveness. Competing needs for urban services require recreation planners and administrators to sharpen their goals, if they are to compete with other agencies for funds in an era of scarce resources.

New federal and state guidelines call for more sophisticated plans based on the expressed values of citizens. These changes require a better grasp of what goals are and how they can be used in the planning process.

Despite the common use of goals and objectives in many plans, these terms are seldom defined or related in a systematic way. The result is contradictory statements that border on platitudes, instead of useful criteria for the development of policy or measurement of performance. The problem is serious. What is at stake is the ability of a planner or an administrator to justify programs or projects based on these goals.

All too often, attempts to formulate goals and objectives are omitted from most planning efforts or given token attention. In the haste to cope with urgent problems, there is a tendency to plunge into the planning process at the program or project level without knowledge of community values and needs as shown in Appendix H. This usually results in conflict, duplication of effort, and the failure of many programs to accomplish their intended purpose.

Goals and objectives are essential to the preparation and implementation of a recreation plan. If lay people, professionals, and decision makers do not understand and accept the justification for goals and objectives in the planning process, other dimensions of a planning effort will be unsuccessful.

Defining Goals and Objectives

Any attempt at goal formulation involves semantic problems. It is important to develop a set of common definitions to establish a framework for communication with citizens, staff members, or other agencies. If this is not done, most goal formulation efforts become frustrating exercises in communication instead of planning for the provision of leisure services.

A goal is an orientation. It provides the community with a direction. In this sense, a goal is an ideal and should be expressed in abstract terms. It is a value to be sought, not an object to be measured or achieved, e.g., the quality of life. Conversely, an objective is an end or point to be reached. It is capable of attainment and measurement, e.g., diversity.

In general, goals are universal and lasting, while objectives can change, e.g., growth. *Goals* are a statement of desirable conditions toward which society should be directed, while *objectives* are the stated purposes of a planning unit or agency capable of planning and taking action. Normally, goals and objectives are considered as "ends," and policies, programs, practices, and standards are considered as "means." For example, 10 acres of park land per 1000 residents should not be considered an end. It is only one measure that can be used to evaluate the attainment of an objective.

Role of Goals in the Planning Process

Plans should be prepared in terms of goals. The planning process is organized into five stages: survey and analysis, goal formulation, development of alternatives, implementation, and revision. As part of this process, goal formulation includes these five steps: (1) establishment of the perimeter of concern, (2) establishment of the range of choice, (3) examination of the relationships of goals, (4) evaluation of goals or sets of goals, and (5) adoption of goals as public policy.

Once goals are adopted by a community, they are converted to objectives. Where standards apply, they provide detailed specifications to describe or measure attainment. For example, if the goal is "quality of life" and the objective "diversity," under the area of leisure

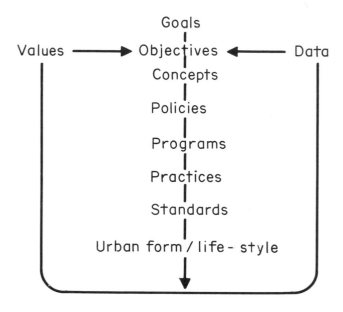

FIGURE 13.1   Goal system.

services one policy might be to "provide a range of recreation opportunities to meet the needs of all residents." Detailed standards or criteria can measure the attainment of this objective in terms of the quantity and quality of land, facilities, or program.

The next step in the planning process is to develop alternatives and a course of action to implement the objectives. This involves a series of *practices,* e.g., development plans and proposals for financing, operation, and maintenance. These practices are part of *programs* which are time-phased ways to describe and allocate resources. The program represents a broad classification for applying practices which work toward specific objectives, e.g., beautification or human development.

Figure 13.1 shows these relationships as a system based on continuing inputs of values and data. In practice, goals would seldom change while everything else might because of new or different values and data. The result of this process at the community scale is urban form and life-style to include the recreation planning objectives and relationships described in Chapters 1 and 2.

Goals and Values

Goals are conditioned by values which the community holds to be important. These values are expressed in the marketplace, voting booth, public meetings, and by citizen participation in the planning or decision process. Social research methods can be used to describe these values and translate their meaning into public policy. These methods can also be used to test possible goals and objectives for community support.

Responsive planning and representative government suggest a public opinion sample prior to goal formulation. If this is not possible, a "representative" citizens' group can develop "preliminary goals" by judgment and subject them to public hearings by the park and recreation commission. The difficulties and the time lost by this approach prompt most communities to sample public opinion first and then formulate goals based on this expression of community values.

Sound planning should be based on an accepted social purpose. The determination of this purpose becomes an important step in the planning process. Planning is the opposite of improvising. It is organized foresight and corrective hindsight. As a process, it needs realistic goals and objectives to create a common ground for compromise and cooperation. The usefulness of the plan will depend on acceptance of the goals and objectives by all concerned or the plan will lack public support. A lack of public support is usually a signal of conflicting values, internal inconsistencies, or needless ambiguity in the goal formulation process (Figure 13.2).

Policy: The Critical Link

Most plans are not implemented because they lack the catalyst of policy to move between ends and means in a consistent manner. *Policy* is a governing principle or course of action. It is the broad framework for guiding governmental action. Policies take ideas from the conceptual level of abstraction and express them in statements of intent or action. The rapid pace of change in most cities suggests the administrative flexibility of policy plans. At the same time, it requires an explanation of political decisions inconsistent with an established policy. This is a more adaptable approach to coping with change than the traditional park and recreation plan.

It makes little sense for cities and suburbs with rapidly changing populations to prepare long-range plans without the flexible dimension of policy. In light of new leisure patterns, design concepts, and management techniques, many cities may have been blessed because their traditional master plans were not implemented.

The merits of policy planning for coping with rapid change have already relegated most recreation plans without a policy dimension to the area of site or project

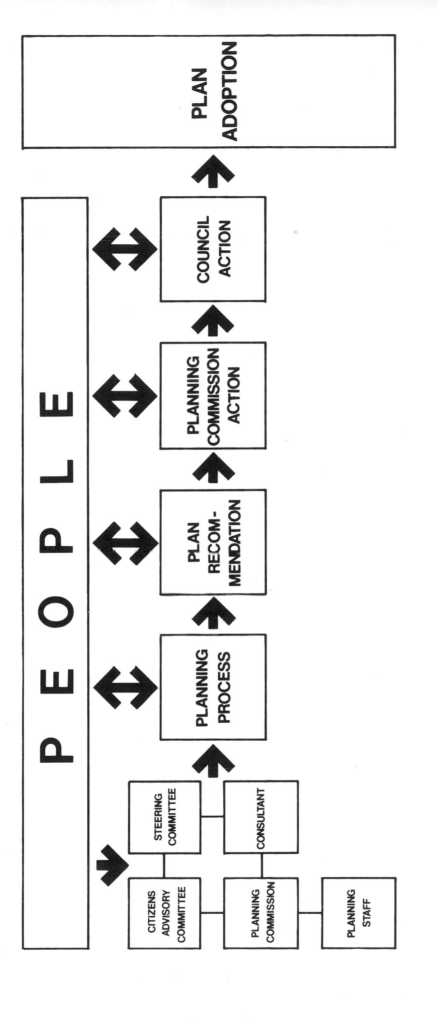

PEOPLE

STEERING COMMITTEE

CITIZENS ADVISORY COMMITTEE

CONSULTANT

PLANNING COMMISSION

PLANNING STAFF

PLANNING PROCESS

PLAN RECOMMENDATION

PLANNING COMMISSION ACTION

COUNCIL ACTION

PLAN ADOPTION

WHO IS INVOLVED ▪▪ DECISION PROCESS ▪▪ RESOLUTION

FIGURE 13.2   Public involvement in planning and decision process/County of Kauai, Hawaii.

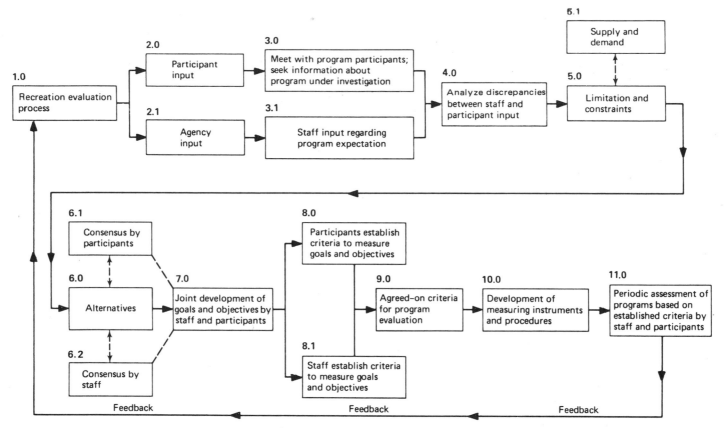

FIGURE 13.3 Evaluation system for leisure services.

planning. The national trend is toward policy plans instead of the traditional project type of master plan. Cities that avoid this approach to planning will make their task of coping with rapid change even more difficult.

Policy plans do have limitations. They require a high degree of consensus from community leaders and citizens. This requires public participation in the planning process to a much greater degree than the physical plan. If policy is to serve as a critical link between means and ends, it requires a systematic sample of public opinion and sensitivity to community values or priorities.

If the purpose of a city's general plan or capital improvement budget is to reflect public policy and rational decisions, serve as a tool for effective management, or allocate scarce resources to competing needs; the virtues of a flexible, policy-oriented approach to recreation are evident. To neglect this approach is to deny the realities of recreation planning in the 1980s.

Evaluating Goals and Policies

Once goals and policies are established, they should be continually evaluated to reflect the changing values, priorities, or needs of a community. Most approaches parallel the model shown in Figure 13.3 and the measures of effectiveness concepts outlined in Chapter 6.

The purpose of an evaluation system is to (1) determine to what extent the goals, objectives, or policies of a plan are being achieved, and (2) assess what needs to be changed to minimize the gaps between performance and objectives. The intent of evaluation is well accepted, but the process is often controversial because of the different characteristics of actors in the planning process shown in Table 13.1. These differences often become exaggerated when considered by the different groups shown in Table 13.2.

The best way to understand or reconcile these differences is to (1) monitor the effectiveness of leisure services, (2) encourage formal involvement of appropriate groups to help formulate or revise goals, (3) give equal weight to agency and citizen values, (4) seek citizen participation at the neighborhood level and from special interest groups, and (5) communicate on a regular basis with these groups. This type of effort is not common in most communities because it demands a commitment of professional time and community participation. Experience suggests the benefits of this effort exceed the costs and may be the only way to provide effective leisure opportunities in cities.

TABLE 13.1 | CHARACTERISTICS OF ACTORS IN THE PLANNING PROCESS

Characteristics	Planner	Decision maker	Individual
Technical training	Professional	None	None
Objectives	Public interest	Special interest	Self-interest
Time horizons	Long range	Short range	Immediate
Salary/time	Full	Partial	Intermittent
Orientation	Benefit	Cost	Cost
Approach	Systematic	Political	Emotional
Responsibility	No	Yes	No
Authority	No	Yes	No
Salary	Yes	None	None
Age	−30	50+	30+
Income	Middle	High	Low

TABLE 13.2 | GOALS OF ACTORS IN THE PLANNING PROCESS

Group	Goals or objectives
Community decision makers	Pride and status Cohesion and social betterment Reduction of juvenile delinquency Increase in citizen health and safety Beautification: aesthetic betterment and balance Increase in "culture" Community betterment: achievement of the good city
Suppliers of public recreation	Happiness or enjoyment Personal growth and self-improvement Physical and mental health Public safety Integration and socialization Citizenship and democratic values
Users of public recreation	Group interaction and sociability Relief from normal roles and surroundings Search for status Competition, reality testing, self-evaluation Variety, excitement, challenge

Source: Abstracted from a review of the literature by Gans, 1957, and Gold, 1973.

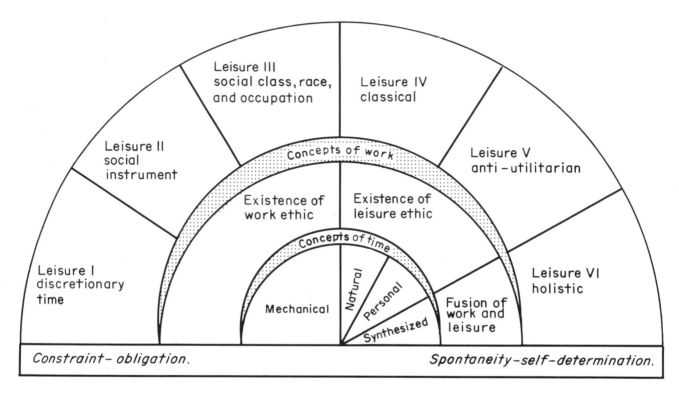

FIGURE 13.4   Concepts of leisure.

ILLUSTRATIVE GOAL SYSTEMS

In practice, most cities translate the above concepts into goal systems with different orientations to fit their needs. No typical case is described because it may not exist, and it is capricious to project a standard set of goals for the same reasons that it is to use similar recreation standards. However, three examples are outlined here to show what is possible.

Human Service Orientation

The human service orientation to goal formulation parallels the concepts and principles described in Chapter 2. It is an evolving approach based on human development as the primary goal of leisure services. This approach implies a cultural change in human values and leisure life-style that departs from the Puritan ethic. It acknowledges the concepts of time, work, and leisure shown in Figure 13.4.

The basic difference between the human service and traditional goal orientation of most communities is a value orientation which sees the public agency as a catalyst instead of in a direct service role. Recreation opportunities are provided with the public agency becoming a facilitator rather than the exclusive provider of activities. This strategy enables individuals and organizations to develop their own leisure opportunities and assume responsibility for the outcomes or objectives. Some of the recreation objectives include those shown in Table 13.3.

Another way of viewing this approach is by the components shown in Table 13.4. Note the sensitivity of this leisure service delivery system to family or life cycle, socioeconomic status, individual preference, and geographic location. It also acknowledges the social, physical, and institutional variables which could have a critical bearing on leisure opportunities in cities. The following goals of Culver City, California illustrate the human service orientation:

I To assume the role of community catalyst and organizer causing needed actions to occur from within the communi-

TABLE 13.3 | OBJECTIVES OF HUMAN SERVICE ORIENTATION

Physical	Psychological	Social	Intellectual/educational	Spiritual
Relief of tension	Anticipation	Interpersonal relationships	Mastery	Ecstasy
Relaxation	Reflection	Friendships	Discovery	Mind expansion
Exercise	Challenge	Trust	Learning	Transcendence
Motor skill development	Accomplishment	Companionship	Insight	Revelation
Rehabilitation	Excitement	Involvement	Intensified skills	Release
Fitness	Achievement	Fellowship	New experience	Contemplation
Coordination	Aesthetic appreciation	Communication	Develop avocations	Meditation
Physical growth	Self-image	Group and family unity	Cultural awareness	Wonderment
Muscle tone	Introspection	Develop sense of community	Learning about one's self	
Rejuvenation	Security	Compatibility	Evaluation	
Testing of body capabilities	Pleasure	Appreciation	Synthesis	
	Self-confidence	Cultural sharing	Problem-solving	
	Self-actualization	Concern for others		
	Enjoyment	Belonging		
	Exhilaration	Interaction		
	Self-expression			

Source: James F. Murphy and Dennis R. Howard, *Delivery of Community Leisure Services: A Holistic Approach,* Lea & Febiger, 1977, pp. 116 and 121. Reprinted with permission.

TABLE 13.4 | COMPONENTS OF A LEISURE SERVICE DELIVERY SYSTEM

Social components	Physical components	Participant components	Agency components
Ethnicity	Climate	Human needs	Goals
Cultural heritage	Transportation system	Motivation	Objectives
Social class	Topography	Individual self-concept	Philosophy
Race	Business and industry	Age	Organizational structure
Family	Schools	Sex	Leadership
Mores/folkways	Churches	Experience	Recreation areas and facilities
Religion	Environmental quality	Attitudes	
Health	Population density/crowdedness	Interests	Open space
Sanitation		Desires	Locality
Education		Goals	Priorities
Allied humor		Competencies	Financial support and distribution
Service resources		Capabilities	
Justice/courts			Equipment

Source: James F. Murphy and Dennis R. Howard, *Delivery of Community Leisure Services: A Holistic Approach,* Lea & Febiger, 1977, pp. 116 and 121. Reprinted with permission.

ty and encourage and participate in similar efforts to better serve the needs of the total community.

II To accept a humanistic ethic as our parks and recreation central value system and to revise services to emphasize human development, human welfare and social action.

III To encourage and participate in efforts to preserve our environment and open space and eliminate all forms of environmental pollution which detract from city beautification, such as elimination of unsightly billboards, utility installations and excessive noise.

IV To gain support for park, open space and recreation needs, the Parks and Recreation Department must become an effective educational force. The Department must become proficient in influencing the development of public policy at all levels, including the city council, departments such as Planning and Redevelopment, the school district, the community college and regional government.

V Provide meaningful and balanced recreational opportunities for Culver City residents.

VI To become a leading participant in the major social movements of our day with specific emphasis on the need for equal opportunities for all Americans, including racial and ethnic minorities, minorities based on age and minorities based on sex.

Neighborhood Renewal Orientation

This approach is more pragmatic than the human service orientation and most useful at the neighborhood scale. Chapter 12 describes the needs analysis method used for an inner-city neighborhood park in Decatur, Illinois (Stone and Taylor, 1976). In this context, the objectives of the new park illustrate this orientation:

- The park should be readily accessible to its potential users—physically, psychologically, and socially.
- The park should be a part of, not apart from, the rest of the neighborhood; the park spaces should be woven into the fabric of residential areas.
- It should be designed to contribute to neighborhood safety and security.
- It should provide features and facilities responding to preferences of current and future populations.
- It should contribute to the environmental quality of the neighborhood.
- Its design should promote involvement of residents in each successive stage to encourage proprietary feelings.
- Its activity spaces should be distributed and arranged so that they reduce conflict and discord and promote better intra-neighborhood relations.

The objectives of the proposed park should provide answers to questions such as (1) Can you get to the park easily? (2) Why do you want to go there? (3) Is it enjoyable, safe? (4) What does it do for the neighborhood? (5) Are there opportunities for active and passive recreation, outdoor activities, multi-age or interest use, organized group activities, and year-round use?

Examples of the design program and products of this approach are outlined in Chapter 12. This approach is sensitive to current user needs at the neighborhood level. It emphasizes land and facilities instead of program and implies government plays a major role in providing adequate leisure opportunities.

Conservation and Open Space Orientation

Many cities and states have mandated a conservation or open space element of the comprehensive plan that includes parks and recreation. These elements usually have a resource instead of a user orientation with a focus on land and facilities. However, it is possible to include many aspects of the human service or renewal orientations. Appendix H abstracts selected goals and objectives from the open space and recreation elements of the general plan for Davis, California, to illustrate this approach.

From Platitudes to Reality

Formulating objectives and policies is the most vital and frustrating part of the planning process. If planning is to be effective, it should be guided by credible goals and objectives. The policy links between objectives and programs to attain these objectives should be clear.

The purpose of a goal-oriented approach to recreation planning is to relate ends and means and sort out different levels of abstraction that confuse citizens and professionals. For example, a "goal" which can be reached is really not a goal because its level of abstraction is not high enough. Likewise, a standard is not a goal because its level of abstraction is too low.

Viewed in this manner, goals, objectives, and policies become more than platitudes. They provide measurable guidelines that condition the planning and decision process. They convert vague hopes into detailed directions. This approach to recreation planning is far from perfect, but it can provide a constructive alternative for coping with change.

14 | SELECTION OF ALTERNATIVES

After a community has examined its recreation resources, identified problems or potentials, projected needs, and formulated goals and objectives, it is faced with selecting alternatives to reach these objectives. The conceptual problem is establishing a range of options. The methodological problem is developing a technique to rank these options. The challenge is to apply criteria or techniques that allow the values of people and professionals to focus on alternatives which can be implemented over time.

STRATEGIES AND METHODS

This chapter outlines some basic strategies and methods for selecting alternatives at both the systems and site level of recreation planning. Illustrative case studies show several techniques that can be adapted to particular situations. They describe successful applications of different strategies or approaches to the problem. There is no technique that fits all situations, nor is there evidence to prove any single technique is best. At this stage in the evolution of recreation planning, many techniques should be considered, adapted, or synthesized to fit the specific needs of each situation.

Levels of Generalization

The level of generalization is central to selecting alternatives. In all cases, it should reflect the concepts described in Chapter 4 and be constructed to take advantage of unforeseen opportunities, new knowledge, and changing community attitudes. At the systems level, proposals or options should be mapped in general terms. Specific locations for facilities or projects should not be indicated in detail to give decision makers a reasonable degree of flexibility.

This strategy is based on the concepts of advocacy and pluralism described in Chapter 13 that suggest that "right" choice or decision is a matter of *value*, not fact. In most cases, the decision process will be influenced by the factors shown in Figure 14.1. Controversy and compromise are an expected part of this process.

Establishing a Range of Choice

The process of establishing a range of choice parallels the concepts detailed in Chapters 7 and 13. The problem is to aggregate a large number of options into similar or substitutable recreation opportunities that can be sup-

ported by public and private efforts. The classification of spaces and activities described in Chapters 7 and 8 can establish a range of choice in the context of resource and use quality.

One approach is to establish a gradient or scale of choice with extremes and a mean, such as high, low, and medium, or minimum, maximum, and average. Another approach is to establish time or responsibility targets such as short- or long-range options and public or private responsibilities for various types of opportunities. Other techniques focus on measures of user satisfaction or need outlined in Chapters 10 and 12.

Common Techniques

Techniques commonly used to select alternatives require a combination of analytical methods, citizen participation, and agency review. Integrating these components at the beginning of the process will minimize delay, misunderstanding, or polarization and result in options that reflect the values of all concerned. Each technique is briefly described here.

SYSTEMS MODELS   Systems analysis is a way to study the relationships or relative worth of the components of a system. It is one effective way to visualize complexity or reduce the variables of urban recreation planning to a manageable set of inputs (land, development, or programs) and outputs (human service, community development, or environmental management). With this method, it is possible to view a city as an ecosystem in which leisure takes place as a part of living and is provided for through a system of public and private opportunities that begin with the home environment and extend to the region.

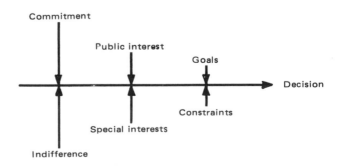

FIGURE 14.1   The decision process.

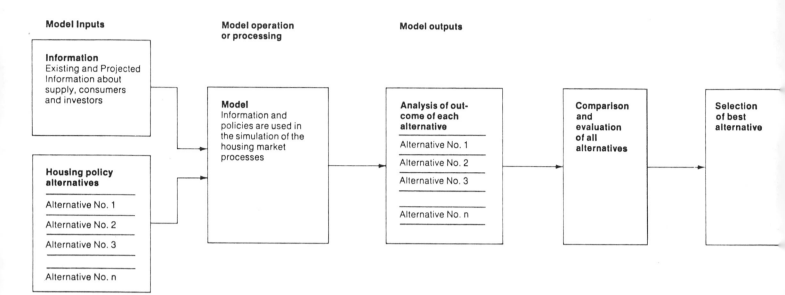

FIGURE 14.2   Model of housing policy alternatives/San Francisco.

Systems models have been commonly used to consider alternatives in other fields such as housing or health. Figure 14.2 shows a typical model for considering housing alternatives. A model is a representation of relationships. The representation may be physical or symbolic.

Physical models of recreation designs are common, but generally cannot show the social or humanistic dimensions of the project or system. Physical models also have limitations in the number of variables that can be considered. Conversely, symbolic models can (1) represent a large number of physical or social relationships, (2) manipulate variables, and (3) simulate possible actions which might be costly or controversial in practice.

Figure 14.3 shows one type of symbolic representation that could assess alternatives with the types of performance criteria or measures of effectiveness described in Chapter 6. The inputs could include leisure time, land, labor, and capital. The outputs could include physical fitness, urban beautification, neighborhood identity, and public safety.

A major problem with models occurs when the builders believe the model is "reality" when models are only a crude representation of reality. Models do not teach us anything. However, by following the steps we have programmed into them, they may produce results which show fallacies in our thinking about a problem. Decision makers and planners should approach models with skepticism and critically question the assumptions and results. They should consider the model a tool to help evaluate alternatives, not an end in itself.

PROGRAM BUDGETING   Program budgeting, or PPBS (planning-programming-budgeting-system), is a systematic technique for considering alternative ways to allocate resources to attain objectives in a cost-effective manner. It is a bridge between the planning and budget process. PPBS is a technique by which needs are identified, objectives are determined, priorities are established, and resources are employed to implement or consider the results of implementing a plan or policy. It requires explicit answers to these questions:

1   What is the social, environment, or economic problem we are attempting to solve?
2   What is our objective?
3   How can the problem best be solved?
4   How can we attain our objective?
5   What are the alternative ways of reaching the objective?
6   What results do we expect to achieve?
7   How do we measure these results?
8   What will the results cost this year and in future years?
9   How will we pay for it?
10   Who will pay and who will benefit?

At the local government level, PPBS requires (1) relating output to program objectives, (2) specifying the resources required, and (3) achieving a balance or consistency between programs. In practice, PPBS offers the opportunity to:

1 Develop measures of program effectiveness (criteria).

2 Develop program objectives (alternatives).

3 Compare alternatives (systems analysis).

4 Select an alternative (decision).

5 Describe the fiscal implications of this choice (capital budget).

PPBS is a tool for (1) developing the short- and long-range missions of any agency (goals), (2) coordinating interdependent efforts (programs), (3) determining the quantifiable outputs of those efforts (program objectives), and (4) estimating the multiyear budgets and costs of obtaining program objectives (capital budget).

In terms of time, scale, or jurisdiction, PPBS requires the (1) establishment of a comprehensive set of objectives, (2) identification of program categories to achieve these objectives, and (3) relation of these programs to the six-year capital improvement budget of a community. This task is not easy because it requires translating principle or policy into reality that someone must pay for over time.

CRITICAL PATH METHOD The critical path method (CPM) is a way to consider alternatives with reference to the time and parties involved in the planning or decision process. It is also a logical way to consider alternatives or implement the recommendations of a recreation plan.

CPM can be used to describe who does what and when. It is a way to sort out responsibility and time.

GAMING SIMULATION Gaming simulation is a technique that allows people to play roles and study the consequences of their actions and interactions. It is a way to (1) analyze the social impact of policies or practices, (2) compress time or scale, (3) identify actors and issues in the planning process, (4) evaluate planning methods or test innovative ideas, and (5) involve the public in the planning process. The game can also be used to popularize, refine, or establish the credibility of a proposed recreation plan, or any aspect of a plan.

Recreation planning games range from computer simulations to home exercises. There are usually two or more sides with conflicting objectives, a model of the environment, and a set of rules to manipulate the model. There is a preparation, a play, and an analysis phase to each game. The outcome, who wins or loses, is less important than the process.

Several sophisticated gaming models, such as METRO, have been developed for considering land use issues. Figure 14.4 shows an example of METRO that can be adapted to recreation planning issues. Some experimental games oriented to recreation planning include COPING (Gold, 1976), YOU ARE THE DIRECTOR (ABAG, 1973), and FFES/CHARGES (Gold, 1979). These games force the players to make choices among possible options and establish priorities related to cost. They are useful to help describe the recreation needs of special populations or specific neighborhoods that can be generalized at the community or regional level.

FIGURE 14.3 Symbolic model for recreation planning.

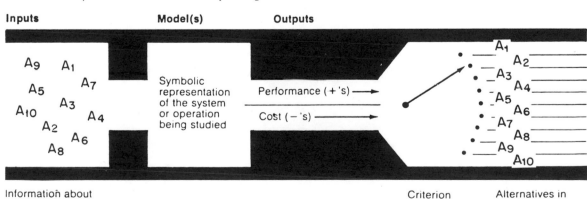

Inputs

Model(s)

Outputs

Information about alternatives

Symbolic representation of the system or operation being studied

Performance (+ 's) ⟶

Cost (− 's) ⟶

Criterion

Alternatives in order of preference

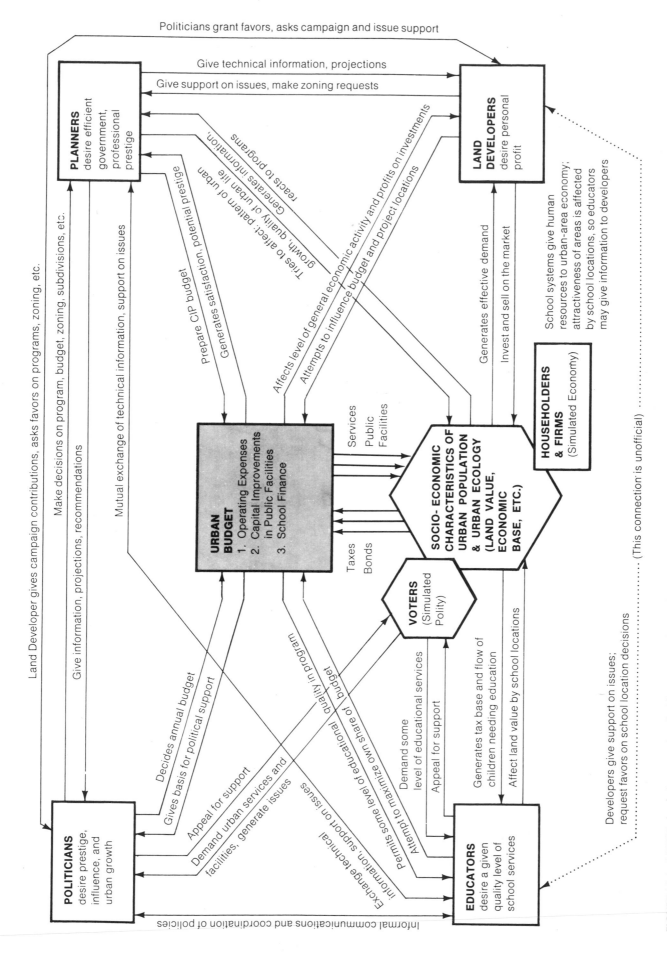

FIGURE 14.4 METRO simulation. *(Reprinted with permission from Policy Analysis in Local Government, by Kenneth L. Kraemer, © 1973 by International City Management Association, Washington, D.C. Based on model developed by Richard D. Duke for Tri-County Regional Planning Commission, Lansing, Michigan, 1966.)*

SCENARIOS   A scenario is a description of the future that envisions the way things will be, given a set of events, conditions, or actions. It can be used at the neighborhood or community scale to study or dramatize choices. It can also be used to portray the future character of a recreation area or system. Scenarios are best for dealing with philosophical issues or events that depend on the critical choices of decisionmakers. They are also a way of exploring alternative sets of conditions that might characterize a system of recreation opportunities.

Scenarios are commonly used with the previous methods to study the qualitative aspects of a range of choices or value orientations. They start with philosophical assumptions, introduce social or physical factors, and depict a range of choice from worst to best.

For example, one could take the reality checks described in Chapter 2 and write a scenario that outlines different ways to cope with these problems and opportunities. This would be a bold way of popularizing the potential impact of different approaches to recreation planning described in Chapter 3. Scenarios are no substitute for systematic studies. However, they are one way of considering the implications of a major shift in public policy.

MEDIA AND PARTICIPATION   The use of mass media and citizen participation in selecting alternatives is essential in all the above techniques, but it can be a technique in itself. For example, given the challenge of involving 10 million people in the New York or Los Angeles metropolitan areas in the recreation planning process to select alternatives, a direct approach is to *ask* them, using any or all of these successful techniques:

Public Hearings   The public hearing, town meeting, or neighborhood forum is a way to solicit views on alternatives. These meetings should be held at an appropriate time and place to encourage a majority of residents to attend. Meetings should be at the convenience of the public instead of officials or agencies. They should include provisions for public transit, baby-sitting, and bilingual interpretation and should present a balance of all views. Meetings should be widely publicized in advance and a summary should be part of the public record.

Mass Media   The use of television, radio, and newspapers to cover public meetings or increase public awareness of alternatives is an effective way to reach the metropolitan constituency for urban parks and recreation. Talk shows, interviews, debates, and documentaries can have a significant impact on public opinion. They are a low-cost and very effective way to solicit public opinion on alternatives. Although public reaction to the media may not necessarily represent all values in a community, it can bring out hidden values not possible in systematic surveys of public opinon. The potential of the mass media to consider alternatives or influence the decision process on major issues at the metropolitan scale is significant and should be used.

Displays and Exhibits   Most communities do not take advantage of public or private space for communicating alternatives or involving people in the recreation planning process. A fixed or mobile exhibit of proposed projects or possible options with a way for people to respond to these ideas is a cost-effective way to solicit public opinion and increase awareness.

Demonstration Areas   The provision of temporary or permanent demonstration areas to dramatize what is possible for a neighborhood or the entire community is an exciting way to involve the public in the selection of alternatives. The use of mobile equipment, experimental apparatus, and innovative designs or programs in demonstration areas is a pragmatic way to sort out alternatives.

The best way to find out what works is to try it in a demonstration situation. The risk is minimal and the rewards great, if the public is made aware of the demonstration objective. Demonstration becomes a vehicle for testing and allows the public to select alternatives in practice before a large-scale commitment of public funds is made.

Surveys   The value of field surveys, questionnaires, home interviews, and telephone surveys to assess public opinion on alternatives is described in Chapter 7. Beyond these formal methods of obtaining public response are a wide range of informal methods including telephone answering services, suggestion boxes, and onsite interviews to help assess user reaction to traditional or innovative ideas.

Preliminary Plans   Alternative policies, design concepts, and program ideas can be published as preliminary plans in local newspapers. These plans can be oriented to special populations such as senior citizens, children, or ethnic groups. They should invite constructive comment and criticism. All too often alternatives are presented in a format few people can understand. They intimidate instead of involve people. The way to avoid this is to publish different versions of preliminary plans for special

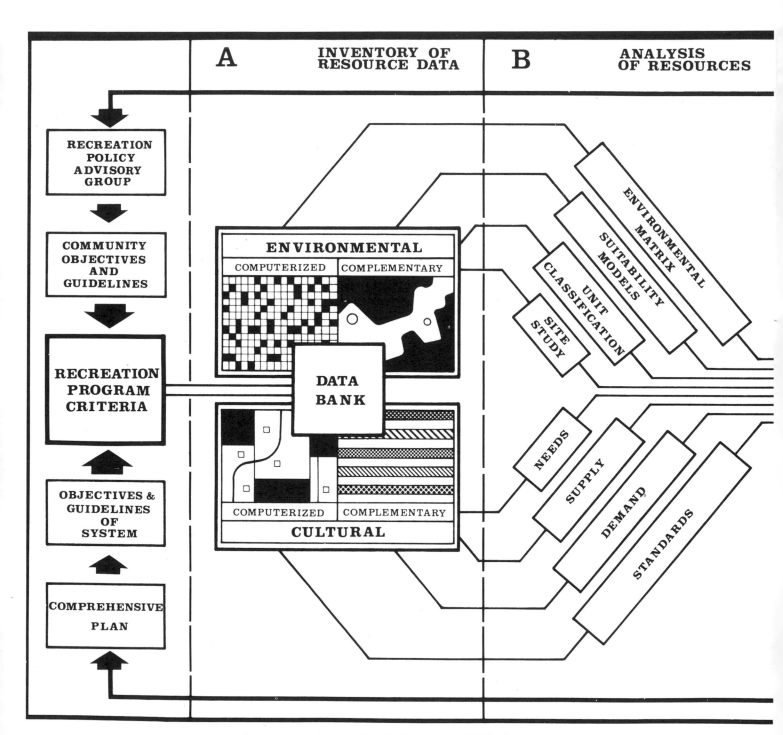

FIGURE 14.5   Recreation site evaluation planning process/Santa Barbara County, California.

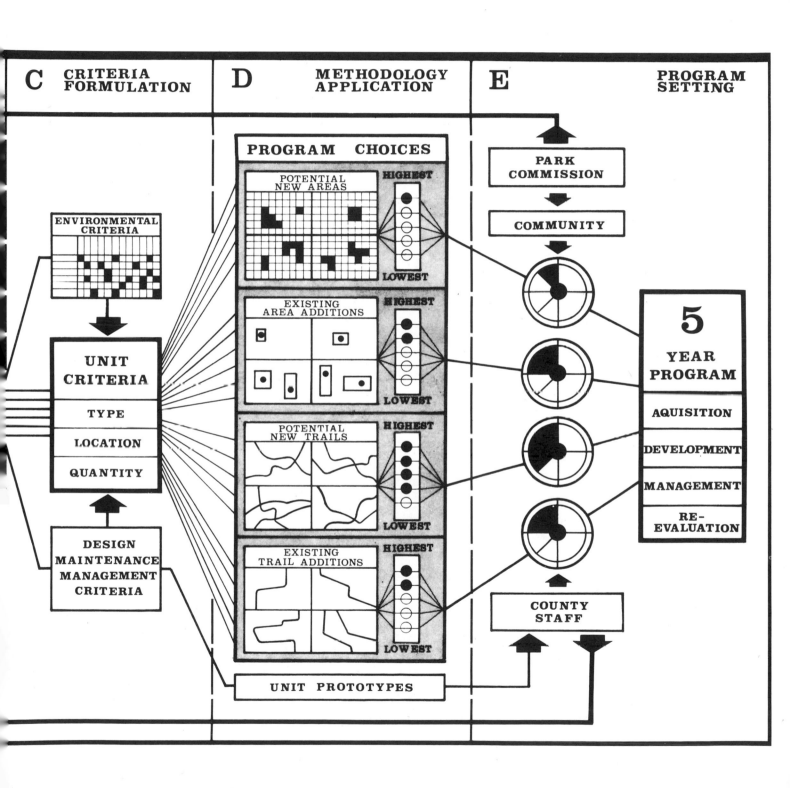

C CRITERIA FORMULATION

D METHODOLOGY APPLICATION

E PROGRAM SETTING

PROGRAM CHOICES

POTENTIAL NEW AREAS
HIGHEST
LOWEST

EXISTING AREA ADDITIONS
HIGHEST
LOWEST

POTENTIAL NEW TRAILS
HIGHEST
LOWEST

EXISTING TRAIL ADDITIONS
HIGHEST
LOWEST

ENVIRONMENTAL CRITERIA

UNIT CRITERIA
TYPE
LOCATION
QUANTITY

DESIGN MAINTENANCE MANAGEMENT CRITERIA

UNIT PROTOTYPES

PARK COMMISSION

COMMUNITY

COUNTY STAFF

5 YEAR PROGRAM
AQUISITION
DEVELOPMENT
MANAGEMENT
RE-EVALUATION

COUNTYWIDE MAPS

RAW DATA MAP COMPUTER PRINTOUT

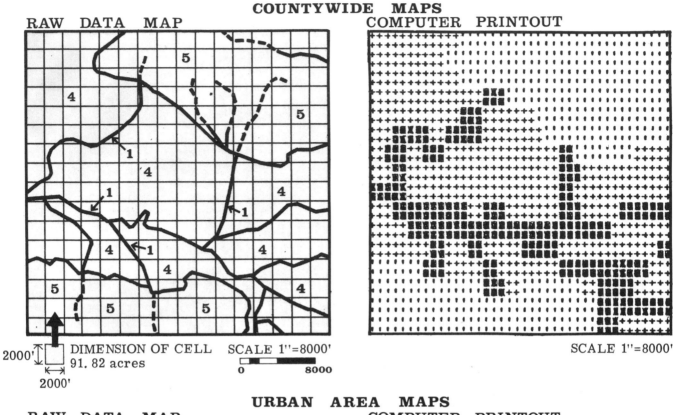

DIMENSION OF CELL SCALE 1"=8000'
91.82 acres
2000'

SCALE 1"=8000'

URBAN AREA MAPS

RAW DATA MAP COMPUTER PRINTOUT

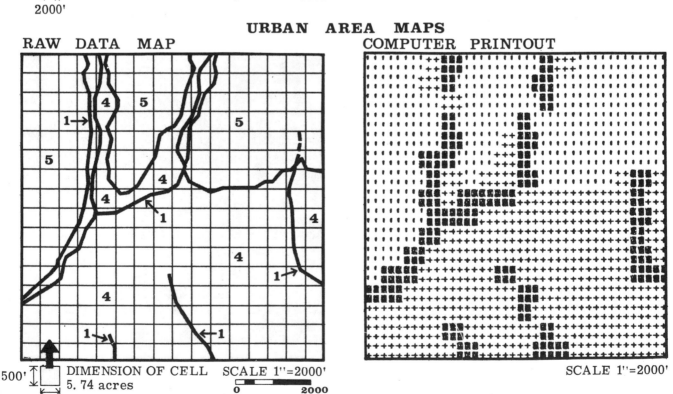

DIMENSION OF CELL SCALE 1"=2000'
5.74 acres
500'

SCALE 1"=2000'

FIGURE 14.6 Computer mapping technique/Santa Barbara County, California.

TABLE 14.1 | TRAIL EVALUATION CRITERIA

I Number and character of intersections

High 6 No intersections
5 One minor intersection
4 One major intersection, or a few minor intersections
3 Several intersections
2 Several major intersections
Low 1 Many major intersections or railroad crossings

II Visual quality (high 6, low 1)
One point for each favorable condition of:

Scale of area Visual variety
Scale of elements Visual integrity
Visual enclosure Other parameters

III Land use type

High 6 Publicly owned, underdeveloped land, existing park
5 Mostly publicly owned
4 Publicly owned, but with restrictions
3 Privately owned residential or agricultural
2 Sensitive agriculture or highly restrictive
Low 1 Special ownership; for example, Vandenburg A.F.B.

IV Number of owners

High 6 1 owner/mile
5 2–5 owners/mile
4 6–15 owners/mile
3 16–30 owners/mile
2 31–50 owners/mile
Low 1 Over 50 owners/mile

V Type of facilities (at terminus points)

High 6 Major existing parks
5 Minor existing parks
4 One park and one school or other recreation facility
3 One school only
2 Near to recreation or school facility
Low 1 No facilities at either terminus

VI System compatibility

High 6 Connecting two existing parks or within a park
5–2 Connections to various levels of recreation facilities
Low 1 Connecting no recreation units

VII Biological impact

Trail locations were overlaid on the tolerance intensity of environmental biology printout maps and scored according to the biologic sensitivity of the zones they traversed.

Tolerant to many activities: 6   Very sensitive: 1

VIII Geological impact

Trail locations were overlaid on the geologic problem index printout maps and scored for their relative safety from geologic hazards.

IX Physical condition

High 6 Good surface, good lighting, safe environs
5–2 Decreasing degrees of safety
Low 1 Poorly lit, poor surface, obstructions, drainage problems

X Potential number of users

High 6 Located through high-density residential areas; busy tourist areas
5–2 Decreasing degrees of potential users
Low 1 Near very few or no residences; connecting insignificant termini

XI Composition of users

High 6 Diverse age groups
5–2 Decreasing degrees of user diversity
Low 1 Small, specialized groups of users

XII Kinetic environmental experience

High 6 Enjoyable movement over terrain
5–2 Decreasing degrees of trail use enjoyment
Low 1 Disturbing noises, smells, unfavorable climatic conditions, difficult maneuvering.

TABLE 14.2 | SCORING MATRIX

LOMPOC URBAN AREA — BIKE TRAILS													
Scoring key — Basic scoring: 1 = Low; 6 = High (1–6). May be used when individual variable is extremely important for evaluation (±3).	No. and character of intersections	Visual quality	Land use type	No. of owners	Type of facilities	System compatibility	Biological impact	Geologic impact	Physical condition	Potential no. users	Composition of users	Kinetic environmental experience	Total score	Rank
# TRAIL NAME														
1 Ocean Beach Park Trail	6	5	6	6	6	6	2	3	3	2	3	5	53	3
2 Casmalia Road Trail	5	4	1	1	3	1	2	5	4	3	4	2	35	10
3 Santa Ynez River Trail	6	4	5	3	3	3	3	5	3	4	4	4	47	8
4 Correctional Institute Trail	6	5	2	1	5	5	4	5	3	4	4	4	48	7
5 Cabrillo Highway Trail	4	3	4	5	5	4	4	5	4	5	3	4	50	5
6 Kenneth Adam Park Trail	6	5	2	2	5	5	5	5	3	4	5	5	52	4
7 Santa Ynez River—"A" Street Trail	5	4	5	5	5	5	3	5	3	5	5	5	55	2
8 Riverside Drive Trail	6	3	3	3	3	3	5	5	4	5	5	4	49	6
9 River Park Trail	6	4	5	5	5	5	3	5	3	5	5	5	56	1
10 Cabrillo Highway South Trail	4	4	4	4	3	3	4	3	4	3	3	4	43	9
LOMPOC URBAN AREA — HIKING AND EQUESTRIAN TRAILS														
1 Ocean Beach Trail	6	4	2	−2	5	5	1	4	3	3	3	5	38	3
2 Santa Ynez River Trail	6	4	5	3	3	4	3	5	3	4	4	4	48	2
3 Kenneth Adam Park Trail	5	4	3	5	5	5	6	5	2	4	5	4	53	1

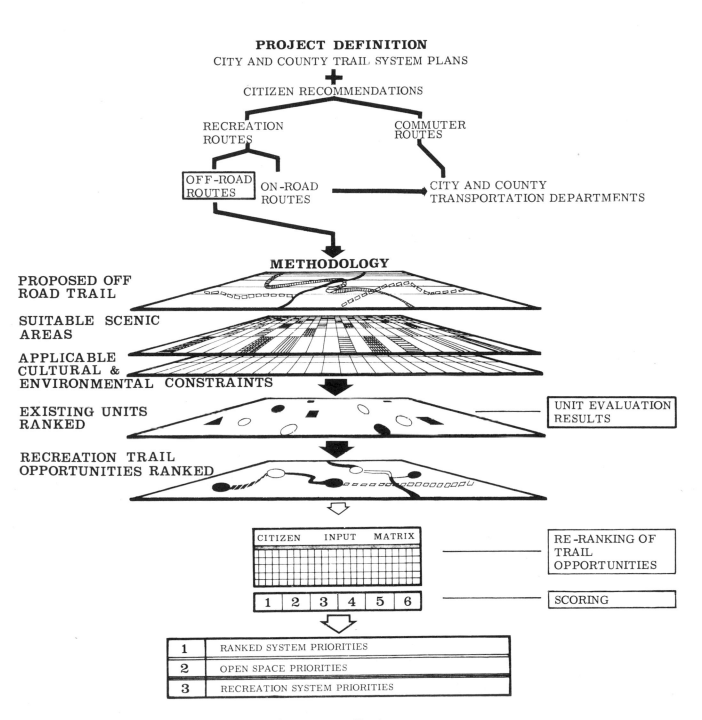

FIGURE 14.7   Recreation trail ranking system/Santa Barbara County, California.

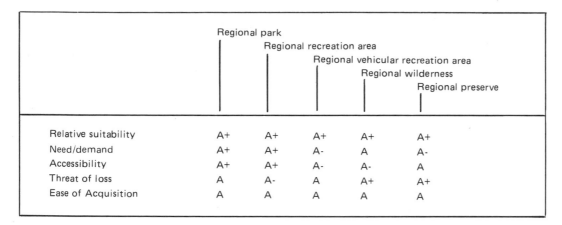

	Regional park	Regional recreation area	Regional vehicular recreation area	Regional wilderness	Regional preserve
Relative suitability	A+	A+	A+	A+	A+
Need/demand	A+	A+	A-	A	A-
Accessibility	A+	A+	A-	A-	A
Threat of loss	A	A-	A	A+	A+
Ease of Acquisition	A	A	A	A	A

FIGURE 14.8 Criteria weighting and park type/East Bay Regional Park District, California.

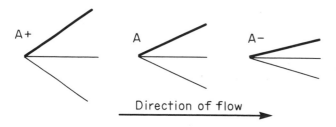

FIGURE 14.9 Visual weighting of acquisition criteria/East Bay Regional Park District, California.

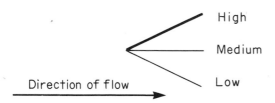

FIGURE 14.10 Visual ranking of acquisition/East Bay Regional Park District, California.

populations to encourage the widest range of candid comment.

Beware of any plan that does not indicate alternatives prior to recommending one, because this may be a signal of (1) relative lack of citizen participation, (2) planners or special interests attempting to superimpose their values on the community, and (3) an unsophisticated approach to the planning process based on traditional methods. In a pluralistic society, alternatives are essential if recreation planning is to be responsive to human needs. Planners who claim they do not know what the public wants

may not have made a sincere attempt to measure public opinion.

ILLUSTRATIVE APPLICATIONS

Four examples are described here to show the spectrum of techniques possible. The common thread in each is a high level of citizen participation and systematic way to assess the differences between major alternatives. No technique can or should fit all situations, but there are aspects of each example that can be combined with the previous methods to select alternatives.

Weighted Criteria Method

At the county level, one example of a sophisticated methodology has been developed for Santa Barbara County (1974). It uses a computerized model to evaluate the impact of development alternatives with weighted criteria. The major components of this method are (1) an inventory of natural and cultural resources, (2) analysis of those resources as they relate to recreation, (3) formulation of planning criteria, (4) application of the methodology to select alternatives, and (5) program setting with the community and elected officials. This process is shown in Figure 14.5.

This process is used to rank the relative priority of all potential sites (areas) and linkages (trails) in the county. It establishes detailed criteria for evaluating each project. For example, all supply and demand data is mapped as shown in Figure 14.6. Each project is evaluated with criteria such as those shown in Table 14.1, which applies only to trails. This information is translated into the matrix shown in Table 14.2 and evaluated in the process shown in Figure 14.7.

Railroad Sorting System

Faced with the challenge of selecting regional park sites to fit a system within the projected financial capacity of the district, Overview (1973) developed a methodology for the East Bay Regional Park District in California that is similar to the system used to sort railroad cars. The method is based on this four-step process:

Step 1 *Determining Initial Eligibility*. Each site is evaluated in terms of the classification system described in Chapter 8. An area must meet the purpose, minimum standards, and management policies established for each type of park or it is eliminated from any further consideration.

Step 2 *Applying the Parkland Acquisition Criteria*. Five criteria are used to evaluate each potential area: relative suitability, need/demand, accessibility, threat of loss, and ease of acquisition. Each site is rated high, medium, or low depending on how well it meets the criteria. The ranking process includes a wide range of objective and subjective judgments.

Step 3 *Applying the Priority System*. Applying the parkland acquisition criteria to derive a priority ranking for each site follows this procedure: (a) "weighting" the five parkland acquisition criteria in terms of their relative importance for selection of parklands in each category, (b) combining the weight of each criterion with the ranking of a site, (c) running each site through the sytstem for each parkland category to develop a list of sites in order of importance, and (d) grouping the sites for each parkland category into priority groups for acquisition.

Figure 14.8 shows the criteria weighting for each criteria and park type. These weights are the following: above average importance (A+), average importance (A), and below average importance (A−). These weights are changed into graphics analagous to numerical values. Instead of large, medium, and small numbers, the relative weight of the criteria is portrayed graphically by a large, medium, or small distance, as shown in Figure 14.9.

The graphic process for evaluating each proposed site is similar to the way a train moves through a railroad yard. The course of the train is determined by switches which transfer the train from one track to another. The course of a park site being evaluated is determined by one "switch" for each of the five acquisition criteria. Each switch presents a "choice" representing the high, medium, or low ranking of a potential park site in terms of a particular parkland acquisition criterion shown in Figure 14.10.

The visual weighting of criteria for each parkland category is represented graphically by the distance (spread) between the arms of the switch as shown in Figure 14.9. These weighted switches, one for each of the five acquisition criteria, are arranged end to end, left to right in a flowchart similar to a railroad yard.

The site enters at the left and moves to the right "switching" at each switch depending on its high, medium, or low ranking for the criterion represented by that switch. The higher the site ends up at the right edge of the flowchart, the higher its priority in relation to the other proposed acquisitions of the same parkland

FIGURE 14.11 Regional park flowchart/East Bay Regional Park District, California.

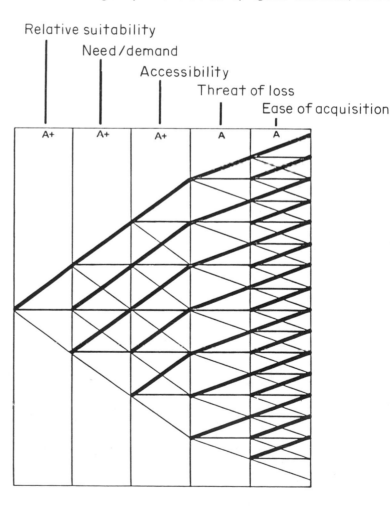

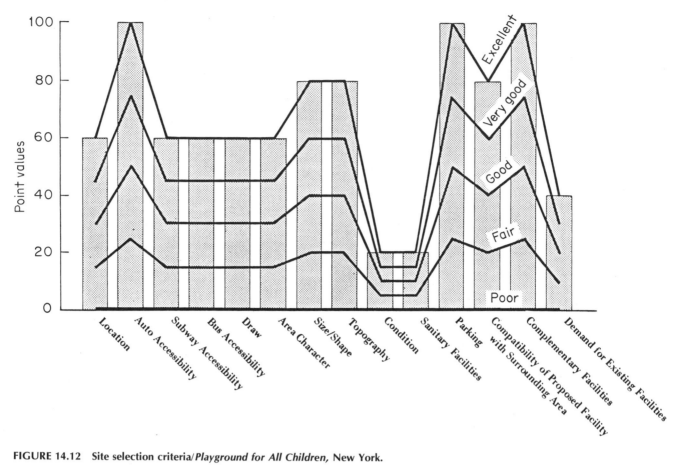

FIGURE 14.12   Site selection criteria/*Playground for All Children*, New York.

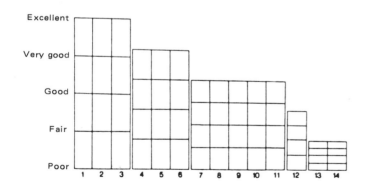

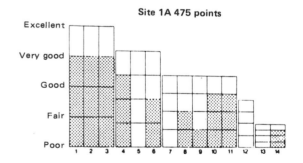

Site 1A 475 points

Site 1B 580 points

1. Accessibility by automobile
2. Parking
3. Complementary facilities
4. Compatibility of proposed facility with surrounding area
5. Size/shape
6. Topography
7. Location
8. Draw
9. Area character
10. Accessibility by subway
11. Accessibility by bus
12. Demand for existing facilities
13. Condition
14. Sanitary facilities

FIGURE 14.13   Graphic comparison of sites/*Playground for All Children*, New York. Criteria used in evaluating the sites are shown in descending order of importance.

Tuolumne Meadows

⑦

Legend

- ▪■▪ BUILDING
- ━━ PAVED ROAD
- ━ ━ DIRT ROAD
- ----- TRAIL
- MEADOW
- FOREST

0 500 1000
Scale in Feet

← north

To TIOGA PASS

Tuolumne Lodge

Dana Fork

Lyell Fork

120

Walk-in Campground

Stables

Store

Campground

Parsons Lodge

Lake

To YOSEMITE VALLEY

TUOLUMNE MEADOWS

TIOGA

8560 8540 8620 8640 8620 8600 8580 8620 8640 8600 8580

Activities

permitted at Tuolumne Meadows will include:

- A Hiking
- B Backpacking
- C Cross-country skiing
- D Snowshoeing
- E Swimming in river
- F Fishing
- G Rafting
- H Tent camping
- I Walk-in camping
- J Vehicle camping
- K Picnicking
- L Sightseeing
- M Horseback riding

Services

provided at Tuolumne Meadows will include:

- a Accommodations
- b Cafeteria food service
- c Restaurant food service
- d Grocery sales
- e Recreational equipment rental
- f Recreational equipment sales
- g Emergency medical service
- h Gift sales
- i Gas and oil service
- j Auto repair and towing
- k Post office
- l Laundry
- m Alcoholic beverage sales
- n Photography instruction
- o Commercial guided tours
- p Mountaineering instruction
- q Clothing sales
- r Bike rental
- s Horse rental
- t Pack animal rental

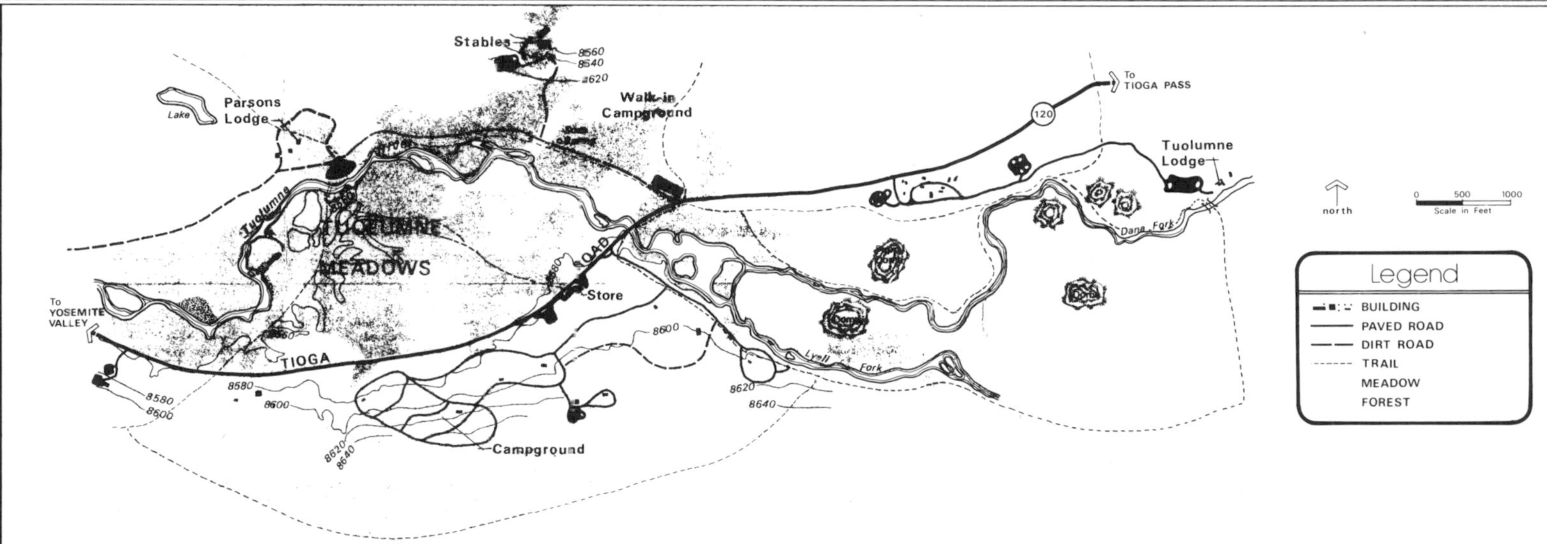

A

1. All facilities for VISITOR USE will be removed from Tuolumne Meadows
2. The CAMPGROUNDS will be removed, but walk-in camping will be allowed
3. The STORE will be removed
4. PARSONS LODGE will be removed
5. All ACCOMMODATIONS will be removed
6. All ROADS will be removed
7. The STABLES will be removed
8. WINTER USE will be allowed, but no facilities will be provided
9. All OFFICES and HOUSING will be removed

B

10. Tuolumne Meadows will be a minor VISITOR USE area
11. The CAMPGROUND will be reduced in size
12. The CAMPGROUND will be converted to walk-in camping only
13. Campground sites that impact the river or the meadow will be eliminated
14. The walk-in campground will be expanded
15. The STORE will be moved to the campground
16. PARSONS LODGE will be retained and used as a winter ski shelter
17. a hostel
18. The number of ACCOMMODATIONS will be reduced

19. Accommodations will remain as tent cabins
20. ROADS and trails that cross the meadow will be removed
21. WINTER USE will be allowed, but only minimal facilities will be provided
9. All OFFICES and HOUSING will be removed

C

22. Tuolumne Meadows will be a major VISITOR USE area
23. The CAMPGROUND will be retained
12. The CAMPGROUND will be converted to walk-in camping only
24. The walk-in campground will be maintained at its present capacity
25. The STORE structure will be winterized and the store will remain open year round
26. PARSONS LODGE will be retained but not used
27. The number of ACCOMMODATIONS will remain the same
28. Accommodations will be winterized
29. ROADS that cross the meadow will be removed, but trails will be retained in their existing location
30. The STABLES will be retained at its present capacity
31. WINTER USE will be encouraged and additional facilities will be provided
32. OFFICES and HOUSING will be provided only for visitor services and resource protection employees

D

22. Tuolumne Meadows will be a major VISITOR USE area
33. The CAMPGROUND will be expanded
34. The walk-in campground will be reduced
35. The STORE will be expanded
36. PARSONS LODGE will be retained and used for interpretation or other park purposes
37. The number of ACCOMMODATIONS will be increased
38. Accommodations will be improved, but not winterized
39. All ROADS and trails will be retained
40. ROADS that cross the meadow will be relocated to bypass the meadow
41. The STABLES will be relocated to the south side of the meadow
42. The STABLES will be expanded
43. OFFICES and HOUSING will be provided for all employees working at Tuolumne Meadows

Existing Conditions

At TUOLUMNE MEADOWS there are:

- Campground (600 sites)
- Walk-in campground (50 sites)
- Mountaineering and climbing instruction
- Post office
- Stables
- Minor maintenance area
- Grocery store and fast food service
- Alcoholic beverage sales
- Lodge (tent cabins)
- Restaurant food service
- Service station and towing
- Ranger station
- Climbing and backpacking equipment sales
- Parsons Lodge (historic stone structure not presently used)
- Lembert Cabin (historic structure at Soda Springs)
- Research station

Tuolumne Meadows is a major take off point for backcountry and High Sierra Camp users.

The grocery store and fast food service, lodge, and restaurant food service structures are tent frame structures. Canvas is removed during the winter.

FIGURE 14.14 Workbook options/Yosemite National Park, California.

235

type. Figure 14.11 shows the flowchart format for a regional park.

Step 4 *Determining Acquisition Boundaries.* Once a site is designated suitable for acquisition as a regional park, the mimimum and preferred boundaries are determined with these eight guidelines: The parcel (a) provides suitable space for an essential activity or facility, (b) is essential for access, staging, or internal circulation, (c) contains improvements appropriate for immediate regional parkland use, (d) contains valuable natural resource features, (e) lies within a logical operational area, (f) is threatened by development or other irreversible changes, (g) has an owner willing to sell at a fair price, and (h) could stand alone and function effectively as a park if the preferred acquisition could not be completed.

Point Value Method

At the site, or project, scale, alternatives can be considered with a point value method based on design criteria. This method was used to select the best site for a playground to serve disabled children in New York City (HUD, 1976). It represents a humanistic and systematic approach to selecting alternatives that demonstrates what is possible given this challenging set of variables.

With 12 possible locations and 14 site selection criteria, each site was evaluated with a scoring system. Figure 14.12 shows each *criterion*. Those considered most important are given the maximum value of 100. An evaluation gradient of excellent to poor is established.

Point scores are assigned by dividing the maximum value of a criterion into four equal parts, with poor equal to zero, fair equal to one-quarter, good equal to one-half the maximum value, and so forth. The evaluations are assigned numerical values and the number totaled to yield a score for each site. Figure 14.13 shows a graphic comparison of this data.

Workbook Method

Perhaps no bolder approach to assessing design alternatives has been attempted than outlined in *The Workbook* developed for the preparation of the Yosemite National Park Master Plan (National Park Service, 1975). Given the challenge of involving a nationwide public to help select the best range of alternatives for a superlative natural area, the National Park Service developed a workbook method that allows people to systematically select options from four alternatives.

Each alternative represents a different type of park experience and environment. Each option is grouped under one alternative and is compatible with every other option on the worksheet. The options are also grouped by a general location with lists of possible activities and services that could be provided. A map of each area and description of existing conditions is also provided with a detailed workbook of instructions, facts, and planning objectives for the entire park (Figure 14.14).

This is an elaborate approach to citizen involvement in selecting alternatives. It could be adapted to the neighborhood or community level. It is premature to evaluate the utility of this method, but it would appear to hold much promise, especially at the regional or metropolitan level to help select alternatives or cluster options that imply an alternative. In effect, this method prompts the planner to outline options and allows people a systematic way to respond to those options.

15 IMPLEMENTATION

Once alternatives are translated into recommended policy options, the last stage in the planning process is to detail ways to implement and revise the plan over time. This requires coping with the present and continually rethinking the future. The effort implies two levels of action: (1) a pragmatic concern for the present or immediate future that focuses on responsibility, capital budgeting, project design, and citizen participation, and (2) a strategic concern for the long-range future that focuses on probable changes in recreation activities, institutions, or spaces.

Both levels of action require a sense of urgency and vision. These are not easy times to cope with the present or plan for the future because of dramatic changes taking place in American society. These changes will affect the present and future course of recreation planning. The reality checks described in Chapter 2 provide an unparalleled set of rationales and opportunities to change the process and products of recreation planning. Appendix J translates these reality checks into local actions or policy options (HCRS, 1978).

This chapter synthesizes these reality checks and policy options to outline an agenda for the present and future. It summarizes the ideas in this book to help provide a needed bridge between recreation planning and site design. This bridge extends to those detailed aspects of park and recreation administration, management, and program covered in other books listed in the Bibliography.

COPING WITH THE PRESENT

Two critical aspects of coping with the present are open space preservation and development programming. They have no substitute or success formula. Both are difficult in times of public austerity and shifting levels of public responsibility for providing local recreation services. They are the essence of implementing a recreation plan and should be approached with the most critical insight and realistic perspective possible.

Open Space Preservation

The relationships between open space, people, cities, and leisure are described in Chapter 2. This chapter summarizes some basic planning principles and design concepts of open space preservation at the systems scale. It also outlines some methods of preserving open space in cities.

PLANNING PRINCIPLES   *Open Space* is a general term covering many classifications of land use. The common denominator is space characterized as a landscape, whether it is natural or man-made. Open space can integrate or separate urban functions, activities, or areas. It has the single and multipurpose potential to provide opportunities for (1) resource production, (2) scenic protection, (3) conservation, (4) outdoor recreation, (5) public health and safety, and (6) development control.

Although many legalistic definitions are described in federal and state laws, a working definition of open space is: all land and water in an urban area not covered by buildings; or any undeveloped or predominantly undeveloped land in an urban area which has value for park and recreation purposes, conservation of land and other natural resources, or historic or scenic purposes.

The functions and classification of open space are described in Chapter 4. Some philosophical and practical justifications of urban open space are described in Chapter 2. Open space preservation ultimately becomes a question of public regulation and private restraint. The act of prohibiting development of vacant land or creating open spaces in developed areas suggests the systems scale approach shown in Figure 15.1 and a site-scale constraint-oriented approach shown in Figure 15.2. At both scales, these principles of open space preservation should be observed:

1 Space alone does not constitute service or opportunity. The visual and functional aspects of space are more important than arbitrary standards or philosophical justification.

2 Open spaces that are not used in a visual or functional sense will not have a constituency and be difficult to justify for public acquisition.

3 Open spaces that are used for several purposes, to include recreation, will have broad public support and be a cost-effective investment of public funds.

4 Urban open spaces should be viewed as places to enjoy the basic qualities of urban living instead of an escape from the city. The potential for interaction of people in a public environment should be a primary recreational justification of open spaces.

5 People should identify with open spaces and be encouraged to participate in their design, development, and management.

DESIGN CONCEPTS   These principles can be applied in three basic design concepts for open space that relate to urban form and function. A summary of each concept follows.

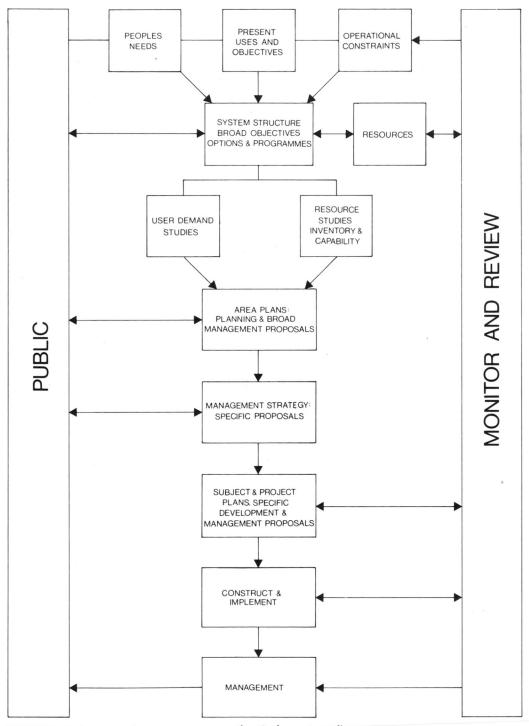

FIGURE 15.1   Systems scale open space preservation/Canberra, Australia.

1 *Expediency concept.* Land becomes public open space because it happens to be available or is given as a gift. No advance planning is done and open space preservation is viewed as an opportunistic effort. Government units act independently to meet their needs or objectives. No pattern or system of open space emerges by design. Linkage between spaces, access, and management are not coordinated at the metropolitan or regional level.

2 *Design concept.* Land becomes public open space because of natural constraints or potential recreation resources. Open space is used to shape urban development into four alternative forms: (a) concentric rings, (b) wedges and channels, (c) containers, and (d) recreation cores. Advance planning and regional cooperation are required. A strong pattern of open space and developed areas emerges with the possibility of coordinated linkages, access, and management by a regional park authority. The four alternatives are shown in Figure 15.3, and a summary of each follows.

a *Concentric rings alternative.* The rings of open space become more extensive as their distance from the urban core increases. The responsibility for acquiring, developing, and managing the outlying rings rests with the state or federal government. Each ring becomes an increment or barrier for urban development and different levels of urban density.

b *Wedges and channels alternative.* Open space is in corridors that parallel the drainage or road pattern. A radial pattern of spaces expands as they move away from the core. The system parallels the direction of urban development and provides maximum access for recreation users to the edge of these corridors. This pattern also relates well to mass transit systems for access to large regional parks located in these corridors.

c *Containers alternative.* Open space is used to limit and define urban growth. It becomes a container or context for urban development and does not necessarily relate to the drainage or road pattern. Open space is a buffer to separate or integrate different types of land use. Recreation access or resources are incidental to the overall land use pattern. The emphasis is on linear parks and local management of these spaces.

d *Recreation cores alternative.* Open space serves as the focal point for urban development. Emphasis is on large and small spaces to preserve specific sites or provide specialized opportunities. Access and linkage are secondary to providing for local needs. A regional

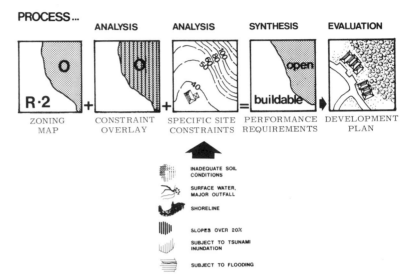

FIGURE 15.2 Site scale open space preservation. The constraint districts are the development restriction zones of the general plan/Kauai, Hawaii.

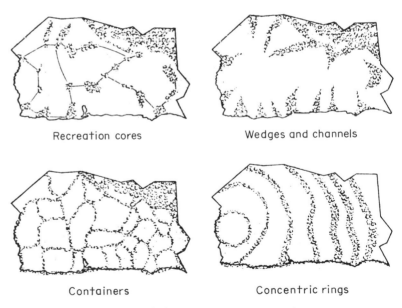

FIGURE 15.3 **Open space design concepts: systems scale/Orange County, California.**

park authority is possible for the large spaces, but local systems are more probable because of the nature of these spaces.

3 *Natural features concept.* The preservation of natural features such as flood plains, wildlife habitat, or landmarks are the primary objective of planning. Natural

TABLE 15.1 | METHODS FOR PRESERVING OPEN SPACE

Acquisition of Fee

Purchase
  Purchase with life tenancy
  Lease purchase
  Excess condemnation
  Official map
  Purchase and leaseback
Gift with life tenancy
Trade or transfer
Tax foreclosures
Street closing
Redevelopment process
Subdivision dedication
Private purchase or gift

Acquisition of Less Than Fee

Conservation easements
Development rights
Public easements

Scenic easements
Purchase and resale without certain rights
Compensable regulations

Zoning

Protective zoning
Aesthetic zoning
Agricultural zoning
Zoning for large lots
Zoning for planned unit development
Private restrictive covenants
Slope conservation restrictions

Property Tax Concessions

By contract
Tax abatement for hunting/fishing rights
Tax exemptions
Tax deductions for gifts

TABLE 15.2 | BENEFITS AND COSTS OF OPEN SPACE

Quantifiable Benefits*

Recreation user satisfaction
Natural resource and lease income
Savings from compact growth
  Energy conservation
  Reduction in cost of government services
Savings in transportation costs
Preventing development in hazardous area
Tourism and related economic industries or services
Agricultural industries and services
Increased land values of adjacent properties
Decreased levels of crime and violence
Attraction and retention of desirable development

Nonquantifiable Benefits †

Improvement in mental and physical health
Reduction in levels of air, noise, or water pollution

Increased recreation opportunities for the disadvantaged
Maintenance of rural atmosphere
Increased community identity and imagibility
Preservation of scenic, historic, or cultural features
Retention of options for future growth

Quantifiable Costs*

Land acquisition
Development of recreation facilities
Maintenance and operation of recreation facilities

Nonquantifiable Costs †

Impacts on tax base
Impacts on housing market
Opportunities forgone for development

*Quantifiable in an objective sense, because of available data, measures, or precedent.

†Nonquantifiable to date because of a lack of available data, measures, or precedent and the intangible nature of these factors.

processes and landscape character instead of recreation access, urban growth directions, or road patterns suggest which lands should receive priority consideration for open space preservation. A regional management authority normally provides these resource-oriented recreation opportunities.

METHODS OF OPEN SPACE PRESERVATION   There is no need to belabor our lack of national commitment to preserve open space in cities. In most cases, the problem is ethical instead of legal or economic. It is more a matter of local will or attitude than a lack of techniques or methods.

Table 15.1 outlines methods of preserving open space. The legal tools to implement these methods are detailed in many sources. The benefits and costs of open space have also been documented in many studies listed in the bibliography. In almost every case, the benefits of open space exceed the costs over time. Table 15.2 categorizes these benefits and costs.

Development Programming

Once a framework and locations for open space are established, the task of projecting development, program, and management of these spaces assumes major importance in the planning and budgeting process (Figure 15.4). This book will not cover the topics of recreation program and management because they are detailed in many other sources. However, it is important to summarize three aspects of development programming that are links between long-range systems planning and project design or management.

INCREMENTAL IMPLEMENTATION   The traditional approach to implementation is linear and total. The entire project is usually completed at the earliest possible time, normally within the next capital budget. Government assumes total responsibility for the entire project and there is little citizens or the private sector is expected to do.

An incremental approach is possible that separates a project into major components such as land, development, program, maintenance, and administration. Each component can be expressed in units and responsibilities which can represent the combined efforts of the public and private sector.

For example, Table 15.3 shows a resource allocation matrix for a hypothetical neighborhood. This approach emphasizes flexibility, demonstration, and citizen participation. It is based on the strategy of people estab-

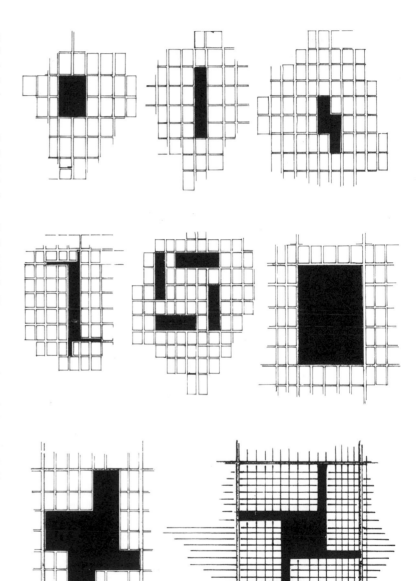

FIGURE 15.4   Open space design concepts: site scale.

TABLE 15.3 | RECREATION RESOURCE ALLOCATION MATRIX*

Two-year cycles	I		II		III		IV		V		Resource totals
Each year	1	2	3	4	5	6	7	8	9	10	
Land	200	—	—	—	25	25	25	25	25	25	350†
Development	—	50	25	25	20	20	20	20	20	20	220
Program	—	25	50	50	50	50	50	50	‡	‡	325
Maintenance	—	15	15	15	‡	‡	‡	‡	‡	‡	45
Administration	—	10	10	10	5	5	5	5	5	5	60
Totals	200	100	100	100	100	100	100	100	50	50	1000

*Based on $1 million in public funds (units of $1000).
†One acre of land in high-density area.
‡Voluntary resident effort.

lishing priorities and planners evaluating the cost-effectiveness of a project before it is initiated and in process.

This approach should help to (1) minimize a misallocation of resources, (2) expedite local project planning, (3) directly involve people in the planning or design process, (4) maximize unforeseen opportunities, and (5) produce tangible results that can be evaluated before more resources are allocated to a project.

This approach emphasizes flexibility and choice to determine what will best accommodate local needs and priorities. It assumes preferences or priorities may change. This approach also shows people what trade-offs are possible with voluntary effort to extend limited public funds. It establishes a framework for public and private effort that is the basis of self-generated parks.

ENVIRONMENTAL AND SOCIAL IMPACT REPORTS The preparation of an environmental impact report (EIR) on recreation projects or the recreation element of a comprehensive plan is required in many states. This requirement is being extended in some states to include social impact reports (SIR). The detailed guidelines for an EIR/SIR vary in different states and are constantly being revised. However, the basic process is well established in practice and should be a critical part of implementing a recreation plan or analyzing alternatives prior to the implementation stage.

The objective of these reports is to provide decision makers and the public with a statement of full disclosure in terms they can understand. The process should trans-

late technical information into positive and negative impacts that can be considered in the decision process.

The EIR/SIR is not an instrument for approval or disapproval. It does not endorse or condemn a project. It is an objective way to study and report the primary and secondary impacts of a proposed action and describe ways to mitigate these impacts. It is also a way to avoid future management problems, make other agencies aware of proposals, and encourage citizen participation in the planning process.

For example, Figure 15.5 shows the environmental impact of a highway on a park in terms of noise levels. Similar studies should be made to describe the visual impacts of highways on parks or how they affect levels of user access and air pollution. Conversely, the environmental impact of a park on the landscape or adjacent land use should be described in an environmental impact report that is part of the project plan (Figure 15.6). Figure 15.7 illustrates an integrated process that combines social and environmental impact assessment.

RENEWAL OF EXISTING SPACES The renewal of existing public and private recreation spaces is a major opportunity. It is a cost-effective approach to making the best use of existing facilities. In many cities, the existing parks are obsolete. They no longer meet the needs of people because of radical changes in the population or life-style of a planning area. Changes in leisure technology, energy use, mobility patterns, family income, and the cost of acquiring, developing, or managing urban parks

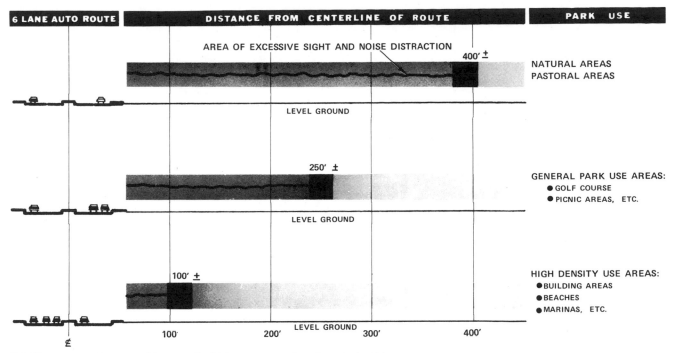

FIGURE 15.5 Environmental impact of a highway on a park/Jackson Park, Chicago.

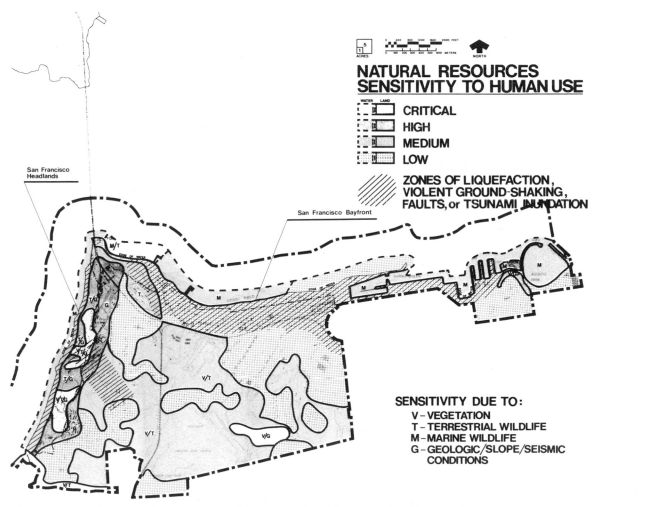

FIGURE 15.6 Environmental impact of park/Golden Gate National Recreation Area, San Francisco.

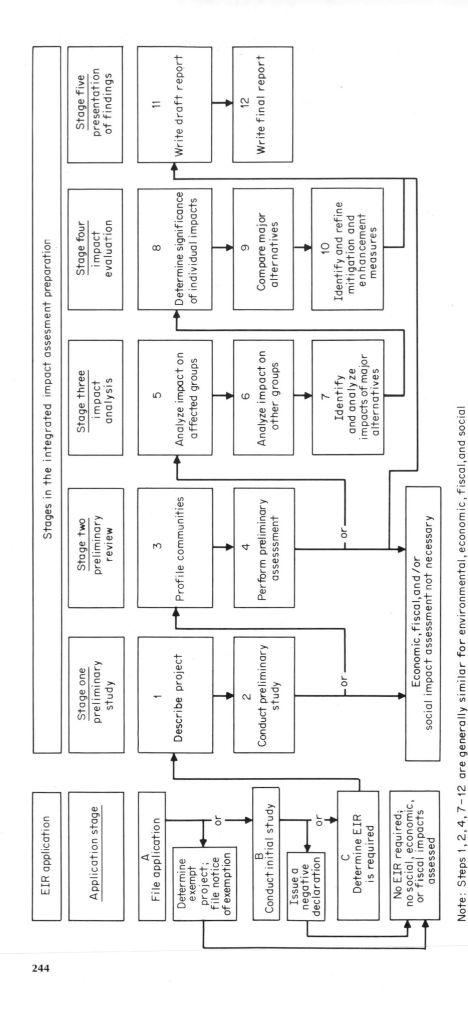

Stages in the integrated impact assessment preparation

| EIR application | | Stage one preliminary study | Stage two preliminary review | Stage three impact analysis | Stage four impact evaluation | Stage five presentation of findings |

Application stage

A
File application

Determine exempt project; file notice of exemption

B
Conduct initial study

Issue a negative declaration

C
Determine EIR is required

No EIR required; no social, economic, or fiscal impacts assessed

1 Describe project

2 Conduct preliminary study

or

Economic, fiscal, and/or social impact assessment not necessary

3 Profile communities

4 Perform preliminary assesssment

or

5 Analyze impact on affected groups

6 Analyze impact on other groups

7 Identify and analyze impacts of major alternatives

8 Determine significance of individual impacts

9 Compare major alternatives

10 Identify and refine mitigation and enhancement measures

11 Write draft report

12 Write final report

Note: Steps 1, 2, 4, 7–12 are generally similar for environmental, economic, fiscal, and social impact assessment. Steps 3, 5, 6 are unique to social impact assessment.

FIGURE 15.7 Integrated environmental and social impact report process/Sacramento County, California.

244

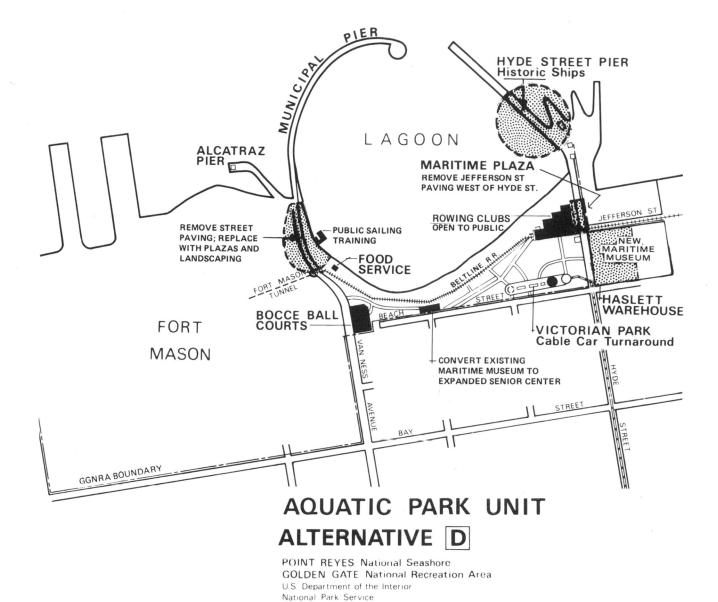

MUNICIPAL PIER

HYDE STREET PIER
Historic Ships

LAGOON

ALCATRAZ
PIER

MARITIME PLAZA
REMOVE JEFFERSON ST
PAVING WEST OF HYDE ST.

ROWING CLUBS
OPEN TO PUBLIC

JEFFERSON ST.

REMOVE STREET
PAVING; REPLACE
WITH PLAZAS AND
LANDSCAPING

PUBLIC SAILING
TRAINING

NEW
MARITIME
MUSEUM

FOOD
SERVICE

FORT MASON
TUNNEL

BELTLINE R.R.

STREET

HASLETT
WAREHOUSE

FORT
MASON

BOCCE BALL
COURTS

BEACH

VAN NESS

VICTORIAN PARK
Cable Car Turnaround

CONVERT EXISTING
MARITIME MUSEUM TO
EXPANDED SENIOR CENTER

AVENUE

BAY

HYDE

STREET

STREET

GGNRA BOUNDARY

AQUATIC PARK UNIT
ALTERNATIVE D

POINT REYES National Seashore
GOLDEN GATE National Recreation Area
U.S. Department of the Interior
National Park Service

FIGURE 15.8   Renewal of existing parks/Golden Gate National Recreation Area, San Francisco.

suggest priority be given to the renewal of existing spaces before additional spaces are acquired.

The effort can include the reuse of historic buildings or districts. Dumps, parking lots, obsolete industrial buildings, surplus military installations, and abandoned cemeteries can also be recycled. Figures 15.8 and 15.9 illustrate what is possible. A new federal program (Urban Park and Recreation Recovery Act of 1978) provides substantial assistance to eligible cities for renewing urban parks. The strategy of renewal of existing spaces before acquisition of new ones makes environmental and economic sense. It is a logical way to cope with the present and begin rethinking the future.

RETHINKING THE FUTURE

It is a time for great optimism in the field of parks and recreation because after years of romanticism profes-

sionals and public agencies are beginning to cope with reality. Changing values, technology, the energy crisis, and inflation are forcing cities to do out of necessity what they might have done by choice. The traditional approach to providing open space and leisure services is no longer acceptable in many communities seeking alternatives because of a fiscal crisis or changing life-styles and populations.

A new generation of recreation plans is evolving that offers some hopeful alternatives. These alternatives are based on the ideas of future-oriented professionals who have been (1) calling for a redefinition of leisure services in cities, (2) describing the phenomenon of nonuse of local parks, (3) projecting a cost-revenue crisis in government, (4) urging realistic citizen participation in the planning process for urban parks, (5) pleading for more research and demonstration programs in park planning and design, and (6) suggesting it is not how much but how good urban parks are.

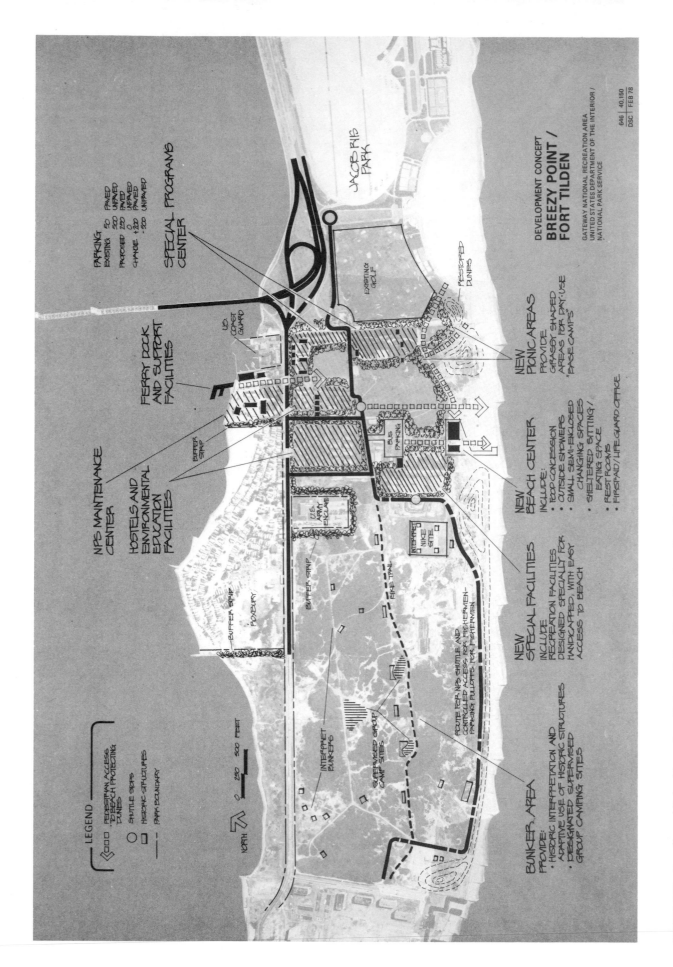

LEGEND

⟨⟨⟨ PEDESTRIAN ACCESS TO BEACH PROTECTING DUNES
◯ SHUTTLE STOPS
▢ HISTORIC STRUCTURES
––– PARK BOUNDARY

NORTH
0 250 500 FEET

PARKING
EXISTING   50   PAVED
            500 UNPAVED
PROPOSED   220 PAVED
CHANGE   +170 PAVED
           -500 UNPAVED

SPECIAL PROGRAMS CENTER

FERRY DOCK AND SUPPORT FACILITIES

NPS MAINTENANCE CENTER

HOSTELS AND ENVIRONMENTAL EDUCATION FACILITIES

U.S. COAST GUARD

BUFFER STRIP

BUFFER STRIP

FOXBURY

BUFFER STRIP

U.S. ARMY ENCLAVE

BUFFER STRIP

INTERPRET BUNKERS

SUPERVISED GROUP CAMP SITES

BIKE TRAIL

INTERPRET NIKE SITE

BUS PARKING

NEW PICNIC AREAS
PROVIDE:
GRASSY SHADED AREAS FOR DAY-USE "BASE CAMPS"

NEW BEACH CENTER
INCLUDE:
• FOOD CONCESSION
• OUTSIDE SHOWERS
• SMALL SEMI-ENCLOSED CHANGING SPACES
• SHELTERED SITTING / EATING SPACE
• REST ROOMS
• FIRST-AID / LIFE-GUARD OFFICE

NEW SPECIAL FACILITIES
INCLUDE:
RECREATION FACILITIES DESIGNED SPECIALLY FOR HANDICAPPED, WITH EASY ACCESS TO BEACH

ROUTE FOR NPS SHUTTLE AND CONTROLLED ACCESS FOR FISHERMEN
PARKING PULLOUTS FOR FISHERMEN

BUNKER AREA
PROVIDE:
• HISTORIC INTERPRETATION AND ADAPTIVE USE OF HISTORIC STRUCTURES
• DESIGNATED SUPERVISED GROUP CAMPING SITES

EXISTING GOLF

RESTORED DUNES

JACOB RIIS PARK

DEVELOPMENT CONCEPT
BREEZY POINT / FORT TILDEN

GATEWAY NATIONAL RECREATION AREA
UNITED STATES DEPARTMENT OF THE INTERIOR / NATIONAL PARK SERVICE

646 | 40,150
DSC | FEB 78

FIGURE 15.9 Recycling public land for park use/Gateway National Recreation Area, New York.

The major challenge of recreation planning in the 1980s and beyond will be coping with change. The recreation standards and concepts of eighteenth-century England or nineteenth-century America may not apply to Urban America in the twentieth-century. A critical summary of the state of the art reveals:

- Recreation planning and design has been dominated by the use of arbitrary standards and irrelevant concepts. Most of the ideas in current use are premised on the thinking of the 1930s about recreation and open space in cities.

- The park and recreation field is essentially retrospective and romantic in the way it approaches problem solving. Most recreation plans do not acknowledge or accommodate significant changes or trends in leisure life-styles, legislation, technology, or values.

- Demonstration and innovation are the exception in most communities. Studies of user behavior are not evident in most recreation plans. Parks and recreation is still not considered an experimental field with credible definitions, measures, or a theoretical foundation.

- The objectives of many public park and recreation systems better accommodate the needs of the supplier than the user.

- Most recreation plans still assume an emphasis on youth, unlimited growth, increasing personal income and mobility, cheap energy, and unlimited public budgets. They project a past that may not be realistic in light of current trends toward an aging society, growth management, decreasing real income, and a growing energy crisis.

There are some hopeful exceptions to these conclusions illustrated by the examples in this book. These examples show what is possible in a wide range of situations. They respond to the reality checks and policy options recreation planning must consider in the 1980s and beyond.

These examples offer needed alternatives to help improve the state of the art. They represent a range of concepts and methods that will require the vision and social purpose which characterized the early years of the Park and Recreation Movement. They require a commitment to research and demonstration to find new ways of providing leisure opportunities in cities.

Change and Innovation

If change were to take place with equal force or speed, it might allow projection or prediction. But now change is uneven and subject to great forward leaps. A breakthrough in one area can have profound impact in other areas. Who anticipated these items we now take for granted: automobiles, space flights, income taxes, billboards, air conditioning, enclosed shoppings malls, fast-food restaurants, computers, penicillin, hydrogen bombs, dune buggies, neon lights, disposable diapers, color television, collective bargaining, credit cards, social security, vending machines, supermarkets, tranquilizers, detergents, and suburbia?

Each item has had a significant influence on urban life. Combined, they have created a need for people to cope with change, which is the fundamental cause of most urban problems. Some of these problems now include: a taxpayers' revolt, an energy crisis, racial polarization, juvenile delinquency, traffic congestion, water and air pollution, urban blight, inflation, diminishing open space, crime, water shortages, inadequate schools, bankrupt cities, and slums.

Beyond the present is an uncertain future where innovation and technology may solve some problems, but create still more. Who is considering the future impact on leisure patterns of: increased lifespan, disease eradication, mind-altering drugs, birth control, space travel, weather control, cybernation, guaranteed minimum wage, and flextime work schedules?

In the context of urban parks and recreation, just 10 years ago who envisioned: skateboard parks, racquetball centers, mainstreaming the handicapped, unisex toilets, inflatable buildings, water scooters, giant slides, electronic games, hang gliders, disco golf courses, computer tennis court reservations, trickle irrigation systems, plastic snow, astroturf, surf machines, and solar heated pools?

More important, who is thinking about the possible impacts of these items on the park and recreation experience or agency: legalization of marijuana, nude sunbathing, an aging society, social impact reports, surplus schools, growth management, a major recession, a sustained energy crisis, and zero-based budgeting?

Scenarios of the Future

One way to focus on the possible implications of change and innovation is with scenarios of the future. Scenarios can be used in a recreation plan to describe the planning context or impact of an implementation program. For example, these scenarios of the future seem possible:

TRADITIONAL VIEW By the year 2000, population density, mobility, and personal income will double. The workweek will decline and people will retire at 60. An energy crisis and economic depression will not occur. Growth and affluence will continue with an unlimited consumption of resources. Simple forms of recreation will continue, but more specialized and expensive activities will gain mass appeal. The work ethic will prevail and leisure time will be used to escape from cities to the country.

HUMANISTIC VIEW The humanistic view envisions a future where there is little distinction between work and leisure. Work, in an affluent society, will become a privilege for a few and mass leisure will be socially acceptable. Work will become people-oriented instead of object-oriented. The emphasis of society will be on human services instead of things. Education systems will prepare people for a life of leisure instead of work. A leisure ethic will replace the work ethic and humanism will replace materialism. The question will no longer be the production of wealth, but the fair distribution of wealth. Open space will be a public trust for future generations instead of a speculative commodity to be exploited for profit.

PESSIMISTIC VIEW The pessimistic view sees the future as one of complexity, scarcity, and turmoil with mass leisure as a problem in an industrialized world with diminishing resources and competing needs. Technology, combined with an accelerating pace of change, will subject recreation to "future shock." Our relationship with things will become more temporary. The "throwaway culture and transience" described by Toffler (1970) in *Future Shock* will become a way of life for many. Open space preservation will be an opportunity foregone or a luxury beyond the reach of most communities.

OPTIMISTIC VIEW New work attitudes, life-styles, and ethics will shape our leisure patterns. Three-day workweeks and flextime schedules will level peak use. Work sharing, extended vacations, sabbaticals, and early retirement will allow extensive travel and participation in local recreation programs. Work will be done at home, or workers will live close to where they work in new towns or recycled cities. Cottage industries will bring work and leisure environments together again. Gasoline shortages will force people to rediscover urban parks. Inflation and declining real income will force people to rediscover simple activities. Managed open space will create the environmental framework and social focus of cities. Open space and parks will be considered an essential of urban living to be provided by community action and sophisticated long-range planning.

Other scenarios of the future have been developed by using the Delphi Technique to solicit the independent views of a panel of experts. Table 15.4 abstracts the results of a recent study (U.S. Forest Service, 1974). A panel of 904 experts from all aspects of natural resource management were asked to list the most significant events that would occur by the year 2050.

New Dimensions of Recreation

Regardless of which events occur in the long-range future, a spectrum of new activities, institutions, and spaces is evolving that should be considered now in the preparation of recreation plans. These items represent some dramatic new dimensions for the provision of leisure opportunities in cities. They illustrate what is needed and possible, if we are bold enough to depart from the conventional approach to urban recreation planning.

NEW ACTIVITIES A new generation of activities will become common in or near cities. These activities will require new spaces, management techniques, and sophisticated program leadership. Many of these activities will be self-directed, noncompetitive, and energy conserving in the use of land or facilities. They will symbolize dramatic changes in life-style, ethics, or attitudes toward people and the environment.

A sampling of the new activities includes: ballooning, ski-touring, windsurfing, put/take fishing, landsailing, psychodrama, turf-skiing, spinnaker-flying, New Games, water-walking, ski-bobbing, hot tubbing, flingbee, snurfing, spelunking, para-sailing, camera hunting, parcourse fitness, yoga, Rolfing, wind-skating, flikerball, disco-skating, and swingball tennis.

NEW INSTITUTIONS A new type of institution will develop to accommodate the life-styles and leisure needs of the future. Human development and environmental management will become the expanded focus of public park and recreation agencies. The arts, leisure, and education will be closely coordinated in departments of life enrichment. Among the new institutions of the future will be the following:

Public Utilities To provide leisure services in the same way as gas, water, electricity, and mail are delivered to local communities.

Recreation Franchises Private contractors will provide revenue-producing services, e.g., tennis, golf, or marinas.

TABLE 15.4 | SCENARIOS OF THE FUTURE

Natural Resource Management

1980

1 Economic incentives to encourage management of private land for fish and wildlife.

1985

2 Tax credit to private landowners who provide scenic amenities.

1990

3 Federal land, water, and air use plan established.

2000

4 National land-use zoning policy established.
5 Preempted public recreation land replaced with comparable land.
6 Coordinated environmental planning between government and private enterprise.
7 Most marine and estuarine areas managed for fish and wildlife habitat.

2030

8 Electrical power rationed by national priorities.

After 2050

9 National per-capita land requirement established.
10 Some natural and man-made lakes heated for swimming.
11 Viable international agreement on allocation of the world natural resources.
12 Shoreline along navigable rivers placed in public ownership.
13 All intensively developed recreation facilities under public management.

Never Occur

14 All water and land recreation resources under federal control.
15 Cease construction of new highways.
16 All recreation facilities provided by commercial enterprise.

Population-Workforce-Leisure

1985

1 Companies will consult employees on what sort of recreation activities would be best for their physical and mental health.
2 Most people work a 4-day, 32-hour week.

1990

3 Public schools open year-round with staggered vacations.
4 U.S. census of population includes questions on the recreation activities and needs.
5 Most homes have video-tape systems.

2000

6 Employers given tax incentives to include recreation facilities in plants.
7 Five hundred miles is a reasonable one-way distance to travel for a weekend.
8 Average retirement age is 50 years.
9 "Weekends" distributed throughout the week.
10 Leisure is an accepted life-style.
11 Public schools function to serve the recreation needs of the entire community.

12 Attempt to control population through tax incentives.
13 Middle-class Americans vacation on other continents as commonly as they vacation in the United States today.

2030

14 Most middle-income families own their own vacation home.

After 2050

15 Nationwide mandatory population control.
16 The average worker has a 3-month annual vacation.
17 The average lifespan is 100 years.
18 Twenty percent of the available workforce used to produce goods and services for the entire population.
19 Average entry into the workforce at 25 years of age.

Never Occur

20 Compulsory genetic measures initiated to improve the human race.

Urban Environments

1985

1 Special fishing areas established in urban areas for the handicapped, elderly, and children.

1990

2 Small private aircraft excluded from metropolitan airports.

2000

3 Cemetery land and other open land in urban areas used for recreation.
4 Simulated indoor environments available that provide recreational opportunities now available only in the outdoors.
5 All water reservoirs open to public recreation.
6 Only non-air-polluting vehicles allowed in urban areas.
7 Artificial turf used in most public field sports areas and on some golf courses.
8 Green space preserved between most metropolitan areas.
9 Some city parks or parts of parks enclosed in all-weather protective bubbles.
10 Computers used to direct and control movements of individual transportation units.

2020

11 Most metropolitan areas provide adequate outdoor-recreation opportunities so that most urban residents do not feel the need to go to the country for recreation.

2050

12 "Camping" available in multistory structures similar to parking garages.

After 2050

13 Roofs of many downtown buildings used as public playgrounds.
14 New urban growth displaced to relatively uninhabited regions.
15 High-speed public-transit systems built between most urban areas and major rural recreation facilities.
16 Most city blocks have a minipark or play lot.
17 Ninety percent of the U.S. population lives in urban areas.
18 Apartment structures designed so that they can be detached and moved to recreational areas.
19 Self-contained floating cities with year-round residents.
20 Self-contained underwater cities.

Never Occur

21 Transparent roofs cover most cities.

Source: Elwood Shafer, George Moeller, and Russell Getty, *Future Leisure Environments,* U.S. Forest Service Research Paper NE-301, 1974.

Contract Services Private contractors will provide many of the planning, design, management, maintenance, and program services now provided by the public sector in most communities.

Commercial Enterprises Private concessionaires will provide community and regional theme or amusement parks on public land.

Company Resorts Private corporations will provide special park and recreation opportunities for their employees in or near cities. They will also provide onsite exercise rooms or facilities to improve the physical fitness of employees.

Leisure Cooperatives Individuals, neighborhoods, and organizations or social groups will join together to provide specialized leisure opportunities or equipment for their members, e.g., sailboats or swimming pools.

Leisure Counselors Public and private specialists will advise people on alternative ways and places to use their time budgets in the same manner as investment counselors now advise people on how to spend their discretionary income.

Day-Care Centers Public and private places will provide supervised care for children while parents are participating in recreational activities at the community and neighborhood level.

Community Colleges Local colleges will assume a dominant role in providing arts, cultural, and human development programs for adults. Their facilities will be integrated with park and recreation facilities to serve the entire community.

NEW CONCEPTS We need new ways to think about leisure in cities. For example, we have traditionally considered only *public* land and water for outdoor recreation, but new approaches to design, management, and program offer these exciting possibilities:

Air Rights Using space over public and private urban development for leisure opportunities. We can deck over freeways, railroad yards, warehouses, and parking lots for recreational use (Figure 15.10).

Underground Spaces Developing underground malls, plazas, and pathways that have multiuse recreational potentials.

Risk Recreation Providing activities and places that encourage physical and mental challenge or self-confidence.

Self-Programmed Recreation Encouraging simple, energy-conserving, noncompetitive activities such as New Games or parcourse fitness.

Recycling Existing Parks Renewing existing parks that no longer meet the needs of users to include a major emphasis on adventure playgrounds, community gardens, and water- or energy-conserving landscapes.

Reuse of Existing Buildings Converting abandoned or obsolete buildings to public or private recreational uses, e.g., theaters, factories, or supermarkets.

Self-Generated Parks Encouraging residents to help design, develop, and maintain neighborhood parks.

Rooftop Spaces Making intensive use of rooftops for public and private recreational opportunities (Figure 15.11).

Recreational Retailing Combining amusement parks with shopping centers.

Reuse of Cemeteries Redeveloping or opening cemeteries for passive recreational use, arboretums, and wildlife preserves.

Urban Campgrounds. Providing campgrounds in urban parks for tourists.

High-Rise Recreation Structures Building or redeveloping high-rise structures for recreational use, e.g., tennis clubs, hostels, or play areas.

Pneumatic Structures Providing air-supported structures for special events or temporary facilities in changing neighborhoods.

Joint Use of Facilities Using private clubs, marinas, golf courses, shopping centers, and industrial parks for public programs (Figure 15.12).

Public/Private Opportunities Considering the entire city as a recreation place to include places such as streets, theaters, bars, restaurants, libraries, museums, historic districts, private plazas, and flea markets where people

FIGURE 15.10   Air rights for parks/Seattle, Washington.

FIGURE 15.11 Rooftop Garden, Kaiser Medical Center/Oakland, California.

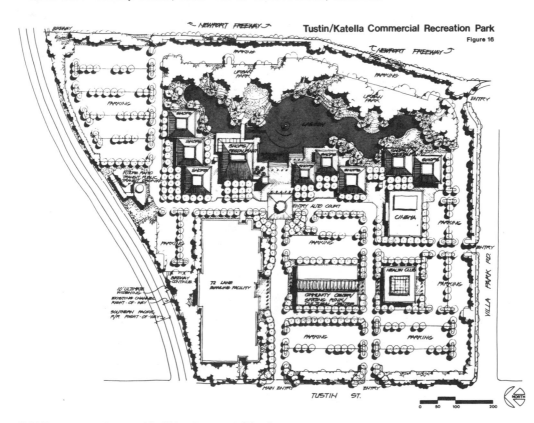

FIGURE 15.12 Joint use of facilities/Orange, California.

1 C.B.D.
2 CORRIDOR
3 NEW CENTER
4 UNIVERSITY PARK
5 FOREST PARK
6 RIVERFRONT

FIGURE 15.13 Design framework for the inner city/Detroit, Michigan.

FIGURE 15.14   Urban living in a park setting/Victoria Mews Condominiums, San Francisco. Condominiums occupy an entire city block on one of the sunniest slopes of Potrero Hill. A private stream meanders down an extensively landscaped hillside to the middle level, which includes a swimming pool, saunas, and hot tubs, offering a panoramic view of the city skyline. While below, a Verandah Club and tennis courts complete this dramatic exterior hillside design.

can experience diversity, pleasure, or enrichment (Figure 15.13).

We can build cities in parks, instead of parks in cities. The idea of parks or recreation as an isolated set of spaces or experiences in cities in passé. Past distinctions between indoor and outdoor spaces and public vs. private opportunities are fading with new concepts that integrate space and services to serve the needs of people living in cities (Figure 15.14).

A Beginning

The only way to approach the future is with hope and optimism: *hope,* because of many recreation planners and designers committed to creating better leisure environments and people who want to enjoy urban life in these environments; *optimism,* because of what is beginning to happen in our legal system, government, universities, schools, businesses, and in the minds of people.

The pessimistic view that large cities and urban parks, recreation, and open space are a lost cause or that small communities do not have the resources to implement some of these ideas is distorted in light of what is possible in practice. There has never been a better time for innovation and demonstration in recreation planning and design, if we will try to understand and invent the future. There is much to be done. Here are some places to begin:

1 Study the *future* as well as the past and present to see if we are thinking boldly enough about current issues and trends. We teach courses in the history of recreation and planning; why not the future?

2 Develop a more *humanistic* or people-serving concept of urban parks and recreation. It is time to balance our emphasis on the resource with a serious concern for the user.

3 Broaden our *interpretation* of urban recreation in time,

space, and attitude. There is no rule that says parks must be public, square, horizontal, and dull places that do not relate to people.

4 Encourage the *private* sector to provide high-quality services. Government cannot and will not be able to do the whole job.

5 Consider recreation planning an *experimental* field with a major emphasis on research, demonstration, and innovation to develop new products and services.

6 Link our efforts to improve the quality of urban parks to the energy crisis, changing needs, priorities, and life-styles of *people* living in cities to include those with the greatest needs for leisure services, e.g., the poor, senior citizens, physically handicapped, and mentally retarded.

7 Challenge the assumptions, concepts, and *standards* traditionally used to provide leisure opportunities in cities. One mark of professionalism is self-criticism.

8 Understand that the best way to preserve wilderness areas from overuse is to improve the *quality* of life and environment in cities. By placing a priority on urban open space, we can solve, instead of perpetuating, these two problems.

9 Develop objective measures to assess the *effectiveness* of urban leisure services. It is difficult to do research or rationalize public funds for the support of parks and recreation without credible measures.

10 Train or retrain a new kind of enlightened *professional* in recreation planning and design to meet the challenges and opportunities of the future.

We are beginning to realize the potentials of living with nature in an era of limits. Of all our resources, the most precious is human awareness. This awareness is causing us to reexamine the purpose of life and ask what fulfillment really means. Urban parks, recreation, and open space offer society unique opportunities for this examination. They can provide the time, place, and means by which people can achieve self-discovery that leads to self-respect and a better society.

APPENDIX A | NATIONAL URBAN RECREATION STUDY

SUMMARY OF FINDINGS

1 People in all urban areas want a well-balanced system of urban recreation opportunities which includes close-to-home neighborhood facilities and programs for all segments of the population.

- Most people want recreation close-to-home, but recreation opportunities are often poorly-distributed in urban areas.

- Recreation in urban areas includes a wide array of programs provided by many organizations in a variety of locations. Urban recreation opportunities encompass participatory and spectator sports, environmental education, arts and cultural programs, "just relaxing" in the parks, and many others. These opportunities are provided by local governments, schools, private voluntary groups, and commercial organizations. They are found in parks, community and senior citizens centers, service centers of non-profit, voluntary agencies, and in other public and private facilities.

2 A wide variety of open space areas with substantial scenic, cultural, environmental, agricultural, and recreational values remain in and near our cities. While threats to remaining open space areas due to continued urban expansion into the countryside are very real, acquisition of these areas can meet only a small portion of total recreation needs.

- A large number of potential open space and recreation sites exist in the study areas, within and outside cities, but the primary values of most open space sites are environmental and economic rather than recreational.

- Open space acquisition on the fringe of urban areas, such as that involved in creation of new National Recreation Areas, is frequently justified on the basis of providing recreation opportunities for urban residents, but does not meet the highest priority recreation needs of most city dwellers.

3 Existing and potential recreation resources are not being fully utilized.

- The city itself is a recreation resource—its streets, its museums, its churches, its gathering places all provide recreation opportunities.

- Many city parks and recreation facilities are under-utilized because of limited activity programming, poor staffing, deteriorated conditions or bad locations.

- Water supply reservoirs, utility corridors, abandoned railroad rights-of-way, and decaying waterfronts all have potential to be *re-used* for recreation.

- Schools, community centers, churches, and public buildings have unrealized potential for recreation use in conjunction with their primary functions.

4 Good management, well-trained staff, and adequate financial support are the keys to providing good recreation services.

- Satisfaction with recreation opportunities in the urban areas studied was more dependent on the existence of good programs and imaginative leadership than on large acreages or elaborate facilities.

5 Lack of coordination among recreation providers at every level of government is a serious barrier to more efficient and responsive urban recreation programs.

- Few urban areas have effective mechanisms for coordination of recreation services and facilities. In some cities, fiscal conditions discourage coordination that can create more effective and efficient recreation services. For example, several joint school-park and recreation programs have been discontinued due to lack of funds.

- At the metropolitan level, lack of common land use goals and strategies makes protection of identified regional open space very difficult.

6 The greatest urban recreation deficiencies for land and facilities exist in the inner cores of the nation's largest cities.

- In the growing cities, the greatest need is for development of new park land and facilities; in the older cities, lack of funds for programs and maintenance has restricted recreation opportunities and has resulted in the loss of large investments in park facilities as these facilities deteriorate and become unusable.

- Recreation deficiencies in the large, economically hard-pressed cities are unlikely to be corrected through local efforts or through existing Federal programs since parks and recreation agencies in these cities are having difficulty competing for public dollars. These cities are often receiving less money to provide recreation services than they did five years ago.

7 As local dollars for parks and recreation become more scarce, localities have turned for help, not to the States, but to the Federal Government.

- Very few States direct their own financial resources to urban recreation.

- The major Federal programs providing funds for parks and recreation, either directly or indirectly are: the Land and Water Conservation Fund, General Revenue Sharing,

Source: Abstracted from U.S. Department of the Interior, Heritage Conservation and Recreation Service, *National Urban Recreation Study: Executive Report*, 1978, pp. 10–11.

Community Development Block Grants, and the Comprehensive Employment and Training Act. Most of these programs are not designed specifically to enhance urban recreation, but they make substantial impacts on urban recreation programs.

- The Land and Water Conservation Fund—the major categorical grant program for recreation—provides almost twice as much money per capita to suburban areas as to central cities. Only 16% of the State and local share of the Fund has been expended in central cities containing 30% of the national population.
- General Revenue Sharing and the Community Development Block Grant Program are used least for recreation in the older economically hard-pressed cities which use these Federal funds for more urgent and essential needs.
- The Comprehensive Employment and Training Act program has enabled many park and recreation agencies in economically hard-pressed cities to maintain recreation services that they would have been unable to provide with local funds alone. However, use of the CETA Program, which was not specifically intended to meet park and recreation manpower needs, has had unintended, adverse consequences on the quality of recreation services provided.

8   No coherent national urban policy exists that considers urban recreation.

- Current Federal policy emphasizes State and local discretion in use of revenue sharing, block and single-purpose, categorical grants for urban recreation. The targeting of these funds to meet critical urban needs is thus largely a function of State and local priorities. The Federal Government promotes coordination of these grant and planning programs mainly through Statewide, metropolitan and areawide A-95 clearinghouses. Thus, while a national policy does exist, based on State and local discretion and coordination, the lack of an explicit national policy on meeting urban recreation needs has resulted in piecemeal and sometimes conflicting efforts.
- The lack of a coherent policy results in uneven application of Federal programs to urban recreation problems. Conflicting or uncoordinated goals and strategies at the Federal level produce gaps and overlaps in local use of Federal dollars. The effects of Federal dollars could be made much more positive by a unified approach which encourages Federal, State, and local cooperation in addressing critical urban recreation problems.

9   Current national recreation programs do not effectively address priority open space and recreation needs of urban areas.

- Federal programs directed at land protection have had little impact on continued loss of valuable open space resources in and near cities. The emphasis has been on full-fee acquisition of threatened lands and resources rather than on alternative land protection strategies.
- Federal support for urban recreation comes primarily from community development, manpower, and human services programs that are not primarily directed toward recreation, but are, nevertheless, major influences on community and neighborhood programs.

APPENDIX B | GUIDELINES FOR STATE OUTDOOR RECREATION PLANS

2 *Requirements of the Land and Water Conservation Fund Act of 1965, as Amended.* The Land and Water Conservation Fund Act of 1965, as amended, requires a Statewide Comprehensive Outdoor Recreation Plan (SCORP) from each State prior to consideration by the Secretary of the Interior for financial assistance for acquisition or development projects.

3 *General Objectives.* The SCORP guidelines are designed to provide each State maximum opportunity and flexibility to devise and carry out its own planning process for development and implementation of its plan. The SCORP should be:

   a *Action-Oriented.* The SCORP will be geared to the requirements of the decisionmaking process, contain actions that the State proposed to undertake directly, and consider actions of the Federal government, local governments, and the private sector.

   b *Comprehensive.* The SCORP will analyze the entire range of recreation resources and programs that are significant in providing outdoor opportunities within the State. The scope and content of the SCORP are to be influenced by the unique conditions within each State, and solutions sought which best fit its individual needs.

   c *A Continuing Process.* Planning is a continuous process by which wants and needs are recognized and identified, and means are sought to satisfy them. The SCORP will not be a static document, but a continuing record of the findings and decisions resulting from a planning process that will result in an effective guide to future actions.

4 *SCORP Planning Process.* The SCORP cycle begins and ends with broad-based public participation. The first step is to determine citizen reaction (including public officials) to the adequacy of existing recreation opportunities, and further to solicit ideas and opinions as to what needs to be done and in what priority. Participation by the public is obtained at other critical points throughout the cycle as well. Figure B.1 presents a diagrammatic concept of a continuous planning process with citizen participation occurring at appropriate points in the cycle.

5 **b** *Policy Plan.* The Land and Water Conservation Fund (L&WCF) Act requires as a condition for State participation in the Fund program an acceptable Statewide Comprehensive Outdoor Recreation Plan (SCORP). The SCORP Policy Plan is developed through a cyclical pattern similar to that in Figure B.1. A preliminary step is determining outdoor recreation needs. This is accomplished by comparing existing opportunities (as defined in terms of resources and developed facilities) with what is wanted and needed (based on public opinion surveys and similar data). Later, once needs are deter-

mined, the next step is to decide which options or alternatives are available to the State in meeting the needs identified. Public input is again sought as final consideration of issues and actions are sifted out. The Policy Plan then sets forth in a concise manner the program of actions and priorities recommended, subject to a final public review and approval by the Governor or the State Liason Officer (SLO). SCORP Policy Plans will contain the following elements:

 (1) *State Issues.* A qualitative overview of State outdoor recreation issues based on input from public participation programs and other available planning information. This section should define problem areas requiring State, local and Federal action, such as apparent deficiencies in recreational opportunities in specific areas, or by types of activities. It should also identify data gaps or other deficiencies in information needs but, at the same time, should include judgemental statements on issues for which no quantitative data are readily available. The overview should provide a comprehensive picture of State concerns as a preliminary step towards a more detailed analysis of specific needs and problems which follow in the planning process.

 (2) *Assessment of Resources.* An assessment of public resources which provides significant outdoor recreation opportunities, and the potential for addition to and further development of such resources. Also, to be taken into account are those *private resources*

Source: Abstracted from U.S. Department of the Interior, Heritage Recreation and Conservation Service, *Outdoor Recreation Grants-in-Aid Manual,* part 630, chap. 1, revision of Dec. 7, 1978.

FIGURE B.1 **SCORP planning process.**

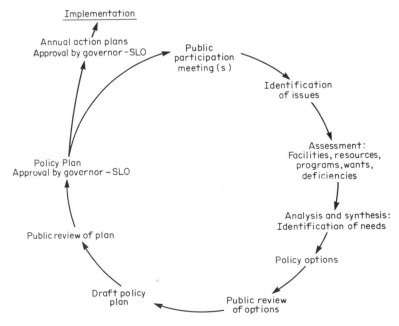

which provide such opportunities, or which have an important potential for recreational use. The level of detail required in this assessment is optional, but it should provide a meaningful picture of existing and potential recreational opportunities in the State.

(3) *Analysis of Demand.* An indication of how people now recreate—including visitors, as well as residents—and a prediction of citizen demand by significant outdoor recreation activities. Demand predictions should rely heavily on the expressed desires of the citizenry obtained from the participation process. The manner in which any necessary supporting surveys are conducted, and their level of detail, is up to each State but should provide a solid basis for projecting future requirements for land and facilities.

(4) *Analysis of Future Needs.* A statement of existing and estimated future requirements for outdoor recreation lands, water, and facilities related to major types of outdoor recreation activities. Again, the methodology to be employed in determining needs is not prescribed, but a description of the method employed should accompany the conclusions.

(5) *Identification of Options.* An identification of those options (special problems and opportunities) that should be considered in determining future outdoor recreation actions. This is a critical point in the planning process in which public advice and consent should be obtained or sought.

(6) *SCORP Recommendations and Policies.* A statement of the recommendations and policies adopted by the State. This will include measures to be taken to deal with specific issues identified in the planning process, establish general priorities as a guide for specific actions, and guidelines and standards recommended for selection of specific actions to be undertaken to implement to SCORP.

c *Action Plan.* A statement of those actions to be taken, as approved by the Governor or SLO, and according to an annual schedule, to carry out the policies and recommendations of the Policy Plan. Actions should cover the entire range of measures by which the State proposes to influence the provision of outdoor recreation interests, including legislation, planning, technical and financial assistance, research and education etc., as well as direct programs to be funded. The process of selection for the issues and actions to be undertaken should be explained.

APPENDIX C

1. SELECTING A PROFESSIONAL PLANNING CONSULTANT

A RECOMMENDED PROCEDURE The following basic procedural steps are recommended as an ethical, business-like, and systematic approach to the task of selecting a planning firm. **1.** Define the nature of the planning work or development problem sufficiently to permit proper choice of consultants to be considered for the work. **2.** Consider the general qualifications of a number of firms which appear to be capable of meeting the requirements of the assignment. The size of the planning firm is not an indication of competence or suitability for the particular planning work or project being considered. (A community or private organization which needs help in identifying sources of planning consulting services may obtain information from the American Institute of Planners, the American Society of Consulting Planners or the official planning assistance agency in its state) **3.** Choose for interviews one or more (preferably not more than three) firms which are believed to be the best qualified. **4.** Interview the selected firms separately, explaining fully the proposed assignment and the selection procedure to be followed. Carefully examine the qualifications of each firm by interviewing not more than one at a time, scheduling at least an hour for each interview and spacing interviews to allow adequate time for deliberation on each firm. Take into account especially the following criteria:

(a) **Experience and Reputation.** Since planning problems are usually very complex, it is essential that the client be fully satisfied that the firm has had a varied experience. This will enable it to put the client's problems in the proper perspective. Direct experience in planning, in either a consulting or public planning agency capacity, is a reliable source of know-how in the planning field, where success may depend upon the application of solutions successfully attempted elsewhere.

(b) **Background of Personnel Available.** A professional planning education on the part of personnel to be assigned is important, but this should not be the exclusive criterion used in selection. Many professionals in allied fields such as architecture, engineering, social or political science, have achieved a high level of excellence in planning on the strength of many years of relevant experience. Impressive academic credentials alone in allied fields, without planning experience, usually should not be considered a substitute for such experience.

(c) **Workload.** Reputable firms do not overload their staffs with responsiblity for more projects than they can comfortably discharge. Frequently, at the time of the selection process, the client has no control over the precise time when the program will start. This is especially true in federally-assisted programs, where the time gap between approval of the program and authorization to proceed can sometimes exceed one year.

Source: "Selecting a Professional Planning Consultant and Administration of the RFP, as recommended by the American Institute of Planners and the American Society of Consulting Planners," 1973. The American Institute of Planners is now the American Planning Association. Qualified professionals are also members of the American Institute of Certified Planners (AICP).

Therefore, unless the program is to commence immediately, the client's best assurance that the proper staff will be available at the appointed time is the firm's reputation for promptness of performance and effectiveness of work.

(d) **Availability of All Required Fields of Expertise.** Complex planning programs may require special expertise which a given firm may prefer to subcontract or perform in association with another. In such instances, the availability and reputation of all subcontractors or associate team members should be as carefully considered as that of the principal contractor.

(e) **Professional Responsibility.** Membership of at least one of the firm's principals in the American Institute of Planners, or of the firm as a whole in the American Society of Consulting Planners, offers assurance that the firm's conduct is governed by a strict Code of Professional Responsibility.

(f) **Social Responsibility.** Reputable firms encourage and provide equal opportunities of employment for qualified women and members of all minority groups.
5. List the firms you have interviewed in order of desirability, based on capability for carrying out the assignment. **6.** Contact your first choice and agree upon a detailed program of work and a mutually satisfactory fee. This should be the first time there is any discussion of fee. **7.** In the event that it is found impossible to agree upon the work program, fee or other contract details, notify the firm in writing that negotiations are being discontinued. Then begin negotiation with the next firm on the list.

ADDITIONAL CONSIDERATIONS Some pitfalls exist that can stall or frustrate negotiations. Once recognized, they can be readily avoided. Here are four examples:

1 Avoid Mass Interview: It is possible to interview too many consulting firms. The proper use of pre-interview selection techniques will enable the client to interview a few qualified consulting firms in depth and provide sufficient data for a sound selection decision. A successful pre-interview selection process should provide consulting firms an opportunity to submit information which would explain the nature and extent of services, innovative approaches, if any, and availability for future work. In order for such information to be most relevant to the client's problems, a short prospectus describing the problem or the proposed planning program should be made available to all prospective consultants. The client should also make every effort to determine the experience of prior clients with consultants being considered.

2 Avoid Competitive Bidding: Members of both the American Institute of Planners and the American Society of Consulting Planners are prohibited by their adopted Codes of Professional Responsibility from competitively soliciting or bidding for planning work. Clients are advised not to deprive themselves of competent professional assistance by insisting on a bid in competition with others. Competition is, of course, desirable; but it should be on the basis of professional competence and experience. Specific work assignments and fees should be discussed only after a consultant is selected. This should not be deemed to preclude the consultant from citing cost experience elsewhere on projects of similar magnitude and complexity or from discussing a likely cost range, it being understood that the final cost will be a function of the final scope of services agreed upon. If the client is subject to budgetary restraints, he should make them known to all pre-selected consultants.

3 Avoid Non-Written Agreements: For the protection of both client and firm, the client should always execute a written agreement with a planning consulting firm. As a minimum, this agreement should specify the work to be done. Although special demands of the consulting firm may arise during the course of a work program, the firm cannot be expected to do work outside of its contract with the client, unless the contract fee is amended accordingly.

4 Avoid "Loss-Leader" Services: The prime purpose of the firm selected to do planning work should be planning. Clients who select planning firms to do planning work should avoid supporting the practice of "loss-leader services." This practice seeks to provide cut-rate planning services in anticipation of securing future contracts for other types of professional services.

5 Avoid Penalty Clauses, Performance Bonds, or Other So-Called "Incentive" Features: These are unnecessary provisions in a professional service agreement. Such devices can provoke a reduction in the quality of service to the client and place emphasis upon less important aspects of the agreement.

MUTUAL RESPONSIBILITY The client has his responsibilities in the selection and hiring of a planning consulting firm as outlined here. Equally important to the client, however, is the professional obligation of the planning consulting firm to perform its work competently and in a professional manner. The American Institute of Planners and the American Society of Consulting Planners govern the ethical conduct of their members through the establishment and maintenance of standards of professional competence and behavior embodied in their Codes of Professional Responsibility, as mentioned earlier. These codes set forth the consultant's role in contract negotiations and his responsibilities to his client.

Services and Fees of a Professional Planning Firm

GENERAL CONSIDERATIONS It is not possible to establish standard fee schedules to govern the charges of professional planning consulting firms. Variables may be based on the extent and breadth of a consultant's education and experience as well as on the variety, quality, and character of his work. A consultant with an established reputation may demand higher fees than one less well known. A consultant may be more competent in certain areas of professional work, or more innovative, than others and may be worth higher fees because of the special ser-

vices which he can render. The scale, complexity and importance of the work also will be factors in charges of a consulting firm.

The basic standard of compensation should be the value of the planning firm's services to the client. In general, fees are based on the scope and complexity of the work as measured by the time of professional personnel required to successfully complete it; the experience, education, training and reputation of the firm's personnel; and the kind and quality of planning service which the firm is prepared to provide. Though it is impossible to set standard fees, it is feasible to outline criteria and factors involved in establishing fees. These factors and criteria are outlined here under four major headings:

I Major types of services performed
II Types of financial arrangements
III Cost factors
IV Professional ethics

I MAJOR TYPES OF SERVICES PERFORMED The following list is not intended to be complete; rather it is representative of planning consultant services.

(a) Reconnaissance Surveys and Work Program Development: This may include working with state and local officials and agencies in surveying needs and opportunities relating to physical, social and economic development and structuring a work program outlining the kinds of planning activities that should be undertaken to deal with the issues identified.

(b) Planning Agency Organization and Administration: This may involve advising planning agencies in staffing, organizing and developing programs required to carry out a variety of planning and development related activities. It could involve services offered in-residence on a continuing or periodic basis.

(c) Preparation of Long- and Short-range Plans, Policies and Programs: This would include analyzing development problems in depth, establishing objectives, shaping alternative policies and programs, and evaluating their impact as a basis for preparing comprehensive community and regional plans.

(d) Technical Assistance and Special Planning Studies: Such work might involve the provision of advice on urgent development problems or on matters dealing with such issues as intergovernmental relations or federal aids; or it could pertain to special functional areas of concern at all government levels (e.g., annexation policies, feasibility studies, business area development, job training programs, low-income housing and urban renewal strategies, programming and budgeting aspects of developmental programs, and recommendations on development codes and ordinances).

(e) Project Planning: This involves the preparation of specific plans for areas under unified control such as new communities, shopping centers, college campuses, industrial parks, urban renewal and other similar projects.

(f) Provision of Assistance and Testimony in Court Cases: Often consultants assist in preparing cases in zoning and planning-related development litigation and in providing expert testimony. Whether working for a public or private client, a key element of these services is the ability of the consulting firm to provide advice based on an understanding of community interelationships that focus on public policy development decisions. The range of services which a firm is in a position to provide will depend upon the disciplines and experience encompassed by its personnel.

The work involved in performing planning services may relate to the following 12 areas of professional specialization recognized by the American Institute of Planners and the American Society of Consulting Planners.

1 Administration for planning and development.
2 Comprehensive physical planning.
3 Resource development.
4 Social planning.
5 Transportation planning.
6 Urban design.
7 Research methodology.
8 Economic planning.
9 Environmental sciences planning.
10 Renewal planning.
11 Planning law.
12 Programming and budgeting.

II TYPES OF FINANCIAL ARRANGEMENTS The amount and kinds of work the consultant does will depend upon the size and complexity of the area involved and kind of local staff resources and data available. The following are common financial arrangements used for the provision of planning and related services.

(a) Lump Sum Fee for all Contracted Services: This arrangement is of advantage to the client due to its relative ease of budgeting. However, it can be a problem for the client and the consultant, since it is difficult to anticipate unknown factors which could be involved. In fairness to both parties, there should be a definite statement of time limits and a provision for the adjustment of the fee. It is, of course, necessary that the program and responsibilities of the consultant be carefully specified in enough detail to preclude mutual misunderstanding.

(b) Fixed Fee for Professional Planning Services—Plus Actual Amount of Other Expenses: Beyond a fixed fee, the firm is paid the cost incurred in connection with the work based upon the actual costs incurred. Such costs would include, in addition to payroll and general office overhead, materials, printing and other out-of-pocket costs directly chargeable to the job. It is usual to set a limit of reimbursable costs in the contract providing for this type of financial arrangement, or to provide that such costs shall not be incurred without prior approval of the client.

(c) Fee as Fixed Percentage of Expenses: Compensation is based on the firm's technical payroll, multiplied by an agreed-upon factor, to arrive at the total compensation. This method may be combined with a fixed fee or per diem compensation for the personal services of the consulting firm's staff if considerable time of such staff is required. It is difficult for the client to budget unless a maximum compensation is included. This arrangement has the advantages of removing the greater part of uncertainty from the consulting firm's calculations in a large undertaking while offering the client a simple method of determining and auditing fees as well as maximum feasibility in establishing the scope of services that he needs.

(d) Per Diem Fees: This method may apply to any of the firm's personnel, including its principals. It always requires explicit understanding as to what constitutes a "day" and how travel time and expenses are to be allocated. This arrangement is especially advantageous for irregular or indefinite assignments. Court testimony is a common example.

(e) Contingency Fee: This method involves work by the consulting firm on the basis of compensation to be determined later and measured by the benefits accruing from the service. This is a difficult method for use in planning studies. It requires contractual agreements that will clearly disclose the basis upon which the contingency fees will ultimately be computed. However, this method would be unethical in all cases where the professional planner offers expert testimony or where he is required to appear as an impartial expert rather than as an advocate.

III COST FACTORS In calculating fees, a planning consultant must include the costs of operating a professional office. In addition, there is the time that must be spent in arranging for consulting work and attending professional meetings, as well as time for vacation and illness, none of which time can be charged to a client. Furthermore, every consultant must keep the nucleus of a competent staff in readiness to serve at all times. Basically, the costs of every job include.

(a) Personnel: Principal's time, technical staff time (including that of specialists whether on the staff or under subcontract) and clerical staff time.

(b) General Overhead Costs: Fringe benefits, vacations, illness, rent, telephone, equipment, insurance, taxes, professional memberships and conferences, reference library, and other usual expenses involved in the operation of a professional office.

(c) Other Project Expenses: Such items as travel and subsistence, materials and supplies, or typical subcontractor items such as renderings, models and the like.

IV PROFESSIONAL ETHICS The acceptance of a contract and the manner of compensation impinge directly on the ethics of the planning profession and subject both contractors and consultants to the penalties provided under the AIP Code of Professional Responsibility and the ASCP Code of Conduct.

2. SAMPLE AGREEMENT FOR PREPARATION OF A PARK MASTER PLAN

THIS AGREEMENT made this _____ day of _____ 19___ by and between the _____, hereinafter called the OWNER, and _____, hereinafter called the CONSULTANT.

WITNESSETH:

ARTICLE 1: ADDRESSES

That the OWNER does hereby employ the CONSULTANT to prepare a MASTER PLAN for the property located in _____ _____, containing a total of _____ acres, more or less.

The CONSULTANT will base the final plan of the following legal description, unless otherwise directed in writing by the OWNER:

GIVE
LEGAL
DESCRIPTION

ARTICLE 2: SERVICES

The CONSULTANT agrees to perform professional consultant services to the Parks and Recreation Staff (hereinafter called the STAFF) in preparing the MASTER PLAN which shall include:

1 A detailed office and field study of the site and its immediate environs to determine:

(a) general character as to terrain, vegetation, and man-made features,

(b) suitability or adaptability of portions of the site for the several types of recreational use and development hereinafter proposed, and

(c) detailed characteristic of specific areas as related to specific uses.

2 Submission of preliminary plans and sketches, within ninety _____ days after authorization to proceed and topographical material has been received from the STAFF, and submission of the report text for review by the STAFF prior to printing.

3 Availability for conferences with the STAFF, other consulting landscape architects, the Parks Commission, and any other persons, agencies, or organizations designated by the Director of the Parks and Recreation Department (herinafter called the DIRECTOR).

Source: Robert D. Buechner, *The Use of Consultants,* Arlington, Va.: National Recreation and Park Association, 1970, pp. 21–27. Reprinted with permission.

4 Submission of a final MASTER PLAN to be published in document form and to contain maps, sketches, and photographs, together with explanatory and descriptive text. The maps shall include, but are not limited to:

(a) A comprehensive development map of the total site, including one full-scale colored rendering for presentation purposes.

(b) Section maps detailing feature areas.

All maps shall be drawn at such a scale as to be readable at group presentations and legible when reduced to document size.

This document will be printed by quality lithographic methods and _____ copies furnished to the OWNER. Additional copies will be furnished upon request at reproduction and handling costs. One "mylar" copy of each map at full scale, will be furnished the OWNER. The MASTER PLAN shall be submitted within _____ days after receipt of the preliminary plans and sketches. The CONSULTANT and the OWNER each reserve the right to offer for sale to the general public copies of the MASTER PLAN at a price based upon production and handling costs.

5 In the preparation of this MASTER PLAN, it is understood that the **design theme** will be determined by the DIRECTOR, and that consideration will be given to the following recreational facilities, and also to any other facilities, which may appear feasible to the STAFF during the preparation of said Plan.

(a) Horse trail system, including overnight shelter(s), corrals, and feed station, pack trip center with stables, corrals, and parking areas,

(b) Hiking trail system, with rest shelters,

(c) Entrances and park road system for circulation and access to feature areas, scenic parkway with parking overlooks, if proven feasible,

(d) Organized group camps for scheduled stays,

(e) Overnight tent and travel trailer camps,

(f) Family and group picnic areas,

(g) Special interest facilities, cycle cross-country course, etc.

(h) Interpretive areas and facilities—museum and amphitheater and nature trails,

(i) Concession facilities—supplies and refreshments, snack bars, dining,

(j) Administration, maintenance, service and residence areas, control facilities, and

(k) Complementary facilities—water supply and distribution, sanitary facilities and sewage disposal, trash disposal, and parking.

6 Submission of a supplement to the MASTER PLAN, which will consist of a report containing preliminary cost estimates for construction of all proposed facilities, a suggested priority program in five (5) year increments covering a fifteen (15) year period including preliminary cost estimates, and such other recommendations as may be appropriate as supplementary information. Twenty-five (25) copies of this Supplementary Report, produced by duplicator methods, will be submitted.

7 Formal presentation of the completed MASTER PLAN to the Commission and Board.

ARTICLE 3: PAYMENT

In consideration of the above named services, the OWNER agrees to pay the CONSULTANT the sum of $ _____ (including all travel, printing, and duplicating expenses), payable in four (4) equal installments of $ _____, at twenty-five percent (25), fifty percent (50%), seventy-five percent (75%), and one-hundred percent (100%) of the project completion as determined by the OWNER, the final payment to be within _____ days following delivery of the completed MASTER PLAN to the OWNER.

ARTICLE 4: ITEMS SUPPLIED AND EXTRA WORK

(a) The OWNER shall provide topographic and aerial photography maps, with the scale, contour interval, coverage, and accuracy to be determined by the OWNER and that the STAFF will make available to the CONSULTANT all of its maps and final data pertinent to the project and the advice and guidance of its staff and consultants.

(b) It is understood and agreed that all available information relating to the status of mining claims, archaeological, and hydrological investigations, and rights-of-way outside the park will be made available to the CONSULTANT.

(c) If, during the progress of the work, and upon written authority of the DIRECTOR, the OWNER finds it desirable or necessary to cause the CONSULTANT to perform additional services other than those defined in Article 2 (and Article 4, if applicable), the payment for such additional work shall be as follows:

Principal _____ @ $_____/ mile
Employees _____ @ $_____/ hr.
(specify)
Mileage @ _____/ mile
Direct Charges _____ @ at cost
(Phone, transp., etc.)

ARTICLE 5: ABANDONMENT OF PROJECT

If the owner finds it necessary to abandon the project, the CONSULTANT shall be compensated for all work completed under Article 2 and 4. Scheduled items not completed, but upon which work has been performed, shall be paid for upon basis of estimated extent of completion.

ARTICLE 6: OTHER PARTIES

Neither the OWNER nor the CONSULTANT shall assign, sublet, or transfer his interest in this agreement without written consent of the other.

ARTICLE 7. TERMINATION

(a) This Agreement shall be terminated at any time by the OWNER or the CONSULTANT upon giving _____ days' written notice. Termination by the OWNER shall comply with Article 5.

(b) This Agreement, unless previously terminated by written notice, shall be terminated by the final payment for the finished work.

IN WITNESS WHEREOF, we have executed this agreement the day and year first above written.

CITY, COUNTY, STATE OR OTHER AGENCY

By _____
Chairman   Date
By _____
Consultant   Date

ATTEST: _____
Clerk   Date

APPENDIX D

1. RECREATION SPACE CLASSIFICATION SYSTEM

Orientation	Function	Space, design, and service area	Example
Home-oriented space	Should meet aesthetic qualities and accommodate informal activities of an active and passive nature, i.e., sitting, reading, gardening, sunning, children's play, and family activity	Varies according to housing type; immediately adjacent or within 500 feet of each dwelling unit	Front and back yards, driveways, sidewalks, porch, balconies, workshops, play rooms, recreation rooms
Home cluster or sub-neighborhood common space	Especially important in high-density areas, providing visual relief and aesthetic qualities for similar activities to those mentioned above, as well as meeting areas for small informal groups, walking, jogging, and dog walking	Must be visually accessible; varies from 500 square feet to 2 acres; designed to be as flexible and adaptable as possible; will serve an area of 100 yards to ¼ mile radius	Vacant lots, cul-de-sacs, boulevards, green belts, walkways, trails, play lots, rest areas, vest-pocket parks, parkettes
Neighborhood space	Should accommodate neighborhood interest preferences; may include sports areas for minor leagues, outdoor skating rinks, water play, as well as special events and informal passive activities	Space should be associated with an elementary school; varies from 4 to 20 acres; will serve 5000 people within an area of ¼ to ½ mile radius	Neighborhood parks or park-school combinations; play fields for baseball, soccer, and football; adventure playgrounds, wading pools, neighborhood centers
Community space	Should accommodate social, cultural, educational, and physical activities of particular interest to the community; multi-purpose, year round, day/night activities; low-level competitive sports with limited spectator space	Space should be associated with a secondary school; varies from 15 to 20 acres; will serve several neighborhoods or 15,000 to 25,000 people within a radius of ½ to 1½ miles; accessible by walking, cycling, and public transit	Community park or park-school combinations; facilities for playgrounds, recreation center, meeting rooms, and library; track and field areas, sports fields, arena, and swimming pool
Citywide space	Should provide specialized facilities for the use of a wide segment of the population; will accommodate the preservation of unique historical, cultural, or natural areas	Parks can be 25 to 200 acres; accessible to all residents by private and public transportation; should not exceed ½ hour driving time; should be linked to other open space	Major city parks and areas left in their natural state; beaches, trails, and picnic areas; fair grounds, civic centers, and major sports facilities
Regional space	Specialized areas for conservation and preservation of naturalized resources; usually involves more time-consuming activities, i.e., day-long picnics and family camping	Up to 500 acres or more, serving two or more municipalities; if possible accessible by public transportation; within 20 miles or 1 hour driving time of high-density areas	Conservation areas, botanical gardens, regional and provincial parks; wild life sanctuaries and naturalized reserves; scenic drives and waterway systems; air fields, ski areas, zoos, and museums

Source: Adapted from *Guidelines for Developing Public Recreation Facility Standards,* Ministry of Culture and Recreation, Sports and Fitness Division, Ontario, Canada, 1976, pp. 32–33.

2. CLASSIFICATION OF PARK AND RECREATION AREAS

THE FOLLOWING CLASSIFICATIONS ARE RECOMMENDED:

Playlots   The playlot is a small area intended for children up to 6 or 7 years of age. It is essentially a substitute for the backyard and thus normally provided only in high-density areas such as apartment or tenement districts. Playlots are expensive to maintain and difficult to administer but serve an important function in the dense inner city areas. They range in size from 2,500 square feet up to 1 acre and usually feature play apparatus, a paved area for wheeled toys, benches, sand areas, a small wading or spray pool, and landscape treatment. They should be located within a block or super-block or near the center of a housing development. Children should not be required to cross a major arterial street to reach the playlot.

Vest Pocket or Mini-Parks   There has been great emphasis of late on the vest pocket parks, which are usually vacant lots converted to recreation use. In some instances, such parks may become permanent features in the neighborhood but should be supportive to adequate open space for all needed facilities. Vest pocket parks may serve children only, senior citizens only, or all age groups, depending on the needs in the neighborhood. The size and location is determined more by the availability of vacant land than any other factor. Vest pocket parks may feature children's play areas, quiet game areas, landscaping, and some sports activities such as multi-purpose courts if space allows.

Neighborhood Parks   The neighborhood parks should, if possible, adjoin the public elementary schools, which usually serve about a square mile of urban area and a total population ranging from 2,000 to 10,000. It is desirable to locate the areas for active recreation such as ball diamonds and play areas toward the interior of the site so the perimeter can be landscaped to buffer sound, provide a greater measure of safety, and prevent glare from night lighting. Operating agencies should give much more consideration to the inclusion of night lighting for outdoor facilities because it greatly extends use and tends to reduce vandalism.

Recreation facilities for adults should be provided in the park portion of the site, in accordance with the desires of the people. Such facilities as sitting areas, shuffleboard, and horseshoe courts should be located in the shade. Tables for games such as chess, checkers, and cards, and perhaps some picnic tables are

desirable. The site and the school building should be designed to attract the people of the neighborhood and make it a center for education, recreation, and for cultural activities. **The recommended standard for neighborhood parks is 2.5 acres per 1000 with a minimum size of 5 acres.**

District Parks   The district parks supplement the neighborhood parks in providing the near-at-hand recreation facilities needed by the urban population. These larger sites should, if possible, adjoin the public junior and senior high schools. They also encompass the activities formerly included in the "playfield." While the neighborhood sites should be designed to attract and serve the entire neighborhood populations, there are certain recreation facilities needed which require more space than the neighborhood sites should accommodate. Thus, the need for the district park. Other facilities may include a tennis complex, swimming pool, multi-purpose courts, community center, and adequate off-street parking. Parks of this type are best located on or near thoroughfares, easily accessible and distributed so they are within about one to three miles of each home. The increased mobility of teenagers who heavily utilize the district parks tends to widen the radius of the service area. **The recommended standard for district parks is 2.5 acres per 1000, with a minimum size of 20 acres.**

Large Urban or Metropolitan Parks   Such parks are normally acquired to provide the urban dweller with an opportunity to get away from the noise and congestion of the city without having to travel a great distance. A central location is desirable but not always possible and the large urban park is often located near or outside the city limits.

A minimum of 100 acres is required with 250 to 1,000 acres being more desirable. This park may feature wooded areas, varying topography and water features, picnic areas, boating and swimming, a nature center, nature, hiking and riding trails, day camps, and some sports facilities on a less formal basis than the district park.

The large urban park usually serves those within a 30-minute drive, which may be 50,000 to 100,000 people. **The recommended standard for large urban parks is 5 acres per 1000 and a minimum size of 100 acres.**

Regional Parks   These parks serve the people of a large region—usually those within an hour's travel time. The size and location will vary but at least 250 acres is recommended and may go up to several thousand acres. The responsibility for providing these extraurban parks generally falls upon the county or a regional authority. Even within the jurisdiction responsible for

Source: Abstracted from Robert D. Buechner (ed.), *National Park, Recreation and Open Space Standards*, National Recreation and Park Association, 1971, pp. 25–29. Reprinted with permission.

these parks there may be variances in the type of development included in a regional park. Some are left primarily in their "natural state" while others will have both natural areas and extensive development. They should not, under any circumstances, take the place of neighborhood or district parks. As the metropolitan area expands there is often pressure to put facilities in the regional park that are not in keeping with the philosophy or purpose of the park. This is actually an example of one type of park development *encroaching upon another*. It is easy to succumb to this pressure because the parkland is there when urban sprawl arrives. If proper location and development of neighborhood and district parks is achieved, such pressure need not exist.

Some of the facilities normally found in the regional park are campgrounds, picnic areas, nature centers, trail systems, water areas, a golf course, a miniature train, botanical gardens, and in some cases sports fields. **The recommended standard for regional parks is 20 acres per 1000, with a minimum size of 250 acres.**

SPECIAL FACILITIES

Parkways and Scenic Corridors   These are essentially elongated parks with a road extending throughout their length. They are usually restricted to non-commercial traffic. The parkway generally serves to connect large units in the park system or to provide a pleasant means of travel within the city and between the city and an outlying region. In some communities, what were once beautiful scenic drives have become major traffic arterials or high-speed thruways, yeilding under pressure of commuter traffic. This should not be condoned, and can often be avoided through proper design and speed restrictions.

The parkway usually follows stream or river alignments, shorelines of large lakes, or natural wooded areas. Thus, its location and size is dependent upon the availability and location of these resources. Where this kind of resource does not exist naturally, **it is recommended that a parkway effect or scenic drive be created through proper landscape design and planting.** Although no specific acreage standard is applicable, **a minimum right-of-way of 300 feet is recommended; with portions being much wider for scenic vistas and other recreation development.**

Swimming Pools   Swimming pools, like golf courses, will draw from considerable distances—especially when there are not enough pools to serve the community.

It is highly desirable to include indoor or indoor-outdoor pools in junior and/or senior high schools, and these should be available for elementary school use so swimming can be taught at an early age.

In determining the number of pools required to serve a community, **the standard of 15 square feet of water surface for each 3 percent of the population is recommended.** This is the same as 450 sq. feet per 1000 people. Obviously the configuration of the pool determines its exact water surface area, but the average 50-meter pool will be about 9,000 square feet, thus serving a population of 20,000. A 25-meter pool will serve 10,000 people. The deck space should be at least twice the area of the water surface.

Portable pools are proving popular in land- and facility-deficient inner city areas. They are not without some problems—but many well constructed models are available. Some prerequisites for portable pools are a firm base (such as a paved area), nearby restroom facilities, an adequate water supply, and space for storage during the winter months.

Although swimming is generally thought of as a summertime, outdoor activity, new design trends such as the air-supported roof have liberated the indoor-outdoor concept. Depending on the geographical location, outdoor pools may only be in operation 25-30 percent of the year. The indoor-outdoor pool provides year-round use and is especially important for expanded learn-to-swim programs during the school year.

Golf Courses   **One 18-hole daily fee golf course is recommended for each 25,000 of the population.** A daily fee course may include semi-private courses that charge green fees comparable to public courses and draw from the golfing element that play the public courses.

The size of the site will depend primarily on the terrain, vegetation, and shape of the parcel of land. Generally, 75 to 90 acres are required for 9 holes and 120 to 180 acres for 18 holes. A golf course architect should be retained to design *any* new course and every effort should be made to follow the plans explicitly without cutting corners.

The average golfer may travel 25 miles or more to play an attractive, properly maintained course. It is often desirable to locate a course within or adjacent to a large urban or regional park, but not essential. Although a golf course does not have large capacity for use (350-400 golfers/day or about 80,000 rounds per year may be expected) compared to many other recreation areas, the fact that "open space" is created by its existence should be a factor in determining feasibility.

Par-3 golf courses continue to be popular. They should be considered as supplementary to regulation courses and not as substitutes. Par-3 courses offer opportunities for beginners to improve their game, and they serve some who do not have time for a full round on a regulation course and those who cannot meet the physical demands of walking a full-length 18-hole course. They also take some of the load off the regulation courses. A 9-hole, par-3 course can be built on 15 to 25 acres. Where possible, it is recommended that a par-3 course adjoin a regulation course in order that one manager can take charge of both courses and to combine and simplify the operation and maintenance of two courses.

Additionally, the NRPA recommends that the following concepts and trends be considered to best meet the golfing needs of the present and future:

- Small towns or cities that cannot justify expenditures or obtain adequate land for a full 18-hole course should consider the par-3 or par-3 executive course (has some par 4 holes).

- A par-3 course should be built for youth play and teaching. High schools should include a golf practice hole as part of their site plan.

- Consideration should be given to a full-length 9- or 18-hole course for novices, or "duffers" to ease the pressure and speed up play on other courses.

- Special programs should be developed to teach golf to inner-city residents (especially youth) and transport them to public golf courses.

- In cases where it is not feasible or financially expedient to light an entire course, consideration should be given to lighting the last 3 or 4 holes for extended playing time.

3. PARKLAND CLASSIFICATION SYSTEM

REGIONAL PARK AND REGIONAL SHORELINE PARK

Purpose and Goals

A Regional Park or a Regional Shoreline Park is a spacious area of scenic or natural character in which a variety of recreational experiences and facilities are provided for the purpose of making the out-of-doors available for public enjoyment and education.

Minimum Standards

For an area to be considered suitable for designation as a Regional Park or a Regional Shoreline Park, it must possess the following characteristics:

1 The area must have *either* of the following features:

   a To be suitable for a *Regional Park,* it must contain a minimum area of 500 acres, either in a single block, or in a series of smaller units with the smallest unit being at least 100 acres and with the potential for linking the units with a trail, scenic road, or transit system; *or*

   b *To be suitable for a Regional Shoreline Park,* it must contain a minimum area (including tidelands and marshes) of 100 acres, either in a single block, or in a series of smaller units stretching along the bay shoreline with the potential existing for linking the units with a trail, scenic road, transit system, or ferry system.

2 Seventy to ninety percent of the area suitable for a *Regional Park* and sixty to eighty percent of the area suitable for a *Regional Shoreline Park* must have a scenic or natural character. This portion should be designated a Natural Environment Unit for planning and management purposes.

3 Ten to thirty percent of the area suitable for a *Regional Park* and twenty to forty percent of the area suitable for a *Regional Shoreline Park* must be usable for accommodating a variety of recreational activities and not possess any significant environmental features that would conflict with the development of recreational facilities. This portion should be designated an Outdoor Recreation Unit for planning and management purposes.

Source: Policies for Planning, part 2, Master Plan, East Bay Regional Park District, Oakland, Calif. Prepared by Overview, 1973. pp. 27–37. The classifications for regional wilderness, regional preserve, and open space reserve are not described here.

Planning and Management Guidelines (Natural Environment Unit)

PLANNING AND DEVELOPMENT POLICIES

1 Development should be for the purpose of making the unit available for public enjoyment in a manner consistent with the preservation of natural values. Facilities might include such things as access roads, trails, and basic but not elaborate development necessary for camping and related outdoor activities.

2 A Natural Environment Unit may contain a Preserve Unit or a Trail Link; any such unit should be planned and managed according to the guidelines applying specifically to it. A Natural Environment Unit may not contain any staging units.

RESOURCE MANAGEMENT AND USE POLICIES

1 The primary management objective should be to provide for a variety of recreation experience in the out-of-doors, while preserving, or when necessary establishing, scenic landscape conditions. Users should be encouraged to enjoy the unit "as-is" in an outdoor environment where man is a visitor.

2 Forest and land management techniques such as tree cutting, controlled burning, reforestation and planting programs, and cattle grazing may be used to preserve, maintain, or re-create the desired environmental setting.

3 In periods of extreme fire hazard, all or some portion of the Natural Environment Unit may be closed to public use in order to protect the land and to insure the safety of the public.

4 Typical recreation activities within the unit might include such things as hiking, fishing, camping, picnicking, nature study, boating, and horseback riding.

Planning Management Guidelines (Outdoor Recreation Unit)

PLANNING AND DEVELOPMENT POLICIES

1 The Outdoor Recreation Unit should contain all the substantial recreational development that is to be provided within a Regional Park. Development should include a broad range of facilities such as campgrounds, picnic areas, snack stands, nature interpretive facilities, equestrian complexes, road networks, beaches, bathhouses, turfed meadows, and fishing piers.

2 Facilities which would involve major modifications of the land, forests, or waters, which are attractions in themselves and do not directly enhance the public's enjoyment of the outdoor environment, or which would provide for indoor or formalized recreation facilities, should not be developed within an Outdoor Recreation Unit.

3 All facilities should be designed to harmonize in appearance with the surrounding natural landscape.

4 The Outdoor Recreation Unit may contain the staging facilities for a Wilderness Unit, Preserve Unit, or Trail Link if these elements are part of, or adjacent to, the Regional Park.

5 Whenever feasible, an internal transportation system rather than a traditional road system should be utilized for movement within the unit.

RESOURCE MANAGEMENT AND USE POLICIES

1 The primary management objective for an Outdoor Recreation Unit should be to accommodate the more structured outdoor recreational activities and to thereby preserve the Natural Environment Unit for unstructured enjoyment of the out-of-doors.

2 The Unit should be managed to provide an appearance that harmonizes with the surrounding natural landscape as much as possible. This may require extensive maintenance because of the probable heavy use of the unit.

3 Reforestation or planting may be necessary to provide an attractive environmental setting and should use indigenous vegetation wherever possible.

REGIONAL RECREATION AREA AND REGIONAL SHORELINE RECREATION AREA

Purpose and Goals

A Regional Recreation Area or a Regional Shoreline Recreation Area is an area developed for the purpose of providing for varied and intensive forms of outdoor recreational activities.

Minimum Standards

For an area to be considered suitable for designation as a Regional Recreation Area or a Regional Shoreline Recreation Area, it must possess the following characteristics:

1 The area must have *either* of the following features:

   a To be suitable for a *Regional Recreation Area,* it must contain a minimum of 100 acres, except where the design criteria for a specific recreational facility (as noted in Minimum Standard No. 2-b) require more area;

this acreage can be either in a single block or in a series of smaller units with the smallest unit being at least 20 acres and with the potential existing for linking the units with a trail, scenic road, or transit system; *or*

   b To be suitable for a *Regional Shoreline Recreation Area,* it must contain a minimum (including tidelands and marshes) of 50 acres, except where the design criteria for a specific recreational facility (as noted in Minimum Standard No. 2-b) require more area; this acreage can be either in a single block or in a series of smaller units stretching along the bay shoreline with the potential existing for linking the units with a trail, scenic road, transit system, or ferry system.

2 The area must have *either* of the following features:

   a The land must not possess any significant or delicate environmental features that would conflict with the intensive development of recreational facilties; *or*

   b The land must be capable of withstanding intensive human impact and have the resource characteristics (including size) required by the design criteria for a specific recreational facility (such as a quarry that could be used for a swimming lake, an area of varied terrain suitable for an off-road vehicle recreation area, or a calm lagoon useful for a small-boat marina and sailing area).

Planning and Management Guidelines

PLANNING AND DEVELOPMENT POLICIES

1 The area should be planned and developed to provide whatever degree of facility development is necessary to accommodate many and varied forms of recreation. Large crowds should be expected, so heavy capital investment and substantial alteration of the environment may be necessary to facilitate intensive public use of the area.

2 Wherever feasible, nature interpretive facilities should be provided within a Regional Recreation Area. Marshes, wildlife refuge areas, ponds, and other similar facilities may be artificially created for this purpose.

3 In order to provide a wide range of activities for many people, development might include such things as parking areas, swimming beaches, marinas, bathhouses, man-made lakes, playing fields, and eating facilities.

RESOURCE MANAGEMENT AND USE POLICIES

1 The primary management objective should be to accommodate large crowds enjoying many types of outdoor recreational activities. Extensive maintenance may be necessary to achieve this objective.

2 High quality routine maintenance should be provided in order to provide pleasant recreational experiences to a large number of people in a relatively small area.

APPENDIX E

1. ILLUSTRATIVE CITIZEN SURVEY QUESTIONNAIRE ON RECREATION

The 1973 St. Petersburg Questionnaire
*INDICATES QUESTION THAT EVERYONE SURVEYED IS ASKED.

Hello, my name is _____. I work for the St. Petersburg Parks and Recreation Department. As mentioned in the letter we sent to your household this past week, we would like to know your opinion of the pools, parks, and recreational centers in your neighborhood.

(ONLY IF RESPONDENT MENTIONS THAT HE DID RECEIVE OR SEE THE LETTER SENT TO THE HOUSEHOLD OR THAT HE DID NOT RECEIVE OR SEE THE LETTER SENT, MARK APPROPRIATE RESPONSE.)

Received letter   Yes _____   No _____

Is your telephone number _____?

Is your address _____?

(IF NO TO EITHER ADDRESS OR TELEPHONE CONCLUDE THE INTERVIEW.)

(IF THEY WISH TO VERIFY SURVEY, ASK THEM TO CALL _____ AT 894-2111, EXTENSION 269.)

(IF RESPONDENT IS TOO BUSY TO TALK NOW, SAY:)

I'll call back later. What time is convenient for you? _____

(IF RESPONDENT AGREES TO INTERVIEW THEN CONTINUE.)

*Q1   Are you 16 years or older?   Yes _____   No _____

*Q2   Are you a member of this household?
Yes _____   No _____

*Q3   How would you rate the pool, park, and recreational facilities?
Excellent _____   Fair _____   No Opinion _____
Good _____   Poor _____   Don't know _____

(IF OPINION IS "POOR" ASK:)

Would you tell me why you say that, please? _____
_____
_____

*Q4   Did anyone in your household use these facilities (NAME EACH FACILITY) during the past month?

(a) _____ Pool   Yes _____ · No ___
    _____   Don't know _____
(b) _____ Park   Yes _____ No ___
    _____   Don't know _____
(c) _____ Center Yes _____ No
    _____   Don't know _____

(IF YES TO a, b, OR c, ASK:)

*Q5   Would you tell me which members of the household used these facilities and which members did not? I need to know the age and sex of each person, whether or not he or she used them.

(IF RESPONDENT IS UNDER 16 YEARS, OR NOT A MEMBER OF THE HOUSEHOLD, SAY:)

*Q6   Did anyone in the household use any other public recreational facilities during the past month?

Yes _____   No _____   Don't know _____

(IF YES, ASK:)
Which ones were they and who used them?

(ENTER OTHER FACILITIES ON SPREAD SHEET FOR EACH USER. IF NO ONE IN HOUSEHOLD USED ANY OTHER FACILITY (Q4 and Q6) GO TO Q13.)

(FOR Q7 THROUGH Q11 READ QUESTIONS FOR EACH HOUSEHOLD FACILITY USER AND ENTER ANSWER ON SPREAD SHEET BEFORE GOING ON TO NEXT HOUSEHOLD USER.)

Is the mother or father of the household at home?

Yes _____   No _____

(IF NEITHER IS AT HOME, SAY:)

Is some other adult at home?   Yes ___   No ___

Source: Harry P. Hatry et al., *How Effective Are Your Community Services?* Washington, D.C.: Urban Institute, 1977, pp. 279–283. Reprinted with permission.

SPREAD SHEET

Q5		Q5 & Q6	Q7	Q8	Q9	Q10	Q11
SEX	AGE	FACILITY	NUMBER OF TIMES USED LAST MONTH	LENGTH OF STAY	ACTIVITY ENJOYED MOST	METHOD OF TRANSPORTATION	TRANSPORTATION TIME ONE-WAY
		Pool					
		Park					
		Center					
		Pool					
		Park					
		Center					
		Pool					
		Park					
		Center					
		Pool					
		Park					
		Center					

(IF THE ADULT CANNOT BE REACHED ASK WHAT TIME AN ADULT WILL BE HOME. IF THERE IS NO ADULT, CONCLUDE THE INTERVIEW.)

   (ENTER THE SEX AND AGE OF EACH HOUSEHOLD MEMBER ON THE SPREAD SHEET.)

*Q7   About how many times did (household member) use (facility name) in the past month?

   (ENTER ON SPREAD SHEET.)

*Q8   How many hours did he/she stay on the average?

   (ENTER ON SPREAD SHEET.)

*Q9   Which single activity does he/she enjoy doing most when he/she goes there?

   (ENTER ON SPREAD SHEET.)

*Q10   What means of transportation did he/she usually use to to get there?

   (ENTER ON SPREAD SHEET. USE CATEGORIES: WALK, CAR, CAB, PUBLIC BUS, BIKE, MOTOR-BIKE, OTHER.)

Q11   How many minutes does it take to get there on the average?

   (ENTER ON SPREAD SHEET.)

(Q12 IS FOR USERS ONLY.)

Q12 How do you think your household members rate the facilities that they have used during the past month? (DO NOT READ.)

(WRITE IN NAMES OF EACH FACILITY LISTED ON RATING TABLE.)

(SURVEY ONLY THOSE FACILITIES WHERE NO ATTENDANCE BY ANYONE IN THE HOUSEHOLD. NAMES OF FACILITIES WILL BE PREVIOUSLY ENTERED FOR Q13 AND Q14.)

*Q13 Would you give me the reasons why during the last month your household did not use

(NAMES OF FACILITIES)	(REASONS)
a _____	_____
b _____	_____
c _____	_____

Q14 Let me read a list of possible reasons in case we have overlooked some. For (facility). . . .

(READ REASONS. INDICATE RESPONSE BY CHECK MARK IN BOX.)

	NAMES OF FACILITIES		
	POOL	PARK	CENTER
a Don't know about facility or its programs			
b Not open the right times			
c Too far away			
d It's too crowded			
e It's not attractive			
f Costs too much to go there			
g Too dangerous there			
h Do not like other users			
i Personal health			
j Activities not interesting			

(IF CHECKED ASK WHAT WOULD BE INTERESTING.)

k Too busy			
l Other (SPECIFY)			

*Q15 Are there any recreational activities or programs that you would add or change in the city which would improve recreation for your household?

Yes _____ No _____
Don't know _____ No opinion _____

(IF YES)

What additions or changes would you make?

_____

_____

(IF RESPONSE IS "DON'T KNOW" THEN SUGGEST THESE CHANGES TO RESPONDENT.)

Would you like to have more variety in the program being offered?

Yes _____ No _____ Don't know _____

(IF YES ASK)
What new programs would you like to see added?

_____

(POSSIBLE SUGGESTIONS INCLUDE: SEWING CLASSES, CARD GAMES, WRESTLING, JUDO, DANCING, ETC.)

Would you like to see more facilities available, such as:

Tennis courts	Yes _____	No _____
Ball diamonds	Yes _____	No _____
Handball courts	Yes _____	No _____
Swimming pools	Yes _____	No _____
Shuffleboard courts	Yes _____	No _____
Other _____		

*Q16 How many different people in your household have played golf in the last 12 months? _____

(IF RESPONDENT PLAYS GOLF ASK:)

Q17 What kinds of waiting times do you experience?

Usually too long _____
Occasionally too long _____
Not usually a problem _____
Don't know _____

RATING TABLE

FACILITY NAME	CHARACTERISTICS	VERY GOOD	GOOD	FAIR	POOR	DON'T KNOW
	i) Hours of operation					
	ii) Cleanliness					
	iii) Condition of equipment					
	iv) Helpfulness and attitude of personnel					
	v) Amount of space					
	vi) Safety					
	vii) Overall rating					
	i) Hours of operation					
	ii) Cleanliness					
	iii) Condition of equipment					
	iv) Helpfulness and attitude of personnel					
	v) Amount of space					
	vi) Safety					
	vii) Overall rating					
	i) Hours of operation					
	ii) Cleanliness					
	iii) Condition of equipment					
	iv) Helpfulness and attitude of personnel					
	v) Amount of space					
	vi) Safety					
	vii) Overall rating					
	i) Hours of operation					
	ii) Cleanliness					
	iii) Condition of equipment					
	iv) Helpfulness and attitude of personnel					
	v) Amount of space					
	vi) Safety					
	vii) Overall rating					

Q18 Has the cost of greens fees restricted your golfing:

> A great deal _____
> Somewhat _____
> Not much _____
> (DON'T READ) → Don't know _____

Now I have some general questions to complete the questionnaire. As mentioned in the letter, your replies will be strictly confidential.

*Q19 Does the household have a family vehicle like a car or truck?

Yes _____   No _____

Don't know _____   Won't say _____

*Q20 What was the last grade or class the head of the household completed in school?

_____ Grade 8 or less
_____ High school, incomplete
_____ High school, completed
_____ Technical, trade or business
_____ College, university, incomplete
_____ College, university, graduate
_____ Don't know
_____ Won't say

*Q21 Do you own or are you buying or do you rent the place you live in?

_____ Own (buying)
_____ Rent
_____ Other
_____ Don't know
_____ Won't say

*Q22 How many years have you lived in the neighborhood?

_____

Don't know _____   Won't say _____

*Q23 Can you tell me approximately what is the level of income for all members of your household, that is, before any taxes? What is the total annual income?

Below $5,000 _____
Between $5,000 and $10,000 _____
Between $10,000 and $15,000 _____
Over $15,000 _____
Don't know _____
Won't say _____

*Q24 Do you consider yourself of a White _____, Black _____, or of another race _____?

Don't know _____   Won't say _____

2. ILLUSTRATIVE SURVEY OF USERS OF RECREATION FACILITIES

Adapted from Nashville and St. Petersburg User Surveys

Facility Name_____Date_____

READ EACH QUESTION. CHOOSE AND CIRCLE THE NUMBER TO THE LEFT OF THE RESPONSE THAT BEST APPLIES TO YOU.

1 Where did you find out about this facility?

(1) Newspaper
(2) Television
(3) Friends and neighbors
(4) City published information
(5) Phone book
(6) Other; specify_____

2 How did you get here?

(1) Own car
(2) Other person's car
(3) Motorcycle
(4) Bus
(5) Bike
(6) Walked
(7) Other; specify_____

3 How long did it take to get here?

(1) Less than 10 minutes
(2) 10–19 minutes
(3) 20–29 minutes
(4) 30–39 minutes
(5) 40–49 minutes
(6) 50–59 minutes
(7) 60 or more

4 About how often have you come here during the past 12 months?

(1) This is my first visit
(2) Almost daily

Source: Harry P. Hatry et al., *How Effective Are Your Community Services?* Washington, D.C.: Urban Institute, 1977, pp. 285–286. Reprinted with permission.

(3) At least once a week
(4) At least once a month
(5) Less than once a month

5 How long do you usually stay at this facility?

(1) Less than 1/2 hour
(2) 1/2 or more, but not 1 hour
(3) 1 hour or more, but not 2 hours
(4) 2 hours or more, but not 4 hours
(5) 4 hours or more

How would you rate the following?

	Excellent	Good	Fair	Poor
6 Hours of operation	1	2	3	4
7 Cleanliness	1	2	3	4
8 Condition of equipment	1	2	3	4
9 Availability of equipment	1	2	3	4
10 Amount of space (lack of crowdedness)	1	2	3	4
11 Safety conditions (including feeling of security)	1	2	3	4
12 Physical attractiveness	1	2	3	4
13 Variety of programs	1	2	3	4
14 Helpfulness and attitude of personnel	1	2	3	4
15 Parking area	1	2	3	4
16 Restrooms	1	2	3	4
17 Convenience to your home	1	2	3	4
18 Amount of supervision	1	2	3	4

19 Is there anything else you particularly like about this facility?

_____

20 Is there anything else you particularly dislike about this facility?

_____

21 How would you rate this facility overall?

(1) Excellent   (3) Fair
(2) Good   (4) Poor

22 Do you have any suggestions for improving this facility?

_____

_____

_____

23 How long have you lived in _____ ____ ?

(1) Less than 3 months
(2) 3–12 months
(3) 1–5 years
(4) More than 5 years
(5) Not a resident

24 Home address (or nearest intersection to your home):

_____

25 What is your age?

(1) Less than 14   (5) 35–49
(2) 14–18   (6) 50–64
(3) 19–24   (7) Over 65
(4) 25–34

26 What is your sex and race?

(1) White male
(2) White female
(3) Nonwhite male
(4) Nonwhite female

27 Which of the following comes closest to your total household income before taxes last year?

(1) Under $5,000
(2) $5,000 to 7,999
(3) $8,000 to 9,999
(4) $10,000 to 14,999
(5) $15,000 and over

APPENDIX F | NATURAL RESOURCE MANAGEMENT POLICIES

	Preservation zone	Protection zone	Enhancement zone
Land and Water Management			
Geology and Soil Erosion	Allow natural earth movement and erosion to take its course.	When important resources and visitor safety are directly threatened, attempt to inhibit natural destructive processes, including land movement and cliff erosion.	When important resources and visitor safety are directly threatened, attempt to inhibit natural destructive processes, including land movement and cliff erosion.
	Correct and prevent man-induced erosion.	Correct and prevent man-induced erosion.	Correct and prevent man-induced erosion.
Water Quality	Upgrade water quality and wastewater facilities as needed.	Upgrade water quality and wastewater facilities as needed.	Maintain water quality and wastewater facilities.
Vegetation Management			
Grazing	No livestock grazing.	Livestock grazing permitted. Eliminate all overgrazing and phase out grazing operations from unsuitable range sites.	No livestock grazing.
Role of Fire	Explore prescribed burning in conjunction with other management techniques to maintain resource diversity and contrast, and to prevent significant long-term buildup of combustible materials.	Explore prescribed burning in conjunction with other management techniques to maintain resource diversity and contrast, and to prevent significant long-term buildup of combustible materials.	No prescribed burning.
Exotics	Eliminate exotic plants where feasible. No planting of exotics permitted.	Control exotic plants where their spread threatens important recreational resources and native plant communities. Planting of exotics for specific recreational sites permitted.	No control of exotic plants. Planting of exotics permitted.
Herbicides	Utilize, wherever feasible, non-chemical management techniques.	Utilize, wherever feasible, non-chemical management techniques.	Utilize, wherever feasible, non-chemical management techniques.
Wildlife Management			
Unnatural Populations	Maintain animal populations at levels that ensure the vitality of the group, protect vegetation, and minimize contact with park visitors.	Maintain animal populations at levels that ensure the vitality of the group, protect vegetation, and minimize contact with park visitors.	Maintain animal populations at levels that ensure the vitality of the group, protect vegetation, and minimize contact with park visitors.
Exotics	Eliminate exotic animal species where feasible.	Manage level of exotic species to ensure protection of natural and recreational resources and visitor safety.	Manage level of exotic species to ensure protection of natural and recreational resources and visitor safety.
Fragile Habitats	Identify and protect fragile habitats.	Identify and protect fragile habitats.	Identify and protect fragile habitats.
Management of Threatened and Endangered Species			
	Identify and protect threatened and endangered species.	Identify and protect threatened and endangered species.	Identify and protect threatened and endangered species.

Source: U.S. Department of the Interior, National Park Service, *Assessment of Alternatives for the General Management Plan,* Golden Gate National Recreation Area (GGNRA) and Point Reyes National Seashore, California, Washington, D.C.: Government Printing Office, 1977, pp. 54–55.

APPENDIX G | PARK, RECREATION, AND OPEN SPACE STANDARDS

1. RECREATION STANDARDS: POPULATION RATIO METHOD

BY CLASSIFICATION AND POPULATION RATIO

Classification	Acres/ 1000 people	Size range	Population served	Service area
Playlots	*	2500 sq ft to 1 acre	500–2500	Subneighborhood
Vest pocket parks	*	2500 sq ft to 1 acre	500–2500	Subneighborhood
Neighborhood parks	2.5	Min. 5 acres up to 20 acres	2000–10,000	¼–½ mile
District parks	2.5	20–100 acres	10,000–50,000	½–3 miles
Large urban parks	5.0	100+ acres	One for ea. 50,000	Within ½ hr driving time
Regional parks	20.0	250+ acres	Serves entire population in smaller communities; should be distributed throughout larger metro areas.	Within 1 hr driving time
Special areas and Facilities	*	Includes parkways, beaches, plazas, historical sites, flood plains, downtown malls, and small parks, tree lawns, etc. *No standard is applicable.*		

*Not applicable.

SPACE STANDARDS FOR NEIGHBORHOOD PARKS
Suggested space standards for various units within the park. The *minimum* size is 5 acres.

Facility or unit	Area in acres	
	Park adjoining school	Separate park
Play apparatus area—preschool	.25	.25
Play apparatus area—older children	.25	.25
Paved multipurpose courts	.50	.50
Recreation center building	*	.25
Sports fields	*	5.00
Senior citizens' area	.50	.50
Quiet areas and outdoor classroom	1.00	1.00
Open or "free play" area	.50	.50
Family picnic area	1.00	1.00
Off-street parking	*	2.30†
Subtotal	4.00	11.55
Landscaping (buffer and special areas)	2.50	3.00
Undesignated space (10%)	.65	1.45
Total	7.15	16.00

*Provided by elementary school.

†Based on 25 cars @ 400 sq ft per car.

Source: Abstracted from Robert D. Buechner (Ed.). *National Park, Recreation and Open Space Standards,* National Recreation and Park Association, 1971, pp. 12–15, 34–39. Reprinted with permission.

SPACE STANDARDS FOR DISTRICT PARKS
Suggested space requirements for various units within the park. The *minimum* size is 20 acres.

	Area in acres	
Facility or unit	**Park adjoining school**	**Separate park**
Play apparatus area—preschool	.35	.35
Play apparatus—older children	.35	.35
Paved multipurpose courts	1.25	1.75
Tennis complex	1.00	1.00
Recreation center building	*	1.00
Sports fields	1.00	10.00
Senior citizens' complex	1.90	1.90
Open or "free play" area	2.00	2.00
Archery range	.75	.75
Swimming pool	1.00	1.00
Outdoor theater	.50	.50
Ice rink (artificial)	1.00	1.00
Family picnic area	2.00	2.00
Outdoor classroom area	1.00	1.00
Golf practice hole	*	.75
Off-street parking	1.50	3.00†
Subtotal	15.60	28.35
Landscaping (buffer and special areas)	3.00	6.00
Undesignated space (10%)	1.86	3.43
Total	20.46	37.78

*Provided by Jr. or Sr. High School

†Based on 330 cars @ 400 sq ft per car

STANDARDS FOR SPECIAL FACILITIES

Facility (outdoor)	**Standard/1000 people**	**Comment**
Baseball diamonds	1 per 6000	Regulation 90 ft
Softball diamonds (and/or youth diamonds)	1 per 3000	
Tennis courts	1 per 2000	(Best in battery of 4)
Basketball courts	1 per 500	
Swimming pools—25m	1 per 10,000	Based on 15 sq ft of
Swimming pools—50m	1 per 20,000	water for ea. 3% of pop.
Skating rinks (artificial)	1 per 30,000	
Neighborhood centers	1 per 10,000	
Community centers	1 per 25,000	
Outdoor theaters (noncommercial)	1 per 20,000	
Shooting ranges	1 per 50,000	Complete complex incl. high-power, small-bore, trap and skeet, field archery, etc.
Golf courses (18 hole)	1 per 25,000	

Note: All of the above-mentioned facilities are desirable in small communities, even though their population may actually be less than the standard. Every effort should be made to light all facilities for night use, thus extending their utility.

STANDARDS FOR RECREATION FACILITIES—DADE COUNTY, FLORIDA

| Facility | User group age | Standards | | | Facility and acres | | | |
		Spatial facility	Per number persons in user group	Minimum facility	Within park, total acres	Outside park, total acres	Service* area	Miscellaneous
Lighted league play ball diamonds†	10–40	1	6,000	1	2.2	4.5	2–3 miles	Adjacent to high school, buffered from residential property
Lighted regulation tennis courts	12–64	1	4,000	6	3.5	4.5	2–3 miles	
Light shuffleboard courts	60+	1	1,000	12	0.5	1.0		Provide sheltered sitting area adjacent courts; near public transit and major arterials
Regulation basketball courts	12–19	1	500	2	0.4	0.6	0.5 miles	
Swimming pools	6–15	1800 sq ft	1,000	1	0.6	0.8	1–1.5 miles	Optimum pool size 5,000 sq ft shallow wading areas separate from diving pool
Play apparatus areas	3–12	1	500	1	0.2	0.3	0.5 mile	Includes sitting areas, playground equipment for children, small open areas for free play
Golf courses (private included)‡	All ages	18 holes	50,000	1	110–150	110–150	30-min driving time	Rectangle most desirable shape extending north to south, gently rolling terrain preferred
Picnic grounds	All ages	1 acre	6,000				30-min max. driving time	Located in natural beauty areas preferably adjacent to bodies of water, well-shaded, well-buffered from surrounding conflicting uses
Beaches‡	All ages	0.2-acre sand and 50-ft shore line	1,000	1	2.5	2.5	30-min max. driving time	
Boat ramps	All ages	2 linear ft	1,000	200′	6.5	8		Minimum 0.6 parking space per linear ft of ramp

*Includes acreage for auxiliary facilities.   †Primarily 60 to 75 foot combination diamonds.   ‡Peak season tourist population as well as resident population.
Source: Ibid., pp. 34–35.

PARK AREA STANDARDS—ELMHURST, ILLINOIS

Neighborhood Playlot
- Size: At least 1 acre preferred
- Service area: 1/4 mile or less
- Location: High density neighborhoods where typical private yards do not exist
- Usual facilities: Paved area, playground apparatus area for small children; usually private responsibility.

Neighborhood Park
- Area per 1000 persons: 3 acres
- Size: 5–10 acres, not including parking
- Service area: 1/2 mile or as limited by geographical barriers
- Location: Preferably adjacent to elementary schools or near the center of the neighborhood
- Usual facilities: Softball/baseball fields, multiple-use paved areas, playground apparatus areas, landscaped areas, and picnic areas. Small field-house. Minimum of automobile parking.

District Park
- Area per 1000 persons: 3 acres
- Size: 10–30 acres
- Service area: 1 mile
- Location: Preferably near the center of 4 or 5 neighborhoods
- Usual facilities: Facilities of neighborhood park, tennis courts, football and soccer fields, lighting for evening use, community center/recreation buildings and swimming pool. Substantial parking areas. Skating rinks, sledding hill, and natural areas.

Large Park
- Area per 1000 persons: 5 acres
- Size: 100–400 acres
- Service area: 3–5 miles
- Location: Wherever appropriate sites can be secured with natural features
- Usual facilities: District park facilities, large rustic areas and picnic areas, facilities for hiking, field archery, golf, and water related recreations, many of which could be revenue producing facilities.

Parkways and Special Areas
- Area per 1000 persons: 2 acres
- Size: Size varies depending on use of the area and land available
- Service area: The whole community
- Location: Along waterways and to provide aesthetic treatment for civic buildings and other public facilities
- Usual facilities: Landscaped areas but possible to include picnic and playground facilities, zoo, hobby center, museum, golf course, and others depending on function and characteristics of the park.

Reservations and Regional Parks
- Size: Several hundred to several thousand acres
- Service area: Entire urban area
- Location: On the fringe of urban development at appropriate sites, preferably within one hour's driving time
- Usual facilities: Water resources, rustic areas, camping, nature study, bridle paths, picnicking and other facilities not requiring intensive development, usually the responsibility of a regional or state park authority.

Specific Facility Standards*

- 9-hole golf courses: 1 9-hole public course for every 25,000 persons. 45 acres for regular play, 20 acres for Par 3; located within the District
- 18-hole golf courses: 1 18-hole public course for every 50,000 persons. Minimum size 120 acres including area for club house, parking and service areas, preferably located in a county park within 10 miles
- Community centers: 1 for every 20,000 persons. 1 game room for every 10,000; 1 arts and crafts room for every 10,000; 1 club room and multiple use room for every 4,000; 1 indoor swimming pool for every 50,000; each center would include gymnasium, kitchen, office, and service facilities
- Arenas, coliseums, or cultural center: 1 for every 50,000 persons; should be combined with a community center. Include facilities for music, art, and dramatic interests
- Camping facilities: 1 group camp for every 25,000 population about one-hour distance from Elmhurst. Ideal size: 500–1,000 acres, suitable for long term camping, school camping, and family camping
- Water related facilities: 5 acres of water surface for each 2,000 people, boat storage, rental, and launching ramps desired. Public ownership of all stream banks within the District
- Softball diamonds: 1 for every 3,000 persons, 1/2 lighted
- Baseball diamonds: 1 official regulation lighted diamond for every 30,000 persons. 1 junior diamond for every 3,000 persons. 1/4 lighted
- Football, soccer fields, handball courts: 1 for every 10,000 persons. 1/2 lighted
- Tennis courts: 1 lighted court for every 1,500 persons
- Picnic areas: 3 acres of picnic areas for every 1,000 persons. 4-16 picnic tables per acre at each location, and space for horseshoes, informal softball, and other field games
- Ice skating rinks: Area 100' × 200' for free skating plus area 85' × 200' for hockey, lighted for night use; warming area; located in district parks
- Community swimming pools: 1 pool for every 20,000 persons. 8,000–10,000 square feet of water surface and double that in deck space
- Neighborhood swimming pools: 1 pool for every 5,000 persons outside community pool service area (would be considered where a neighborhood is isolated from the community pool). 4,000 square feet of water surface and 8,000 square feet of deck

*Standards refer to all community facilities, regardless of ownership.

Source: California Committee Planning for Recreation, Park Areas and Facilities, *Guide for Planning Recreation Parks in California*, Sacramento: Recreation Commission, 1956, pp. 36–38.

CITYWIDE RECREATION FACILITIES. Suggested
Space Standards—Service Population of 100,000

	Facilities	Total acreage, including parking	Parking provided†	
			Number of automobiles	Acreage required
	Cultural Center (adjoining a major educational institution when practical)			
A	Drama and music center (auditorium seating 1000; intimate hall for chamber music)*	10	300	2.1
B	Outdoor theater*	20	600	4.2
C	Junior museum (science, crafts, art center)* ...	15	30	.2
D	Museum; art center with art gallery and studios for painting, sculpture, and crafts; floral display hall*	15	300	2.1
E	Landscaping: 25 percent of total acreage of items starred*	15	—	—
		75	1,230	8.6
	Recreation Park			
F	Open meadow area	30	—	—
G	Natural areas, trails, lake or water course	45	150	1.0
H	Picnic and barbecue areas (family and group)	30	300	2.1
I	Day and weekend camping (family and group)	30	300	2.1
J	Golf courses (one 18-hole course = 160 acres) Four courses provided on following basis: One 18-hole course for 20,000 population, plus one 18-hole course for each 30,000 thereafter	640	1,600	11.2
K	Children's wonderland (combined with children's zoo)*	5	100	.7
L	Play area for preschool children and apparatus section (four or each, widely separated)*	3	—	—
M	Adaptable space for circus, carnivals, outdoor conventions*	20	600	4.2
N	Corporation yard	10	—	—
E	Landscaping: 25 percent of total acreage of items starred	70	—	—
		883	3,050	21.3
	Sports Center			
P	Stadium, swimming pool, athletic fields, courts	50	1,300	9.0
	Civic Center			
	Administrative offices, auditorium and exhibition hall	30	600	4.2

Plazas and Squares

20 percent of commercial district

Greenbelts

Strip parks and tree-lined walks connecting squares, neighborhood recreation centers, community and citywide recreation parks, and the civic center
Tree-lined boulevards and pathways linking larger parks
Waterfront developments along ocean, bays, lakes, and rivers

*Includes parking space.
†The parking standard proposed assumes joint use of parking areas. Allowance of 300 square feet per automobile.
Source: California Committee Planning for Recreation, Park Areas and Facilities, *Guide for Planning Recreation Parks in California,* Sacramento: Recreation Commission, 1956, pp. 64–65.

2. RECREATION STANDARDS: DEMAND PROJECTION METHOD

MARICOPA COUNTY, ARIZONA, SYSTEM PLAN

1 *Population distribution maps were made for 1960 and 1980.* Data for 1958 (adjusted to 1960) and 1980 was adapted from the reports of the Advance Planning Task Force of the City of Phoenix and Maricopa County. The figures 664,000 for 1960 and 1,440,000 for 1980 were used consistently.

2 *Regions of use were plotted.* Points equidistant both in time and distance between the five proposed regional parks were located on a Maricopa County map. Time/distance lines, at 15-minute intervals, were plotted from McDowell Regional Park outward to a time/distance interval of one hour's driving time. The geographic area thus created was called the "region of use." Although not the only recreation "choice" factor, it was concrete and measurable.

3 *Population socio-economic characteristics were correlated with density of population.* The socio-economic characteristics of median age, median family income, median number of years of education and occupation were graphically plotted on maps of the Phoenix Urban Area to determine the dominant 1960 characteristics of three density groups: low (0–4.9 persons per acre), medium (5–19.9 persons per acre) and high (20 persons per acre up).

4 *The 1980 population 12 years of age and over was computed according to low, medium, and high density.* For the McDowell region of use the results were: low density, 39,420; medium density, 185,420; county rural, 16,790. (Throughout the report, county rural areas were equated as to socio-economic characteristics with high density urban areas.) The total population for 1980 of 242,000 was not by itself significant.

5 *The effect on participation rates of the socio-economic characteristics of each density group was derived from studies of the Outdoor Recreation Resources Review Commission (ORRRC).* This was accomplished by a complicated computer analysis which "weighted" the effect on recreation participation of each of the four socio-economic characteristics of age, income, education and occupation. The result was in the form of "percent participating" in each of the three density groups.

6 *The "percent participating" figures for picnicking were*

then multiplied by the population in each McDowell density group, set forth in 4 above. The products of these three multiplications were then totaled to give the total number of participants in picnicking for the McDowell region of use in 1980. This total number was of persons 12 years of age and over—one of the limitations of the ORRRC studies. This figure was 130,000.

7 *The number of user days per participant for a three-month peak period was multiplied times the number of participants.* According to ORRRC, each participant will spend 3.8 days picnicking during a three-month peak period. Thus the total number of participants, 130,000, was multiplied by 3.8 to give 494,000 user days for a three-month peak period of picnicking.

8 *The number of user days in a three-month peak was divided by 3 to give a one-month peak of 164,502.*

9 *From this figure, a peak weekend day was derived, or 10,281.* To arrive at this figure, 164,502 was multiplied by 25% to give total user days for a one-week peak. This result was again multiplied by 25% to give a peak weekend day since 50% of the use during a week is on the weekend.

10 *The number of users on a peak weekend day was reduced to the number of "picnicking units."* The average size of a family (excluding those under 12) in the McDowell region of use was found to be 2.5 persons. Thus the users on a peak weekend day, 10,281, was divided by 2.5 to give the number of family units who need picnicking facilities—4,112.

11 *The total amount of acres for picnicking was then calculated.* Using the "standard" of 10 family units per acre—or 1/10 acre per unit—it was calculated, by multiplying by 4,112, that 411.2 acres should be planned for picnicking for the McDowell region of use.

12 *The number of picnicking facilities existing or planned in the McDowell region of use was deducted from the number of facilities required to get the net number needed.* An analysis of the McDowell region of use showed that no significant picnicking facilities existed or were planned. Therefore, the net need was the same as the gross need—411.2 acres.

13 *Since it must be assumed that McDowell Regional Park will fulfill the outdoor recreation needs of the people living within the McDowell region of use, the facilities needed by the region of use are the same as those which must be provided in the regional park.*

Source: Abstracted from Robert D. Buechner (Ed.) *National Park Recreation and Open Space Standards,* National Recreation and Park Association, 1971, pp. 46–47. Reprinted with permission.

3. RECREATION STANDARDS: RECREATION EXPERIENCE METHOD

HUMANISTIC AND SUPPORT CONSIDERATIONS FOR ENHANCEMENT OF THE RECREATION EXPERIENCE

Example 1

Recreation experience	Consideration	Standard	Necessary	Desirable	Optional
Physical Recreation Outdoor Juvenile low-organized games and free play	Drinking water	Year-round access to source of drinking water; distance to source no greater than 150 feet; water quality to meet Penna. Dept. of Environmental Resources Standards	X		
	Sanitary provisions	Year-round access to restroom facilities; distance to facilities no greater than 300 feet; sanitary system to be approved by Penna. Dept. of Environmental Resources	X		
	Refuse control	If on public land, durable, waterproof and rodent proof waste containers to be provided no greater than 150 feet apart; containers to be regularly inspected and emptied	X		
	Protection from climate/weather	Access to shade, rain and/or wind control elements (convenient vegetation such as a shade tree or wind-break may be adequate, a structural shelter not necessarily required)		X	

Example 2

Recreation experience desired	Examples of activities	Quantitative standard	Responsible agency
Physical Recreation (Outdoor)			
Specialized individual and dual sports	Target shooting, flying, soaring, auto or motor-bike racing, equestrian activities, etc.	Specialized facilities depending upon interest group or organization	Commercial, semipublic, public
Environment-Related Activities (Outdoor)			
Water activities	Power boating, water skiing, fishing, scuba diving, sailing, etc.	Large pollution-free lake(s) at least 100 acres in size, with boat ramps and marinas, plus county-wide pollution and water quality controls on all recreational water bodies and streams	Public
Winter activities	Ice boating, downhill skiing, tobogganing, snowmobile racing, etc.	Downhill ski area with snow-making capabilities, or refrigerated toboggan chutes and runs, or snowmobile race course; all with spectator facilities—facilities provided as interest warrants	Public, commercial

Example 2 (continued)

| Unstructured quiet activities | Hiking, pleasure driving, bicycling, etc. | Countywide open space corridors linking all regional hike/bike systems and scenic roads all tying into state system | Public, commercial |
| Outing sports and activities | Hunting, camping, picnicking, hosteling, etc. | At least 700 acres of predominately natural public land adequately managed for hunting, day and overnight camping, picnicking, etc., plus a county hostel system | Public, commercial |

Source: Abstracted from Monty Christiansen, *Application of a Recreation Experience Components Concept for Comprehensive Recreation Planning,* vols. 1 and 2, Harrisburg, Pa.: Dept. of Community Affairs, Bureau of Recreation and Conservation, 1975, p. 83 (Example 1) and p. 41 (Example 2).

Example 3

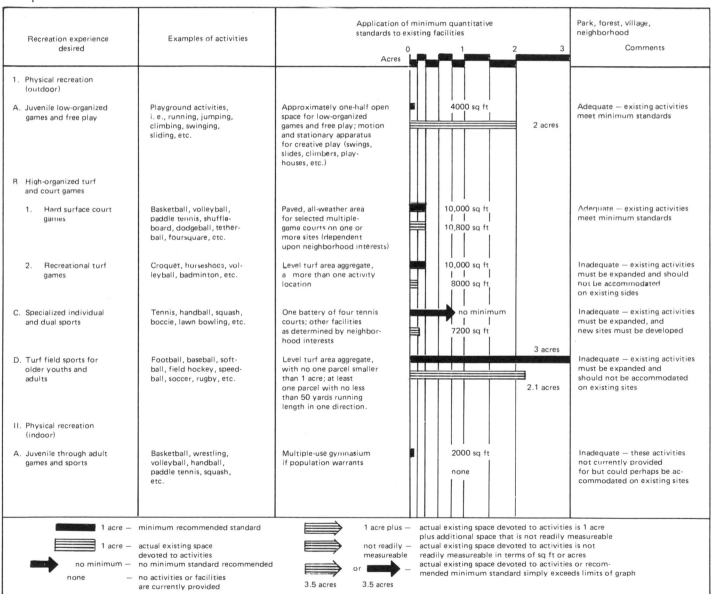

Recreation experience desired	Examples of activities	Application of minimum quantitative standards to existing facilities	Park, forest, village, neighborhood Comments
1. Physical recreation (outdoor)			
A. Juvenile low-organized games and free play	Playground activities, i. e., running, jumping, climbing, swinging, sliding, etc.	Approximately one-half open space for low-organized games and free play; motion and stationary apparatus for creative play (swings, slides, climbers, playhouses, etc.)	Adequate — existing activities meet minimum standards
B High-organized turf and court games			
1. Hard surface court games	Basketball, volleyball, paddle tennis, shuffleboard, dodgeball, tetherball, foursquare, etc.	Paved, all-weather area for selected multiple-game courts on one or more sites (dependent upon neighborhood interests)	Adequate — existing activities meet minimum standards
2. Recreational turf games	Croquet, horseshoes, volleyball, badminton, etc.	Level turf area aggregate, a more than one activity location	Inadequate — existing activities must be expanded and should not be accommodated on existing sides
C. Specialized individual and dual sports	Tennis, handball, squash, boccie, lawn bowling, etc.	One battery of four tennis courts; other facilities as determined by neighborhood interests	Inadequate — existing activities must be expanded, and new sites must be developed
D. Turf field sports for older youths and adults	Football, baseball, softball, field hockey, speedball, soccer, rugby, etc.	Level turf area aggregate, with no one parcel smaller than 1 acre; at least one parcel with no less than 50 yards running length in one direction.	Inadequate — existing activities must be expanded and should not be accommodated on existing sites
II. Physical recreation (indoor)			
A. Juvenile through adult games and sports	Basketball, wrestling, volleyball, handball, paddle tennis, squash, etc.	Multiple-use gymnasium if population warrants	Inadequate — these activities not currently provided for but could perhaps be accommodated on existing sites

Legend:

- ▬ 1 acre — minimum recommended standard
- ▤ 1 acre — actual existing space devoted to activities
- ➡ no minimum — no minimum standard recommended
- none — no activities or facilities are currently provided
- ⇨ 1 acre plus — actual existing space devoted to activities is 1 acre plus additional space that is not readily measureable
- ⇨ not readily measureable — actual existing space devoted to activities is not readily measureable in terms of sq ft or acres
- ⇨ or ➡ — actual existing space devoted to activities or recommended minimum standard simply exceeds limits of graph
- 3.5 acres   3.5 acres

APPENDIX H

1. COMMUNITY NEEDS AND VALUES

Health and safety needs	Hazards	Environments in which threats from fire, flood, earthquake, unfenced heights, deep water are minimized.
	Crime	Protection from criminal activities, such as assault, burglary, car theft.
	Traffic	Protection from traffic, especially in residential areas with children, old people.
	Aid	Easy access to emergency services, police, fire, and ambulances.
	Health	Sufficient sun, light, clean air, pure water, sanitation, trash and garbage control to maintain public health standards.
	Exercise	Adequate space and facilities for walking, jogging, cycling, and active sports.
Livability needs	Space	Adequate space to engage in desired activities.
	Quiet	Ambient noise and vibration levels to carry out desired activities; sleeping, talking, reading, and relaxing.
	Light	Sufficient light for activities such as reading, shopping, driving; avoidance of excessive light or glare where darkness is valued, e.g., in residential areas at night.
	Climate	Climate controls that protect people from or reduce unacceptable heat, cold, wind, sun, rain, fog, or drought.
Access needs	Regional access	Access to jobs, services, schools, shops, recreational, and transportation facilities.
	Cycle and pedestrian	Safe and pleasant conditions for cyclists and pedestrians to circulate within and between communities.
	Public access	Sufficient public access to valued resources, such as shorelines, beaches, lakes, rivers, viewpoints.
	Orientation	Visible access or clear signing of important and desirable facilities and destinations.
Identity needs	Conservation	Environments which are familiar, stable, predictable, where severe disruptions of continuity do not take place, are not threatened, or are managed with full participation.
	Territory	Places which people and communities feel "belong" to them, for which they can care and feel responsible, even if they are not owned.
	Expression	Environments which allow and encourage the expression of personal, family, community, or cultural identities.
	Mastery	Environments which are responsive, which can be easily changed to accommodate changing needs.
	Choice	Individual, family, and community freedom to express particular desires or to explore alternative lifestyles.
	Privacy	Protection from intruding eyes, noise, and distracting events for desired activities, personal, family and community life.

Source: Developed in cooperation with Donald Appleyard, Department of Landscape Architecture, University of California, Berkeley, 1977.

	Social contact	Interaction, help in times of trouble, adequate choice of friends and neighbors.
	Participation	Participation in the process of analyzing community needs, policy formation, planning and design decisions.
	Power	The chance to make decisions which affect personal or group environments.
Aesthetic and symbolic needs	Attractiveness	Environments which are pleasurable and inviting to the senses; sight, sound, smell, and touch.
	Imageability	Environments which are unique, vital, vivid, and distinctive.
	Purity	Environments which are ordered, simple structured, clean, and well-maintained.
	Natural character	Environments related to nature by natural materials open air, vegetation, views.
	Sense of place and history	Environments which have a strong sense of identity, whose history is significant and evident.
Community needs	Justice	Equitable distribution of amenities and services to all population groups and areas.
	Pluralism	Tolerance of different life-styles, expressions, and tastes.
	Resource conservation	Conservation of natural, energy, atmospheric resources.
	Economy	Low capital-costs for easily maintained and durable environments.

2. OPEN SPACE/RECREATION GOALS AND OBJECTIVES

THE CREATION, ACQUISITION, AND PRESERVATION OF OPEN SPACE

1 Maintenance of community scale and identity

   a Identification of open space areas which may be used to prevent the blending of distinct urban areas

   b Development of methods of controlling urban expansion

2 Maximization of opportunities for future decisions on urban growth

   a Identification of existing open spaces which are threatened by urban expansion

   b Avoidance of premature commitment of potential open space lands to other uses by timing the development of public facilities and services to guide rather than to precipitate growth

   c Development of methods of preserving open space

3 Achievement of a sense of natural openness as an integral part of urban surroundings

   a Development of programs to ensure that various types of open space are available and reasonably accessible for people of all ages and social and economic groups, and for all geographic areas of the community

   b Investigation of methods to provide for the integration of public and private open spaces in each development

4 Coordination of the location and development of open spaces with other land uses so that they enhance one another and together contribute to a satisfying urban environment for the people of the community

   a Relation of the amount and type of open space to the present and future needs of the city and its population

   b Acquisition of open space lands in advance of development in order to facilitate site planning for future development

   c Assignment of equal priority to programs for acquisition, development, and maintenance of open space land in established areas to that given programs for advance acquisition in less-developed areas

5 Establishment of policies and plans relating to open space which will offer the greatest benefit return to the community

   a Acquisition of open space lands in advance of development in order to take advantage of reasonable land costs

   b Planning with sufficient flexibility to take advantage of financial opportunities which might arise

6 Preservation and conservation of natural features, resources, and amenities, and expansion of resources and similar assets as the city grows in order to maintain and enhance its unique character

   a Preservation of open lands in their natural state in order to ensure their maintenance as wildlife and fish habitats, natural drainage areas, and areas of passive recreation and outdoor education

   b Preservation and enhancement of the community's natural resources in acquiring and planning parks and other open spaces

7 Preservation of options with regard to agricultural land, considering it for other uses only when it demonstrated that it is required to meet the internal needs of Davis citizens and then only to the extent necessary

   a Avoidance of premature commitment of agricultural lands to other uses by timing the development of public facilities and services to guide rather than to precipitate growth

   b Consideration of the unique quality of prime agricultural land when weighing the decision to commit such land irreversibly to other uses

   c Basing of decisions to rezone open space and agricultural lands on a careful evaluation of land use capabilities and resources in the Davis area, as well as on the environmental and economic consequences of the proposed zoning change

   d Rezoning of open space or agricultural lands for other uses based on community needs and the amount of land already zoned for development

8 Development and expansion of recreational open space land and facilities in order to provide for the happiness, health, safety, and well being of each member and segment of the community

   a Determination of the demand for recreational open space by area and needs of residents

   b Development of programs to ensure adequate recreational open space to meet the public demand

Source: Abstracted from the Open Space and Recreation Elements of the General Plan for Davis, California, 1978. Illustrative goals, objectives, and supporting policies or practices are shown in outline format.

c Development of programs to create needed small open spaces

9 Establishment of policies and plans relating to private open spaces

   a Development of standards to ensure that necessary amounts and types of open spaces are available for each Land Use category

THE CONTINUING CREATION AND MAINTENANCE OF AN ENVIRONMENT THAT ENCOMPASSES AREAS, FACILITIES, AND ACTIVITIES TO MEET THE DIVERSE RECREATIONAL NEEDS OF DAVIS RESIDENTS

1 Acquisition and development of sufficient lands to meet the recreational needs of citizens

   a Development of standards for the acquisition, maintenance, and renovation of parks to serve the needs of all Davis residents

   b Determination of the types and sizes of parks, and areas to be served by each

2 Creation of a series of parks that serve as focal points for the surrounding neighborhoods

   a Centralization of such parks within a neighborhood

   b Provision for indoor and outdoor activities and programs directed toward the needs of the neighborhood served

   c Provision for a continuous system of interconnected bikeways in and out of the city for both transportation and recreation use

3 Protection and preservation of natural habitats existing with the city to provide wilderness areas, with a minimal number of appropriately designed facilities compatible with a wild area

4 Creation of programs and facilities to enrich the lives of all the city's residents

   a Provision for programs emphasizing the innate creativity of human beings and their need for self-expression and recognition

   b Coordination of recreation programs with other city programs

5 Construction of parks with originality and innovation in design that will provide challenge and self-renewal to the viewer and user

   a Investigation of alternative methods of park design

   b Investigation of feasibility of establishing neighborhood design standards through preplanning of neighborhoods with parks

6 Provision of adequate shade in Davis parks through the use of shade trees and/or man-made shelters

   a Provision for a two-step tree-planting program with fast-growing, if less-desirable, shade trees intermixed with more-desirable, slow-growing shade trees

   b Construction of shelters, such as arbors, lattice work canopies, canopies, etc., in conjunction with the planting of trees for future shade

7 Development of parks with night-use capability

   a Development of night-use standards to be incorporated in overall park standards

   b Provision of sufficient night lighting, with attention to the rights of surrounding residents

8 Provision of adequate furnishings in parks for the maximum comfort of the user

9 Inclusion where appropriate of bikeways, walkways, and equestrian trails in parks

   a Development of park plans to provide for accessibility by all modes of transportation

   b Provision for recreational walking, bicycle riding, and horseback riding

10 Encouragement of involvement of citizen groups in the development and maintenance of specialized use areas, such as the landfill areas

11 Provision of programs and activities designed to meet the recreational needs of the residents of Davis

   a Provision of programs and activities to meet the needs of the city as a whole as well as those of specific interest groups

   b Periodic community evaluation to ensure that programs and activities continue to meet the changing needs and interests of the community

APPENDIX I

1. NEEDS-RESOURCE INDEX MODEL

MODEL

$$\left[\frac{\left(\dfrac{N_1 + N_2}{2}\right) + \left(\dfrac{N_3 + N_4}{2}\right) + \left(N_5\right) + \left(\dfrac{N_6 + N_7}{2}\right)}{4} \right] -$$

$$\left[\frac{R_1 + R_2}{2} \right] = \text{comparative priority of need}$$

where N_1 = median family income

N_2 = % of families below poverty level

N_3 = population density

N_4 = average household size

N_5 = juvenile probation referrals rate

N_6 = target age group density

N_7 = target age group as a % of total population

R_1 = park acreage

R_2 = park facilities

Assumptions

The equation developed above is based on four assumptions.

1 That there are distinct characteristics which identify the need for and resources of parks and recreation services and facilities

2 That these characteristics can be quantified

3 That analysis can be keyed to specific geographic subareas within the City

4 That the seven need and the four resource indicators adequately define the demand and supply of parks and recreation services and facilities

Source: Adapted from City of San Jose, *Quantitative Approach to Needs Assessment/San Jose Park and Recreation Department,* Evaluation Unit, Office of Fiscal Affairs, San Jose, Calif., November 1974.

Limitations

The model and methodology has these limitations.

1 *Untested assumptions.* The model is based on a set of assumptions about the relationship of specific indicators to what we have defined as the comparative priority of need. To the extent that any indicator is not highly correlated with the need for community-provided recreation services, its inclusion in the analysis may distort the final ranking of neighborhoods.

2 *Boundary definitions.* A major assumption made in the development of the methodology is that the provision of parks and recreation services is keyed to specific geographic areas in the city. Indeed, the whole concept of the neighborhood and district parks hinges on a definition of geographic subareas within the city.

The analysis attempted to define subareas so that an acceptable compromise could be made between area definitions that were relevant to the provision of parks and recreation services and that related to available data. The 37 areas defined as neighborhoods, while relevant to capital facilities planning, are not directly applicable for program planning at specific facilities. Thus the data, while relevant for program planning, is not in a form that can be easily used for that purpose.

Subarea boundaries, as we have defined them, necessitate that data be aggregated to disaggregated to conform to neighborhood boundaries. Most data is keyed to census tracts or to specific physical facilities. As neighborhoods are aggregations of census tracts, the neighborhood score for any specific indicator becomes a function of a series of approximations.

The important point is that the usefulness of data based on a series of approximations is limited. If the subarea is large, the overall score may obscure significant variations within the subarea. A distribution of data which is skewed and is represented by average or median scores distorts perceptions of actual conditions within a neighborhood.

3 *Weighting.* It has been assumed for preliminary analysis of the data that all indicators considered are of equal importance. However, it is likely that some variables are more significant than others in defining the "need" for and "resources" of parks and recreation services and facilities.

To the extent that the relative significance of specific indicators is not determined, a distortion of the overall comparative priority ranking will exist.

2. NEEDS ANALYSIS: EFFECTIVE POPULATION METHOD

PARK AND RECREATION ACREAGE AND INVESTMENT ANALYSIS

The approach used is a variation of the "needs/resources" technique which several cities have employed in their park and recreation studies. That technique usually gives each of a city's subareas an index of recreation need and an index of recreation resources, standardizes the scores, and then compares the needs index with the resources index to determine a priority rating for each area. While that result shows which areas are the most deficient, it does not say directly *how much* more deficient one area is than another—and it does not say how much of the future investment each should get. In contrast, the refinement developed in the present study *does* address both these questions.

COMPUTING EFFECTIVE POPULATION

The relative need for neighborhood-and community-level public parks and recreation was expressed by computing an "effective population" for each study area. To obtain this, the actual 1970 population was adjusted according to three indicators of recreation need:

1 The percentage of persons under 18 years of age
2 The percentage of persons below the poverty line
3 The percentage of housing units in multi-family buildings
It would have been better to use the proportion of *persons*, rather than units, in multiple dwellings, but that data was unavailable by tract.

Assumed demand ratios were used to compute for each area and for Oakland as a whole an age score, an income score, and a housing score:

$$\text{Age score} = \%\ 18\text{ or over} + 3\ (\%\text{ under }18)$$
$$\text{Income score} = \%\text{ above poverty line} + 2\ (\%\text{ below poverty line})$$
$$\text{Housing score} = \%\text{ one-family units} + 1.25\ (\%\text{ multi-family units})$$

(The choice of ratios was made jointly by the City Planning Department and the director of Parks and Recreation. The decision basically was judgmental though available literature was consulted. The latter included national survey data by ORRRC on participation rates by age, and certain recommendations in the American Public Health Association book, *Planning the Neighborhood.*)

Source: Adapted from *Open Space, Conservation and Recreation Plan,* City of Oakland, Calif. Appendix 1, pp. 101-103, 1976.

The scores for each area were then converted into *relative* scores by comparing them with the corresponding citywide scores:

$$\text{Relative age score for Area A} = \frac{\text{Area A age score}}{\text{citywide age score}}$$

$$\text{Relative income score for Area A} = \frac{\text{Area A income score}}{\text{citywide income score}}$$

$$\text{Relative housing score for Area A} = \frac{\text{Area A housing score}}{\text{citywide housing score}}$$

If Area A has a higher percentage of people under 18, persons below the poverty line, or multifamily units than does Oakland as a whole, its relative age, income or housing score will be greater than 1.00. If it has a lower percentage than Oakland as a whole, its relative score will be less than 1.00.

For each study area, the relative scores were then multiplied by each other, and by the actual area population, to yield the area's effective population:

$$\begin{aligned}\text{Effective population of Area A} = &\ \text{relative age score for Area A} \times \\ &\ \text{relative income score for Area A} \times \text{relative housing score for Area A} \times \text{actual population of Area A}\end{aligned}$$

If an area has a higher-than-average percentage of young people, poor people, and multi-family units, its effective population will be bigger than its actual population. The reverse will be true if it has lower-than-average percentages.

The effective populations of the various study areas add up to the actual population of Oakland as a whole.

DETERMINING EXISTING ACREAGE AND INVESTMENT

In general, acreage and investment were counted for land and/or facilities which were acquired, built, or budgeted through fiscal year 1974–75. For estimating investment in land, a standard figure of $1.50 per square foot was used in all sections of Oakland. It was felt that reflecting area-by-area land value differences would have biased the analysis, since land price in itself serves no recreational purpose. It is the amount (and quality) of the space which is important. The investment in improvements at each city site was estimated by the Office of Parks and Recreation. For school playgrounds a standard improvement cost of $1 per square foot was used.

The investment figures were generally in 1972 dollars, except that for a few sites budgeted after 1972 the actual budget figures were used. The acreage and investment totals exclude school gyms and other school buildings. Operating and maintenance costs were not counted as investment.

For the analysis of *usable neighborhood and community sites,* acreage and investment were counted for public school playgrounds, recreation centers, and other usable neighborhood and community parks and recreation areas—and those portions of citywide or regional public sites which are also substantially usable at the neighborhood or community level. Determination of the latter was based on site-by-site judgments by the Office of Parks and Recreation and the City Planning Department.

Some conceptual problems arose where a neighborhood or community site is located at the edge of a study area. In such a case the site may effectively serve only part of that area—while also serving, though, a portion of the adjoining area. In general, however, the study areas are big enough that situations like this largely cancel each other out. In nearly every case, therefore, each site (or portion thereof for a site which actually straddles an area boundary) was simply counted in the study area where it is physically located. However, Lakeside Park—which is physically in the Westlake, Roosevelt, and McChesney study areas—was split up among them roughly in proportion to the amounts of close-by benefited area in each rather than the percentages of the park itself.

CALCULATING ACREAGE AND INVESTMENT RATIOS

To determine per capita acreage or investment, the total amount of acreage or investment was divided by the effective population (or, for figures on Oakland as a whole, by the actual population). The resulting per capita figures directly indicate the study areas' relative sufficiency in aggregate acreage or investment, as compared with local needs.

COMPUTING FUTURE INVESTMENT SHARES BY AREA

For future investment in neighborhood and community parks and recreation, a special allocation model was developed. This assumed that the more deficient an area is now compared to the "best-off" area—the one with the highest per capita investment—the bigger the share it should get of future investment.

Each area was assigned an allocation score based on that relationship:

$$\text{Allocation score for Area A} = \frac{\text{per capita investment in best-off area}}{\text{per capita investment in Area A}}$$

This means, for example, that if Area A now has only half as much investment per capita as the best-off area, it gets an allocation score of 2.00.

(The formula gives all the study areas *some* share in the future allocation, since even the best off area itself gets a score of 1.00.)

Because the study areas vary greatly in population, it was then necessary to weight each area's allocation score by its effective population:

Weighted allocation score for Area A = allocation score for Area A × effective population of Area A

Finally, the weighted scores for all the areas were added up, and each area's figure was computed as a percentage of this total. That percentage is the area's implied share of future neighborhood and community park and recreation investment:

$$\% \text{ share for Area A} = \frac{\text{weighted allocation score for Area A}}{\sum_{i=A}^{n} \text{weighted allocation scores for Areas A through } n}$$

An alternative method which might be used in future would involve setting some desirable *standard* for aggregate investment per capita. Allocation scores would then be assigned in proportion to each area's per capita "gap," if below that standard.

APPENDIX J | LOCAL ACTIONS AND POLICY OPTIONS

A CONSERVE OPEN SPACE FOR ITS NATURAL, CULTURAL, AND RECREATIONAL VALUES.

Develop procedures for public-private conservation of open space, through mechanisms such as free acquisition, purchase of easement, management strategies, or establishment of regional resource conservation and recreation authorities with independent taxing and management roles.

Transfer derelict land, tax delinquent land, surplus highway rights-of-way, and other land not presently in productive use to park agencies through land exchange, purchase, or long-term, no-fee leases.

Make maximum use of lands associated with public water supply reservoirs to meet urban recreation needs.

Adopt regulations for new residential, business, or industrial development and redevelopment which require either the dedication of park lands, provision of recreation facilities, or payment of money to public recreation fund.

Work intensively with the private sector to encourage donations or bargain sales.

Work closely with conservation groups to conserve open space.

B PROVIDE FINANCIAL SUPPORT FOR PARKS AND RECREATION.

Evaluate user fee policies and identify ways to increase recreation revenues through user fees and concession royalties.

Earmark a portion of local tax revenues for parks and recreation

Hire grants experts to ensure that the local government is taking advantage of all appropriate nonlocal sources of assistance.

C PROVIDE CLOSE-TO-HOME RECREATION OPPORTUNITIES.

Establish priorities which recognize the location of potential users when considering new recreation land acquisition.

Use streets closed to traffic, rooftops, parking lots, utility rights-of-way, water supply reservoirs, etc., to provide nearby recreation in heavily developed and densely populated areas.

Use mobile recreation units where appropriate.

D ENCOURAGE JOINT USE OF EXISTING PHYSICAL RESOURCES.

Utilize school buildings that have been closed because of declining enrollments for recreation.

Consider the potential for joint recreation use in the planning stages for all new or expanded school and park facilities.

Develop reciprocal, no-fee policies which encourage both park use by school groups and school use by park groups.

Assist in providing services required to open up school facilities to the public for recreational purposes after school hours; this will overcome present constraints on joint-use owing to prohibitive custodial and maintenance costs.

Encourage use of schools by nonpublic recreation providers.

Encourage joint-use for recreation, wherever possible, on lands and facilities committed to other private and public purposes, including federal properties, utility rights-of-way, and the property of institutions and private corporations.

Develop model contracts (between park and recreation agencies, schools, community colleges, and other public and private agencies now providing some type of recreation services) as a means of standardizing and simplifying the techniques for joint facility development and programming.

Encourage use of local park and recreation facilities for a wider range of human delivery services (i.e., health information, consumer protection, nutrition, bookmobiles, etc.).

E ENSURE THAT RECREATION FACILITIES ARE WELL MANAGED AND WELL MAINTAINED, AND THAT QUALITY RECREATION PROGRAMS ARE AVAILABLE, BY EMPLOYING AN ADEQUATE NUMBER OF WELL-TRAINED STAFF.

Develop, with universities and colleges, well-planned curricula and intern programs to train recreation professionals to deal with the unique problems and opportunities associated with urban recreation.

Provide support for in-service training to create greater job mobility and career ladders in parks and recreation. Specialists from other nonpark and recreation disciplines could participate in the program.

Increase use of neighborhood residents as recreation leaders and aides by recruiting staff from neighborhoods in which they will work, and by developing flexible recruitment standards which will allow use of nonprofessionals with neighborhood experience.

Contract for services with nonprofit agencies for recreation programming, and with private-for-profit agencies for operation and maintenance, when savings can be achieved without lowering service levels.

Source: Abstracted from U.S. Department of the Interior, Heritage Recreation and Conservation Service, *National Urban Recreation Study: Executive Report*, 1978, pp. 108–114.

Contract with nonprofit community organizations for development, operation, and maintenance of neighborhood facilities. Encourage use of neighborhood residents in these activities, especially of unemployed youth.

Utilize private-nonprofit agencies to help recruit volunteers.

Recruit, train, and place volunteers to provide program assistance and light maintenance. Establish a separate volunteer unit in the park and recreation agency. Use neighborhood organizations and residents, whenever possible.

Create a summer internship program to use undergraduate recreation majors as volunteers.

Develop meaningful, highly visible volunteer recognition programs which express appreciation for citizen-volunteer services.

Establish programs which provide training and work-release opportunities in parks for inmates of local correction institutions and work-parole opportunities for juvenile offenders. These programs could provide both horticultural and maintenance staffing for park departments and rehabilitation for working participants.

Participate with the state and federal governments in joint implementation of youth conservation programs, and encourage support and participation by conservation, environmental, and community organizations.

Support all alternative staffing resources with training, supervision, supplies, and community recognition.

F REDUCE DETERRENTS TO THE FULL UTILIZATION OF EXISTING URBAN RECREATION FACILITIES AND PROGRAMS.

Encourage residents to assume responsibility for making neighborhood parks safe by giving them a role in park supervision and/or maintenance.

Sentence vandals caught destroying park property to repair the effects of their vandalism.

Develop park-oriented crime prevention courses for integration into public safety and law enforcement curricula at state and local colleges and universities.

Develop and promote use of an in-service seminar package on park security problems and methods for the continuing education of police and recreation professionals.

Improve police-community relations in parks by greater involvement of police officers and police academy cadets in the supervision of youth recreation activities under the police athletic league and other programs.

Design park facilities which discourage crime and vandalism without reducing recreation, aesthetic, and environmental benefits.

Coordinate park planning and public transit planning to ensure that new parks are accessible by public transit.

Improve public transit service to parks during weekends and evenings, times of peak recreation use.

Plan for maximum pedestrian and bicycle access to new parks, as an alternative to automobile access.

Develop master plans for trails to be used as guides in creating comprehensive recreation and transportation systems for pedestrian and all nonmotorized vehicles.

Ensure that transit-dependent people have real input to the transportation planning process.

Provide recreation leaders with sensitivity training on conducting recreation programs for members of special populations.

Increase the awareness of all park and recreation employees to the needs and desires of special populations.

Fund outreach and transportation services for those with special needs as part of a coordinated approach by all public and private agencies.

Develop a comprehensive inventory and plan for all parks and physical improvements as a first step toward removing or modifying architectural barriers for the physically handicapped.

Provide specialized staff and equipment for the handicapped, seniors, and young children to help them make better use of park facilities and programs.

Develop programs to lease portions of parks to private groups for recreation use.

Expand local efforts to inform citizens of existing recreation opportunities and issues, with emphasis on reaching residents such as the handicapped or economically disadvantaged who do not regularly participate in recreation programs, as well as informing regular users of new programs, schedules, and use-related problems.

Utilize the techniques described in "How Effective Are Your Community Recreation Services?" (BOR, 1973) to determine who the users of recreation services are and what citizen desires and preferences are not being served.

G PROVIDE APPROPRIATE AND RESPONSIVE RECREATION SERVICES THROUGH SOUND PLANNING.

Employ professionals to do recreation services planning, as well as facility planning, on a continuing basis.

Improve coordination between planning and implementation efforts to ensure realistic plans and responsive action to meet identified needs.

Coordinate recreation planning with other human service

planning; coordinate park and facility planning with overall land use planning.

Conduct citizen participation and preference surveys to determine recreation deficiencies.

Create user advisory councils at neighborhood or community levels to ensure citizen participation in the planning process.

Create recreation coordinating councils at the jurisdication level composed of all public and private (commercial and voluntary) recreation providers to coordinate recreation service delivery.

Create metropolitanwide planning bodies, composed of park and recreation agencies, schools, and other public and private park and recreation providers, to coordinate park and recreation acquisition and development.

Develop formal working ties, with environmental and conservation groups, to help in planning and implementing open space protection and park development programs.

H MAKE ENVIRONMENTAL EDUCATION AND MANAGEMENT AN INTEGRAL PART OF URBAN PARK AND RECREATION POLICIES AND PROGRAMS.

Adopt policies and provide in-service training programs that result in sound environmental management.

Use local parks as year-round, close-to-home urban environmental laboratories for all age groups to study natural systems. Use other facilities such as waste water treatment centers, streets, and utilities to study the interaction between human beings and their environment.

Broaden the scope of interpretive programming to address local environmental issues; sponsor public forums on land use planning, energy conservation, and environmental management programs to involve the public in the decision-making process.

Sponsor cooperative programs for environmental improvement in park lands with civic and youth organizations, special populations (senior citizens, handicapped, juvenile offenders, etc.), and other local government and private agencies.

Develop cooperative programs between resource agencies and local educational advisors so that park and recreation resources become an instrument for environmental teaching as an extension of the standard academic program.

Conduct teacher/parent workshops on the use of park lands for environmental education.

Provide internship opportunities in natural resource agencies to train CETA-funded urban personnel in environmental interpretation.

I STRENGTHEN THE ROLE OF THE CULTURAL ARTS IN URBAN RECREATION.

Encourage urban recreation programming to include quality art opportunitites by using imaginative, locally available talent of public and private institutions, organizations, and individuals.

Use CETA funds to hire people to develop arts programs in parks and community centers.

Appoint an arts committee to do an inventory of public and private facilities with potential for public recreation and art program use. Such a survey could also identify facility deficiencies and needs.

Develop more arts-in-the-parks programs, combining such features as citizen mural programs, regularly scheduled art shows and sales, mobile performance stages, etc.

Develop a highly qualified cultural arts staff with responsibility for developing program ideas which can be used throughout park systems; for training recreation staff to upgrade their arts programming skill; and for planning and implementing a sequenced series of major arts events.

Consider passage of a local entertainment tax to finance public arts facilites and/or programs.

GLOSSARY

This glossary describes the terms used in this book. It is based on *A Glossary of Terms Used by the Bureau of Outdoor Recreation* (1975), *Glossary of Recreation and Park Terms* (Sessoms, 1972), the glossary in *Urban Recreation Planning* (Gold, 1973), *The Language of Cities* (Abrams, 1971), *Encyclopedia of Urban Planning* (Whittick, 1974), and the accepted or common use of selected terms.

Activity-Day   Twelve activity hours, which may be aggregated continuously, intermittently, or simultaneously by one or more persons.

Activity-Hour   An accumulation of 60 minutes by one or more persons for a special recreation activity.

Activity-Occasion   Participation by one person in an activity without relation to the duration of such participation.

Benefit-Cost Ratio   An economic indicator of efficiency derived from dividing benefits by costs.

Carrying Capacity   The natural, physical, or social capability of a recreation area to withstand use and provide a desired quality of recreation experience, or the amount of recreation use of a resource which is most appropriate for the protection of the resource and satisfaction of the participant.

Central City   The largest city of a standard metropolitan statistical area (SMSA), which gives the SMSA its name and has a population of 50,000 or more.

Commercial Recreation   Recreation conducted by a business enterprise for profit and open to the public on a fee or charge basis.

Community Park   An area that provides recreation opportunities for two or more neighborhoods.

Comprehensive Plan   An official document adopted by a local government that describes general policies for the desirable physical, social, and economic development of a city.

Concession   An authorization granted by a government agency to a commercial enterprise to operate visitor facilities and services.

Ecosystem   An interdependent community of living organisms and their environment.

Environment   The aggregate of surrounding space, conditions, and influences affecting the life and development of an organism, society, or individual behavior.

Expressed Demand   Use of existing recreation opportunities conditioned by factors such as access, cost, information, and experience.

Extensive Recreation   Activities that are usually dispersed over a large area and require few or no facilities.

Inner City   Neighborhoods which surround the central business district of a metropolitan area and are generally in the geographic core of the central city of an SMSA.

Intensive Recreation   Activities that can take place in a limited amount of space.

Landscape   An outdoor area with man-made and natural characteristics.

Latent Demand   Recreation demand inherent in the population, but not reflected in the use of existing facilities; additional participation will occur if opportunities are available.

Leisure   Any portion of individual's time not occupied by employment or essential activities.

Neighborhood   A residential area with a social, physical, and political identity.

Neighborhood Park   An area that provides recreation opportunities within walking distance of residents.

Objective   An aim or end of action, a point to be reached.

Open Space   Land and water in an urban area which is not covered by cars or buildings; or any undeveloped land in an urban area which has value for park and recreation purposes, conservation of natural resources, or historic or scenic purposes.

Outdoor Recreation   Leisure time activities which utilize an outdoor area or facility.

Outdoor Recreation Resources   Land and water resources capable of providing outdoor recreation opportunities.

Park   Public or private land set aside for aesthetic, educational, recreational, or cultural use.

Participation Rate   The number of times a person takes part in a given recreation activity over a specific period of time.

Plan   A course of action which can be implemented to accomplish stated objectives and which someone intends to implement.

Planning   The systematic collection, organization, and processing of information to facilitate decision making.

Policy   A governing principle or course of action; or a general guide to conduct which is subject to modification.

Program   A time-phased plan for resource allocation and specifying how to achieve stated objectives.

Program Objective   Specific results to be attained by the planned commitment of resources.

Rational Decision   One which considers all possible courses of action to attain desired ends, identifies and evaluates the consequences of each alternative, and selects the preferred alternatives in terms of most valued ends.

Recreation   Any leisure time activity pursued for its own sake or what happens to a person as a result of a recreation experience.

Recreation Area   Any public or private space set aside or primarily oriented to recreation uses.

Recreation Demand   The amount and kinds of recreation opportunities an individual or population subgroup desires (latent demand) or uses (expressed demand) in a given time period, place, or planning unit.

Recreation Facilities   Buildings and other physical features or improvements designed, constructed, and managed for recreation use.

Recreation Need   The difference between current recreation demand and the existing supply of opportunities expressed in terms of land, facilities, or programs.

Recreation Planning   A process that relates the leisure time of people to space. The use of information to facilitate decision making that results in the allocation of resources to accommodate the current and future leisure needs of a population and planning area.

Recreation Programs   Recreation opportunities which result from the organized or planned use of recreation resources that normally require scheduling, facilities, and supervision or leadership.

Recreation Resources   Land and water areas and associated facilities, people, organizations, and financial support that provide opportunities for recreation.

Recreation Standard   The measure of quantity and quality considered as a desirable goal for the provision of recreation areas and facilities.

Recreation Supply   The quantity, quality, and effectiveness of existing or potential recreation resources.

Self-Generated Park A recreational space primarily initiated, planned, designed, developed, and managed by the users.

Social Indicator A measure of human welfare in terms of the opportunity or accommodation for a public or private good or service.

Suburb An incorporated residential area outside the existing political boundaries of the central city.

Standard A measure for relating an allocation of resources to existing or potential needs as determined by stated goals, objectives, and policies.

Standard Metropolitan Statistical Area (SMSA) An integrated social and economic unit which contains at least one central city of 50,000 or more inhabitants.

Supplier A public agency or private firm that provides park and recreation spaces, facilities, or services.

Urban Area A city or town having a population of 2500 or more persons.

Urbanized Area A central city and surrounding settled area as defined by the Bureau of the Census in 1980.

User Preference The voluntary choice of an activity, area, or experience to fulfill a recreation desire or need.

User Satisfaction The fulfillment of a recreation desire and preference normally conditioned by the user's background, activities available, facilities, and design or management of the area.

Visit The entry of one person into a recreation area or site to carry on one or more recreation activities.

Visitation The total number of persons entering and using a recreation area over a specified period of time.

Visitor One who enters a recreation area for enjoyment of the opportunities provided.

Visitor-Day Twelve visitor hours, which may be aggregated continuously, intermittently, or simultaneously by one or more persons.

Visitor-Hour The presence of one or more persons on lands or waters, generally recognized as providing outdoor recreation for continuous, intermittent, or simultaneous periods of time aggregating 60 minutes.

BIBLIOGRAPHY

This is a selected bibliography of the literature on urban recreation planning. The bibliography emphasizes recent research, government publications, and professional texts. The primary emphasis is on relationships between the resource, user, and supplier and the implications these relationships can have for the planning, management, and support of urban parks, recreation facilities, and programs.

References have not been selected to represent any particular point of view or approach, but rather to indicate a basic list of available and authoritative material on this topic which can lead to other sources. This bibliography also serves as a guide to government agencies and scholarly publications which are currently publishing material on this topic. Items are categorized for convenience and to minimize duplication. Any source used in this book but not listed here is included in the list of credits or noted as the source of the appropriate figure or table. These references provide the theoretical and pragmatic foundation for the concepts, methods, and examples in each chapter.

General Background (History, Philosophy, Urban Parks, Current Issues)

Bannon, Joseph J. 1976. *Leisure Resources: Comprehensive Planning.* Englewood Cliffs, N.J.: Prentice-Hall.

Brown, Robert, and **Fisk, Donald.** 1973. "Recreation Planning and Analysis in Local Government." *Municipal Year Book,* 54–60.

Dunn, Diana. 1974. *Open Space and Recreation Opportunity in America's Inner Cities.* U.S. Department of Housing and Urban Development.

French, Jere S. 1973. *Urban Green.* Dubuque, Iowa: Kendall-Hunt.

Gray, David, and **Donald Pelegrino.** 1973. *Reflections on the Recreation and Park Movement: A Book of Readings.* Dubuque, Iowa: Brown.

Greben, Seymour, and **David E. Gray.** 1974. "Future Perspectives." *Parks and Recreation,* June: 11–19.

Gold, Seymour M. 1974. "Deviant Behavior in Urban Parks." In *Journal of Health, Physical Education and Recreation,* 45 (November): 50–52.

———. 1976. "The Fate of Urban Parks." In *Parks and Recreation,* October: 13–18. Also published as "Where Will People Play?" *Planning,* (August 1976): 8–11, and as "Urban Parks: An Endangered Species." *California Parks and Recreation,* February 1977: 25–34.

———. 1975. "The Green Revolution in Urban America." *Parks and Recreation,* February: 26–28.

———. 1977. "Neighborhood Parks: The Nonuse Phenomenon." *Evaluation Quarterly,* 2 (May): 319–327.

———. 1972. "Nonuse of Neighborhood Parks." *Journal of the American Institute of Planners,* 38 (November): 369–378.

———. 1977. "Planning Neighborhood Parks for Use." *Ekistics,* 43 (February): 84–86.

———. 1977. "Recreation Planning for Energy Conservation." *International Journal of Environmental Studies,* 10 (April): 173–180.

———. 1975. "Titanic Effect on Parks and Recreation." *Parks and Recreation,* June: 23–25.

———. 1973. *Urban Recreation Planning.* Philadelphia: Lea & Febiger.

Guggenheimer, Elinor. 1969. *Planning for Parks and Recreation Needs in Urban Areas.* Center for New York City Affairs, New School for Social Research. New York: Twayne.

Jacobs, Jane. 1961. *The Death and Life of Great American Cities.* New York: Random House.

Kando, Thomas M. 1975. *Leisure and Popular Culture in Transition.* St. Louis: Mosby.

Kaplan, Max. 1975. *Leisure: Theory and Policy.* New York: Wiley.

Kraus, Richard, and **Joseph E. Curtis.** 1977. *Creative Administration in Recreation and Parks.* St. Louis: Mosby.

Lutzin, Sidney, and **Edward H. Storey** (Eds.). 1973 *Managing Municipal Leisure Services.* Washington, D.C.: International City Management Association.

Murphy, James F. 1974. *Concept of Leisure: Philosophical Implications.* Englewood Cliffs, N.J.: Prentice-Hall.

———. 1975. *Recreation and Leisure Service: A Humanistic Perspective.* Dubuque, Iowa: Brown.

National League of Cities. 1968. *Recreation in the Nation's Cities: Problems and Approaches.* Prepared for the U.S. Department of the Interior, Bureau of Outdoor Recreation.

National Recreation and Park Association. 1971. *Modernizing Urban Park and Recreation Systems.* Proceedings from a National Forum, Houston, October: 18–19.

———. 1969. *Parks and Recreation in the Urban Crises.* Proceedings from a National Forum, Washington, D.C. March: 19–21.

———. 1971. *Urban Study Status Report: A Progress Report.*

Premo, M. J., (Ed.). 1968 *Parks and Recreation in the Urban Crisis.* Report of the National Forum on Urban Affairs, Arlington, Va.: National Recreation and Park Association.

Rutledge, Albert J. 1971. *Anatomy of a Park.* New York: McGraw-Hill.

Strong, A. L. 1965. *Open Space for Urban America.* U.S. Department of Housing and Urban Development.

U.S. Department of Housing and Urban Development. 1974. *Urban Recreation.* Prepared for the Nationwide Outdoor Recreation Plan by the Interdepartmental Work Group on Urban Recreation, HUD-CD-41

U.S. Department of the Interior, Heritage Conservation and Recreation Service. 1978. *Analysis of Federal Recreation and Recreation-Related Programs.* National Urban Recreation Study Technical Report No. 6.

———. 1978. *National Urban Recreation Study: Bibliography.* Technical Report No. 13.

————. 1978. *National Urban Recreation Study: Executive Report.*

U.S. Department of Interior, Bureau of Outdoor Recreation. 1973. *Final Environmental Statement on Nationwide Outdoor Recreation Plan.*

————. 1973. *Outdoor Recreation: A Legacy for America.*

U.S. Outdoor Recreation Resources Review Commission. 1962. *The Future of Outdoor Recreation in Metropolitan Regions of the United States,* ORRRC Study Report 21 (3 vols).

————. 1962. *Outdoor Recreation for America.*

————. 1962. *Outdoor Recreation Literature: A Survey,* ORRRC Study Report 27.

Verhoven, Peter J., Jr. 1975. *An Evaluation of Policy-Related Research in the Field of Municipal Recreation and Parks: Final Report, Volume 3: Bibliography,* Prepared with support from U.S. National Science Foundation /RANN, by National Recreation and Park Association, Arlington, Va.

Whyte, William H. 1968. *The Last Landscape.* Garden City, N.Y.: Doubleday.

Wurman, Richard S., et al. 1972. *The Nature of Recreation.* Cambridge, Mass.: M.I.T.

Recreation Need *(Theoretical Concepts, Methods, Standards, Deficiency, Case Studies)*

Bradshaw, J. 1972. "The Concept of Social Need." *New Society,* 30 (March): 640–643.

Buechner, Robert D. (Ed.). 1971. *National Park, Recreation and Open Space Standards.* Washington, D.C.: National Recreation and Park Association.

Butler, George D. 1967. *Introduction to Community Recreation.* New York: McGraw-Hill.

————. 1962. *Standards for Municipal Recreation Areas.* New York: National Recreation Association.

California Committee on Planning for Recreation, Park Areas and Facilities. 1956. *Guide for Planning Recreation Parks in California.* Sacramento: Recreation Commission.

Christiansen, Monty. 1975. *Application of a Recreation Experience Components Concept for Comprehensive Recreation Planning.* Harrisburg, Pa.: Department of Community Affairs, Bureau of Recreation and Conservation, Leisure Technical Assistance Publication Program, vols. 1 & 2.

Craig, W. 1972. "Recreational Activity Patterns in a Small Negro Urban Community: The Role of the Cultural Base." *Economic Geography,* 48, 1: 107–115.

Hendee, J. C. 1969. "Rural Urban Differences Reflected in Outdoor Recreation Participation." *Journal of Leisure Research,* 4 (Winter): 333–341.

Hendricks, J. 1971. "Leisure Participation as Influenced by Urban Residence Patterns." *Sociology and Social Research,* 55, 4: 414–428.

Hoinville, G. 1971. "Evaluating Community Preferences." *Environment and Planning,* 3: 33–50.

LaPage, W. G. 1971. *Cultural "Fogweed" and Outdoor Recreation Research.* Proceedings, Forest Recreation Symposium, U.S. Forest Service, Upper Darby, Pa., 186–193.

————. 1970. "The Mythology of Outdoor Recreation Planning." *Southern Lumberman,* 221, 2752: 118–121.

Maryland National Park and Planning Commission. 1977. *Park, Recreation and Open Space Plan.* Silver Spring, Md.

McVeigh, T. 1971. *Social Indicators: A Bibliography.* Monticello, Ill.: Council of Planning Libraries Exchange Bibliography, no. 215.

Mercer, David. 1973. "The Concept of Recreational Need.' *Journal of Leisure Research,* 5 (Winter): 35–50.

Michelson, W. 1970. *Man and His Urban Environment: A Sociological Approach.* Reading, Mass.: Addison-Wesley.

Paaswell, R. E. 1972. "Problems of the Poor in an Auto Owning Environment." *International Journal of Environmental Studies,* 3: 253–257.

Plessas, D. J. and **R. Fein.** 1972. "An Evaluation of Social Indicators." *Journal of the American Institute of Planners,* 38, 1: 43–51.

Shafer, E. L., Jr., and **G. Moeller.** 1971. *Predicting Quantitative and Qualitative Values of Recreation Participation.* Proceedings, Forest Recreation Symposium. U.S. Forest Service, Upper Darby, Pa., 5–22.

Staley, Edwin J. 1969. "Determining Neighborhood Recreation Priorities: An Instrument." *Journal of Leisure Research,* 1 (Winter): 69–74.

Stone, Susan C., and **John W. Taylor.** 1976. *Inner City Turnaround.* Urbana: University of Illinois.

Webb, E. J., et al. 1970. *Unobtrusive Measures: Nonreactive Research in the Social Sciences.* Chicago: Rand McNally.

Recreation Behavior *(User Preference and Satisfaction, Case Studies)*

Appleyard, D., and **M. Lintell.** 1962. "The Environmental Quality of City Streets: The Residents' Viewpoint." *Journal of the American Institute of Planners,* 38: 84–101.

Bangs, H. P., and **S. Mahler.** 1970. "Users of Local Parks." *Journal of the American Institute of Planners,* 36, (September): 330–334.

Bechtel, R. B. 1972. The Public Housing Environment: A Few Surprises," in W. J. Mitchell (Ed.). *Environmental Design: Research and Practice.* Los Angeles: University of California, 13-1-1 to 13-1-9.

Cheek, Neil H., Donald R. Field, and **Rabel J. Burdge.** 1976. *Leisure and Recreation Places.* Ann Arbor: Science Publishers.

Converse, Phillip E., and **John P. Robinson.** 1966. *Summary of United States Time Use Survey.* Ann Arbor: University of Michigan, Survey Research Center.

Cooper, C. 1971. "St. Francis Square: Attitudes of Its Residents." *American Institute of Architects Journal,* 53: 22–27.

Driver, B. L. (Ed.). 1970. *Elements of Outdoor Recreation Planning.* Ann Arbor: University Microfilms. Also published in paperback by University of Michigan Press, 1974.

Gans, Herbert. 1957. "Recreation Planning for Leisure Behavior: A Goal-Oriented Approach," Unpublished Ph.D. dissertation, University of Pennsylvania.

Gold, Seymour M. 1977. "Social and Economic Benefits of Trees in Cities," *Journal of Forestry,* February: 84–86. See also *Human Response to Vegetation in Urban Parks.* Davis: University of California, 1976. Unpublished.

Guggenheimer, E. C. 1969. *Planning for Parks and Recreation Needs in Urban Areas.* New York: Twayne.

Hatry, Harry, and **Diana Dunn.** 1971. *Measuring the Effectiveness of Local Government Services.* Washington, D.C.: Urban Institute. (Also, technical report and appendixes with same title and publisher and no author listed, November 1972.)

————. et al. 1977. *How Effective Are Your Community Services?* Washington, D.C.: Urban Institute and International City Managers Association.

Hester, Randolph T. 1975. *Neighborhood Space.* Stroudsburg, Pa.: Dowden, Hutchinson and Ross.

Lansing, J. B., and **R. W. Marans.** 1969. "Evaluation of Neighborhood Quality." *Journal of the American Institute of Planners,* 35: 195–199.

Mack, Ruth, and **Diana Dunn.** 1965. "Outdoor Recreation," in Robert Dorfman (Ed.) *Measuring the Benefits of Government Investments.* Washington, D.C.: Brookings Institution.

Malt, H. L. 1972. "An Analysis of Public Safety as Related to the Incidence of Crime in Parks and Recreation Areas in Central Cities." for U.S. Department of Housing and Urban Development, (unpublished).

Michelson, W. H. 1970. *Man and His Urban Environment: A Sociological Analysis.* Reading, Mass.: Addison-Wesley.

Peterson, G. L. 1967. "A Model for Preference: Quantitative Analysis of the Perception of the Visual Appearance of Neighborhoods." *Journal of Regional Science,* 7: 19–31.

Robinson, John P. 1977. *Changes in Americans' Use of Time: 1965–1975.* Cleveland: Communication Research Center, Cleveland State University.

————. 1977. *How Americans Use Time.* New York: Praeger.

Sanoff, H., and **M. Sawhney.** 1971. *Residential Livability: A Socio-physical Perspective.* Raleigh: Urban Affairs and Community Service Center, North Carolina State University.

Recreation Demand *(Forecasting Techniques, Demand Models, Case Studies)*

California Department of Parks and Recreation. 1966. *Park and Recreation Information System.* Sacramento, Calif., Planning Monograph No. 2.

Cicchetti, C. J., 1973. *Forecasting Recreation in the United States.* Lexington, Mass.: Heath.

Clawson, M. 1959. *Methods of Measuring Demand for and Value of Outdoor Recreation.* Washington, D.C.: Resources for the Future, Inc., Reprint No. 10.

Clawson, M., and **J. L. Knetsch.** 1966. *Economics of Outdoor Recreation.* Baltimore: Johns Hopkins Press.

Ellis, Jack B., and **Carlton S. Van Doren.** 1966. "A Comparative Evaluation of Gravity and System Theory Models for Statewide Recreational Traffic Flows." *Journal of Regional Science,* 5, 2: 57–69.

Fog, George E. 1975. *Park Planning Guidelines.* Washington, D.C.: National Recreation and Park Assocation; pp 13–21.

National Academy of Sciences. 1975. *Assessing Demand for Outdoor Recreation.* U.S. Bureau of Outdoor Recreation.

National Advisory Council on Regional Recreation Planning. 1959. *A User-Resource Planning Method.* Hidden Valley, Lomis, Calif.

Van Doren, Carlton S., John E., Lewis, and **George Priddle.** 1979. *Land & Leisure : Concepts and Methods in Outdoor Recreation.* Chicago: Maaroufa Press.

Wilkinson, R. F. 1973. "The Use of Models in Predicting the Consumption of Outdoor Recreation." *Journal of Leisure Research,* 5, 3 (Summer): 34–39.

Recreation Economics *(Methodology, Theoretical Perspective, Economic Analysis, Case Studies)*

Becker, Boris W. 1975. "The Pricing of Educational-Recreational Facilities: An Administrative Dilemma." *Journal of Leisure Research,* 7, 2: 86–94.

Brown, William G., and **Farid Narvas.** 1972. "A New Approach to the Evaluation of Non-priced Recreational Resources." *Land Economics,* July.

Clawson, Marion, and **Jack Knetsch.** 1966. *Economics of Outdoor Recreation.* Baltimore: Johns Hopkins Press.

Dorfman, Robert. 1966. *Measuring Benefits of Government Investments.* Washington, D.C.: Brookings Institution.

Gold, S. 1974. "The Distribution of Urban Government Services in Theory and Practice." *Public Finance Quarterly,* 2: 107–130.

Goldberger, A. S. 1964. *Econometric Theory.* New York: Wiley.

Hatry, Harry P., and **Diana Dunn.** 1971. *Measuring the Effectiveness of Local Government Services.* Washington, D.C.: Urban Institute.

Hirsch, W. Z. 1964. "Local Versus Area-Wide Urban Government Services." *National Tax Journal,* December.

————. 1968. "The Supply of Urban Public Services." *Issues in Urban Economics.* Baltimore: Johns Hopkins Press.

James, L. D. 1968. "A Case Study in Income Redistribution from Reservoir Construction." *Water Resources Research,* 4: 499–505.

Kavanaugh, J. M., M. J. Marcus, and **R. M. Gay.** 1973. *Programming Budgeting for Urban Recreation.* New York: Praeger.

Margolis, Julius. 1957. "Secondary Benefits, External Economies, and the Justification of Public Investments." *The Review of Economics and Satistics,* August.

Milliman, J. W. 1972. "Beneficiary Charges—Toward a Unified Theory." in Selma J. Mushkin (Ed.). *Public Prices for Public Products.* Washington, D.C.: Urban Institute.

Milstein, D. 1961. "A Economic Approach to Leisure Analysis." *Social Problems,* Summer.

Mumy, G. E., and **S. H. Hanke.** 1975. "Public Investment Criteria for Under-Priced Public Products." *Economic Review.*

Robinson, Warren C. 1967. "The Simple Economics of Public Outdoor Recreation." *Land Economics,* 3: 71–83.

Seckler, David W. 1966. "On the Use and Abuses of Economic Science in Evaluating Public Outdoor Recreation." *Land Economics,* November.

Shabman, L. A., and **R. J. Kalter.** 1969. "Effects of Public Programs for Outdoor Recreation on Personal Income Distribution." *American Journal of Agricultural Economics,* 51: 1516–19.

U.S. Department of the Interior, Bureau of Outdoor Recreation. 1973. *Outdoor Recreation: A Legacy for America, Appendix A, An Economic Analysis.*

———. 1976. *Evaluation of Public Willingness to Pay User Charges for Use of Outdoor Recreation Areas and Facilities,* Economics Research Associates, San Francisco.

Verhoven, Peter J., Jr. 1975. *An Evaluation of Policy-Related Research in the Field of Municipal Recreation and Parks,* vol. 4, National Recreation and Park Association.

Wennergren, E. Boyd. 1967. "Surrogate Pricing of Outdoor Recreation." *Land Economics,* February: 112–116.

———. 1964. "Valuing Non-market Priced Recreational Resources." *Land Economics,* August.

Wennergren, E. Boyd, and **H. H. Fullerton.** 1972. "Estimating Quality and Location Values of Recreational Resources." *Journal of Leisure Research,* 4 (Summer): 170–183.

Recreation Surveys (*Survey Research Methods, Approaches, Costs, Case Studies*)

Ferriss, Abbott L. 1963. "Applications of Recreation Surveys." *Public Opinion Quarterly,* XXVII (Fall): 433–454.

Field, Donald R. 1973. "The Telephone Interview in Leisure Research." *Journal of Leisure Research,* 5 (Winter): 51–54.

Hatry, Harry P., and **Diana R. Dunn.** 1971. *Measuring the Effectiveness of Local Government Services: Recreation.* Washington, D.C.: Urban Institute.

James, George A., and **Robert K. Henley.** 1968. *Sampling Procedures for Estimating Mass and Dispersed Types of Recreation Use on Large Areas.* U.S. Department of Agriculture, Forest Service Research Paper SE-31.

National League of Cities. 1968. *Recreation in the Nation's Cities: Problems and Approaches.* National Recreation and Park Association.

Shafer, Elwood L., and **John F. Hamilton.** 1967. *A Comparison of Four Survey Techniques Used in Outdoor Recreation Research.* U.S. Department of Agriculture, Forest Service Research Paper NE-86.

Shannon, Alan R., 1975 "A Systems Approach to Recreation Planning." *Parks and Recreation* 10 (September): 32–33.

Staley, Edwin J. 1969. "Determining Neighborhood Recreation Priorities," *Journal of Leisure Research,* Winter: 69–74.

Stephan, Frederick F., and **Philip McCarthy.** 1958. *Sampling Opinions: An Analysis of Survey Procedures.* New York: Wiley.

Webb, Kenneth, and **Harry P. Hatry.** 1973. *Obtaining Citizen Feedback: The Application of Citizen Surveys to Local Governments.* Washington, D.C.: Urban Institute.

Park and Recreation Administration (*Philosophy and Financing of Public Park and Recreation Services*)

Artz, Robert, and **Hubert Bermont** (Eds.). 1970. *New Approaches to Financing Parks and Recreation.* Washington, D.C.: Acropolis, 65–69.

Bannon, Joseph J. 1976. *Leisure Resources: Comprehensive Planning.* Englewood Cliffs, N.J.: Prentice-Hall.

Butler, George D. 1976. *Introduction to Community Recreation.* New York: McGraw-Hill.

Doell, Charles E., and **Louis F. Twardzik.** 1973. *Elements of Park and Recreation Administration.* Minneapolis: Burgess.

Epperson, Arlin F. 1977. *Prive and Commercial Recreation.* New York: Wiley.

Godbey, Geoffrey, and **Stanley Parker.** 1976. *Leisure Studies and Services: An Overview.* Philadelphia: Saunders.

Hines, Thomas I. 1974. *Fees and Charges.* Management Aids Bulletin No. 59, Arlington, Va.: National Recreation and Park Association.

Hjelte, George. 1976. *Policies and Practices in Charging for the Use of Recreation Resources.* Los Angeles: Recreation and Youth Services Planning Council.

Hjelte, George, and **Jay S. Shivers.** 1972. *Public Administration of Recreation Services.* Philadelphia: Lea & Febiger, 315–339.

Kraus, Richard G. 1977. *Recreation Today.* Santa Monica, Calif.: Goodyear.

Kraus, Richard, and Joseph E. Curtis. 1977. *Creative Administration in Recreation and Parks.* St. Louis: Mosby, 213–233.

Lutzin, Sidney, and Edward H. Storey (Eds.). 1973. *Managing Municipal Leisure Services.* Washington, D.C.: International City Management Association, 211–224.

McCormack, John R. 1965. *Park and Recreation Finance.* National Recreation and Park Association.

Meyer, Harold D., Charles K. Brightbill, and H. Douglas Sessoms. 1969. *Community Recreation.* Englewood Cliffs, N.J.: Prentice-Hall.

Michigan Department of Natural Resources, Recreation Services Division. 1977. *Public Preference for Financing Public Recreation.*

——. 1976. *Recreation Fees and Charges at Local Public Facilities in Michigan.*

Murphy, James F. 1974. *Concepts of Leisure: Philosophical Implications.* Englewood Cliffs, N.J.: Prentice-Hall.

——. 1975. *Recreation and Leisure Service: A Humanistic Perspective.* Dubuque, Iowa: Brown.

Murphy, James F., et al. 1973. *Leisure Service Delivery System: A Modern Perspective.* Philadelphia: Lea & Febiger.

Reynolds, Jesse A., and Marion N. Hormachae. 1976. *Public Recreation Administration.* Reston, Va.: Reston, 246–271.

Shake, George L. 1968. *License and Permit Fees.* National Recreation and Park Association.

Stein, Thomas A., and Douglas Sessoms. 1977. *Recreation and Special Populations.* Boston: Holbrook Press.

Van Dusen, Thomas M., and Eugene M. Huhtala. 1966. *Entrance Fees.* National Recreation and Park Association.

Wright, David G. 1966. *Admission Fees.* National Recreation and Park Association.

Citizen Participation (Case Studies)

Gold Seymour M. 1976. "Coping," "You Are the Director," and "Fees and Charges." Recreation planning games, unpublished.

U.S. Department of the Interior, National Park Service. 1975. *Workbook for Yosemite National Park Master Plan.* San Francisco, Calif.

Open Space Preservation *(Development Controls, Resource Analysis, Acquisition Methods, Costs, Case Studies)*

American Law Institute. 1975. *A Model Land Development Code.* Washington, D.C.

Conservation Foundation. 1967. *Three Approaches to Environmental Resource Analysis.* Washington, D.C. Prepared by the Landscape Architecture Research Office, Harvard University.

Coughlin, Robert, Thomas Plaut, and Ann Louise Strong. 1978. *Land Acquisition Methods for the Preservation of Urban Open Space.* National Urban Recreation Study Technical Report No. 4, U.S. Department of the Interior, Heritage Recreation and Conservation Service.

Einsweiler, Robert C., and Associates. 1978. *Use of Regulatory Powers in Protecting Urban Open Space.* National Urban Recreation Study Technical Report No. 5, U.S. Department of the Interior, Heritage Recreation and Conservation Service.

Hagman, Donald, and Dean Miaczymski. 1977. *Windfalls of Wipeouts.* Chicago: American Society of Planning Officials.

Heckscher, August (with Phyllis Robinson). 1977. *Open Spaces: The Life of American Cities.* New York: Harper & Row.

Lewis, Phillip H. 1961. *Recreation and Open Space in Illinois.* Urbana: State Housing Board.

Little, Charles E. 1975. *Green-Line Parks: An Approach to Preserving Recreational Landscapes in Urban Areas.* Prepared by Environmental Policy Division, Congressional Research Service, Library of Congress for the Subcommittee on Parks and Recreation, Committee on Interior and Insular Affairs, U.S. Senate.

Litton, R. Burton, Jr. 1968. *Forest Landscape Description and Inventories.* Berkeley: California, Pacific Southwest Forest and Range Experiment Station, U.S. Department of Agriculture, U.S. Forest Service, PSW No. 91.

McHarg, Ian L. 1969. *Design with Nature.* Garden City, N.Y.: Natural History Press.

Schaal, H. R. 1972. "Constraint Maps." *Transmission and Distribution,* April.

Shomon, Joseph. 1971. *Open Land for Urban America: Acquisition, Safekeeping and Use.* Baltimore: Johns Hopkins Press.

Strong, Anne Louise. 1965. *Open Space for Urban America.* Urban Renewal Administration, U.S. Department of Housing and Urban Development.

U.S. Department of Agriculture, U.S. Forest Service. 1973. *National Forest Landscape Management,* Vol. 1. See also Vol. 2, *The Visual Management System,* 1974.

U.S. Department of the Interior. 1978. *Urban Open Space: Existing Conditions, Opportunities and Issues.* National Urban Recreation Study Technical Report No. 1.

U.S. Department of the Interior, Bureau of Outdoor Recreation. 1977. *Guidelines for Understanding and Determining Optimum Recreation Carrying Capacity.* Prepared by Urban Research and Development Corporation, Bethlehem, Pa., p. III-3.

U.S. Department of the Interior, National Park Service. 1975. *Scenic Easements.*

Whyte, William. 1959. *Securing Open Space for Urban America: Conservation Easements.* Technical Bulletin No. 36. Washington, D.C.: Urban Land Institute.

——. 1967. *The Last Landscape.* New York: Doubleday.

Wingo, Lowdon (Ed.). 1963. *Cities and Space: The Future Use of Urban Land.* Baltimore: Johns Hopkins Press.

Recreation Services (Programs Facilities, Special Populations, Cooperation, Case Studies)

American Society of Landscape Architects Foundation. 1975. *Barrier-Free Site Design.* McLean, Va.

Artz, Robert. 1970. *School-Community Recreation and Park Cooperation.* Management Aid Bulletin No. 82. Arlington, Va.: National Recreation and Park Association.

Avedon, Elliott. 1974. *Therapeutic Recreation Service: An Applied Behavioral Science Approach.* Englewood Cliffs, N.J.: Prentice-Hall.

Bannon, Joseph J. (Ed.). 1973. *Outreach: Extending Community Service in Urban Areas.* Springfield, Ill.: Charles C Thomas.

Carlson, Bernice, and **David Ginglend.** 1968. *Recreation for Retarded Teenagers and Young Adults.* Nashville: Abingdon.

Howe-Murphy, Roxanne. 1977. "Mainstreaming: The Emergence of the Disabled in the Community." *California Parks and Recreation,* 33, 3: 14–15 & 34.

Kleindienst, Viola K., and **Arthur Weston.** 1978. *The Recreational Sports Program.* Englewood Cliffs, N.J.: Prentice-Hall.

Kraus, Richard. 1973. *Therapeutic Recreation Service: Principles and Practices.* Philadelphia: Saunders.

Nesbitt, John A., Paul D. Brown, and **James F. Murphy** (Eds.). 1970. *Recreation and Leisure Service for the Disadvantaged.* Philadelphia: Lea & Febiger.

Nierman, Wayne. 1972. "The Community School and Recreation." *Journal of Health, Physical Education and Recreation,* 43, 3: 53.

Pomeroy, Janet. 1964. *Recreation for the Physically Handicapped.* New York: Macmillan.

Satterthwaite, Ann. 1978. *Arts and Culture: A New Priority in Urban Recreation.* National Urban Recreation Study Technical Report No. 10. Prepared by National Endowment for the Arts for U.S. Department of the Interior, Heritage Recreation and Conservation Service.

Staley, Edwin. 1974. *School-City Cooperation and Coordination of Recreation and Youth Services in Los Angeles.* Recreation and Youth Services Planning Council, Los Angeles.

Stein, Thomas, and **H. Douglas Sessoms.** 1973. *Recreation and Special Populations.* Boston: Holbrook Press.

U.S. Department of Agriculture, U.S. Forest Service. 1977. *Children, Nature, and the Urban Environment.* Proceedings of a symposium-fair. General Technical Report NE-30. Northeastern Forest and Range Experiment Station, Upper Darby, Pa.

U.S. Department of Health, Education and Welfare, Office of Education. 1978. *Urban-Oriented Environmental Education.* National Urban Recreation Study Technical Report. Prepared for U.S. Department of the Interior by Office of Environmental Education.

U.S. Department of the Interior, Bureau of Outdoor Recreation. 1977. *Recreation for Special People.* Outdoor Recreation Action Report No. 45.

Future Perspective (Trends in Parks and Recreation, Future Leisure Spaces and Services)

Curtis, Joseph E. 1973. "Parks of the Future." *Journal of Health, Physical Education and Recreation,* June: 31–39.

Dunn, Diana R., and **John M. Gulbis.** 1976. "The Risk Revolution." *Parks and Recreation,* August: 12–17.

Fabun, Don. 1967. *Dynamics of Change.* Englewood Cliffs, N.J.: Prentice-Hall.

Fluegelman, Andrew (Ed.). 1976. *The New Games Book.* San Francisco: Headlands Press.

Gold, Seymour M. 1977. "Recreation Planning for Energy Conservation." *International Journal of Environmental Studies,* 10 (April): 173–180.

———. 1976. "The Fate of Urban Parks." *Parks and Recreation,* 11 (October): 13–18. Also reprinted in *California Parks and Recreation,* February 1977: 25–29.

———. 1977. "Municipal Parks and Recreation: Rethinking the Future." *Recreation Canada,* 35, 4: 11–18. Reprinted as "Urban Open Space: 2000," California Parks and Recreation, 34 (December 1978): 14–17 and *Parks and Recreation* (May 1979): 52–57.

———. 1975. "Titanic Effect on Parks and Recreation." *Parks and Recreation,* 10 (June): 23–25.

———. 1973. *Urban Recreation Planning,* Philadelphia: Lea & Febiger.

Goodman, Robert. 1971. *After the Planners.* New York: Simon and Schuster.

Greben, Seymour, and **David E. Gray.** 1974. "Future Perspectives." *Parks and Recreation* (June): 11–19.

Kando, Thomas M. 1975. *Leisure and Popular Culture in Transition.* St. Louis: Mosby.

Martin, W. H., and **S. Mason.** 1976. "Leisure 1980 and Beyond." *Long Range Planning,* April: 58–64.

Michael, Donald N. 1968. *The Unprepared Society: Planning for a Precarious Future.* New York: Harper & Row.

Murphy, J. F. 1972. "The Counter Culture of Leisure." *Parks and Recreation,* 7: 34.

National Recreation and Park Association. 1978. *Parks and Recreation: Special Issue on Future Trends.* 13 (May): 25–45.

Reich, Charles A. 1970. *Greening of America.* New York: Random House.

Schumacher, E. F. 1973. *Small is Beautiful.* New York: Harper & Row.

Shafer, Elwood, George H. Moeller, and **Russel E. Getty.** 1974. *Future Leisure Environments.* U.S. Forest Service Research Paper NE-301, Northeastern Forest Experiment Station, Upper Darby, Pa.

Toffler, Alvin. 1970. *Future Shock.* New York: Random House.

Watt, Kenneth E. 1974. *The Titanic Effect.* Stamford, Conn.: Sinauer Associates.

ILLUSTRATION CREDITS

The author expresses his thanks to the public agencies, consultants, and professionals who contributed illustrations to this book. To minimize duplication, the detailed reference for illustrations not listed here is in the bibliography or on each figure. Many items are from government documents or recreation plans prepared by consultants for government agencies. Where appropriate, the principal consultant and agency are listed to provide a source for additional information.

Fig. 1.1 *Parks and Recreation Master Plan.* Department of Parks and Recreation, Edmonton, Alberta, Canada, 1978, p. 24.
Fig. 1.2 *America's Park and Recreation Heritage: A Chronology.* Prepared by Carlton S. Van Doren and Louis Hodges, Department of Recreation and Parks, Texas A&M University for U.S. Department of the Interior, Bureau of Outdoor Recreation, Washington, D.C.: Government Printing Office, 1975, p. 19.
Fig. 1.3 Alice Watson (Ed.). *America Was Beautiful.* Barre, Mass.: Barre Publishers, pp. 26 and 34. From original volume *Picturesque America*, New York: Appleton, 1872 and 1874. Reprinted with permission.
Fig. 1.4 *Plan and Program for the Preservation of the Vieux Carré.* Bureau of Governmental Research, City of New Orleans, La., 1968, pp. 43 and 163.
Fig. 1.5 Courtesy of Parcourse Ltd., San Francisco, 1978. Reprinted with permission.
Fig. 1.6 *Master Plan of Parks.* Coalinga-Huron Recreation and Parks District, Colinga, Calif. Prepared by Recreation Land Planners, Placentia, Calif., 1975.
Fig. 1.7 Ibid.
Fig. 1.8 *Parks, Recreation and Open Space Plan: Interim Report.* Planning Department, Santa Cruz County, Calif. Prepared by Duncan and Jones, Berkeley, and Ribera and Sue, Oakland, Calif., 1971.
Fig. 1.9 *Master Plan of Parks, Recreation and Cultural Facilities.* Orange, Calif. Prepared by POD, Inc., Orange, Calif., 1975.
Fig. 1.10 *Master Development Plan.* Melbourne and Metropolitan Board of Works, Melbourne, Australia. Prepared by Kenneth J. Polokowski, Center for Environmental Studies, University of Melbourne, 1977.
Fig. 1.11 *Master Plan Point Reyes National Seashore.* U.S. Department of the Interior, National Park Service, Western Service Center, Denver, Colo., 1973, p. 4.
Fig. 1.12 Ibid., p. 7.
Fig. 1.13 Golden Gate National Recreation Area Planning Team, U.S. Department of the Interior, National Park Service, San Francisco, 1975.
Fig. 1.14 *Long Beach Shoreline Plan.* Planning Department, Long Beach, Calif. Prepared by the SWA Group, formerly Sasaki, Walker Associates Planning Consultants, 1976.
Fig. 1.15 *Urban Recreational Open Space.* Ministry of Housing, Ontario, Canada. Prepared by J. R. Wright, et al., Center for Resource Development, University of Guelph, 1976, p. 53.
Fig. 1.16 *Recreational Open Space Planning and Site Design.* Canadian Parks and Recreation Association. Prepared by Jack Wright, Department of Recreology, University of Ottawa, Ontario, Canada, 1976.
Fig. 1.17 *Shelby Farms Plan.* Shelby Farms Planning Board,

Memphis, Tenn. Prepared by Garret Eckbo and Associates, San Francisco; Royston, Hanamoto, Beck and Abey, Mill Valley; Williams and Mocine, Sausalito; John Cone and Environmental Impact Planning Associates, 1975.
Fig. 2.1 *The Nation's Capital: A Plan for the Year 2000.* National Capital Planning Commission and Regional Planning Council, 1961.
Fig. 2.2 *Delivery of Community Leisure Services.* James F. Murphy and Dennis R. Howard, Philadelphia: Lea and Febiger, 1977, p. 134. Reprinted with permission.
Fig. 2.3 *New Landscapes for Recreation.* American Society of Landscape Architects, Washington, D.C., 1972.
Fig. 2.4 *Neighborhood Space.* Randolph T. Hester, Jr., p. 61. Adapted from Kevin Lynch, *The Image of the City*, Cambridge, Mass.: MIT Press, 1960, p. 19. Reprinted with permission.
Fig. 2.5 *The Visual Environment of Los Angeles.* Department of City Planning, Los Angeles, 1971, p. 6.
Fig. 2.6 Courtesy of East Bay Regional Park District, Oakland, California.
Fig. 2.7 *Ralston Creek Park Playground.* Arvada, Colo. Prepared by EDAW Inc., Ft. Collins, Colo., 1976.
Fig. 2.8 *Urban Recreation.* U.S. Department of Housing and Urban Development, Washington, D.C.: Government Printing Office, 1974, p. 31.
Fig. 2.9 Courtesy of East Bay Regional Park District, Oakland, Calif.
Fig. 2.10 Ibid.
Fig. 2.11 *Project WEY: Washington Environmental Yard.* Robin Moore Designer, University of California Laboratory School, Berkeley, 1972. Reprinted with permission.
Fig. 2.12 Richard C. Johns and Cathy Parde, "Human Services: Can Parks and Recreation Afford It?" *California Parks and Recreation,* May 1978, p. 11.
Fig. 2.13 Joseph M. Garvey, "Touch and See," *Parks and Recreation,* November 1969, p. 21.
Fig. 2.14 Courtesy Department of Recreation and Parks, Los Angeles.
Fig. 2.15 *Outdoor Recreation for America.* Outdoor Recreation Resources Review Commission, Washington, D.C.: Government Printing Office, 1962, p. 83.
Fig. 3.1 *Parks, Recreation and Open Space Plan.* Planning Department, Santa Cruz County, Calif. Prepared by Duncan and Jones, Berkeley; and Ribera and Sue, Oakland, 1972, p. 16.
Fig. 3.2 *Batiquitos Lagoon Regional Park Masterplan.* Parks and Recreation Department, San Diego County, Calif. Prepared by John Sue Associates, Oakland, Calif. 1976, p. 71.
Fig. 3.3 *General Plan for Parks.* Department of Planning and Conservation. Evanston, Ill., 1965, p. 54.
Fig. 3.4 *Concept Plan for Open Space and Conservation: Benefit-Cost Analysis.* Planning Department, Orange County, Calif. Prepared by Williams-Kuebelbeck and Associates, Inc., Newport Beach, Calif., 1973, pp. IV-30.
Fig. 3.5 *Ontario Recreation Survey: Tourism and Outdoor Recreation Planning Study.* Progress Report No. 2, Secretary for Resources Development, Toronto, Ontario, Canada, 1974, pp. 15–19.
Fig. 3.6 *Robson Square Plan.* Department of Public Works, Government of British Columbia. Prepared by Arthur Erickson Architects and Cornelia Hahn Oberlander, Landscape Architect. Photography by Simon Scott, Vancouver, British Columbia, Canada, 1975.

Fig. 3.7 *User Resource Planning Method.* National Advisory Council on Regional Recreation Planning, Hidden Valley, Loomis, Calif., 1959, p. 35.

Fig. 3.8 Thomas L. Burton, *Making Man's Environment: Leisure,* Van Nostrand Reinhold, Toronto, Canada, 1975. Reprinted with permission.

Fig. 3.9 *Crow Creek/Sunset Park.* Department of Housing and Community Development, Cheyenne, Wyoming. Prepared by EDAW Inc., Fort Collins, Colo., 1977.

Fig. 4.1 *Conservation, Recreation and Open Space Elements: Lake Tahoe Region.* Tahoe Regional Planning Agency, South Lake Tahoe, Calif. Prepared by EDAW Inc., San Francisco, in association with Economics Research Associates, San Francisco, and Ira Michael Heyman, Berkeley, 1973, p. 53.

Fig. 4.2 Same as Figure 3.1, p. 32.

Fig. 4.3 *Regional Open Space Element.* Association of Bay Area Governments, Berkeley, Calif., 1969, p. 3.

Fig. 4.4 Same as Figure 3.1, p. 32.

Fig. 4.5 Same as Figure 2.5, p. 9.

Fig. 4.6 *Park Plan: Neighborhood Parks.* Department of Planning and Conservation, Evanston, Ill., 1964, p. 7.

Fig. 4.7 S. D. Marquis, "A Systems Approach to Communities and Planning Areas" (unpublished manuscript), Institue for Community Development, Michigan State University, East Lansing, 1963.

Fig. 4.8 *Downtown Design Plan.* City of Santa Rosa and Downtown Development Association, Santa Rosa, Calif. Prepared by EDAW, Inc. San Francisco, 1977.

Fig. 4.9 *Central City District Plan 1972/1990.* Department of City Planning, Los Angeles. Based on preliminary development plan by Wallage McHarg, Roberts and Todd, Los Angeles, 1972.

Fig. 4.10 Ibid.

Fig. 4.11 *General Plan Guidelines.* Council on Intergovernmental Relations, State of California. Prepared by Sydney H. Williams, Williams and Mocine, San Francisco, 1973.

Fig. 4.12 *Guidelines for Local Recreation Planning.* Department of State Planning, Baltimore, 1976, p. 13.

Figs. 5.1 to 5.5 *Data Collection Summary.* Golden Gate National Recreation Area, South Unit, National Park Service, San Francisco. Prepared by Royston, Hanamoto, Beck and Abey. Mill Valley, Calif., 1975, pp. 103–106.

Fig. 5.6 *Reference Manual on Population and Housing Statistics.* U.S. Department of Commerce, Bureau of the Census, Washington, D.C., 1978, 26.

Fig. 5.7 Ibid., p. 31.

Fig. 5.8 Phillip E. Converse and John P. Robinson. *Summary of United States Time Use Survey.* Survey Research Center, University of Michigan, Ann Arbor, 1966.

Fig. 5.9 *Inner City Turnaround.* Housing Authority, Decatur, Ill. Prepared by Susan C. Stone and John W. Taylor, Housing Research and Development Program, University of Illinois, Urbana, 1976, p. 99.

Fig. 5.10 Golden Gate National Recreational Area Planning Team, U.S. Department of the Interior, National Park Service, San Francisco, 1975.

Fig. 6.1 Same as Figure 1.1, p. 26.

Fig. 6.2 *Community Facilities: Parks and Open Space.* Metropolitan Area Regional Planning Commission, Jackson, Mich. Prepared by Harland Bartholomew and Associates, St. Louis, 1970, p. 14.

Fig. 6.3 *Draft Environmental Statement: General Management Plan.* Gateway National Recreational Area, New York/New Jersey, Denver Service Center, National Park Service, U.S. Department of the Interior, 1978, p. 43.

Fig. 6.4 Seymour M. Gold, "Social and Economic Benefits of Trees in Cities," *Journal of Forestry* (February 1977): pp. 84–86. Also *Human Response to Vegetation in Urban Parks,* University of California, Davis, 1976, pp. 44–46.

Fig. 6.5 Harry Hatry and Diana Dunn. *Measuring the Effectiveness of Local Government Services,* Urban Institute, Washington, D.C., 1972, p. 51. Reprinted with permission.

Fig. 6.6 L. Hale Mescrow, David T. Pompel, Jr., and Charles M. Reich, "Benefit-Cost Evaluation," *Parks and Recreation,* February 1975, pp. 29–31. Abstract of study prepared for Parks and Recreation Department, Eugene, Oregon, by Northwest Research Analysts.

Figs. 7.1 to 7.4 Same as Figure 1.11, pp. 10, 14, 18, 23.

Fig. 7.5 Courtesy Illinois Department of Conservation.

Fig. 7.6 Ibid.

Fig. 7.7 Concord Pavillion, Parks Department, Concord, Calif.

Fig. 7.8 *Assessing Demand for Outdoor Recreation.* Bureau of Outdoor Recreation, U.S. Department of the Interior, Washington, D.C., 1975, p. 12. Prepared by the National Academy of Sciences.

Fig. 7.9 Kenneth Webb and Harry P. Hatry, *Obtaining Citizen Feedback: The Application of Citizen Surveys to Local Governments.* Washington, D.C.: The Urban Institute, 1973, p. 44. Reprinted with permission.

Fig. 7.10 Same as Figure 1.9, pp. 9–10.

Fig. 8.1 Same as Figure 4.1, p. 4.

Fig. 8.2 *General Plan.* Department of Planning, Ojai, Calif. Prepared by Williams and Mocine, Sausilito, 1974.

Fig. 8.3 *Park, Recreation and Open Space Master Plan.* Maryland—National Capital Park and Planning Commission, Silver Spring, 1977, p. 86.

Fig. 8.4 *Three Approaches to Environmental Resource Analysis.* Conservation Foundation, Washington, D.C. Prepared by Landscape Architecture Research Office, Graduate School of Design, Harvard University, 1967. Tables 8.4 to 8.6 abstract the procedure described in pp. 9–13, 36–37, 60–65. Reprinted with permission.

Fig. 8.5 Ibid.

Fig. 8.6 *Environmental Resources Management Element of General Plan.* Planning Department, Sonoma County, Calif., 1975, p. 23.

Fig. 8.7 Same as Figure 1.10.

Fig. 8.8 *Regional Open Space Plan: Summary.* San Francisco Bay Region, Association of Bay Area Governments, Berkeley, 1972, p. V. Prepared by Angus McDonald of McDonald & Company in Association with EDAW, Inc., San Francisco.

Fig. 8.9 Same as Figure 3.7, p. 42.

Fig. 8.10 *Recreation Element of Comprehensive Plan.* Park Department, Santa Barbara County, Calif. Royston, Hanamoto, Beck and Abey, Mill Valley, Calif., 1974.

Fig. 8.11 *Ibid.*

Fig. 9.1 A. H. Maslow, *Motivation and Personality.* New York, Harper and Row, 1964, p. 146. Reprinted with permission.

Fig. 9.2 *Bikeways.* Planning and Environment Commission, New South Wales, Australia. Prepared by Planning Workshop, North Sydney, 1976, p. 13.

Fig. 9.3 Same as Figure 1.1, p. 43.

Fig. 9.4 Same as Figure 1.1, p. 38.

Fig. 9.5 Same as Figure 6.3, p. 12.
Fig. 9.6 *Challenge of Leisure.* Southern California Research Council, Pomona College, Claremont, 1967, pp. 16–17.
Fig. 9.7 *Implications of Community Center Development.* Department of Tourism and Recreation, Canberra, A.C.T., Australia. Prepared by Planning Workshop and Management Consultants, 1974, p. 49.
Fig. 9.8 *Park Needs Study.* Park Department, Whittier, Calif., 1977, p. 15. Prepared by POD, Inc., Orange, Calif.
Fig. 9.9 Same as Figure 3.4, pp. VI–6.
Fig. 9.10 *Recreation Master Plan.* Indian Bend, Washington, Maricopa County, Ariz. Prepared by U.S. Army Engineer District, Corps of Engineers, Los Angeles, 1975.
Fig. 9.11 *Park and Recreation Information System.* California Department of Parks and Recreation, Planning Monograph No. 2, Sacramento, 1966, p. 45.
Fig. 9.12 Ibid., p. 10.
Fig. 10.1 Same as Figure 2.15, p. 45.
Fig. 10.2 Ibid., p. 40.
Fig. 10.3 Ibid., p. 44.
Fig. 10.4 J. B. Ellis, D. N. Milstein and H. E. Koening, "Physical Systems Analysis of Socio-Economic Situations," 1964. In *Outdoor Recreation Demand Study,* Michigan Department of Conservation, Technical Report No. 6, 1966, p. 6.3.
Fig. 10.5 Same as Figure 9.11, p. xii.
Fig. 10.6 Same as Figure 10.4, p. 5.3.
Fig. 10.7 *Guidelines for Understanding and Determining Optimum Recreation Carrying Capacity.* U.S. Department of the Interior, Bureau of Outdoor Recreation, Prepared by Urban Research and Development Corporation, Bethlehem, Pa., 1977, p. iii–3.
Fig. 10.8 *Assessment of Alternatives for the General Management Plan.* Golden Gate National Recreation Area/Point Reyes National Seashore, Calif., U.S. Department of the Interior, National Park Service, Government Printing Office, Region 8, 1977, p. 24.
Fig. 10.9 Ibid., p. 56.
Fig. 10.10 Adapted from "Demand Methodology," Conrad R. Lickel, *Guideline,* National Recreation and Park Association, 1973. Also described in Fogg (1975) and *Statewide Outdoor Recreation Plan,* Bureau of State Parks, Department of Forest and Waters, Penna. 1970.
Fig. 10.11 George E. Fogg. *Park Planning Guidelines.* Washington, D.C.: National Recreation and Park Association, 1975, p. 21. Reprinted with permission.
Fig. 10.12 Alan R. Shannon. 1975. "A Systems Approach to Recreation Planning," *Parks and Recreation* 10 (September) 9:32–33.
Fig. 11.1 *Community Facilities, Parks and Open Space.* Jackson Metropolitan Area Regional Planning Commission, Jackson, Mich. Prepared by Harland Batholomew and Associates, 1970, p. 9.
Fig. 11.2 *Standards for Parks.* Department of Planning and Conservation, Evanston, Ill., 1964, p. 17.
Fig. 11.3 *How Will America Grow?* Citizen's Advisory Committee on Environmental Quality, Washington, D.C.: Government Printing Office, 1976, p. 15.
Fig. 11.4 Seymour M. Gold. *Urban Recreation Planning,* 1973, Philadelphia: Lea and Febiger, pp. 212, 218.
Fig. 11.5 *Application of a Recreation-Experience Components Concept for Comprehensive Recreation Planning.* Department

of Community Affairs, Bureau of Recreation and Conservation, Harrisburg, Pa. Prepared by Monty Christiansen, Penn State University, June 1975, p. 19.
Fig. 11.6 Ibid.
Fig. 12.1 Adapted from "The Concept of Recreation Need," David Mercer. 1973. *Journal of Leisure Research,* 5 (Winter):35–50. After J. Bradshaw. 1972. "The Concept of Social Need," *New Society,* 30 (March): 640–643. Reprinted with permission.
Fig. 12.2 Edwin J. Staley, 1969. "Determining Neighborhood Recreation Priorities: An Instrument," *Journal of Leisure Research,* 1 (Winter): 69–74. Reprinted with permission.
Fig. 12.3 *Quantitative Approach to Needs Assessment.* Parks and Recreation Department, San Jose, Calif. Prepared by Evaluation Unit, Office of Fiscal Affairs, 1974.
Fig. 12.4 *Open Space, Conservation and Recreation.* An Element of the Comprehensive Plan, City Planning Department, Oakland, Calif., 1976, p. 62.
Fig. 12.5 Ibid., p. 66.
Fig. 12.6 Ibid., p. 70.
Fig. 12.7 Same as Figure 8.3, p. xiv.
Fig. 12.8 Ibid., p. 48
Fig. 12.9 Randolph T. Hester, Jr., 1975. *Neighborhood Space: User Needs and Design Responsibility.* Stroudsburg, Pa.: Dowden, Hutchinson and Ross, p. 110. Reprinted with permission.
Fig. 12.10 Ibid., p. 114. Reprinted with permission.
Fig. 12.11 Same as Figure 5.9, p. 143.
Fig. 12.12 Ibid., p. 145.
Fig. 12.13 Ibid., p. 241.
Fig. 13.2 *Wailuku-Kahului General Plan.* Maui County Planning Commission. Prepared by Eckbo, Dean, Austin and Williams, San Francisco, 1972, p. 33.
Fig. 13.3 Joseph Bannon. 1976. *Leisure Resources: Its Comprehensive Planning,* Englewood Cliffs, N.J.: Prentice-Hall, p. 281. Reprinted with permission.
Fig. 13.4 James F. Murphy. 1974. *Concepts of Leisure: Philosophical Implications.* Englewood Cliffs, N.J.: Prentice-Hall, p. 11. Reprinted with permission.
Fig. 14.2 *Status of San Francisco Simulation Model.* Department of City Planning, 1968, p. 3. In Kenneth L. Kraemer, *Policy Analysis in Local Government,* Washington, D.C.: International City Management Association, 1973, p. 68. Reprinted with permission.
Fig. 14.3 Adapted from E. S. Quade and W. I. Boucher (Eds.). *Systems Analysis and Policy Planning.* New York: American Elsevier Publishing Company, 1968, p. 13. In Kraemer, p. 100. Reprinted with permission.
Fig. 14.4 *M.E.T.R.O.* Tri-County Regional Planning Commission, Lansing, Mich., 1966. In Kraemer, p. 126. Game developed by Richard D. Duke.
Fig. 14.5 Same as Figure 8.10.
Fig. 14.6 Ibid.
Fig. 14.7 Ibid.
Fig. 14.8 *Policies for Planning.* Part No. 2 of the Recommended Master Plan for the East Bay Regional Park District, Oakland, Calif., 1973, p. 45. Prepared by OVERVIEW, San Francisco.
Fig. 14.9 Ibid., p. 48.
Fig. 14.10 Ibid., p. 48.
Fig. 14.11 Ibid., p. 49.
Fig. 14.12 *A Playground for All Children: User Groups and Site Selection,* Book No. 1. Department of City Planning, New York.

U.S. Department of Housing and Urban Development, Office of Policy Development and Research, Washington, D.C.: Government Printing Office, 1976, p. 24.

Fig. 14.13 Ibid., p. 40

Fig. 14.14 *The Workbook: Yosemite Master Plan.* U.S. Department of the Interior, National Park Service, Yosemite Planning Team, San Francisco, California, 1975.

Fig. 15.1 *National Capital Open Space System: Interim Report.* National Capital Development Commission, Canberra, Australia, 1976, p. 82.

Fig. 15.2 *Summary of General Plan; Zoning Ordinances and Development Plans.* Planning Department, County of Kauai, Hawaii. Prepared by Eckbo, Dean, Austin & Williams, Honolulu, Hawaii and San Francisco, 1973.

Fig. 15.3 *Interim Open Space and Conservation Element of the Orange County General Plan.* Planning Department, Orange County, Calif., 1972.

Fig. 15.4 Adapted from Jere Stuart French, *Urban Green,* Dubuque, Iowa: Kendall/Hunt Publishing Company, 1973, p. 48. Reprinted with permission.

Fig. 15.5 *Park and Recreational Facilities.* U.S. Department of Transportation, Environmental Development Division, Washington, D.C.: Government Printing Office, 1971, p. 4.

Fig. 15.6 Same as Figure 10.8, p. 454.

Fig. 15.7 *Guidelines for an Integrated Impact Assessment Procedure.* Community Development and Environmental Protection Agency, Sacramento County, Calif. Prepared by Duncan and Jones, Berkeley, 1976, p. 15.

Fig. 15.8 Same as Figure 10.8, p. 97.

Fig. 15.9 Same as Figure 6.3, p. 41.

Fig. 15.10 *Freeway Park.* Seattle Park Department. Adapted from photo by John Normark of Seattle, Washington in *Sunset,* July 1976, p. 54. Design by Lawrence Halprin and Associates, San Francisco.

Fig. 15.11 Photo courtesy of U.S. Department of the Interior, National Park Service, San Francisco. Rooftop Garden, Kaiser Medical Center, Oakland, Calif.

Fig. 15.12 *Master Plan of Parks, Recreation and Cultural Arts Facilities.* Parks, Recreation and Cultural Arts Commission, Orange, Calif. Prepared by POD, Inc., Orange, 1975, p. 57.

Fig. 15.13 *Design Framework for the Inner City: Orchestra Place.* City Plan Commission, Detroit, Mich., 1974. Reprinted with permission.

Fig. 15.14 *Victoria Mews Condominiums.* Portrero Hill, San Francisco. Developed by Ray Bright and Victoria Mews Consortium, design by Richard Meyer, illustration by Chin Ishrimura, landscape design and architecture by David Barovetto of Barovetto, Ruscitto and Barovetto, Sacramento, 1979. Reprinted with permission from *San Francisco Examiner,* May 13, 1979, p. 31.

INDEX